W9-AFZ-631

OPERATING SYSTEMS

A Systematic View

View

Second Edition

OPERATING SYSTEMS
A Systematic View

WILLIAM S. DAVIS
Miami University

▲
▼▼
**ADDISON-WESLEY
PUBLISHING COMPANY**

Reading, Massachusetts ■ Menlo Park, California
London ■ Amsterdam ■ Don Mills, Ontario ■ Sydney

Sponsoring Editor: William B. Gruener
Production Editor: William J. Yskamp

Text Designer: Melinda Grosser
Illustrator: ARVAK
Cover Designer: Ann Scrimgeour Rose
Cover Illustrator: Ann Scrimgeour Rose
Art Coordinator: Joseph K. Vetere

Production Manager: Karen M. Guardino
Production Coordinator: Peter Petraitis

The text of this book was composed in Century Schoolbook by TriStar Graphics

Library of Congress Cataloging in Publication Data

Davis, William S., 1943–
    Operating systems.
    Includes index.
    1. Operating systems (Computers) I. Title
QA76.6.D38   1983   001.64′25   82–3926
ISBN 0–201–11116–0   AACR2

Reprinted with corrections, April 1984

Copyright © 1983 by Addison-Wesley Publishing Company, Inc.

ISBN 0–201–11116–0
DEFGHIJ–DO–8987654

TO CATHY

Preface

The first edition of *Operating Systems: A Systematic View* was published in 1977. The computer field has seen many changes since then. Microcomputers have become everyday machines; we even have personal computer systems today. At the same time, the big mainframes have gotten even bigger, with gigabyte memories supporting nanosecond processors a distinct probability. An operating system is linked to its hardware as perhaps no other software product could be. Thus as computers have changed, operating systems have changed. The intent of this second edition is to update the material to match current technology.

In the preface to the first edition, I made the following statement: "My approach is most definitely *not* theoretical; my intent is to show *why* operating systems are needed and *what*, at a functional 'macro' level they do." The approach and intent of this second edition remain the same. While the material has been updated and many of the examples have been changed, the pace, level, and writing style of the first edition have been retained.

What changes have been made? Part I still contains a discussion of the basic system resources—hardware, software, and data. The material has been updated and rearranged. A key objective was to compare microcomputers and the large mainframes, and give the student some sense how these machines are similar and how they differ.

Part II is an overview of a number of operating system concepts taken, almost without change, from the first edition.

The title of Part III has been changed from "Job Control Language . . ." to "Communicating with the Operating System." A new chapter has been added introducing the general concept of a command or job control language, and illustrating a microcomputer command language (for CP/M®)*; this chapter serves as a lead-in to the DOS and OS Job Control Language material taken from the first edition. A final chapter on libraries and the linkage editor has been added to Part III.

A number of changes have been made in Part IV. The section begins with a chapter on basic operating system concepts using CP/M as an example: microcomputer operating systems can no longer be ignored. As we move on to the large mainframes, the most obvious change since the mid-1970s has been the growing dominance of virtual memory operating systems. The examples covered in the first edition have been essentially retained, but DOS/VS has replaced DOS, and OS/VS1 has replaced OS/MFT. To support these changes, the rest of the material in Part IV has been rearranged. A new chapter gives the student a general introduction to the functions of multiprogramming and time-shared operating systems. Next comes a chapter on the virtual memory concept, essentially taken from the first edition, but with minor modifications. Having set the stage, the chapters on DOS/VS and OS/VS1 follow. The section ends with a chapter on operating system trends that highlights the virtual machine concept and multiprocessing.

The focus of the final section of the text, Part V, is system software. The first edition touched briefly on data communication monitors and data base management systems. Today, these two software packages have moved to "center stage" on many large computer systems. Chapter 19 is devoted to data communication, and Chapter 20 covers the general concepts of data base management systems. Part V ends with a brief overview of commercial software packages.

The new material has been classroom tested, and has met with a very positive response. Although substantial changes have been made, the book is still appropriate for "second-year students in a program oriented toward the *use* of computers rather than toward the design of computers." Professional programmers and systems analysts may find the applied orientation of this text valuable as well. I am excited by this second edition, and hope that you find it both interesting and useful.

Oxford, Ohio   **W.S.D.**
November 1982

---

*CP/M is a Registered Trademark of Digital Research.

Contents
in Brief

Detailed Contents

□ 3 _____ Software and Data

□ 4 _____ Linking the System Components

■ II _____ Operating System Development

□ 5 _____ Single Program Systems

☐ 6 _____ Multiprogramming and Time-Sharing

☐ III _____ Communicating with the Operating System

☐ 7 _____ Command Languages and Job Control Languages

☐ 8 _____ Job Control under IBM's Disk Operating System

☐ **9** _____ **Job Control Language for the IBM
Operating System/360 and System/370 —
JOB and EXEC Statements**

☐ **10** _____ **The DD Statement**

☐ **11** _____ **Libraries and the Linkage Editor**

▇ **IV** _____ Operating System Concepts

☐ **12** _____ Basic Operating System Concepts

☐ **13** _____ Multiuser Systems

☐ 17 _____ IBM System/370 OS/VS1

☐ 18 _____ Trends and Alternatives in Operating System Design

■ V _____ System Software

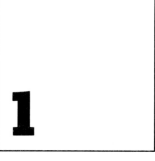

Introduction and Overview

Anyone who has worked with computers for any period of time knows that without software the hardware can do nothing; it's almost a cliché. To most people, however, software means *application* software—programs to compute payroll, or play a game, or compile statistics. This application software is only a part of the story.

Consider a "pure" computer, fresh off the assembly line, with absolutely no scftware in place. Given such a machine, the cliché would *literally* be true; this collection of "iron" could do absolutely *nothing*. It could not read a card. It could not respond to a command from the operator's console, even if the console were attached. It could not load, much less execute an application program. Even with a complete library of application software, this machine could do nothing.

Consider another example. Perhaps you know someone who purchased an inexpensive microcomputer, took it home, plugged it in, turned it on, and spent the next several days trying to get the machine to do something as incredibly simple as adding two plus two. Pure hardware, the "raw iron" is not very easy to use. Pure hardware presents the user with a most unfriendly interface.

It is obvious, however, that most computers are relatively easy to use. At many universities, an inexperienced student can simply walk into the computer center, sit down at a terminal, and begin using the machine. Personal computer systems are commonly used by twelve-year-olds, and small business systems

1

stress ease of use in their advertising. Is it not true that the student, the child, and the nontechnical small business person are communicating with the computer hardware? In most cases, *no,* they are *not* communicating with the hardware. In most cases, insulating the user from the hardware is a special program or group of programs called an *operating system* (Fig. 1.1).

Hardware is rough; it is difficult to deal with. An operating system is a collection of software that sits between the hardware and the application program or the user (Fig. 1.1 again). The operating system deals directly with the hardware. The user or application programmer deals with the hardware through the operating system. This *system software* can be used to smooth over the roughness of the hardware, thus presenting the user with a much simpler, much more friendly interface.

For example, consider the problem of reading a record of data from an external device. At the raw machine level, reading a record might well require

Fig. 1.1
The operating system serves as an interface
between the application software and the
hardware.

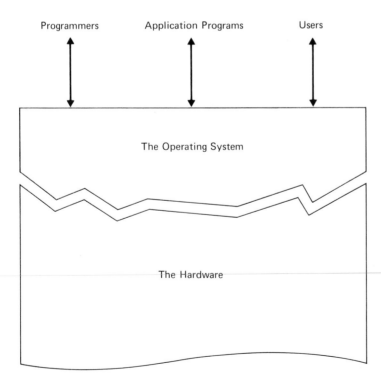

the execution of dozens of precisely coded and precisely timed instructions. The user, however, simply instructs the computer to READ a record; the operating system takes care of the details.

Providing an easy-to-use interface with the hardware is perhaps the most apparent function of an operating system, but there are other, equally important arguments for such software. A modern, computer-based information processing system represents a combination of hardware, software, and data resources. These resources are expensive. Many firms spend millions of dollars each year on hardware, and even more on software development and data management. Because of this high cost, it is essential that these resources be used as efficiently as possible. A modern operating system, particularly on a large machine, is designed to be a *resource manager,* allocating the hardware, software, and data resources to the various users in an efficient manner.

A well-designed operating system is *not* concerned with just hardware or just software or just data management, but with optimizing the way in which *all* of these resources work together in achieving some desired objective. Not all systems have the same objective—a manufacturing process-control system may stress speed of response while an educational system at a university may stress flexibility. Thus not all installations will want the same operating system; "best" is a relative term. In this text, we'll be discussing operating systems not as an end in themselves but as solutions to a number of information processing problems, always keeping system objectives in mind.

The purpose of this book is to give the reader a basic understanding of what an operating system is and how it works. Specific examples of operating system design and implementation will be used to illustrate a number of points; however, we'll try to avoid the bit-level discussion of the intimate working details of the products of any one manufacturer or the theory of operating system design. Our objective is to illustrate the *problems* handled by operating systems and not any single set of solutions to these problems. The text is designed to support a first course in operating systems. The concentration is on the application of this specialized software to a real-world environment; this is *not* a theoretical text.

Our approach in studying operating systems might be described as a systematic or top-down approach. Our starting point is the application programmer's view of the system. We'll consider those features of the operating system (more generally, system software) that the application programmer is most likely to encounter—compilers, a job control or command language, access methods, linkage editors, loaders. Gradually, layer by layer, we'll begin to analyze the operating system in more and more detail until, finally, we investigate the actual hardware/software interface.

Why should the future computer professional study operating systems? Several reasons might be cited. Some of you might become system programmers, and find it necessary to design or modify an operating system. Others might go into systems analysis, management, or consulting, and be assigned the task of selecting an operating system. In either case, the material covered in a first course will serve as a solid foundation for necessary further study.

Not all computer professionals become system programmers, and the selection of an operating system is at best an occasional task. Most computer people deal with applications. Why should they learn about operating systems? One reason might be simple curiosity: most professionals like to know something about all aspects of their field, and computer professionals are no exception. A second argument might be exposure to the design of a large, integrated application. Operating systems are among the largest software packages ever developed. An understanding of how an operating system works can provide valuable insight into the design of any large, computer-based system.

The key argument for learning something about operating systems, however, is that the operating system represents the application programmer's primary interface with the computer. If the programs are to take full advantage of the computer resources, the programmer must understand his or her computer. The operating system is the programmer's interface with the computer. Thus the programmer, to be effective, must understand at least the basics of the operating system. This book is aimed at giving the application specialist just such an understanding.

The book is divided into five parts. Part I, Chapters 2 through 4, covers the basic concepts of software, hardware, and data—the system resources that are managed by an operating system. For many students, much of this material will be review in nature; it's included because subsequent chapters assume a knowledge of this information.

Part II, Chapters 5 and 6, follows the rapidly developing technology of the past two decades and the parallel evolution of operating systems. The concepts of multiprogramming and time-sharing are introduced in this section. Emphasis is placed on the importance of economic factors in these developments.

In Part III, we study modern programmer/system communications, starting (Chapter 7) with a basic discussion of command or job control languages. Next, we consider two of the most commonly used job control languages: IBM's DOS (Chapter 8) and OS (Chapters 9 and 10) JCL.

The products of IBM have been chosen for a very obvious reason—IBM is the dominant force in the computer market. Not all features of the job control languages are covered in this section, only those more commonly used. The intent is to illustrate modern programmer/system communications and not to present an exhaustive course in JCL; the beginning programmer should, however, find the application orientation of this material useful in handling many everyday programming problems. The last chapter in Part III, Chapter 11, deals with a group of operating system or system software modules that the typical application programmer encounters virtually every day—compilers, linkage editors, loaders, and libraries.

In Part IV we turn our attention to a number of commercially available, general-purpose operating systems. The first three chapters are rather general. Chapter 12 concentrates on certain basic concepts (at the microcomputer level), Chapter 13 covers the primary memory management techniques on a large computer system, and Chapter 14 describes virtual memory systems. Chapters 15 through 17 introduce the student to two specific operating systems, both products of IBM. We begin, in Chapter 15, with an analysis of the principles of operation of an IBM System/370 computer. In Chapter 16 we'll cover the DOS/VS operating system; our case study in Chapter 17 will be VS/1. Part IV ends (Chapter 18) with a discussion of anticipated trends in operating system development, including such concepts as multiprocessors and virtual machines.

Most general-purpose operating systems are supplied by the computer manufacturers. In Part V of the text we concentrate on other system software that is often supplied by independent firms. In Chapter 19, we will concentrate on modern data communication monitors, spending some time on the hardware needed to support data communications. Data base management is the subject of Chapter 20. Chapter 21 represents a survey of commercially available system software.

It is assumed that the reader of this text knows how to program in at least one language, and has a solid understanding of computer fundamentals and terminology. A knowledge of assembler language would help, but has not been assumed. Ease in manipulating binary and hexadecimal numbers is *not* essential, although a reasonable grasp of the relationship between binary and hex is assumed in the chapter on System/370 principles of operation. If your number system skills are rusty, read Appendix A.

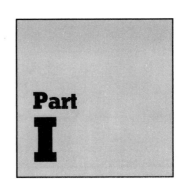

Part

I

The Basic
System Resources

2

Hardware

Overview

This chapter covers the basic hardware components of a computer system. For many readers, the material will be largely review. Reference will be made to the use of binary data within the computer. If you are less than confident of your ability to understand binary concepts, read Appendix A before starting.

We'll begin with a discussion of the computer's mainframe: main memory, the central processing unit, and registers. Human beings access the computer through a variety of input and output devices that are attached to what is frequently called the machine's front end. Secondary storage (tape, disk, drum) occupies the computer's back end. After discussing, briefly, each of these primary computer components, we'll put the pieces together and illustrate a complete computer system.

The Mainframe: Main Memory

A computer is an electronic machine, basically a two-state device: on/off, current/no current. Thus it is not surprising to learn that most computers represent data as a pattern of binary digits, or bits.

How do we go about storing these bits? Almost any device that is capable

9

of holding two states—a light (on/off), a wire (current flowing/no current flowing), an electronic tube (current/no current), a transistor (current/no current), a switch (open/closed)—can be used to store bits. Some devices are better than others, but all could work.

Magnetic core memory, for example, takes advantage of the directional properties of a magnet and of the relationship between electricity and magnetism. It is made from tiny donut-shaped rings (cores) of magnetic material (Fig. 2.1). We've all played with bar magnets as children, and most of us know about the north and south poles of a magnet—magnets possess directional properties.

Unlike a bar magnet, a ring magnet does not have two ends that can be clearly identified as the north and south poles. The ring magnet still has directional properties, however, resulting in clockwise or counterclockwise magnetization, and giving us the necessary two states. We could arbitrarily use the clockwise state (although the other choice would be just as good) to indicate a 1-bit and the counterclockwise state to indicate a 0-bit and design a computer memory around this assumption.

Core memory is fairly fast, with "slow" core being capable of transferring close to two million characters per second, and "fast" core nearly four million characters per second. The cost of core is approximately one-half cent per bit, and until recently, that price was hard to beat. However, newer solid state technologies have begun to produce memory devices that are cost-competitive with core, while offering substantially better performance at transfer rates of over eight million characters per second. Most computer manufacturers are shifting from core to solid state memories on their latest computers.

Fig. 2.1
Core storage.

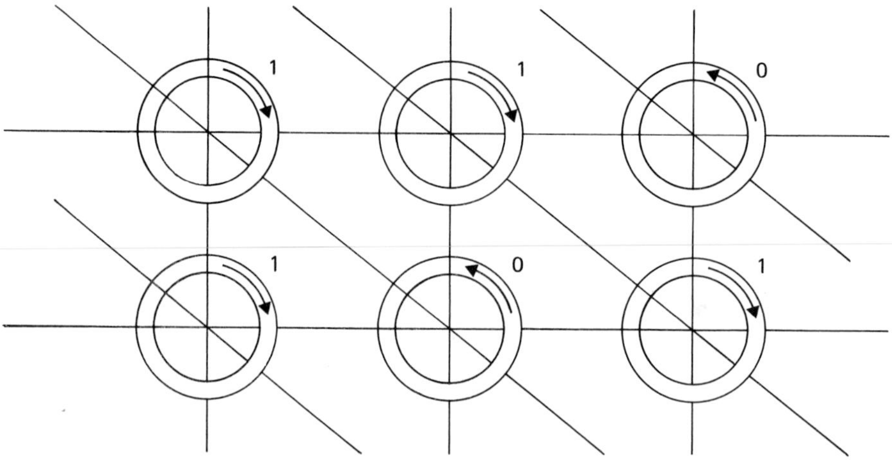

Computer people often refer to a machine's *main memory* as core. In the past, it really was core, and the name made sense. Today, however, most new computers no longer use core, although the term continues to be used to describe the main memory. Over the years, this usage has created a new meaning for the word core—main memory. It will probably continue to be used in this context, in spite of the swing to semiconductor memories.

Individual bits might be stored on cores or on solid state devices but, at any rate, we store bits. These bits can be grouped to form coded characters or binary numbers. Every digital computer has the ability to group bits. Because IBM is the largest supplier of computers in the world, the reader is more apt to have access to an IBM computer than to the product of any other manufacturer; thus we will use the IBM System/370 series of computers as an example of how bits are grouped and *addressed*.

The basic unit of memory on an IBM System/360 or System/370 computer is a set of eight bits called a *byte* (Fig. 2.2). Two codes, EBCDIC and ASCII-8, use eight bits to identify a single character. IBM uses the EBCDIC code, storing one EBCDIC character in each byte.

A very simple addressing scheme is used to allow the programmer to indicate a specific byte location in a program. The bytes are numbered sequentially. The first byte in memory is byte number 0 (Fig. 2.2), the second is number 1, the third is number 2, and so on, until all bytes in a given memory have been numbered.

Not all data in the computer is character data; at times, numeric data is needed. If the computer were limited to groupings of eight bits, the largest number that could be stored would be $(11111111)_2$, which is 255. That is not even big enough to compute take-home pay. Additional data groupings are needed. Thus most computers have the ability to handle a *word* of data.

On an IBM machine, groups of 16 bits or two bytes are wired together to form halfwords (see Fig. 2.2), and groups of 32 bits or four bytes (or two halfwords) are wired together to form (as you may have guessed) fullwords. A half-

Fig. 2.2
Grouping and addressing binary data on an IBM computer.

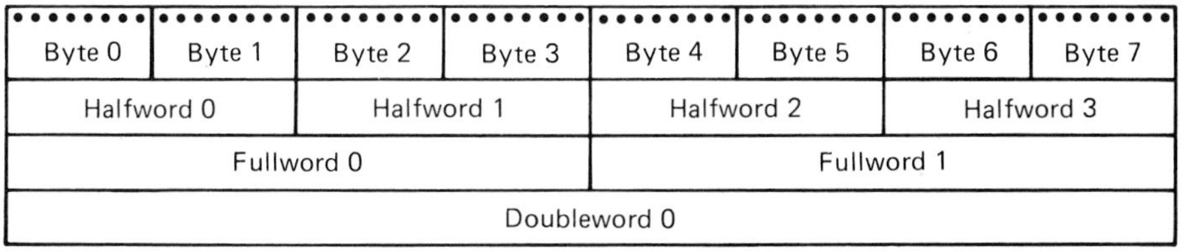

Byte 0	Byte 1	Byte 2	Byte 3	Byte 4	Byte 5	Byte 6	Byte 7
Halfword 0		Halfword 1		Halfword 2		Halfword 3	
Fullword 0				Fullword 1			
Doubleword 0							

word, assuming that the first bit is used as a sign, can hold a maximum value of $(0111111111111111)_2$, which is 32,767. A fullword of 32 bits can hold numbers in excess of two billion!

The Mainframe: The Central Processing Unit

If a computer could be said to have a brain, the *central processing unit* would be that brain. It's in the central processing unit (or CPU) that the computer carries out its arithmetic and logical functions and where the operation of the entire computer system is controlled.

The CPU is divided into two parts (Fig. 2.3): the *control unit* and the *arithmetic and logical unit.* The function of the control unit is to fetch a single instruction from main memory, and to decode it. Once the control unit has figured out what is to be done, control is turned over to the arithmetic and logical unit, which does it. The first step in this cycle is called instruction time, or I-time. The second step, involving the arithmetic and logical unit, is called execution time, or E-time. Completion of both parts represents one *machine cycle* (Fig. 2.4). That's how a computer works: The control unit figures out what is to be done and turns control over to the arithmetic and logical unit, which performs the task and turns control back to the control unit, which decodes the next instruction and returns control to the arithmetic and logical unit, and on and on in a cyclic pattern.

Perhaps the best way to visualize a machine cycle is to look at a familiar, close relative of the computer—the pocket calculator. Let's assume that we have a number in the calculator's memory and wish to add another value to it. Depending on the type of calculator we are using, either we enter the number and push the ADD (or +) button, or we push the ADD (or +) button and enter the number; the result in both cases is the same, a very rapid computation of the correct sum. On the calculator, each action (each instruction) involves two

Fig. 2.3
The central processing unit.

Central Processing Unit	
Control Unit	Arithmetic and Logical Unit

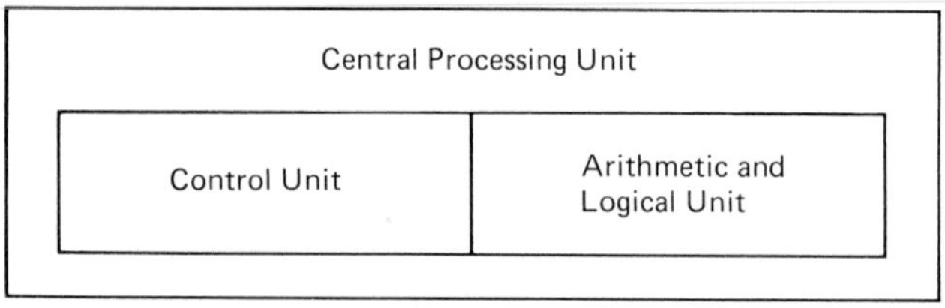

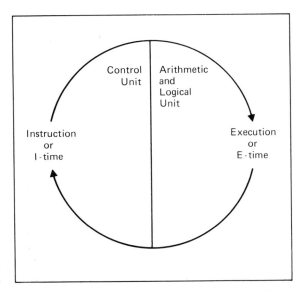

**Fig. 2.4
A machine cycle.**

distinct steps on the part of the person using the machine. First is a "decision" phase ("What should I do next?") analogous to the function of the control unit of the central processing unit. Second is an "action" phase (push the proper button) analogous to the function of the arithmetic and logical unit.

The computer works in much the same way. Rather than using buttons, a computer uses *instructions*. The format of an instruction (Fig. 2.5) is pretty simple, consisting of an operation or op code telling the machine *what* to do (add, subtract, multiply, divide, compare, copy) and a series of operands providing the machine with such information as

1. where in memory data can be found,

2. where in memory an answer is to be placed,

3. the length of an element of data.

A program is simply a series of these instructions stored in main memory. The control unit of the CPU goes into memory, *fetches* one of these instructions, and decodes it. The op code of the instruction tells the machine what to do (this is equivalent to telling it which button to push) and the operands tell the machine what elements of data to do it to. After decoding the instruction,

**Fig. 2.5
An instruction.**

Operation Code or Op Code	Operands

the control unit passes control to the arithmetic and logical unit, which executes the instruction. Then it's back to the control unit, which fetches the next instruction and repeats the cycle.

Note that the program that controls the CPU is stored in main memory; it is a *stored program*. This is a very important concept. The program controls the CPU by guiding it through the right instructions in the right sequence. One program might guide the CPU through the computation and printing of payroll checks. Another might cause the machine to compute an arithmetic average, while still another program might read a magnetic tape and print a list of address labels. Since the program exists only as a pattern of binary 1's and 0's in main memory, it is easy to change. By reading a new program (from cards, tape, or a direct access device) into main memory, a computer that had been processing payroll is transformed into an inventory machine or an accounting machine. By simply changing the program, the same set of hardware can be used for any number of different applications; this *general-purpose* nature of the computer is one of its more powerful features. The ability to work under control of a stored program is what distinguishes a computer from a calculator. On a calculator, a human being must provide the control by actively intervening at *each* step in the process; on a computer, once the process is started the stored program provides "automatic" control, with no need for further human intervention.

The Mainframe: Registers

How does data or an instruction get from main memory to the CPU? On many computers, the answer is "through the registers." A *register* acts as a path or conduit, connecting the two major components of the computer.

Once again, it seems that the best way to explain the functions of a register is by referring to the familiar pocket calculator. We've already seen that the electronic circuits of a calculator are analogous to a CPU. Since most calculators have very limited memory, let's say that our main memory is a sheet of scratch paper. If we wish to add two numbers, it is first necessary to transfer them from the scratch pad (our main memory for this analogy) into the calculator; we do this by keying in the numbers to be added, digit by digit. In effect, we have transferred the data from main memory into a register.

Most computers are designed in a similar manner. Data are first stored in main memory. If two numbers are to be added, one (or both) must first be copied into a register before the ADD instruction can be executed.

Following execution of an ADD on a calculator, the answer is usually displayed (the display is nothing more than a visual copy of what is in the register) so that the operator can copy it to the scratch paper (main memory). Following the execution of an ADD instruction on a computer, the answer is usually dropped into a register, allowing a subsequent instruction to copy it into main memory.

Logically, the registers serve to connect main memory and the CPU. Physically, the registers are part of the CPU on most modern computers. Some machines use general-purpose registers that are available for both addressing and arithmetic. On other computers, the addressing and arithmetic functions are separated. In some cases, the programmer may have access to two special registers called the ACCUMULATOR and the COUNTER, the functions of which should be apparent if you've ever tried to compute a simple average. Many machines have special registers for handling floating-point arithmetic.

The Mainframe: The Whole Package

We have finally reached the point where we can put all the components of a computer together. At the top of Fig. 2.6, we see the central processing unit, better known as the CPU, where all the logical and control functions of the computer are carried out. The CPU is subdivided into two parts: the control unit and the arithmetic and logical unit. The control unit is responsible for figuring out exactly what the computer is to do next; the arithmetic and logical unit is responsible for doing it.

At the bottom of the figure is the computer's main memory, consisting of a series of magnetic or electronic devices, each capable of existing in either of two states (0 or 1). These individual bits are grouped to form bytes, characters, words (depending on the computer manufacturer) or, in general, memory locations. On almost all computers, these memory locations are addressed by assigning them consecutive numbers beginning with 0; we can find the address of a given memory location by simply counting how many memory locations it is away from the first one.

Between the CPU and main memory are a number of registers that serve as pathways or conduits connecting these two components. Registers are actually located in the CPU; Fig. 2.6 illustrates their *logical* position.

According to many sources, the term *central processing unit* should be applied to the entire computer; in other words, everything shown in Fig. 2.6. If this definition were applied, the CPU would actually include main memory and the registers. However, the standard definition clearly limits the term central processing unit to "the interpretation and execution of instructions," which is the meaning assigned to the term in this text. Although the broader definition of the CPU is technically not correct, you'll still find many people using it.

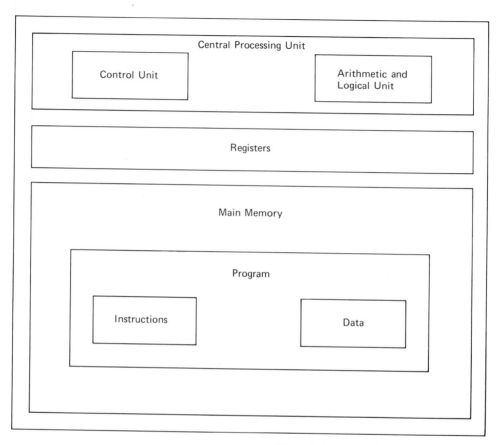

Fig. 2.6
The entire mainframe.

The Front End:
Input and
Output Devices

Human beings communicate with a computer through a variety of *peripheral devices* and media. The punched card is a good example. People sit at a keyboard device, a keypunch, and type one character of data at a time; each character is, in turn, represented on the card as a pattern of punched holes. Once punched, a deck of cards can be loaded into a card reader and input to a computer.

The printer is perhaps the best known of the computer output devices. Inside the computer's main memory, individual characters, lines, or even complete pages of output information are set up under program control, and then sent to the printer. The resulting *hard copy* can be read by a human being.

Other commonly used equipment meets a number of more specialized needs. MICR, which stands for Magnetic Ink Character Recognition, is a banking medium. Checks are imprinted with a magnetic ink indicating the bank's identification number and the account number, with the amount of the check being added after cashing. These magnetic characters are recognized electronically by their different patterns of magnetic intensity. OCR or Optical Character Recognition is an excellent medium for any number of applications in which a limited amount of handwritten or typed information must be read into a computer; the basic mechanism for reading such data takes advantage of the difference in reflectivity of white (paper) and black (the lines) surfaces. Mark sense is a simpler version of this idea, the location of a mark on a sheet of paper determining its meaning—test answer sheets are a good example.

New input/output devices and media are constantly entering the marketplace, and the trend is clearly toward simplicity of use. Consider, for example, the black and white bar code that is printed on most packaged products found in a modern supermarket (Fig. 2.7). This bar code is called the Universal Prod-

Fig. 2.7
**A Universal Product Code (UPC) is printed on
most products offered for sale in the modern
supermarket. (Photo courtesy of Kroger
Company.)**

uct Code, or UPC. It can be read by a simple scanning device (Fig. 2.8) and transmitted directly into a computer, or recorded on a simple cassette tape for later input. Such bar codes can be scanned quickly and accurately by individuals with little or no formal training.

A parallel in the banking industry is the magnetic stripe card (Fig. 2.9). The "stripe" is actually a piece of magnetic recording tape, on which such information as the customer's account number and credit limit can be recorded. To input this information to the computer (at an automatic teller terminal, for example), all the customer need do is insert the card into a slot, right-side-up. What could be simpler?

Perhaps the ultimate in this trend toward simplicity is the rapid emergence of voice response and voice recognition systems. Your local bank may have a system that allows you to call, enter your account number through your push-button telephone, and receive a "spoken" message giving your account balance. That's voice response. Although voice recognition (verbal input) is considerably more difficult, limited systems are in use today, and this technique is almost certain to grow.

The terminal is rapidly becoming the most common of all input/output devices. A basic, printing, keyboard terminal is essentially an electric type-

Fig. 2.8
A bar-code scanner or "light pen." (Photograph
courtesy of Interface Mechanisms, Inc.)

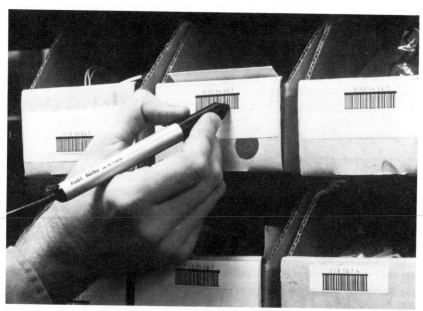

} Magnetic stripe

Authorized Signature

John Doe, Jr.

Property of
The Wurst National Bank
Wurst, Ohio   45000

➡

This
side
toward
machine

Fig. 2.9
A magnetic stripe card.

writer modified for use with a computer. When used as an input device, the
electronic signals that result in the printing of characters are generated by the
user as the keys are depressed. When used as an output device, these signals
come from the computer. CRT (cathode ray tube) terminals (Fig. 2.10) work in
much the same way, except that the characters of data are displayed on a
televisionlike screen rather than being printed.

Fig. 2.10
A cathode-ray-tube (CRT) terminal. (Photograph
courtesy of Control Data Corporation.)

Collectively, all the devices that allow a human being to communicate with a computer serve as the machine's *front end*. Many other devices could be cited, of course, but the brief summary presented above is adequate for our purposes.

The Back End: Secondary Storage

The function of the front-end peripheral devices described above is to support human/computer communication. Compared with computers, people are very slow. Our eyes require characters of a certain minimum size; thus printed or displayed output becomes rather bulky. To put it bluntly, from the computer's perspective, the front end is terribly inefficient.

One of the advantages of a computer system is that, once data have been entered, they can be captured and used again and again without the need for rekeying or rescanning. A modern computer holds a tremendous amount of information, most of which is only rarely (and quite selectively) output for human consumption. These data must be stored somewhere. Since human-readability is not a factor, the ideal medium would be very fast and very compact. Main memory is certainly a possibility, but main memory is simply too expensive to use for anything but the small amount of data being processed by the computer "right now." Thus a number of *secondary storage* devices have been developed. They provide high speed, compact, and relatively low-cost storage for an installation's data bank. Collectively, these secondary storage devices form what is sometimes called the computer system's *back end*.

Magnetic tape is one example. It is a high-speed data storage medium, with transfer rates of 60,000 characters per second and more; modern "hyper-tapes" are capable of transfer rates approaching 800,000 characters per second! Data are stored at very high densities; 800 and 1600 characters *per inch* are common. Thus tape is a compact medium. Even at a "mere" 800 characters per inch, a complete box of 2000 punched cards could be stored in less than 20 feet of tape. A single reel, about the size of an inch-thick record album, holds 2400 feet of tape; thus one reel of tape could easily hold the equivalent of over 100 *boxes* of cards! That is compact.

Magnetic tape is a sequential medium; i.e., in order to read record number 1000, it is first necessary to move the tape past the first 999 records. While perfectly acceptable for certain file update tasks, the sequential nature of tape makes it unsuitable for many current computer applications. Today, tape is most commonly used as a backup medium or for long-term, archival storage.

Imagine a tape cut into a series of strips each containing one hundred records. If record number 1000, and *only* record number 1000, were required, only the strip of tape containing this record would have to be searched. This is the essential concept behind a disk storage unit (Fig. 2.11). Instead of using strips of tape, data are stored in concentric circles on the surface of a disk coated with a magnetic material. To select the proper track, the word used to describe these concentric circles, a movable read/write head is positioned over the desired location. Often, several disk surfaces are stacked together (as in Fig. 2.11) to give added capacity; one position of the read/write heads, covering, in this case, ten tracks, is called a cylinder. (The top and bottom surfaces are not normally used to store data because of the danger of dust causing read errors.)

Reading or writing data on disk is a three step operation. First, the read/write head must be positioned over the proper track; this is called seek time

**Fig. 2.11
A magnetic disk.**

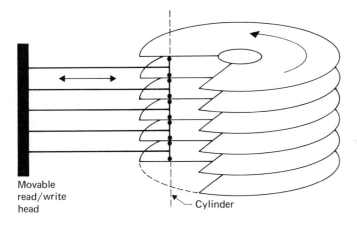

Movable
read/write
head

Cylinder

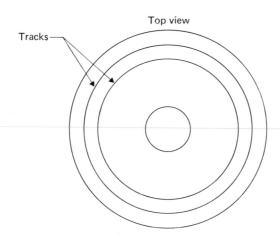

Top view

Tracks

and may involve a movement of anywhere from zero to a few hundred tracks. Once the head is properly positioned, some additional time may expire while the required record rotates beneath the read/write head; this is called rotational delay and may involve as much as one complete rotation. The final component is data transfer time, and represents the time needed to accomplish the actual transfer of data between the disk and the computer, a time which, when compared with seek time and rotational delay, is of minor significance.

On a magnetic drum, data are stored, again in concentric circles called tracks, around the outer surface of a unit shaped like an oil drum. Unlike a disk drive, a drum normally has one read/write head for each track, thus eliminating the need to move the head and, hence, seek time. Drum is faster than disk; disk's big advantage lies in its storage capacity. Because of the speed of drum, this device is enjoying increased popularity on modern virtual storage computer systems, a use we'll analyze in greater detail in Chapter 14.

Traditionally, disk and drum have dominated the direct access market. Lately, however, competition has begun to appear. The "floppy" disk, a slower, less dense, but considerably less expensive alternative to a standard disk drive, is growing in popularity for certain applications—particularly on micro- and minicomputers. Another new approach stores data on a series of "honeycomb-like" cells, with individual cells being retrieved, mounted on a read/write mechanism, and accessed directly; it's a relatively slow but very high-density medium. As the cost of solid state main memory continues to drop, some of these technologies will actually become candidates for bulk storage; perhaps we'll see the day when direct access data storage will in fact be a simple extension of the computer's main memory and thus directly addressable by the CPU itself.

Interfaces, Control Units, and Channels

It is interesting to note the tremendous variety of input, output, and secondary storage devices that can be attached to a computer. A card reader reads cards that contain characters of data represented as a pattern of holes in a column. A bar-code scanner reads black and white lines, and interprets the meaning of the bars based on their relative thickness. A disk device must be told where to position its read/write mechanism before accessing its binary patterns. Each device is different. Each functions by performing a set of unique physical actions. Even the codes used to represent data can vary significantly from device to device. Yet the computer must be able to communicate with *all* these peripherals; it is an electronic Tower of Babel.

The solution to the problem is quite simple: provide a mechanism between the computer and its peripheral devices to "translate." Assume, for example, that the computer in question uses the ASCII code internally. Between this computer and its card reader is a device that controls the card reader and translates the card code into ASCII. Between the computer and its disk is a device that controls the disk drive and translates the disk code to ASCII. Essentially, there is one *interface unit* for each peripheral device. The problem is solved.

On a microcomputer system, that's exactly what happens. If the owner wants to add a diskette unit to the system, a diskette interface board must be purchased and inserted into the system. Once the interface is available, a diskette drive can be attached and used (Fig. 2.12). A printer requires a printer interface. Each new device requires another interface unit. This is one of the limiting factors on the size of a microcomputer system; there are only so many "plugs" or slots into which interface units can be placed, and thus only so many peripheral devices can be added to the system. Another problem is efficiency. Although each input or output device has its own, unique characteristics, there are also several functions that are common to all. On larger computer systems, these two problems are solved by splitting the interface function into two parts. Device-dependent functions are handled by a *control unit,* while device-independent functions are assigned to a *channel.*

The control unit (or interface unit) attached to a disk drive causes the read/write mechanism to be positioned, logically scans the records on the selected track until the requested record is located, performs certain accuracy checks on the data and, in general, controls the disk drive. The control unit attached to a card reader must "tell" the machine to read the next card and, as the columns are scanned, translate the punched card code into the computer's

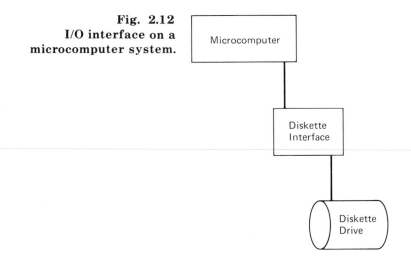

Fig. 2.12
I/O interface on a
microcomputer system.

internal code. Each control unit is different. The control unit is device-dependent; its function is to translate the unique characteristics of a specific device to a common form.

Not all aspects of I/O are device-dependent. For example, there are a number of logical functions that must be performed during any I/O operation. What is really meant when a computer requests the input or transfer of "one card's worth" of information from a card reader? If we assume a standard 80-column card, it means that 80 characters of data are to be moved, one at a time, from the card reader through a control unit, where they are converted into ASCII (or similar coded) form, and then into 80 consecutive memory locations in the computer's main memory.

There are two very important logical functions that must be performed in support of the transfer of data. The first function is counting. How is the equipment to "know" that exactly 80 characters of data have been transferred if it doesn't count them? Counting is a logical function. The other logical function is addressing. Following the transfer of the 40th character from the card to, let's say, memory location 1023, where does the 41st character go? Memory location 1024, obviously. How do we get from 1023 to 1024? Simple. We add 1. Addition is also a logical function.

Within a computer, logical functions are performed by the CPU. Thus on early computers, the CPU was responsible for physically controlling an I/O operation by keeping track of the number of characters transferred and the address of the "next" character in main memory. Many modern computers, particularly minicomputers and other small or mid-sized machines, still use the CPU in this way, attaching control units to a device called an *integrated adapter* (Fig. 2.13), which is physically located in the same "box" as the CPU. These integrated adapters function by "stealing" machine cycles from the CPU to support the character-counting and addressing operations.

There is nothing wrong with cycle stealing; it is a reasonable and fairly inexpensive way of controlling I/O. When the central processing unit is concen-

Fig. 2.13
**On some computers, an integrated adapter is
used to control I/O.**

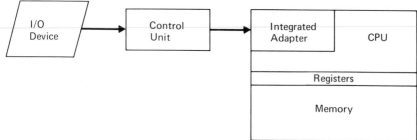

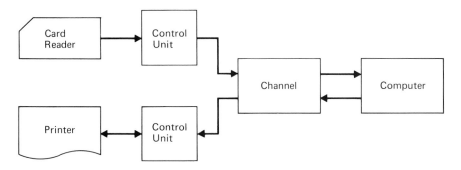

Fig. 2.14
Input and output devices are attached to the
computer through control units and channels.

trating its energies on counting characters and updating addresses, however, it isn't performing useful work on an application program. On a smaller machine, this does not represent a great deal of waste, but as computers become bigger and faster and as more and more input and output devices are attached to the mainframe, controlling each and every I/O operation becomes a burden. The solution to the problem is the channel (Fig. 2.14), which is essentially a special-purpose minicomputer placed between one or more control units and the computer. The channel's functions are to count characters and update main memory addresses, thus taking over responsibility for controlling an I/O operation and freeing the central processing unit to perform other tasks.

Most computers support two different types of channels. The first, called a multiplexer (Fig. 2.15), is designed to attach low-speed I/O devices such as card readers and printers. Compare the speed of a card reader—a rate of perhaps 1000 characters per second—with the speed of a computer, which is capable of manipulating millions of characters per second. Obviously a computer can easily keep up with a number of card readers. The multiplexer allows dozens of low-speed I/O devices to be handled concurrently by overlapping, or multiplexing, their operation, getting one character from a card reader, sending one character to a card punch, sending one character to a printer, and then coming back to the card reader to wait for the next character to be read at the relatively low rate of 1000 characters per second.

High-speed input and output devices, such as magnetic tape, disk, and drum, are normally attached to the computer through a different type of channel called a selector (Fig. 2.15). Unlike the multiplexer channel, a selector channel is designed to handle the transmission of data between main memory and a single I/O device at a time. Because these devices are relatively fast, the advantages of overlapping or multiplexing I/O operations are not as great. In effect, a selector channel serves as a high-speed data path connecting a single I/O device to the computer, with data being transferred in what is known as the burst

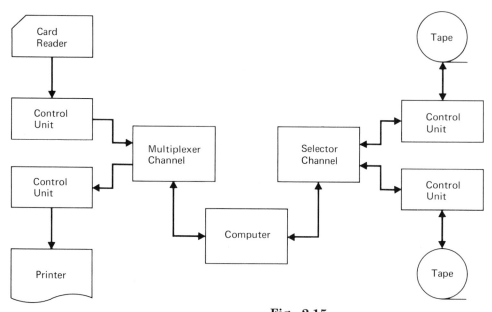

Fig. 2.15
Multiplexer channels are used to connect slower
I/O devices; selector channels are used for high-
speed I/O.

mode. After completing an operation, the channel can then be used to connect the computer to another high-speed I/O device. A selector channel, like its multiplexer counterpart, counts characters and updates addresses, freeing the central processing unit from this responsibility.

Although the so-called high-speed devices (such as tape, drum, and disk) are very fast compared with card readers and printers, they are still quite slow compared with the computer's internal processing speeds. On some extremely fast computers, special selector channels actually overlap a number of high-speed I/O operations; these channels are called block multiplexers.

The Computer System

We have now covered all of the major components of a computer system (see Fig. 2.16). Let's put the pieces together. The system begins with the computer itself, which is subdivided into three major parts: the central processing unit (CPU), registers, and memory. Within memory, we find both program instructions and data; since programs and data are stored as nothing more than a pattern of 1's and 0's on a two-state device such as core (or its equivalent), they

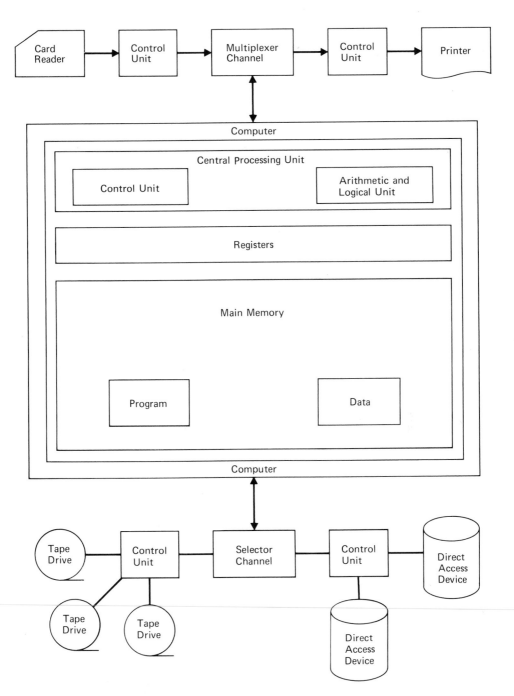

Fig. 2.16
A complete computer system.

are easily changed, allowing the machine to process a number of records and then to switch quickly to another program that can process several "different" records.

The central processing unit is subdivided into two parts: the control unit and the arithmetic and logical unit. The control unit is responsible for getting (fetching) an instruction from memory and decoding it—in other words, for figuring out what the program is to do. Control is then transferred to the arithmetic and logical unit, which executes the specified instruction. Next, it's back to the control unit, where the process is repeated. The registers serve as paths or conduits connecting main memory and the CPU.

Outside the computer, we find low-speed I/O devices such as card readers and printers attached to the computer first through a control unit (Fig. 2.16), and then through a multiplexer channel. A multiplexer channel can multiplex or overlap a number of I/O operations.

High-speed I/O devices such as tape, disk, and drum are attached (Fig. 2.16) first through a control unit and then through a selector channel. A selector channel performs the same counting and addressing functions that a multiplexer does, but it doesn't overlap I/O operations, transmitting data between main memory and one device at a time in burst mode.

All these components together compose a typical computer system. The term system is important, since it implies a collection of different components, all of which must work together to achieve an objective. Without input data, the computer, a data processing machine, would have no data to process. Without control units and channels, the input of data would be impossible. Once in the computer, data are processed through the combined efforts of memory, registers, and the control unit and arithmetic and logical unit of the central processing unit. Of course, without output, there's no point in processing data. Computers work for the benefit of people, not computers; thus if people cannot read and analyze the computer's results, those results are meaningless.

Summary _____

Normally, you will find a summary at the end of each chapter. For this chapter, the discussion of the computer system performs the function of summarizing the material.

Key Words _____

address	central
arithmetic and logical unit	processing unit
back end	(CPU)
byte	channel

computer system
control unit (instruction)
control unit (I/O)
front end
instruction
interface unit
machine cycle
main memory

mainframe
program
register
secondary storage
stored program
system
word

Exercises _____

1. What are the primary components of a computer's mainframe?
2. Why do most digital computers operate on binary data?
3. What is a byte? What is a word?
4. How are a computer's main memory locations addressed?
5. What are the major components of the central processing unit? What functions are performed by each of these components?
6. Describe what happens during a typical machine cycle.
7. Describe the format of a typical, machine-level instruction.
8. What (from the computer's perspective) is a program?
9. What is a stored program? Why is this such an important concept?
10. Describe the function performed by registers.
11. Sketch a typical mainframe, showing the relative positions of all the key components.
12. What function is performed by those devices that are attached to the computer's front end?
13. What is secondary storage? Why is it necessary?
14. Briefly explain how data are accessed on disk.
15. Why is something like an interface unit needed between the computer and an I/O device?
16. What is the function of an I/O control unit?
17. Distinguish between an instruction control unit (CPU) and an I/O control unit.
18. What is the function of an I/O channel?
19. Distinguish between a selector channel and a multiplexer channel.
20. Sketch a complete computer system, showing the relative positions of all the key components.

3

Software and Data

Overview ───────────────────────────────────

A computer is a machine (hardware) that processes data into more useful information under control of a program. All three elements—the hardware, the data, and the software—must be present or the computer system cannot function. In Chapter 2 we discussed the key hardware components of a typical system. In this chapter we turn our attention to the software and the data. In Chapter 4 we will consider the links between these primary system components in greater detail.

We begin with a simple fact—software and data are stored on the hardware. Software is written by programmers, and must be translated to machine-level form before it can be used. Assemblers, compilers, linkage editors, and loaders are some of the tools used to achieve this translation. Once on the machine, software is often stored in a library.

The data enter the system through a variety of input devices. In this chapter, we'll investigate how data elements are grouped and stored within the computer system, concentrating on a number of data management techniques, including various file structures, access methods, and the concept of a data base.

Software and Data: Logical vs. Physical

Hardware is physical; software and data are not. A program consists of a series of instructions—pure logic. Data are facts, mere logical descriptions of reality. On a computer, both software and data exist as nothing more substantial than a pattern of bits, electronic impulses, that can be destroyed or changed in far less than the blink of an eye. One pattern of bits might represent a machine-level instruction. Another might hold EBCDIC or ASCII coded data. Yet another might hold a pure binary integer, or a floating-point number. Physically, there is no way to distinguish among these binary patterns: one pattern of bits looks much like any other pattern of bits. Meaning is derived from the way in which a particular string of bits is used; in other words, meaning is derived by a process of logic. This distinction between the physical and the logical will arise again and again as we study operating system concepts.

Of course, there are clearly understood differences between software and data. One key difference is how these patterns of bits are introduced into the computer system. Let's investigate.

The Source of Software

Programs are written by programmers; you have probably written several yourself. Let's assume that a set of code has been written, and investigate the steps involved in converting that code into a stored program in the computer's main memory.

At the machine level, a program must exist as a pattern of bits. Consider, for example, a simple program segment designed to load values into two registers, add the registers, and store the sum back into main memory. On an IBM System/370 computer, the machine-level code needed to perform this simple logical process might look like the following.

```
0101100000110000110000000000000000
0101100010000001100000000000000100
0001101000110100
0101000000110000110000000000001000
```

Programming, initially, was done in exactly this way; imagine trying to keep track of all those ones and zeros! A single misplaced bit meant a program error. To help lessen the confusion, many programmers began writing programs

Fig. 3.1	HEX	BINARY
Programming	58 30 C000	0101 1000 0011 0000 1100 0000 0000 0000
with manual	58 40 C004	0101 1000 0100 0000 1100 0000 0000 0100
hexadecimal-to-binary	1A 34	0001 1010 0011 0100
conversion.	50 30 C008	0101 0000 0011 0000 1100 0000 0000 1000

in octal or hexadecimal, taking advantage of the ease of conversion to binary and generating the bit strings after writing the entire program (Fig. 3.1). Since this is essentially a table look-up operation, and since computers are good at table look-up operations, it wasn't long before some enterprising programmer hit on the idea of writing a program in binary to do this conversion electronically (Fig. 3.2); thus was born the essential concept of an assembler or compiler program.

The next step in software evolution is not quite as obvious, so be careful. If a program can be written to substitute a binary "01011000" for a hexadecimal "58" by table look-up, why not a program to substitute the same binary operation code for the letter "L"? Certainly, "L" is more like the word "LOAD", the operation in question, than is $(58)_{16}$. And why not use "A" for "ADD" or "S" for "SUBTRACT" or "M" for "MULTIPLY" or "ST" for "STORE"? Such mnemonic codes are incorporated into assembly-level languages as illustrated in Fig. 3.3; the assembler program performs the function of converting the mnemonic instructions into the binary codes required by the computer.

Higher-Level Languages

Even at the assembler level, programming is a tedious and error-prone activity. A first breakthrough from the "code-each-instruction-the-machine-executes" approach came with the use of macros. A macro is an instruction that, when encountered by the assembler program, generates a number of instructions in-

Fig. 3.2
Electronic hexadecimal-to-binary conversion.

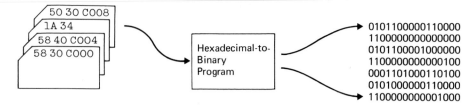

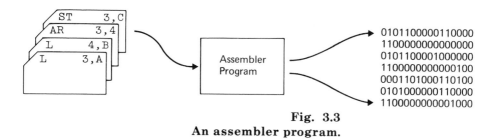

Fig. 3.3
An assembler program.

stead of just one. The first application of macros was probably in the area of input and output, where a number of machine-status bits must be tested and retested to ascertain successful completion of the operation; with macro capability, this set of instructions needed to be coded only once and was then simply incorporated into everyone else's program.

The first true higher-level language was FORTRAN. The basic idea behind a language like FORTRAN is pretty obvious once someone points it out to you. Since the addition of two numbers involves two load instructions, plus an add, and a store, why not write a special program to read something like

```
C = A + B
```

and produce the necessary four instructions (Fig. 3.4)? Human beings think in terms of addition; the load and store functions are strictly for the computer's benefit. With such a scheme, load and store are made transparent, thus simplifying programming. There is of course a cost—a good assembler language programmer can invariably turn out a more efficient program than even the best FORTRAN compiler—but FORTRAN makes the power of the computer available to scientists, engineers, mathematicians, and others who might never have considered using the machine given the limitations of assembler language programming.

Other *compilers* are designed to produce the same output, a binary machine-level program, from a different form of input. COBOL, for example, is a

Fig. 3.4
A FORTRAN compiler.

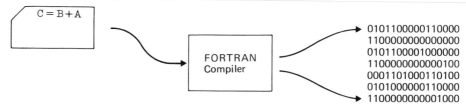

business-oriented language allowing programs to be written in something like the language of business (Fig. 3.5). PL/I combines many of the features of FORTRAN and COBOL. BASIC is an excellent language for the student just learning to program. Many compiler languages are designed to work with the specialized terminology of a given group—the Civil Engineer's COGO is a good example. There are literally thousands of compiler programs in existence today; each one applies a certain set of rules to the interpretation of a programmer's code with the objective of producing a machine-language program.

Object and Load Modules

A program written in programmer code—FORTRAN, COBOL, Assembler—is called a *source* module; source modules cannot be directly executed by any computer. The source module is read and translated by a compiler or assembler program (Fig. 3.6), and the result, a machine language version of the program, is called an *object* module. On many computers, the object module must pass through an additional step before it is ready for execution. Another program, a linkage editor or loader (see Chapter 11), performs a number of functions needed to prepare the program for execution on the computer and produces a *load* module (Fig. 3.6 again).

   Consider this process from a slightly different perspective. A compiler is a program. It reads the programmer's source code as its input, processes or translates this source code, and generates object code as its output. Where does this

Fig. 3.5
A COBOL compiler.

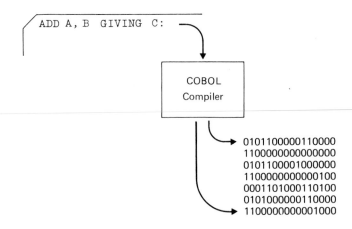

```
ADD A, B  GIVING  C:
```

```
COBOL
Compiler
```

```
0101100000110000
1100000000000000
0101100001000000
1100000000000100
0001101000110100
0101000000110000
1100000000001000
```

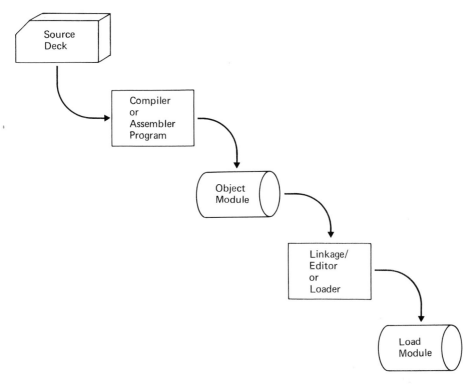

Fig. 3.6
Source, object, and load modules.

output go? Generally, the object module is written to disk, where it is stored on a *library*. Later, the linkage editor reads the object module as *its* input, and processes the object module into a load module. Where does the load module go? Once again, the load module is normally written to disk, where it becomes a member of a library. Later—perhaps microseconds later, perhaps days later—the machine-level load module can be copied from disk (secondary storage) into main memory, and executed by the computer.

The Source of Data

Data enter the computer under the control of a program. In some cases (the computation of a simple average, for example) individual elements of data are read, processed, and forgotten; only the end result (the average) is kept. In other cases a program will read data from an input device and then write the data to secondary storage, thus making them available for later recall.

As an example, consider personnel data being entered by a clerk via a CRT terminal. As the clerk types individual *characters* of data, they must pass through the I/O control unit and the channel before entering the computer. A translation of sorts takes place in these external devices, and, as a result, the program "sees" a string of bits that it can interpret as coded (EBCDIC or AS-CII) characters. The program groups these characters into meaningful sets called *fields*. Related fields are, in turn, grouped to form *records,* and the records are written to secondary storage where they become part of a *file.*

Let's reexamine this standard data hierarchy. A field is a single, meaningful element of data—a name, an address, hours worked, in short, a single, complete piece of data. A field may be any length, from a one-character job classification to a twenty-character name field and beyond. A field may be composed of a number of EBCDIC or ASCII coded characters, or it may be a binary integer, or it may be a floating-point number, or a packed-decimal number. A field is a complete, single element of data.

A record is a collection of related fields. The logic of a program is usually based on the idea of reading one record, processing that data, and writing one record. On a medium such as cards, there is a physical limit to the length of a record; no such limit exists on tape or disk.

A file is a collection of related records. Normally, every record in a file contains the same fields recorded in the same order. If a name is an example of a *field* in a payroll card *record,* the *file* would consist of all the payroll cards, one for each employee. An inventory record would not, obviously, be relevant to the payroll-processing program and, hence, would not be part of the file.

Physically Storing Data

It's very easy to visualize how data are physically stored on punched cards. Each card column contains one character; each card contains a single, complete record; a deck of cards forms a file. Since a punched card is exactly 80 columns long, each record will contain exactly 80 characters. Such records are said to be *fixed length.*

Some disk devices are *sectored*: in other words, the surface is divided into a number of fixed-length sectors (Fig. 3.7). Each sector normally holds a single record. A common sector size on many microcomputer diskette units is 256 bytes. This means that fixed-length, 256-byte records are transferred between main and secondary storage each time the program issues a READ or WRITE instruction.

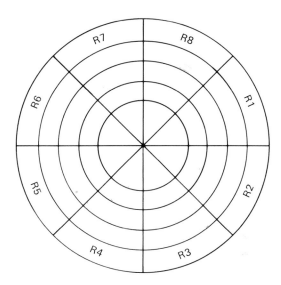

Fig. 3.7
A sectored disk pack.

Tape and nonsectored direct access devices do not restrict the length of records, but fixed-length records, each containing the same number of characters, can still be stored. In fact, it's probably reasonable to assert that most records are fixed length. This is partly due to programming considerations—fixed-length data are easier to work with. Individual fixed-length records on tape are separated by interrecord gaps (Fig. 3.8). Records on a disk, or any direct access device for that matter, are separated by similar gaps; in addition, count fields and, sometimes, keys are associated with each record (Fig. 3.9) to facilitate direct access.

To conserve space on disk or tape, data are often blocked; blocking also improves the efficiency of a program by reducing the number of *physical* reads and writes (seeks on a disk, starts and stops on tape), thus reducing the time spent reading and writing data. Blocking involves grouping several logical records into a single, large physical record (Fig. 3.10). Note carefully the distinction between logical and physical records; a physical record is the entire block, while a logical record is composed of the data needed to complete a single itera-

Fig. 3.8
Fixed-length data on tape.

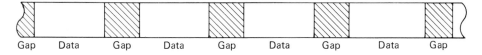

Gap   Data   Gap   Data   Gap   Data   Gap   Data   Gap

With keys

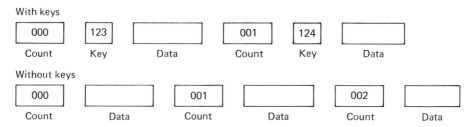

Without keys

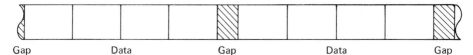

Fig. 3.9
Fixed-length data on disk.

Fig. 3.10
Fixed-length blocked data on tape.

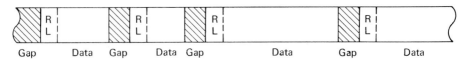

tion of a program. Most input/output devices are designed to handle all the data between two gaps; thus physical records move between the device and the computer. Prior to output, blocks are built in core by putting a series of logical records together. Following input, the physical block must be deblocked into logical records.

Not all data are fixed in length; variable-length data are useful for many applications (Fig. 3.11). To allow for processing of variable-length data, the record length is normally a part of the record (the RL field in Fig. 3.11). Variable-length data can be blocked (Fig. 3.12) or unblocked. A good example of a variable-length record is a student's academic record—almost empty in the first college year but quite long following the senior year. Incidentally, the BL field in Fig. 3.12 is a block length.

Fig. 3.11
Variable-length unblocked data.

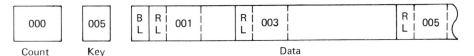

Fig. 3.12
Variable-length blocked data on disk.

Data Management ─────────────────────────

It is not enough merely to store the data on a secondary device; we must be able to retrieve the data as well. Once a file has been created, how can we find it again when we need it? Once a file has been located, how can we find the individual records we need? These are the questions with which *data management* deals.

The telephone book provides a number of excellent examples of what is meant by the term data management. First, how can you be sure that you have the correct phone book? (A New York City directory would not be very useful in locating a Los Angeles number.) The cover clearly identifies the city or area covered by that particular telephone book. Inside the book, data are arranged in alphabetical order; in other words, the book is organized sequentially. Knowing the rules used by the telephone company in organizing the phone book, we can very quickly find the specific name and telephone number that we need.

Our first concern in the discussion of computer data management is one of locating the proper file. Once a file has been found, we must know the rules used to create that file if we want to be able to find individual records. Thus our second concern is to describe some of the more commonly used sets of rules—the access methods.

Locating Files ─────────────────────────

A reel of magnetic tape is called a volume. Typically, each tape file consumes a single volume, although there are multivolume files and multifile volumes. Because people cannot read the data on tape, labels are used to identify files.

A single disk pack or a single drum is also known as a volume; the term volume is used to refer to a single physical unit of some data storage medium. The existence of multiple files on a single volume is the exception on magnetic tape; on a direct access volume, this is the rule rather than the exception. On tape, individual files are preceded by a label. Direct-access files need labels too. Typically on a direct-access volume, the labels of all the files on that volume are grouped at the beginning of the volume, usually on the first cylinder or two. This *volume table of contents* identifies each file and indicates where the file begins, in terms of the actual cylinder and track address.

On most systems, however, there are many different direct-access volumes; disk, for example, is typically installed in clusters, with several drives sharing a common control unit. Before finding a volume's table of contents, we must first find the correct volume. One approach is to search all the volume tables of contents until the one containing the desired file is located. This might work on a small system, but on a larger system with perhaps dozens of direct-access volumes on-line, the task of searching each one in turn would be too time-consuming.

An alternative is to maintain a *catalog* or *index* listing the name and location of each file on the system. This catalog could be stored at a known location on one of the direct access volumes. When a programmer wants a particular file, this catalog can be read into main memory and searched by the computer; through this approach, the proper volume and the location of the file on that volume can be determined.

On some systems, magnetic tape files are cataloged too. Such catalog entries might tell an operator or a tape librarian exactly where a particular tape volume is located (for example, shelf 3, tape 14).

Having located our file, we are now ready to turn our attention to finding a particular record on the file. The key to understanding almost all file organization methods is the relative record address.

The Relative
Record Address

On magnetic tape, we know that records are stored in a fixed sequence. It might be reasonable to number the records, assigning the number 0 to the first record, 1 to the second, 2 to the third, 99 to the hundredth, and so on. We begin with zero because then the first record on the file is located at the start of the file plus 0 records, the second record is at the start plus 1 record, the third is at the start plus 2 records, and so on. We might refer to these numbers as *relative record numbers*; they give the position of a given record relative to the start of the file.

This relative record number, sometimes called a *relative record address,* is not particularly useful on magnetic tape, but it is tremendously useful on a direct-access device. Let's assume that we are working with the drum shown in Fig. 3.13. Five of the tracks on this drum hold a file. There are exactly 100 records on each track; thus, records 0 through 99 are on the first track (*relative track* 0), records 100 through 199 are on relative track 1, records 200 through 299 are on relative track 2, and so on (Fig. 3.13).

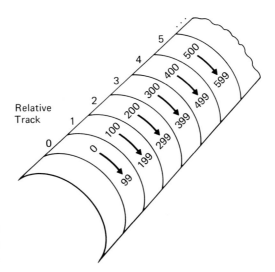

**Fig. 3.13
A file on
magnetic drum.**

Where would you expect to find relative record 432? It should be on relative track 4. How do we know this? Well, records 0–99 are on 0, 100–199 are on 1, 200–299 are on 2, 300–399 are on 3, and 400–499 are on 4. Because record 432 lies between records 400 and 499, it too must be on relative track 4. Also, because record 400 is the first record on track, its position relative to the start of the *track* is 0. Record 401 is relative record 1 on this track, and record 402 is relative record 2 on the track; thus record 432 must be relative record 32 on the track. By knowing a record's relative record number, we can determine its physical location.

Given that there are exactly 100 records on each track in this imaginary file (Fig. 3.13), we might go about computing the address of record number 432 in a different manner. What do we get when we divide 432 by 100? The answer is 4, with a remainder of 32. We want the 32nd record on relative track 4. We can always compute a relative track location simply by dividing a relative record number by the number of records per track. This works for any number of records per track, not just 100. If, for example, a file were stored with exactly 20 records per track, we would divide the relative record number by 20.

Let's refer again to the drum file shown in Fig. 3.13. We now know how to locate a record relative to the beginning of the file. How do we find the *absolute address,* in other words, the actual physical location of the record on the device?

Let's assume that our file starts on track number 50. The first track used by our file is number 50, the second is 51, the third track is 52, and so on. (Don't forget that we start numbering relative tracks at zero.) Given this starting point, we can compile the table on page 42.

Relative Track	Absolute Track
0	50
1	51
2	52
3	53
4	54
5	55
.	.
.	.
.	.

Our file starts on absolute track 50. In every case, if we add the relative track to the address of the start of our file, we arrive at the correct absolute address.

Where does our relative address come from? Knowing the relative record number and the number of records on a track, we can compute it. Where does the absolute address of the start of the file come from? From the volume table of contents. Given these two numbers, the location of the actual track holding our data can be computed, the associated read/write head can be turned on, and the data can be accessed.

In this example, we computed a relative track address because we were working with a drum. If the file had been stored on a disk, we would have computed the relative track and relative cylinder addresses because the physical nature of a disk drive requires both a track and a cylinder location. On a mass storage device, our objective would have been to compute the relative data cartridge. Using core, we would simply multiply the relative record number by the length of the record and compute the relative memory location. Our objective is to compute an address that is compatible with the physical device being used. In every case, however, the starting point is the relative record number.

In the discussion above, the relative record number was always known. Where did it come from? Over the next several pages, we will answer this question for a number of different *file organizations*.

File Organizations

Sequential Files

Cards are read in sequence. A card file is thus a sequential file; data are read in a fixed sequence and there can be no deviation from this fixed sequence.

On tape, individual records are stored in a continuous, unbroken string, determining the order in which data must be processed. Like cards, tape, by its very nature, is a sequential medium, with data being read (or written) in a fixed sequence. One of the biggest problems with using magnetic tape arises from the fact that a human operator must mount tape volumes on a tape drive. This is a source of error and, although the few minutes needed to mount a tape may seem insignificant to us, tape mounting represents a substantial waste of time to a computer capable of executing a million or more instructions per second.

Because of this cost, many firms maintain key *sequential files* on disk. An on-line direct access device also makes a great deal of sense when intermediate results must be stored on a secondary medium. As a result, even though disks and drums are called direct access devices, it is not at all unusual to find sequential files stored on them.

How do we access data sequentially when they are stored on a direct-access device? Simple. The first record on the file is relative record 0, next we have relative record 1, then 2, then 3, and so on. Do you see the pattern? Just add the number 1 to the preceding relative record number. The starting point, the address of the beginning of the file, is in the volume table of contents.

Direct Access Files

Direct access is different. Direct access means that we can go directly (or almost directly) to the single record we want without working through all the records that precede it in the file. The way we use a telephone book is a perfect example of what is meant by the term direct access.

To get a good example of a simple direct-access file, let's take a look at a small store that stocks and sells 5000 different items. Each of these items is assigned a unique part number—0001 through 5000 would make sense. A file is created to hold records for each of these part numbers (Fig. 3.14); individual records might hold the part number, description, stock on hand, selling price, cost, source, and other information.

This file would probably be created sequentially. But look at the relationship between the part number (the logical *key*) and the relative record number (Fig. 3.14). Part number 0001 is relative record 0, part number 0002 is relative record 1, part number 0003 is relative record 2, and so on. The relative record number can be computed directly from the actual key (in this case, the part number) simply by subtracting one. Once we have the relative record number, we can compute the actual location of the record and move the read/write heads directly to the desired cylinder and/or track location, bypassing the intervening records. This is the simplest form of direct access. For this technique to work, there must be one record for every possible actual key; given this restriction, the actual key becomes the relative record number (with a possible slight adjustment, such as subtracting one).

Simple direct access does not always work. What if your school were to decide to create a file of every student's academic record? If the key to the file were the student's social security number (as is often the case), how many rec-

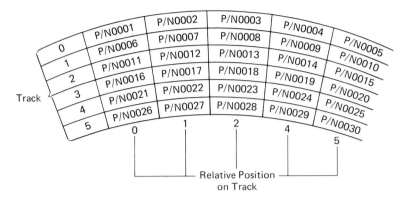

Fig. 3.14
**Simple direct access with the actual key being
(with limited modification) the relative record
address. For simplicity, the individual records
are shown as they might be arranged on a single-
surface disk, with exactly five records on each
track. The "P/N" stands for "part number."**

ords would the school have to allow for in order to use the simple "actual-key equals relative-record-address" approach? Because the social security number is nine digits long, space for 999,999,999 records would be needed! Even if we were to identify carefully the lowest and highest social security numbers among the students in the school, we would still need 100,000 or more records (probably more) to cover even this limited range. If you compare the number of different records needed with the number of students actually attending your school, you will see that a great many record slots would be wasted.

A common solution to this problem is to maintain an *index* showing the relative record number of each record. As the file is created, a table is built showing the actual key and the relative record number of the associated record of data (Fig. 3.15). Normally, this index is kept in sequence by actual key. Later, when a record is to be retrieved, the actual key can be looked up in the index, the matching relative record number found, the actual physical address computed, and the data accessed.

On large files, the index can become so big that it is difficult to maintain. When this happens, a technique known as *randomizing* is sometimes used. The basic idea of randomizing is to take the actual key and grind it through a number of mathematical computations so as to compute a relative record number.

For example, let's say that our actual key is a social security number. The social security number is nine digits long, much too long to use as a relative

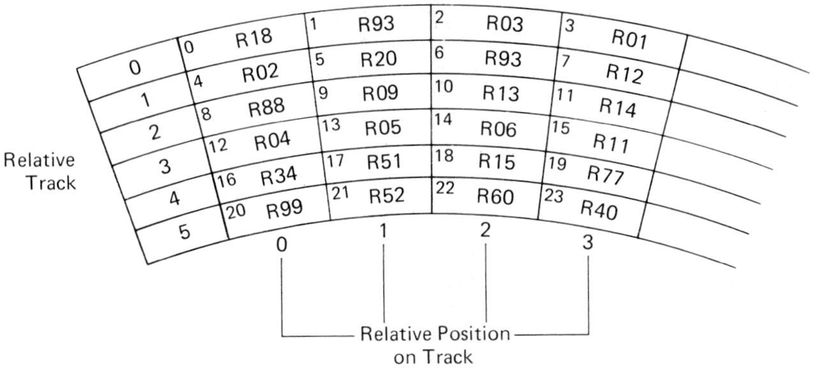

Relative Track: 0, 1, 2, 3, 4, 5

0 R18	1 R93	2 R03	3 R01
4 R02	5 R20	6 R93	7 R12
8 R88	9 R09	10 R13	11 R14
12 R04	13 R05	14 R06	15 R11
16 R34	17 R51	18 R15	19 R77
20 R99	21 R52	22 R60	23 R40

Relative Position on Track: 0, 1, 2, 3

	Index	Computed	
Actual Key	Relative Record Number	Track	Record
01	3	0	3
02	4	1	0
03	2	0	2
04	12	3	0
05	13	3	1
06	14	3	2
09	9	2	1
11	15	3	3
12	7	1	3
13	10	2	2
14	11	2	3
15	18	4	2
18	0	0	0

and so on

Fig. 3.15
Direct access using an index.

record number. But what if we were to create a new number by selecting only the second, fourth, sixth, and eighth digits? Social security number 123–45–6789 would, for example, become relative record number 2468. We now have a 4-digit number, and there are only 9999 possible different 4-digit numbers. This computed key could be used as a relative record number.

A number of techniques exist for indirectly addressing data on a direct-access device. A few of the more popular techniques are

1. *The division/remainder method.* Divide the key by a large constant, usually a prime number close to the total number of records in the file. The remainder, a kind of random number, is the relative record number.

2. *Digit analysis.* A frequency distribution of the occurrence of the digits 0 through 9 by their position in the key is developed. The three or four most evenly distributed key positions are simply used as the relative record number.

3. *Folding.* Break the key into two or more parts and add the parts together, producing a relative record number. A 6-digit key might, for example, be broken into two 3-digit numbers—the first three and the last three–and the sum of these two numbers computed.

4. *Radix transformation.* The key is converted to a number in a different, nondecimal base, and the result is used as a relative record number.

The objective of all these techniques is to produce a series of relative addresses evenly distributed over the entire available space. Some "randomizing" techniques yield both a relative track address and a record number, while others result in a relative track address only; the "RTA only" techniques are designed to get the read/write heads to the proper track that can then be searched until the record with the correct key is found.

The major problem with indirect addressing is *synonyms.* A synonym occurs when two or more records randomize to the same relative address. No randomizing technique will produce a perfect uniform distribution over an entire file. Once a given track is full or once a given record position is occupied, the next key randomizing to that relative address won't fit and must be placed on an overflow track; at retrieval time, the data will not be found in the computed position, necessitating an extra seek and read of the overflow area. A well-designed randomizing technique, custom-made for the data of a specific application, can minimize synonyms (20 percent is a common target); but none, unfortunately, eliminate the problem.

Indexed
Sequential Files

A major problem with the index approach described earlier is the difficulty encountered in maintaining the index. Using an indexed sequential approach, special system software maintains the index.

To create an *indexed sequential file,* data must first be sorted into sequence by key. The individual records are then copied to successive locations on disk, with no space (except for the usual interrecord gaps) between records. As a track is filled, the key of the last record added to the track is placed on a track index. Later, when searching for data, if the actual key is found to be less than the key of the last record on this track, then we know that the record must lie on this track.

As more and more records are added to the file, more and more tracks will be filled, increasing the number of entries in the track index. Eventually all the space on an entire cylinder is filled. When this happens, the key of the last record added to the cylinder is placed in a cylinder index. A cylinder, remember, consists of several tracks.

Moving along to the next cylinder, a new track index is started, containing the key of the last record stored on each of the tracks in this second cylinder. When this cylinder is filled, another entry is made in the cylinder index, and the system moves along to the next cylinder. Note that there is one cylinder index for the entire file and one track index for each cylinder.

Once the file has been created, the records can be accessed either sequentially or directly. How sequential access is achieved should be obvious because the file was created sequentially. To access a record directly is a three-step operation.

1. Get the cylinder index and locate the cylinder holding the desired record.

2. Get the track index associated with this cylinder and identify the track holding the desired record.

3. Move the read/write heads to the indicated cylinder, turn on the head associated with the indicated track, and search for the record with the correct key.

The ability to access data either directly or sequentially is the major advantage cited for the indexed sequential technique. This advantage, of course, also exists with the "actual-key equals relative-record-number" and the "programmer-maintained table-of-contents" approaches.

Chains and Pointers

A well-maintained indexed sequential file is most efficient when processing data sequentially, suffering some inherent inefficiencies when working in the direct mode. A very good organization for a file that is usually accessed directly but must be processed sequentially on occasion involves the use of a chaining technique. A part of each record in the file contains the key and (perhaps) relative address of the next record in sequence (Fig. 3.16); in other words, each record points to the next one. Sequential processing may involve frequent movement of the read/write access arm and, hence, inefficiency, but if such processing is relatively rare, who cares? The file can be organized using the most efficient direct-access technique, thus optimizing its primary use.

Another application of pointers is the linking of logically related records. Assume, for example, that a company maintains a personnel file on all employees.

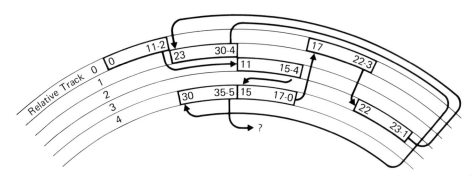

Fig. 3.16
Chaining.

Some of the data in this file—name, social-security number, hourly wage—are used every pay period, while other information is needed only infrequently. Rather than insist that the payroll program provide space for an employee's history of education and training, a separate education and training file is created, with the main personnel record containing a pointer to the associated entry in this new file. Thus a trail to a complete set of data is maintained without creating extremely long, inefficient records. The use of pointers to connect logically related records is common in modern data base management systems.

The
Access Methods

Is it necessary that the programmer be aware of the intimate details of file access in order to write a program? No. Typically, the programmer states, in some formal way as part of the program, that either a sequential file, a direct file, an indexed sequential file, or a virtual file is to be used. The exact procedure for defining the file type varies from language to language and from manufacturer to manufacturer, but once a programmer learns the rules, it is a fairly straightforward procedure.

This definition is subsequently used by the linkage editor program in selecting an *access method,* a special subroutine (normally, vendor-supplied) that is attached to the programmer's object module and that handles many of the details of I/O.

There are many different kinds of access methods available. On an IBM machine, for example, there are two types of sequential access methods: a Queued Sequential Access Method (QSAM), which automatically performs blocking and deblocking, and a Basic Sequential Access Method (BSAM), which leaves these responsibilities to the programmer. The Indexed Sequential Access Method (ISAM) also has both Queued (QISAM) and Basic (BISAM) versions. Only a Basic version (BDAM) is provided for direct access. Virtual files are accessed through VSAM, the Virtual Storage Access Method. BTAM, QTAM, and VTAM allow the program to access files over telecommunication lines, a topic to be covered in Chapter 19.

VSAM

When IBM announced its System/370 series of computers, a series that implements a memory management technique known as virtual memory, a new file structure—the Virtual Storage Access Method or VSAM—was also introduced. Because we assume that most readers of this book are not, at this time, familiar with the intimate details of virtual memory, we won't go deeply into VSAM here, but VSAM does support a different approach to file organization and should, at least, be mentioned.

Under VSAM, data are stored in fixed-length blocks. Within a block, individual logical records can be stored in sequence by some key—employee number, social security number, part number—or in entry sequence (the order in which the records are received). Assuming key sequence, probably the most common approach, an index is maintained indicating the key of the last record in each block. So far, VSAM looks very much like ISAM.

At this point, however, VSAM departs from the ISAM mode, offering some significant improvements. ISAM, with its cylinder and track indexes, is specifically designed for disk files; VSAM uses a "relative byte" address, analogous to a main memory address, to access data, thus making this access method device-independent. Let's repeat that statement: *VSAM is, at least in theory, device-independent!* When disk was the only "DASD" game in town, device independence was no big thing, but technology is changing and VSAM provides the flexibility needed to change with it.

Another major weakness of ISAM is the way file additions and deletions are handled. VSAM spreads "free space" throughout the physical file and VSAM software includes the code needed to rearrange records and pointers, making file updates and data retrieval much more efficient.

Perhaps the biggest potential benefit of the virtual access methods, however, is derived from the relationship of these access methods to virtual memory itself. As we'll see in Chapter 14, the virtual memory concept allows the programmer to address program instructions and data areas which actually reside on some secondary storage device (like disk or drum) as though they were in real core memory. The virtual memory control program takes care of converting these addresses into real addresses; it's like base/displacement addressing one more step removed. Since program instructions are handled in this way, the computer manufacturer is very strongly motivated to make the "disk-to-core" or "drum-to-core" transfer operation as efficient as possible by using special software and, probably, special hardware. VSAM allows data to be treated in much the same way. If computers are going to be designed to make this special kind of I/O as efficient as possible, it makes sense to utilize these extra efficiencies in handling data.

Virtual access methods are in fairly common use today. Their use will continue to grow.

Program Libraries

Like data, a program at the machine level consists of a string of bits. Like data, programs can be stored on any of the common secondary storage devices, using any of the standard organization techniques. Logically, however, programs *are* different. Thus it is not surprising to discover that, at least on most computer systems, a special "file organization" has been developed to store program libraries.

Programs are normally processed in sequence. They are normally loaded into main memory in sequence. It follows that programs are normally stored on a secondary memory in sequence—in essence, a *library* is a special type of sequential file.

A typical configuration for a program library begins with a series of index or identifying records (Fig. 3.17) containing the name of a program and the actual location of the start of the program. The programs themselves, the *members* of the library, follow the index records, one after another. When a program is requested by name, the index is searched, the address of the program is found, and the program is transferred into main memory. IBM calls this kind of library a *partitioned data set* or PDS.

Data Base Management

The fact that a computer is an information processing machine is what makes this machine so valuable. Information is the key to decision making in an organization, and the computer is a warehouse of information. Logically, this information should be available to management, but all too often it is not.

Files have historically been designed to match a specific application. Payroll files contained all the data needed to support the payroll application. Inventory files held only those fields that were necessary to the processing of inventory. The personnel department might maintain a different set of files to keep track of employee progress. This approach is not unique to business: At a

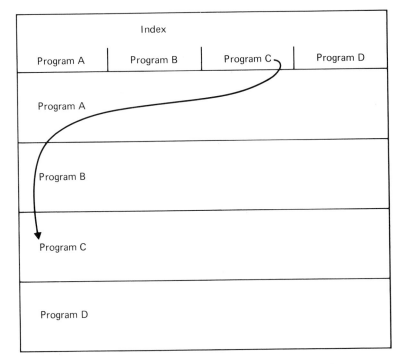

Fig. 3.17
A typical program library.

university there are files for a student's academic record, different files for financial matters, and still other files for housing and financial aid.

On the surface, it makes sense to customize a file to an application, but this does cause problems. Your name and address, for example, probably appear on several different university files. What if you move, marry, or legally change your name? The chances are that the financial files will reflect the change quickly and accurately, but what about the other files? What we have here is *redundant data,* in other words, the same data appearing in several different places. With redundant data, a simple name change must be processed several different times in order to correct every copy; unfortunately, it seems that one or two of the versions are usually incorrect. Redundant data is difficult to maintain; hence it is often inaccurate.

Why not store just a single copy of each student's name and address and allow every program to access it from this single location? In this way, data redundancy would be minimized. Data accuracy would improve because a change, once made, would immediately be available to every program. This is one of the basic ideas behind a concept known as *data base management.*

Using the data base approach, data are treated as an important organizational resource, *not* as the property of an individual programmer or department. The emphasis is on the accuracy and the accessibility of the data. Often, to improve accessibility, logically related elements of data are linked together. Perhaps the best way to illustrate these ideas is through an example.

A university maintains a number of files on every student: academic records, financial records, financial aid records, housing records, and others. Under a data base management system, each student might be assigned a master record (Fig. 3.18) containing such key data as the student's ID number, name, address, class, parents' names and address, major, and so on. Also contained in this record are a number of *pointers* to other records (Fig. 3.18), including this student's academic, financial, and housing records. These pointers might be the relative record numbers of the related records that are located in other physical files on, perhaps, physically separate pieces of equipment.

Fig. 3.18
Data relationships on an integrated data base.

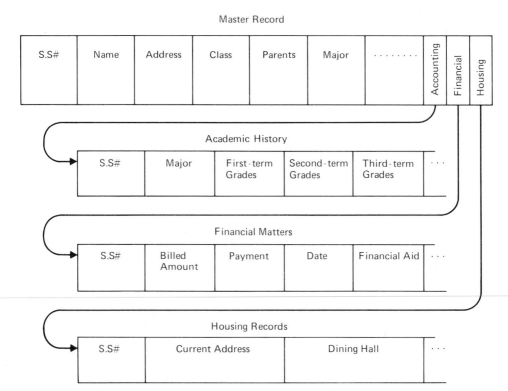

Beginning with this master record, it is possible to collect all the data the university has on any one student. The secondary files can still be processed independently (the academic history file, for example, would be updated each term), accessing the master file record through its key (the social security number in this example) when data such as the student's name and address are required. Because all requests for a name and address will access the same copy, the chances are that the data obtained will be the most accurate and up-to-date information available.

When the records in a data base are connected in this way, they are said to be *integrated.* On a well-planned *integrated data base,* all relevant data can be tracked down and found; in others words, the data are accessible. Building such a data base is not an easy task. Data base design starts with a definition of all of an organization's data resources, identifies key interrelationships between individual elements of data, and then puts the pieces together as an integrated whole rather than as a collection of separate and independent files. The whole point of a data base is to make the data resources of the organization available to whomever needs them.

Physically, the elements of a data base are the same records and files we discussed earlier; the only difference is the integration of these files. A data base management system might use sequential direct, indexed sequential, or virtual files, actually accessing the data through one of the standard access methods. The physical devices are the same too—disk, drum, tape, and mass storage. The pieces are merely put together in a different way.

We'll be covering data base management in far more detail in Chapter 20.

Summary _____

This chapter was a review of a number of key software and data concepts. Software enters a computer system in source module form. The source code is translated, by an assembler or compiler program, to machine-level, object module form. Frequently, one more step is needed to convert the object code to a fully executable load module. Programs are normally stored on a library.

Data enter the system under the control of a program, where the individual characters are grouped to form fields, records and, eventually, files. Physically, the records composing a file can be of fixed or variable length and can be blocked or unblocked. Data management is concerned with the storage and retrieval of the data. Files are located through indexes and/or volume tables of contents; once located, the individual records of the file can be selected by, essentially, "remembering" how the file was created in the first place. We considered a number of different file organizations, including sequential, direct, and indexed sequential. An access method is a subroutine that is added to an application program to implement the rules for record retrieval from a given file organization.

We then briefly described the format of a typical library. The chapter ended with an overview of data base management.

Key Words _____

absolute address	file organization
access method	indexed sequential file
character	library
compiler	load module
data base management	object module
data management	record
direct access	relative record address
field	sequential file
file	source module

Exercises _____

1. Physically, there is no difference between software and data. Explain.
2. Where does software come from?
3. Why must a machine-level program be at a binary level? Be careful; this question relates back to Chapter 2.
4. What is an assembler?
5. What is a compiler?
6. Explain the difference between a source module, an object module, and a load module.
7. Where do data come from?
8. Describe the standard data hierarchy.
9. Sketch or describe the following types of data.
   a) fixed-length unblocked
   b) fixed-length blocked
   c) variable-length unblocked
   d) variable-length blocked
10. What is data management? What are the primary functions performed by data management?

11. Explain the relative record address concept.
12. What is a sequential file organization?
13. What is direct access? Briefly describe several techniques for achieving direct access.
14. What is an access method?
15. What is a library? How is a typical library organized?
16. Briefly explain data base management.

4

Linking the
System Components

Overview

When you consider all the hardware, software, and data components that form a typical computer system, it is very easy to become lost in the details. Often we tend to see a single component at a time, and we miss the essential relationships among them. In this chapter, we will concentrate on how the various components of a computer system are linked.

We begin with the computer's internal components: the CPU, main memory, and registers. Bus lines are used to link these components; the width of a bus line is often a function of the computer's word size. We'll briefly discuss the differences between microcomputers, minicomputers, and the large mainframes, and then review the steps in a typical machine cycle in light of our understanding of the physical links.

Bus lines are also used to attach external devices to the computer system. We'll investigate control units and channels on a large machine, showing how they are attached and what functions they perform. On smaller computers, these functions are usually handled by a variety of interface units; we'll consider the architecture of machines that take this approach as well.

Finally, we'll show how software and data are integrated into the system, illustrating a program-generated request for I/O and the resulting physical control of an I/O device.

Internal Linkage:
The Bus Lines

A computer consists of a number of components that must work together. We have seen how instructions are stored in main memory, transferred to the control unit portion of the CPU during I-time, and executed by the arithmetic and logical unit of the CPU during E-time. We have seen how data are transferred from an input device, through an I/O control unit, through a channel, and eventually into main memory. In our earlier discussions, we have concentrated on how these components are *logically* related; in other words, we have discussed what takes place without really explaining *how* things happen. Obviously, if you think about it, the fact that instructions are transferred between main memory and the CPU implies that there must be some physical connection between these two components. Likewise, a physical connection is needed to support the transfer of data between the channel and the main memory. These physical connections are normally achieved by using special electric cables or links called *bus lines* (Fig. 4.1).

One of the most significant differences between computers is the size of a *word*. A typical mainframe, an IBM System/370, for example, has a word size of 32 bits, while a typical minicomputer, an IBM System/3, for example, has a word size of only 16 bits. Why is word size so important?

Fig. 4.1
**The bus line connecting the internal components
of a typical computer.**

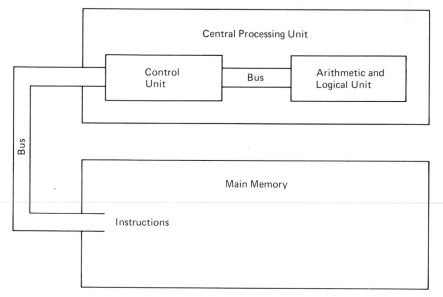

The internal circuitry of a computer is designed around its word size. It makes sense to move data within the computer as quickly as possible. A four-lane bridge can move more cars per hour than a one-lane bridge simply because four cars can cross side by side. Similarly, most bus lines are designed to move several bits in parallel, simply because it's faster. How many bits should be moved at a time? Typically, one word. A 32-bit machine has 32-bit bus lines; a 16-bit machine has 16-bit bus lines; the 32-bit machine will be able to move more bits per second between the CPU and main memory and, hence, will be faster.

A 32-bit address bus can accommodate an address as big as roughly 2 billion. The biggest address possible on a 16-bit bus is just over 32,000. The bigger machine can address, and thus have, considerably more main memory.

What about instructions? A 32-bit bus can carry a bigger instruction than a 16-bit bus. The bigger instruction size means that more bits are available for the operation code. A machine with a 6-bit op code can have only 64 different instructions, while a machine with an 8-bit op code can have as many as 256 different instructions. Thus the large mainframe can have a bigger instruction set; i.e., it can support a greater variety of instructions.

Registers generally hold one word. The internal circuitry of the CPU is usually most efficient when manipulating numbers one word in length. A 32-bit mainframe adds 32-bit numbers; a 16-bit machine adds 16-bit numbers. While the 16-bit machine may be able to add two 32-bit numbers, it will need several machine cycles and may lose a bit in accuracy—the big machine will be both faster and somewhat more accurate. In fact, on huge scientific computers where speed and accuracy are at a premium, word sizes as big as 60 bits are common.

Inside a computer system, bus lines are used to move data from component to component. On most systems, other buses are used to carry addresses and instructions, as well.

In general, the bigger word size of a large mainframe means that the computer will be faster, more accurate (or, at least, more precise), able to address (and thus to have) more main memory, and able to support a larger, more varied instruction set than a smaller machine. The typical mainframe has a word size of 32 bits. The typical mini is a 16-bit machine. A common word size for microcomputers is 8 bits.

A Machine Cycle

Perhaps the easiest way to envision how the various components of a computer are linked is to follow, in detail, a typical machine cycle. The machine we'll be using for this example is pictured in Fig. 4.2. Note that a single bus line links the CPU, the registers (which are physically part of the CPU), and main memory. In main memory is a program and data.

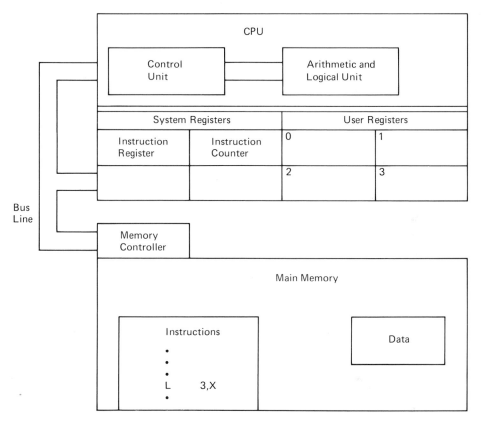

Fig. 4.2
The architecture of a typical computer system.

The registers require a bit more explanation. All are designed to hold a single word of data, but there are two different kinds of registers shown in Fig. 4.2. What is the difference between the system registers and the work registers? The system registers, as the name implies, are used to help control the computer system; they are not, normally, available to the application programmer. The work registers or user registers can be used by the programmer for computations or addressing.

Two of the system registers are of importance to us in this example: the *instruction counter* and the *instruction register*. The function of the instruction counter is to keep track of the next instruction to be executed. The instruction itself is normally fetched from main memory and placed in the instruction register, where the CPU can work on it.

Remember, from Chapter 2, the basic machine cycle. During instruction time or I-time, the control unit portion of the CPU *fetches* the next instruction

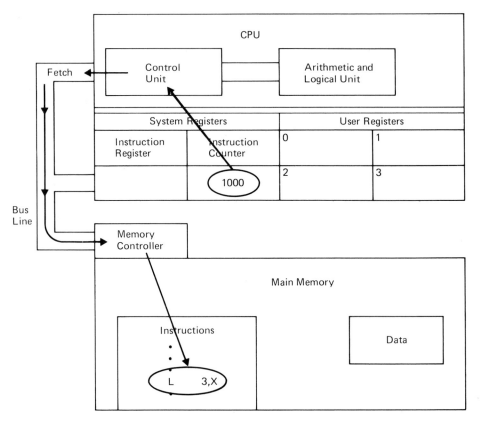

Fig. 4.3
The instruction fetch operation.

to be executed from main memory. The control unit then interprets the instruction and gives control to the arithmetic and logical unit, which executes the instruction. While reasonable, this brief explanation leaves a few questions unanswered.

How does the control unit portion of the CPU know the location of the next instruction to be executed? The answer is quite simple: the address of the next instruction is found in the special system register known as the instruction counter. (Exactly how it gets there is the subject of Chapter 15.) The control unit simply fetches the instruction found at the main memory location specified in the instruction counter register (Fig. 4.3).

How does the instruction get from main memory to the CPU? The location of the instruction is known. The control unit issues a command to memory, over the bus line, to fetch the contents of the specified word. The memory controller, in turn, accepts the command, finds the requested word, and copies the contents of the memory onto the bus. This string of bits moves over the bus line and into the instruction register, where the control unit can work with it (Fig. 4.4).

Once the control unit has verified that the instruction is legal, control is given to the arithmetic and logical unit. Like the control unit, it can directly access the registers; thus the instruction to be executed is known to the arithmetic and logical unit because it resides in the instruction register.

What happens when the arithmetic and logical unit executes the instruction? Let's assume that the instruction calls for the loading of the contents of a

Fig. 4.4
The instruction is copied into the instruction register, and is now available to the CPU. Note that the instruction counter now points to the "next" instruction.

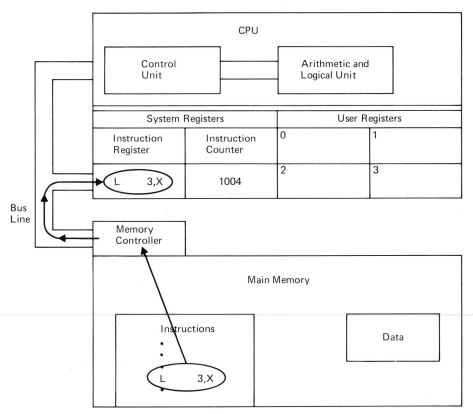

main memory word into a work register. The arithmetic and logical unit would issue, again over the bus line, a command to fetch the contents of the specified main memory location. The memory controller would find the requested word and copy the contents onto the bus line; as a result, a copy of the data would be placed in a work register.

Architectures

Not all computers are designed like the example system described above. Some use a multiple-bus architecture, with separate command bus, address bus, instruction bus, and data bus lines (Fig. 4.5). Others use a "unibus" design, with all components being attached to a single bus line, and all communication taking place over this single electronic link. (Fig. 4.6). The basic idea of what happens during a typical machine cycle, however, does not change with the architecture. The cycle still contains two components—I-time and E-time. Commands, instructions, and data still flow over the bus line or lines. Registers still perform the same "holding" function.

Linking the External Devices

How are the external devices linked to the system? On some machines (particularly microcomputers) that use single bus architecture, the answer is pretty simple. I/O interface units, one for each external or peripheral device, are plugged into the bus line (Fig. 4.6). When the CPU encounters an instruction calling for data from an external device, it sends an appropriate command to

Fig. 4.5
Multiple bus architecture.

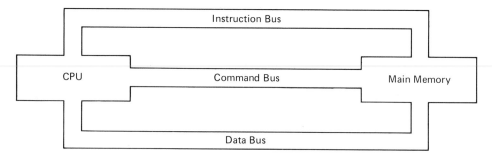

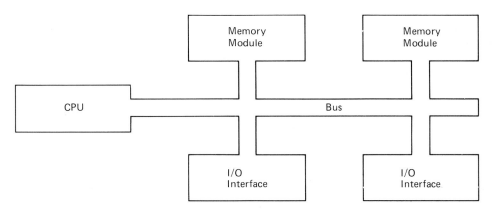

Fig. 4.6
Single bus architecture.

the I/O interface unit. This unit, in turn, communicates with the external device, signaling the processor when it is finished.

It's just a bit more complex on a large computer system. Rather than a simple interface unit for each peripheral, any device-dependent functions are assigned to an *I/O control unit*; a group of control units are subsequently tied to the computer system through a *channel*. How do the channel and the control unit work?

Let's begin with the channel. On a typical system, two bus lines link the channel with the system (Fig. 4.7). As an input or output operation begins, the

Fig. 4.7
Linking the external devices.

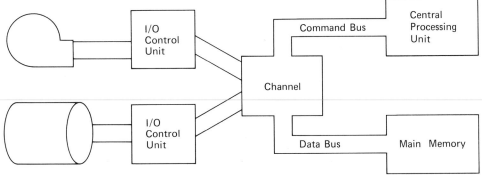

central processing unit sends a "start I/O" command over the command bus. In response, the channel assumes responsibility for the operation, establishing a link with the proper I/O device and controlling the transfer of data into main memory over the data bus. The fact that the channel can directly access main memory without the need for CPU intervention is important, as this frees the CPU to work on some other task. The channel is an independent, asynchronous device.

The channel controls the I/O operation. Because the channel and the CPU are independent, the CPU has no way of knowing when the I/O operation is complete unless the channel tells it. Thus as the last character of data flows across the channel and into main memory (or to the device on output), the channel sends an electronic signal called an *interrupt* across the command bus (Fig. 4.7). The CPU now knows that the requested I/O operating has been completed, and can begin processing the data. We'll consider this interrupt process in considerable detail in Chapter 15.

What about the control unit? Clearly, the I/O control unit is told to "start" by the channel, but what does the control unit actually do? An I/O control unit is capable of executing certain very "primitive" instructions. For example, a disk control unit can cause a disk drive to

1. move the read/write mechanism over a specific cylinder location (seek),
2. turn on a specific read/write head to access a single track on that cylinder,
3. read or write a record on that track by its relative record number or count,
4. read or write a record on that track by logical key.

That's about it. The control unit for a magnetic tape drive would have a different set of primitive commands, including, among others,

1. read the next record,
2. backspace one record,
3. rewind the tape,
4. unload the tape.

In effect, an I/O control unit runs under control of a special type of program, an I/O program or channel program, consisting of primitive commands. Who writes these I/O programs, and where do they reside? Typically, the I/O program is part of the application program, part of the load module in main memory. More specifically, the I/O program is part of the access method, and is added to the load module by the linkage editor.

Perhaps it might be helpful if we backed off one more level and considered the process of communicating with an I/O device in a bit more detail.

Logical vs.
Physical I/O _____

Let's assume that a sequential file exists on disk (Fig. 4.8). As part of the program, a READ instruction is coded; clearly, the programmer wants the "next" record copied from the disk file and into main memory. In response to this command, the disk drive's read/write mechanism is moved over the track containing the "next" record, the "next" record is found, and this record is transferred, over the channel, into main memory.

Think about this process for a bit. What exactly is meant by the "next" record? This is a *logical* concept. In effect, the programmer is saying, "Get me the next record: I don't care what physical steps are involved in finding it."

What steps are involved in physically finding the record? What primitive functions are available to the disk control unit? Essentially, there are three; a disk control unit can

1. seek to a cylinder/track location,

2. search by count,

3. search by key.

The concept of the "next" record is meaningless at this level; if you want to find a record *physically* on disk, you must specify both the cylinder/track location and either a count (relative record number) or a key. The programmer is concerned with *logical* I/O. The device is limited to *physical* I/O. How can we bridge this gap?

Fig. 4.8
Logical versus physical I/O.

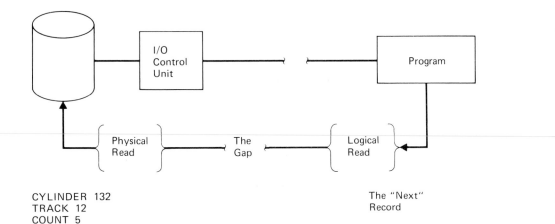

CYLINDER 132
TRACK 12
COUNT 5

The "Next"
Record

The process starts when the application program issues a logical I/O request. What really happens is that control is given to a subroutine, the *access method*. Remember our earlier discussion of access methods in Chapter 3? Typically, these subroutines are added to the programmer's object module during the linkage editor step; thus the access methods are part of the load module that is actually executed on the computer. (Fig. 4.9). The function of the access method is to translate the programmer's logical I/O request into a physical I/O request. The access method normally contains an I/O program or channel program—the primitive commands. Access method logic completes the I/O program.

For example, assume that the program has just finished processing the fifth record in the sequential file. In this specific case, the next record would be the sixth one, which is relative record 5. The access method maintains a counter. It starts the counter at zero (the first record on the file is relative record zero), and adds 1 each time a record is read; thus the counter always indicates the relative record number of the "next" record on the file. When the program started, the file in question was OPENed. At that time, the facilities of data management were used to locate the file; thus the cylinder/track ad-

Fig. 4.9
The access method is part of the load module.

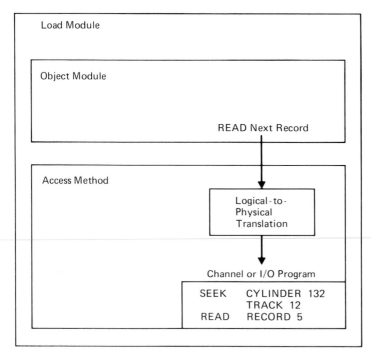

dress of the first record on the file is known. Given the start-of-life address and the relative record number of the desired record, it's a simple task to compute the cylinder/track address and the count of that record. Using this information, a dummy I/O program can be changed to read

1. SEEK CYLINDER 132 TRACK 12

2. READ RECORD COUNT 5

assuming, of course, that 132, 12, and 5 are the correct numbers. Do you see how the *logical* concept of the "next" record, whatever it may be, can be converted to a *physical* location? That's basically what the access method does.

Different access methods, of course, use different rules for achieving this logical-to-physical conversion. ISAM accepts a request for "the record with the key 123456," and uses a series of table look-up operations to convert the request into seek cylinder/track, search by key primitive commands. Under a direct access method, the programmer might provide a relative record number or a key (depending on the technique used); the result, however, is the same: the necessary primitive commands.

Once the physical record location has been determined, the "normal" process of communicating with the I/O device can begin. Typically, the access method asks the operating system to start the I/O operation (we'll analyze the operating system's involvement later in the text). The "start I/O" signal is sent to the channel, which looks back into main memory, finds the channel program (or I/O program), and starts the I/O device. Once the data have been transferred, the CPU is notified via an interrupt, and the program can resume processing. The elements involved in this operation are summarized in Fig. 4.10.

I/O Control and the Operating System _____

Many students are surprised to learn that a task as apparently simple as reading a record from disk can be so complex. In fact, the complexity associated with physical I/O is one of the major reasons why operating systems and systems software came into being. Remember that the basic function of an operating system is to present the programmer an interface that is relatively easy to use. Physical I/O is one of those "rough spots" in the hardware. Access methods were among the first of the programmer aids, and input/ouput control form the core of most modern operating systems. We are, however, getting ahead of ourselves.

In the chapters that follow, we'll be studying key operating system concepts in some detail. Remember that an operating system is a resource manager—its job is to manage the hardware, software, and data resources of a computer system. The intent of this first section of the text was to provide you with a summary of these resources and a brief feel for how they fit together.

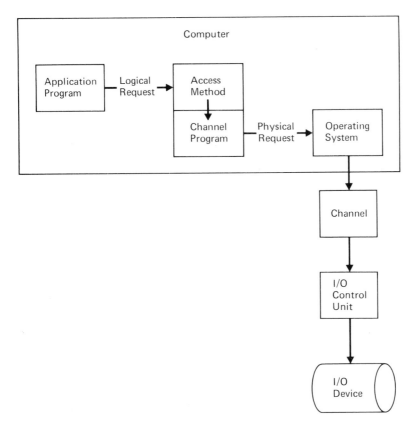

Fig. 4.10
Translating logical I/O requests to physical
I/O operations.

Summary ─────────────────────────────────

The chapter began with a discussion of how the internal components of a computer are linked—bus lines are used. A computer's word size is an important factor in determining the machine's speed, size, precision, and instruction set size; typically, bus lines are one word in width. We then considered what happens during a single machine cycle, describing how instructions and data are moved from main memory into registers via the bus lines.

External devices, channels and control units, are also linked to the system via bus lines. Often, a command bus will link the channel and the CPU, while a data bus links the channel and main memory. The channel can function independently, and thus must signal the CPU when an I/O operation is finished; this electronic signal is called an interrupt.

An I/O control unit executes primitive commands to physically control a peripheral device. These primitive commands must be given to the control unit in the form of an I/O or channel program. Typically, the I/O program is part of the access method, a subroutine that is attached to the application program object module during the linkage editor step. The programmer submits logical I/O requests to the access method. The access method, in turn, translates the logical request to a physical request by completing a dummy I/O program.

Part I of the text was concerned with summarizing the hardware, software, and data resources that are managed by an operating system.

Key Words

access method	instruction register
bus line	interrupt
channel	logical I/O
control unit (I/O)	physical I/O
instruction counter	word

Exercises

1. How are the internal components of a computer linked?

2. Why is word size such an important consideration in rating a computer system?

3. What factors are influenced by a computer's word size? Use the idea of word size to distinguish among microcomputers, minicomputers, and the large mainframes.

4. Describe, in detail, what happens during a machine cycle. What are the instruction counter and the instruction register used for?

5. What is the difference between single bus and multiple bus architecture?

6. How are external devices linked to a microcomputer?

7. How is a channel linked to the computer? Explain the difference between a command bus and a data bus.

8. What is an interrupt? Why, given an independent channel, is something like an interrupt necessary?

9. What are primitive commands? What is a channel program or I/O program?

10. Distinguish between logical and physical I/O.

11. What is an access method? What does an access method do?

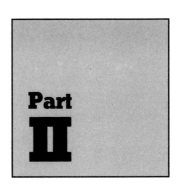

Part

II

Operating System Development

5

Single Program Systems

Overview _____

Many important operating system concepts were developed during the so-
called second generation of data processing—that period covering the 1950s
and the early 1960s when computers came into fairly common use. Computers
were small and, compared with a modern machine, quite slow. Most systems
were operated in what might be called a serial batch mode, i.e., programs executed in sequence, with the program in control of the computer having complete command over all system resources from start to the moment of completion. Second generation computers are, of course, obsolete today, but many of
the techniques described in this chapter remain in common use, particularly on
microcomputer and minicomputer systems.

A key factor during this time period was the movement of electronic data
processing into the business environment. Early computers were largely scientific and military machines, computing ballistic tables and mathematical relationships of interest to the scientist; these applications involve very little input
and output and, because the computations are very difficult, even impossible,
without the aid of the computer, the efficiency of the machine itself was not an
issue. Business, on the other hand, tends to view the computer as another piece
of capital equipment to be used as efficiently as possible; how to get the maximum amount of work from the least amount of equipment became an important consideration. Hardware, being the most obvious component of cost in a

data-processing system, became the focus of cost consciousness; *throughput,* a measure of the amount of work moving through a computer over a given period of time, became an accepted measure of effectiveness. As a result, much of the early system software was concerned with achieving efficient job-to-job transition. The cost of software was also recognized, but largely in hardware terms—a good program was one that achieved a given data processing objective using minimum core for a minimum period of time.

Although largely hardware-oriented, several software concepts intended to shorten program-debug time and simplify the job of the programmer were developed during the second generation—an indication that the cost of the software itself was recognized. In the area of data management, many of the concepts and file organizations discussed in Chapter 3 were products of this period of computer evolution.

In this chapter, we will discuss several of the more important second generation developments, showing how control and support functions evolved to meet specific needs, leading to ideas and techniques crucial to the development of operating systems. Don't forget the primary measure of efficiency being assumed throughout this chapter—throughput; almost invariably, the operating system concepts we'll be discussing were designed to improve the efficiency of the system.

Job-to-Job Transition

On a computer that is used to execute a single program at a time, *job-to-job transition* is an important problem. What happens between the time program A finishes processing and program B begins? Clearly, the computer is not in use; from the standpoint of productivity, this is wasted time. Thus an early objective of system resource management was efficient job-to-job transition.

Setup Minimization

Before any program can be run, it must first be set up (cards loaded in the card reader, the printer loaded with either regular single-part paper or special forms, tapes and disk packs mounted, and so on). This takes time (Fig. 5.1). On a slow

Fig. 5.1
Setup versus run time—a slow machine.

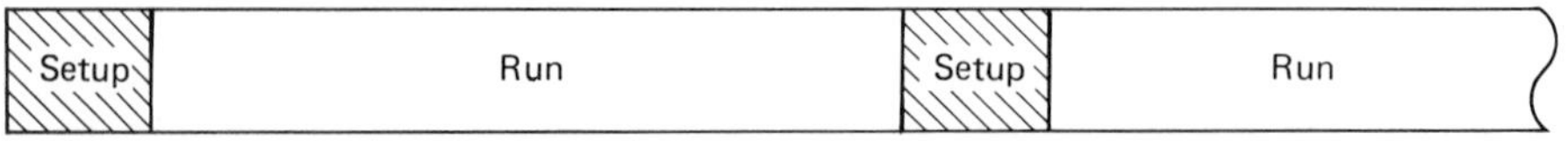

Fig. 5.2
Setup versus run time as computer speed
increases.

machine—say one thousand instructions per second or so—this is no big problem; five minutes of *setup* might be followed by a few hours of computation. As computers became faster, however, setup became a problem. Setup time is not affected by machine speed—if it took five minutes before, it still takes five minutes now—but run time drops by a significant amount as the computer becomes faster. Suddenly, instead of wasting an insignificant five minutes setting up a two-hour job, that five-minute setup is good for only a fifteen-minute job (Fig. 5.2); a substantial percentage of available computer time is blown on a nonproductive activity. Such excessive idle time on an expensive piece of capital equipment is intolerable to a good business person.

Simple elimination of setup is impossible; tape mounts, printer loading, and the other setup activities must be performed. One partial solution, long used in industry for minimizing idle time on production equipment, is *scheduling*. Consider, for example, the following four jobs with varying printer-paper requirements.

Job	Paper
A	1-part
B	4-part
C	1-part
D	4-part

Running these jobs in the given sequence (Fig. 5.3) necessitates three printer-forms changes; changing the sequence to group similar jobs (Fig. 5.4) allows the

Fig. 5.3
Job setups, no scheduling.

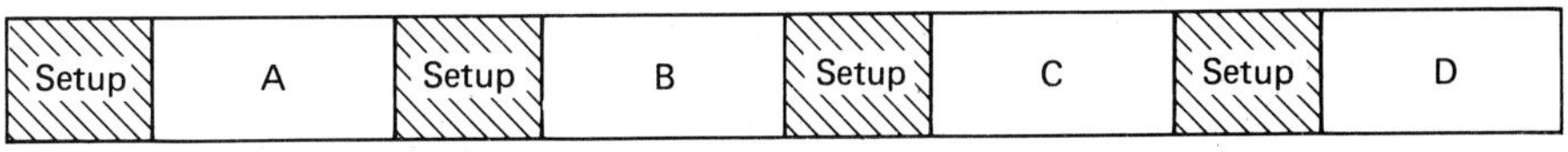

Fig. 5.4
Job setup with scheduling.

same work to be done with only a single forms change, yielding a significant reduction in total setup time. Not all job combinations are so obvious, but the idea of grouping similar jobs to take advantage of common setups is a good one.

Scheduling is often implemented through the use of job classifications. Tests, compilations, and assemblies might, for example, be assigned a classification of A; jobs running under this classification might be restricted to the use of the card reader and printer—single-part paper only. As class A jobs arrive at the computer center, they are simply held until some scheduled time when the entire "batch" is run through the computer with no need for intermediate setups. Other classes—B for tape, C for multiple tapes, D for multipart paper—allow for the grouping of other types of jobs.

How can the operator identify the class of a program deck? One common way is through the use of a job identification card. This card, placed on top of the deck, shows the job class and, perhaps, other information such as the programmer's name and accounting data. Many different card formats have been tried, including different colored cards for each class; the important point is the ability to group like jobs, thus facilitating scheduling to minimize setup. Modern *job control languages* and command languages started with this basic idea of job identification.

Input/output device availability is another basis for scheduling. A job requiring a number of tape drives might, for example, be set up while a job using no tapes is running, thus avoiding the expected idle time for tape mounting. This kind of scheduling is difficult to plan and implement, but a little work and foresight can achieve significant reductions in setup. During the second generation, this planning was facilitated by the programmer's run book, a formal document describing all the operator activity required on a given job.

The opportunity for priority overrides is an important part of any scheduling system—unplanned "hot" jobs do occur in spite of the best planning. Often the job card described above has provision for a priority parameter, aiding the recognition of such jobs.

Before leaving the topic of scheduling, consider for a moment the basic measurement of a computer system—throughput. While a computer is being set up, it is idle; this has a negative impact on system efficiency. The objective of scheduling is to decrease setup time, thus making more time per hour available for processing. The difference between good scheduling and poor scheduling might be an hour per day; ask any business person about the economic value of one hour per day. Good planning, by reducing setup time, improves system efficiency.

Compilation Time and Object Modules

Setup is not the only source of wasted time on a computer; a number of possibilities for substantial waste in run time exist as well. Consider, for example, compilation.

A programmer might prepare the job deck pictured in Fig. 5.5. This is a fairly typical multistep job, with data editing followed by a sort followed by a master file update. All three programs are written in COBOL; thus all three modules must be preceded by a copy of the COBOL compiler program. Just reading all those cards at relatively slow card reader speeds is time-consuming.

Why not store the compiler object module on disk instead of cards? In Fig. 5.6, the COBOL compiler object decks have been replaced by EXEC cards, indicating that a copy of the COBOL compiler is to be loaded from disk. Note also the new version of the sort program—it too has been replaced by an EXEC card followed by a single data card describing the sort fields. Sorting is such a common data processing activity that most firms long ago either purchased, or assigned a programmer to write, a general sort routine and placed this routine, in object module form, on disk, thus making it available to all the programmers

Fig. 5.5
Job deck with compilers in object-module form.

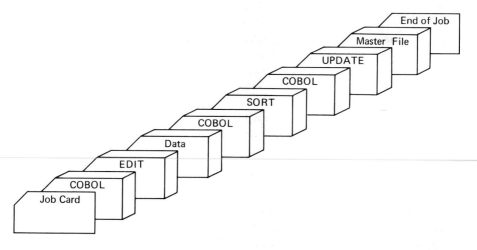

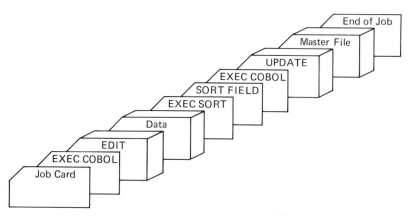

Fig. 5.6
The same job with compilers and the sort routine
stored on disk.

in the data-processing department. The elimination of so many cards, by itself, leads to a significant reduction in total job run time.

Let's pause for a moment and think about those EXEC cards. How does the computer "know" what an EXEC card means? Clearly, since all computer logic is implemented through software, there must be a software module that interprets these commands. For lack of a better term, we'll call it the *control module*. On most computers, this control module is core resident; in other words, it stays in main memory as the application programs are changed. The control module reads and interprets the control cards, and also interprets commands entered through the operator's console (Fig. 5.7). (Note that operator commands can replace the EXEC cards, an approach that is used on many systems even today.)

The compiler and sort object modules are stored on a *library*. A number of special programs are needed to support the library, programs for adding and deleting members and for loading programs from the library into core storage. Programs of the latter variety are called loaders.

What about the compilation process itself? Once a program is completely debugged, compilation, the conversion from programmer language to machine language, is a waste of time, simply producing the same output over and over again. Why not store the program's object module (or load module) on a library? It can be done. A job deck using library modules is illustrated in Fig. 5.8. In addition to cutting the number of cards to be read and replacing slow card input with faster disk input, the compilation operation itself has been eliminated. The use of libraries can significantly reduce program run time, thus increasing the time available for executing other jobs. This increases throughput, subsequently improving system efficiency.

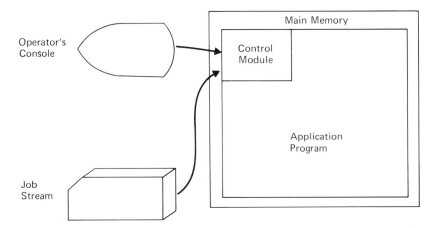

Fig. 5.7
The control module.

We do, of course, pay a cost for this added efficiency. Several new programs are needed—compilers, loaders, linkage editors, and librarians, to name
a few. These programs occupy space on secondary storage and in main memory,
and storage space is expensive. They execute under control of the CPU (just
like any other program), and CPU time is expensive. Consider also the JOB
and EXEC cards, the forerunners of a modern command language. Clearly,
there must be some kind of control program on the computer, the control module, to scan and interpret these commands. What do all these new programs
have in common? They do no "direct" work. They do *not* directly process data;

Fig. 5.8
Job deck with all programs stored
on a library.

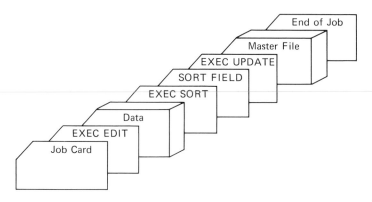

their function is to support the application programs that *do* process the data; they represent system overhead. Although expensive, the benefits gained from this *system software* far outweigh the cost.

On-the-Machine Efficiency

The fact that a computer is set up and running an application program does not necessarily mean that it is being used efficiently. For one thing, there is a tremendous speed disparity between the computer and its I/O devices. To an extent, shifting I/O operations from punched cards to disk by using libraries (see above) helped—disk is much faster than cards. It did not, however, solve the problem, and much of the early system software was developed with on-the-machine efficiency in mind.

The I/O and Computer Speed Disparity

A card reader pushing through 600 cards a minute handles one card in about one-tenth of a second; in this same one-tenth of a second, a microsecond computer is capable of executing something like 100,000 instructions. Most programs are not nearly that large. Put simply, the computer is capable of working at speeds significantly in excess of the ability of its I/O devices to provide data.

This concept is best illustrated by an example. The precise program used in this example is not important; it consists of a read followed by the execution of 100 instructions, followed by a write (Fig. 5.9). The program then repeats. Each cycle involves one read, 100 instructions, and one write, and anything we say about the timing of a single cycle can, by a simple process of multiplication, be applied to any number of cycles.

Our computer is a slow millisecond machine, capable of executing a mere 1000 instructions per second. With card input and printer output, the time needed to complete a single cycle is illustrated in Fig. 5.10. To read one card, our 600-card-a-minute card reader takes 0.1 seconds. At 1200 lines per minute, a single line of output can be written in 0.05 seconds—20 lines per second. On a millisecond machine, 100 instructions consume 0.1 seconds of machine time. Total cycle time is 0.250 seconds. Of this total cycle time, fully 60 percent— 0.150 seconds—is spent on input and output. While input and output are being performed, the CPU, the most expensive component of the data processing system, does nothing. In effect, the CPU is actually used only 40 percent of the time the system is "running"; 60 percent of the time is spent waiting for input and output devices to complete the transfer of data.

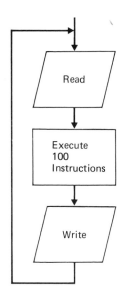

Fig. 5.9
A sample program.

Hardware provides a good solution to this problem, especially on such a slow machine. Magnetic tape can be read at rates in excess of 60,000 characters per second. At this speed, an 80-character card image can be read in slightly more than 0.001 seconds instead of the 0.1 seconds needed by the card reader, while a single 120-character output line could be sent to tape in 0.002 seconds. The speed of the computer is not affected by the fact that faster I/O devices are in use, remaining at 0.100 seconds for the execution of the 100 instructions of this program. Total cycle time works out to 0.103 seconds, with the CPU being active for 0.100 seconds each cycle—roughly 97 percent of the time (Fig. 5.11). Disk or drum could be used as well, with equally dramatic results. These numbers are not intended to be a precise picture of reality but are intended to illustrate orders of magnitude only. The improvement from using fast input and output is not as dramatic on a faster computer, but this example does show the advantages to be gained by using tape and disk.

Fig. 5.10
Program cycle time.

Read one card	0.100 seconds
Execute 100 instructions	0.100 seconds
Print one line	0.050 seconds
Total cycle	0.250 seconds

Run time = 0.100 of each 0.250 seconds = 40%.
CPU idle time = 0.150 of each 0.250 seconds = 60%.

Read one card image	0.001 seconds
Execute 100 instructions	0.100 seconds
Write one record	0.002 seconds
Total cycle	0.103 seconds

Fig. 5.11
Program cycle time
with tape I/O.

Run time = 0.100 of each 0.103 seconds = 97%.

Blocking, Buffering, and Access Methods

The use of tape and disk generally means that data will be blocked to improve the utilization of these media; thus blocks of data must be built in core prior to physical output and logical records must be deblocked following input. Although not really difficult, *blocking* and *deblocking* do represent one more problem for the programmer. To relieve the programmer of much of this burden, access methods were developed. An access method is a system subprogram; a key component of an access method is the code needed to block and deblock data.

A software technique that can lead to significant improvement in system efficiency involves the use of *multiple buffers*. As an example, let's work with data blocked in groups of ten 80-character records. We'll set up two buffers, each 800 characters, the size of a physical record or block, in length. As the program begins, these two buffers are filled and the first logical record is moved from the first buffer into the programmer's work area (Fig. 5.12). As the program completes a cycle and issues a second read instruction, the second logical record is simply moved from the buffer—no physical I/O operation is needed yet. The program continues (see Fig. 5.13 for a flowchart of program logic)

Fig. 5.12
Multiple buffers in a program.

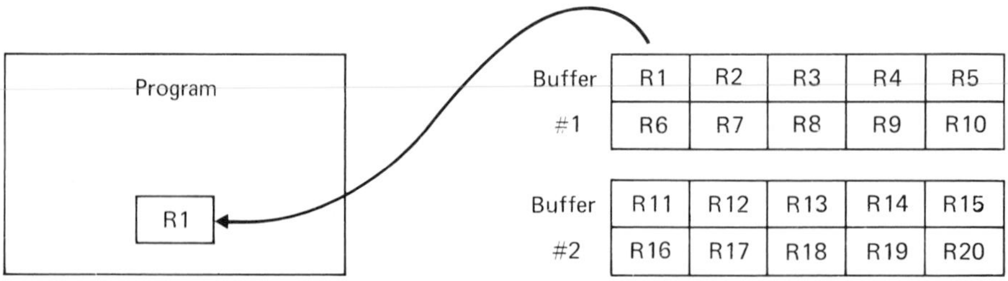

Program		Buffer	R1	R2	R3	R4	R5
		#1	R6	R7	R8	R9	R10
		Buffer	R11	R12	R13	R14	R15
R1		#2	R16	R17	R18	R19	R20

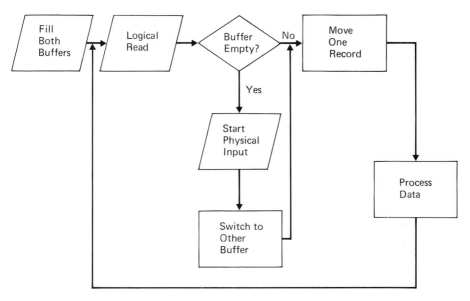

Fig. 5.13
The logic of multiple buffering.

moving data from the first buffer into the work area until the first buffer is emptied; at this point in time—the eleventh read—the program logic switches to buffer number two and concurrently issues a physical read instruction. While the tape or disk drive is doing its (relatively) slow thing, the computer is processing data from the second buffer, in parallel, thus significantly reducing wasted time. When buffer two is exhausted, data are moved from the by now (hopefully) full first buffer while the second buffer is replenished.

The software to support multiple buffering is generally part of the *access method*. The use of more than two buffers is possible—four and even more are sometimes used. With a well-written access method, the programmer is totally oblivious to the problems of blocking, deblocking, and buffering, writing a program as though it were working with simple, unblocked records. Some access methods allow the programmer to process data within the buffer rather than moving records into a work area; this is done by maintaining a pointer for the current record and using relative addressing, all invisible to the programmer. The programmer can concentrate on logical I/O, as many of the details associated with physical I/O are handled by the access method.

How are the access method and buffers added to a program? This is frequently a function of the linkage editor or loader program discussed in an earlier paragraph. Look at the compilation process described in Fig. 5.14. The out-

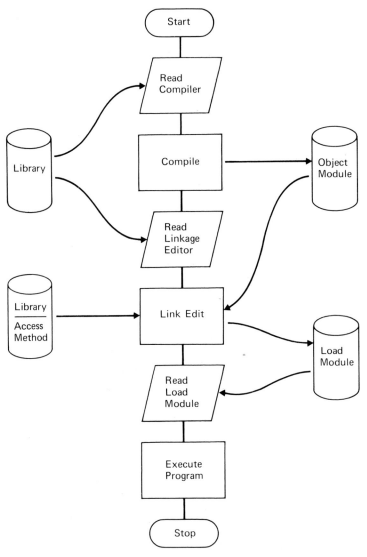

Fig. 5.14
The compile/link edit/execute sequence.

put of the compiler program is, as before, an object module; this object module is written to disk in preparation for the second step in this cycle. The linkage editor adds the access method software and space for buffers to the object module, creating a load module.

Spooling

The use of cards and printers cannot be totally eliminated from data processing. One technique for minimizing the impact of these slow devices is *spooling*. In a simple version of spooling, cards are read, off-line, directly to tape (Fig. 5.15). The tape is then mounted on an on-line drive, allowing the computer to get all its data from the higher speed device. Printer output, rather than going directly to the printer, is spooled to tape for later, off-line printing. Ideally, the programmer should not have to worry about the intermediate storage of the data—spooling should be transparent. Special software is needed to support spooling.

The Input/Output Control System (IOCS)

One of the major topics discussed in Chapter 4 involves bridging the gap between logical and physical I/O. We pointed out that the access method accepts a logical request from the application program and, by setting up an I/O program or channel program, converts the logical request to a physical request. As part of that discussion, we mentioned that the operating system is involved between the access method and the channel, but avoided any discussion of what the operating system actually did. What does the operating system do?

**Fig. 5.15
Spooling.**

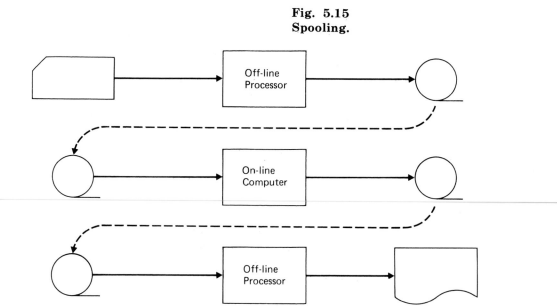

There are a number of tasks that must be performed in support of any I/O operation. Some are very "application"-oriented, including such tasks as blocking or deblocking to *this* program's standard, or converting a logical request to a physical request for *this particular* file organization; such tasks are normally performed in the access method. Other tasks are more "general" in nature: establishing a link with the channel, checking channel status, handling a channel interrupt, and so on. On many systems, these general tasks are grouped to form a system software module called the *input/output control system* or *IOCS*. The input/output control system is a *resident* module read into main memory when the system is started at the beginning of the day and left in place as the system moves from job to job (Fig. 5.16). Application programs, including their access methods, are read into the remaining space in main memory and, upon completion, are replaced by another application program, but the IOCS simply continues to occupy the same main memory until the system is taken down. The input/output control system was perhaps the first of the resident operating system modules, and continues to be a major component of most modern operating systems.

Reconsider the process of converting logical to physical I/O in light of the IOCS. The application program issues a logical READ, and transfers control to

Fig. 5.16
The input/output
control system.

Main Memory

IOCS

Application Program

Access Method

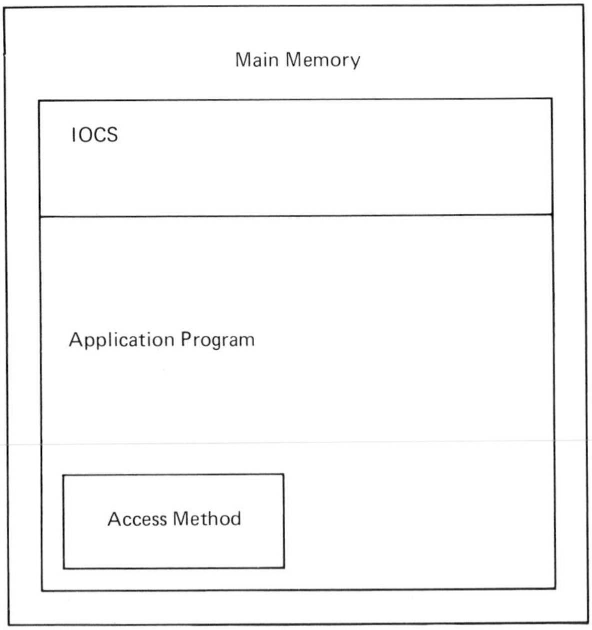

the access method, which interprets the program's request for the system. Eventually, it transfers control to the IOCS, which communicates with the I/O device. Programs change, so the access method must change, too. The physical I/O devices do not change, however, so the IOCS can remain constant.

Checkpoint/Restart

Every programmer has heard horror stories in which the entire set of results from an expected three-hour run is destroyed because of a computer failure or a program or data error occurring two hours and fifty minutes into the run. Such errors are an obvious waste of computer time. The use of *checkpoints* and *restarts* can minimize the impact of these errors. In using this technique, the intermediate results of a program are dumped to tape or disk at regular intervals—perhaps every ten minutes to cite an example; sometimes, a copy of the entire program is included in this dump. Should an error occur, the program is simply restarted at the last checkpoint, a loss of at most ten minutes of processing in our example. The software for checkpoint/restart logic is usually stored on a library and might be added to the load module at link edit time along with access methods and buffers.

Timers

Another problem most programmers have at least heard about is the endless loop, a set of code that simply repeats and repeats without end. An endless loop eats computer time to no good purpose. In the early days of the computer, the programmer was usually present when a program was run; if expected results were not forthcoming in what the programmer knew to be a reasonable period of time, the program was cancelled.

With the programmer not present, this responsibility fell to the operator, who could not be expected to possess an intimate knowledge of each programmer's product. The use of a timer is one solution. With timer control, the programmer is expected to estimate the total runtime of a program, adding this estimate to the other parameters on the job card. If this time estimate is exceeded, the program is terminated.

Memory Management

Another major component of on-the-machine efficiency is memory management. A good program, at least in second generation terms, was one that used no more main memory than it actually needed. Programmers spent a great deal of time trying to squeeze out a last few bytes, and the "good" programmer was one who used core "efficiently."

This was a very realistic concern during the second generation, and it continues to be at least somewhat significant on modern microcomputers and minicomputers. The problem is limited space; not too many years ago, a machine with 100K of main memory was considered "large." Generally, the problem was left to the individual programmer, but some interesting techniques were developed.

Memory Utilization: Overlay Structures

During the second generation, the amount of memory available to the programmer was limited. Careful programming helped, but was not always an adequate solution. What happened, for example, when the programmer was asked to fit an estimated 16K program on an 8K machine?

A few outstanding programmers got around the problem of fitting a 16K program into an 8K machine by using overlays; the basic logic of *overlay structures* is illustrated in Fig. 5.17. The program is broken into a number of modules; let's assume four 4K modules for this example. Module #1, the main or control module, contains a number of work and data storage areas common to the entire program; frequently, the input and output routines are part of this section. The other three sections are pretty much self-contained in that Module #2 is designed to access addresses and fields in Modules #1 and #2 but not in Modules #3 and #4, while Module #3 is restricted to itself and the control section (Module #1) and Module #4 does not access anything in Modules #2 and #3. It takes an outstanding programmer to design and implement such a structure.

Once the structure is set up, it works something like this. The main module (number one) and module number two start in core—that's a total of 8K, filling the entire available storage space. The program progresses through the logic of these two modules until eventually module number two is no longer needed. At this point in time, module number three is read into core right over module number two (Fig. 5.17b), in effect, overlaying the transient module. Next, the final module replaces the third; later, the cycle may start over again. Note that the main control segment remains in core at all times.

This is an example of inventive programming and is not the kind of activity easily implemented with generalized software on a second-generation machine. The concept of overlays is introduced here mainly because it was the ancestor of modern paging and virtual storage software to be discussed in more detail in Chapter 14.

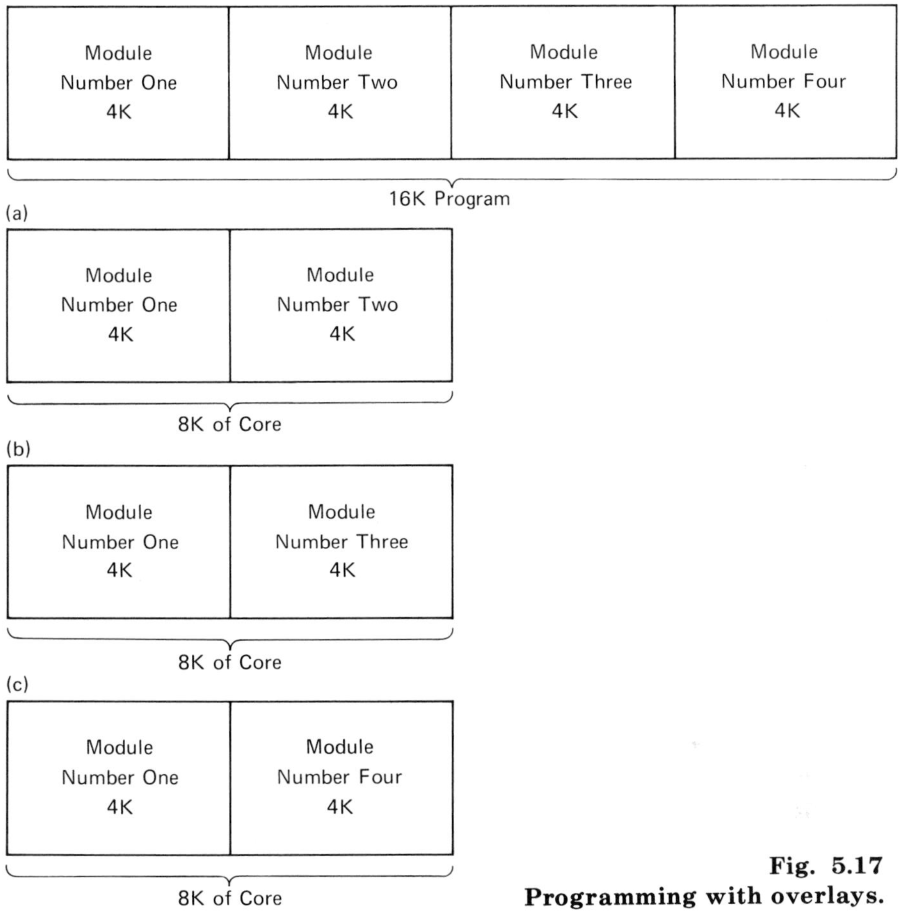

Module Number One 4K	Module Number Two 4K	Module Number Three 4K	Module Number Four 4K

16K Program

(a)

Module Number One 4K	Module Number Two 4K

8K of Core

(b)

Module Number One 4K	Module Number Three 4K

8K of Core

(c)

Module Number One 4K	Module Number Four 4K

8K of Core

Fig. 5.17
Programming with overlays.

Data Management

Many of the techniques and file organizations discussed in Chapter 3 were developed during the computer's second generation. Among the new software for supporting these data management techniques were modules for creating and updating files, routines for maintaining indexes and labels, routines for checking labels, data and library protection programs, randomizing algorithms, and others.

In the early days of computing, the programmer had complete responsibility for all data accessed by a program. Two macros, OPEN and CLOSE, greatly simplified this task, allowing the programmer to ignore many of the details of physical data management. The OPEN macro is coded just prior to the first input or output operation against a given file. The functions of this macro include issuing operator mount messages where appropriate, checking the label on an input file, writing a label to an output file, and in some cases filling a set of input buffers. The CLOSE macro is coded at the end of a program; it writes end-of-file markers and frees any temporary work space on direct access devices. Through these macros, data management and protection features are implemented. Label checking ensures that the proper file is being used. By routing all initial file access through logic not under the application programmer's control, a number of checks and tests can be performed to prevent the intentional or accidental destruction of data or a library.

A Single Program or Serial Batch Operating System

A number of different system software modules have been covered in this chapter. As a summary of this material, let's put the modules together to illustrate what a second generation *operating system* might have looked like.

Main memory (Fig. 5.18) is divided into two primary areas: one holds the "resident operating system" and the other holds a single application program. The operating system portion contains two primary modules. One is the control module, which allows the operator to communicate with the system, interpreting operator commands entered through the console. On many systems, the command language cards (such as JOB and EXEC) that are part of the job stream are read and interpreted by this module. It is through the control module that the operator schedules and cancels (when necessary) application programs. We mentioned this module before; can you see why it is necessary?

The other software module in the operating system region is the input/output control system. The IOCS is responsible for controlling all communication with the external devices.

Outside main memory is a library containing such other system software modules as compilers, the linkage editor, utilities, access methods, and the checkpoint/restart logic. Some experts consider these modules to be part of the operating system; others do not. The key point, however, is that all are system software rather than application software.

How might such a system work? Let's assume that the operator has decided that the time has come to run an assembly and test. A command "LOAD ASSEMBLER" is typed on the console. The command enters the control module, which interprets the request and, using the facilities of the IOCS, causes a copy of the assembler program to be read from the library into main memory. The control program then waits for the next command which, we'll assume, is

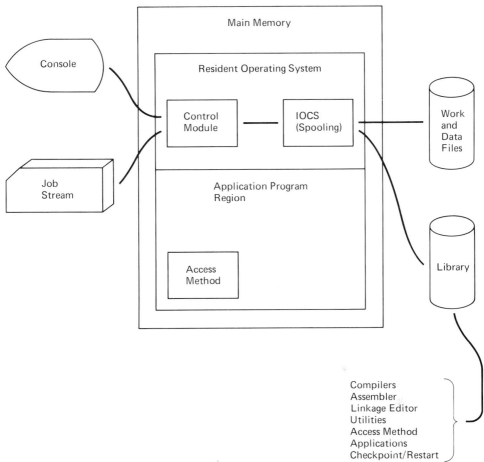

Fig. 5.18
A second generation operating system.

something like "RUN." Control is given to the assembler program, which reads source statements and translates them to object code, placing the object module on a work disk file (with the help of IOCS, of course). When the assembler program completes its task, control is given back to the control module, which waits for the next operator command.

Near the end of the second generation, most computer systems worked in pretty much this way. Even today, modern microcomputer and minicomputer systems running in serial batch mode follow the same pattern. As computers became faster and more powerful, however, new problems began to appear; we'll consider some of these problems in the next chapter.

Summary ————————————————————————————

Reread the discussion of "a single program or serial batch operating system."

Key Words ————————————————————————————

access method	library
blocking	linkage editor
buffering	operating system
checkpoint/restart	overlay structure
control module	scheduling
deblocking	setup
input/output control system	spooling
(IOCS)	system software
job control language	throughput
job-to-job transition	

Exercises ————————————————————————————

1. Define throughput.
2. What is meant by job-to-job transition?
3. What is setup? What effect does setup have on throughput?
4. How does scheduling help to minimize the impact of setup?
5. Why is a control module needed to interpret EXEC commands and other commands?
6. Once a program has been compiled, recompilation is often a waste of time. Why? How can the need for recompilation be avoided?
7. What is system software?
8. What is the speed disparity problem?
9. Explain multiple buffering.
10. Explain spooling.
11. What is an input/output control system? Why is IOCS necessary? What is meant by the term core resident?
12. Explain, briefly, how overlay structures work.
13. Sketch the components of a typical second generation operating system.
14. Explain how a second generation operating system might cause an application program to be loaded and executed.

6

Multiprogramming and Time-Sharing

Overview

In the mid-1960s, computers incorporating Solid Logic Technique (SLT) circuits hit the market. Although a detailed discussion of the intricacies of SLT is beyond the scope of this book, the increased speed made possible by this technology was largely responsible for the development of modern operating systems. The old millisecond speeds of the second generation had been replaced by the microsecond (one million instructions per second) and even the nanosecond; the old solutions—spooling, blocking, multiple buffering—were, by themselves, no longer able to guarantee anything approaching an economically acceptable level of machine utilization. Input and output continued to be as important as ever, but the time needed to complete an I/O operation had become interminable when compared with the almost incomprehensible processing speeds of these newer machines.

One solution was to place more than one program in core at a time, with the CPU turning its attention first to one, then to another, much as a chess master plays 25 or more concurrent chess matches. Multiprogramming and time-sharing, two techniques for achieving this objective, will be discussed in this chapter. The act of sharing a computer's resources among several users creates a number of problems in the allocation of CPU time, memory space, I/O devices, and secondary space. The programs or program modules written to deal with these problems form a key part of a modern operating system.

Throughout this chapter, two terms will be used in referring to the efficiency of a data processing system—*throughput* and *turnaround time.* Throughput, as before, is a measure of the amount of work passing through a computer. Turnaround time is a measure of the elapsed time between job submission and job completion. System objectives might be stated as: "maximize throughput while maintaining a reasonable turnaround" or just "maximize throughput" or "minimize turnaround" or some other combination. It is important to note that these two objectives are often in conflict. In a supermarket, to cite an example, throughput of checkout clerks could be maximized by staffing only one checkout lane, forcing customers to wait in line in order to keep that clerk busy, while the turnaround of customers could be minimized by providing one clerk for each and every customer yielding zero (or almost zero) customer wait time. Obviously, neither solution is acceptable and some compromise is essential; the attitudes and objectives of management play an important part in determining the weight given to throughput and turnaround. The same need to weigh and balance these two objectives is faced in the area of operating system design, a topic to which we'll allude throughout this chapter.

Input/Output vs. Processing Speed in the Third Generation

Consider the 100-instruction program used to introduce the idea of wait time back in Chapter 5. The program in that example ran on a millisecond machine, and we found that by using high-speed I/O devices such as tape and disk coupled with such essentially software techniques as blocking, multiple buffering, and spooling, extremely high levels of CPU utilization could be achieved. Let's take a technological leap and upgrade our computer to a microsecond machine capable of executing 1,000,000 (as opposed to 1000) instructions per second. With the card reader and the printer as our input and output devices (Fig. 6.1) input still takes 0.1 seconds and output takes 0.05 seconds as before, but the time needed to execute 100 instructions drops from 0.1 (100 times 1/1000) to 0.0001 (100 times 1/1,000,000). The total time for a complete program cycle drops to 0.1501 seconds of which, *and this is the important part,* only 0.0001 seconds, less than 0.07 percent of a cycle, belongs to the CPU. The computer, renting for perhaps $100,000 a month, spends over 99.9 percent of its time waiting for I/O devices to finish transferring data! To put these figures in a slightly different perspective, the computer, if actually used in this manner, would be performing useful work for about one minute of each 24-hour day. Total cycle time on the old millisecond machine was, if you remember, some

Read one card	0.1000 seconds
Execute 100 instructions	0.0001 seconds
Print one line	0.0500 seconds
Total cycle	0.1501 seconds

Fig. 6.1 Computer utilization on a microsecond machine.

Percent run time $= \dfrac{0.0001}{0.1501} = 0.00066 = 0.066\%$.

0.2500 seconds; this has been cut to 0.1501 seconds—not quite in half—on the faster machine. But the microsecond machine is 1000 times as fast as its predecessor. And probably ten times as expensive. Why bother with the faster machine?

Faster I/O devices provided an answer before; let's consider them again. A processing time of 0.0001 seconds between a tape read of 0.001 seconds and a 0.002-second tape write (Fig. 6.2) yields a total cycle time of 0.0031 seconds of which only 0.0001, or 3.2 percent, is utilized by the CPU. A scientist or engineer working on a complicated mathematical problem like a moon shot might be willing to pay for the pure speed of a third generation machine, but the business person, given an expectation of only 4 or 5 percent utilization and, at best, a marginal cost justification over the older, slower computers, would probably not buy. Why, to use an analogy, should we invest in 200-mile-per-hour trains when track conditions restrict us to 15 or 20 miles per hour in many places? Speed is desirable, but only if we can utilize it.

Multiprogramming—
One Solution

Let's, just for a moment, drop computers and imagine ourselves running a telephone-answering service. We have one subscriber and, based on past experience, expect only three or four calls each night. Our job, in other words, consists of occasional periods of brief work followed by lengthy waits. What do we do

Fig. 6.2 Utilization using tape.

Read one card image	0.0010 seconds
Execute 100 instructions	0.0001 seconds
Write one record	0.0020 seconds
Total cycle	0.0031 seconds

Percent run time $= \dfrac{0.0001}{0.0031} = 0.032 = 3.2\%$.

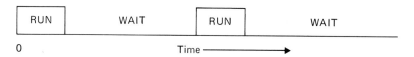

Fig. 6.3
The wait/run time cycle.

with all our spare time? We might read or write or work puzzles. If we were really industrious, we might take on a few more clients, figuring that calls for another would not interfere with our ability to handle those of our first customer. There is, of course, a limit to the number of new clients we can take on; at some point, our phone would become so busy as to discourage potential callers from trying, thus defeating the purpose of our service. But the idea of working on some other task during slack periods is a good one.

Back to computers again. The problem of a relatively brief runtime followed by an extensive wait for completion of an I/O operation is illustrated in Fig. 6.3. Why not use this wait, when the central-processing unit is doing nothing anyway, for some other purpose? Why not put another program into core? Then, when program A starts an I/O operation and enters a wait state, control of the CPU can be turned over to program B (Fig. 6.4). This same logic might be applied to three programs (Fig. 6.5) or four or even more. This basic concept of loading a number of programs into main memory and allowing them to share the CPU is known as *multiprogramming*. One important note of caution—the programs do not execute "simultaneously"; they execute in an overlapped fashion, with the CPU concentrating on only one at a time. The word *concurrent* is used to describe this type of program execution. The distinction between concurrent and simultaneous is subtle, with the former term implying "over the same time period" while the latter means "at the same time." Multiprogramming means the concurrent execution of more than one program on a single computer. All the programs are in memory at the same time (simultaneous core residency), but they share the facilities of the central processing unit in an overlapped manner.

Fig. 6.4
Multiprogramming with two programs.

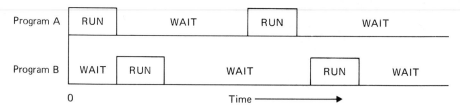

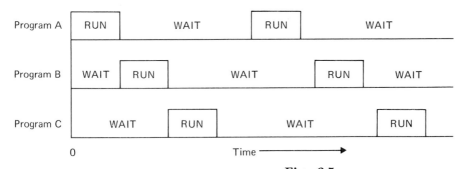

Fig. 6.5
Multiprogramming with three programs.

The benefits arising from multiprogramming should be obvious. Quite simply, time spent waiting for completion of an input or output operation is applied to the solution of some other problem rather than wasted; using multiprogramming techniques, it is theoretically possible to complete four or five or more programs in the same amount of elapsed time that would have been needed to complete just one program in the serial batch mode. Some program interference is inevitable, so this theoretical limit is rarely achieved, but multiprogramming does lead to a significant increase in the amount of work going through a computer (throughput). The economic implications of getting five or six times the work done in the same amount of time were not lost on the business community. Multiprogramming was instrumental in selling modern high-speed computers to business.

Time-Sharing

In addition to its highly positive impact on system throughput, multiprogramming does tend to improve turnaround time as well. If more programs are completed during the same time interval, "my program" will probably come back sooner. There is, however, one problem, at least from a turnaround-time point of view, that multiprogramming does not deal with—the compute-bound job. From the standpoint of throughput, compute-bound jobs are great; they simply sit in core and use the CPU without interruption, adding to the percent utilization statistic. Meanwhile, other jobs wait. As long as throughput is accepted as *the* measure of system effectiveness, this causes no problem, but this is not always the case. In some applications, turnaround (or, perhaps, some other measure such as response time) predominates, and a slightly different approach is needed.

An interactive *time-sharing* system with 50 or more users attempting to solve problems and write programs through terminals is an example of such an application. Typically, the time-sharing user makes rather light demands on the resources of a computer, rarely processing large amounts of data or executing lengthy programs; the only thing that makes time-sharing economically feasible is the fact that computer resources can be shared among many such users. Occasionally, a long-running, compute-bound job will sneak into a time-shared system (a regression analysis, for example) forcing the 49 or more other users to wait; a well-run, time-shared system must be able to deal with this problem.

   With multiple users in core, time-sharing is, as you might expect, quite similar to multiprogramming in its basic mode of operation, but there is one major difference (designed to handle the "long job" problem). A multiprogramming system is driven in a rather passive manner by the input and output timings of the individual programs on the system. Under time-sharing, a program is given a time limit—say one-tenth or one one-hundredth of a second. If, during this interval of time, the program encounters a natural break point (I/O), fine; if, however, no such break occurs, the program is interrupted and placed at the end of the line to wait for another shot at the CPU. Time-sharing is an active technique in that the basic driving mechanism is under control of the system itself and not the individual users of the system.

Software for Multiprogramming and Time-Sharing

The presence of multiple programs in main memory creates a number of problems that are normally handled by software. In the next several pages, we'll take a look at some of these problems and discuss, in general terms, the software solutions. To provide a framework for this discussion, let's break the computer system into the following five parts.

1. CPU time,
2. main memory space,
3. registers,
4. I/O devices,
5. data files and libraries (i.e., secondary storage space).

Multiprogramming and time-sharing create problems in all these areas; an effective operating system must be concerned with optimizing the use of all of them.

   One further point before we continue. There are few pure turnaround or pure throughput systems in existence; most often, some form of compromise between these two objectives is sought. We'll be touching on this point throughout much of the rest of this chapter.

Allocating
CPU Time

What happens when two programs complete an I/O operation at precisely the same instant in time? Both are ready to resume processing (Fig. 6.6) but the CPU is capable of working on only one at a time. Who goes first? The first program in core? the last one? the biggest one? the smallest one? the one that has been in core the longest?

Imagine the following, perhaps more realistic, situation. Some time ago, program A started an I/O operation. Several milliseconds later, as program E is executing, the I/O operation for program A is completed. Two programs, A and E, are ready to go. Which one gets the CPU?

To quote a well-known "law" of data processing and engineering, "If it can happen, it will." Thus any functioning multiprogramming system must be capable of making this crucial *internal priority* decision. One solution might be to print a message on the operator's console describing the situation and asking for a decision. This might take, at best, a few seconds. During these few seconds, a microsecond computer is capable of, in all likelihood, taking *both* programs to their next I/O point. Human reaction times are much too slow.

The usual approach is to write a program to make this decision. Almost any decision rule (last in, first out; first in, first out; biggest first; and so on) can be and probably has been, built into this program. There are good rules and there are bad rules, but the important point is that the decision is made by a program written especially for this purpose.

This small program module is one part of an *operating system*. Often, this software is made *core resident* with a section of main memory being set aside to hold the operating system or *supervisor* program modules. Figure 6.7 shows a sketch of the layout of main storage in a typical multiprogramming system; space for an on-line or resident operating system has been set aside in low core,

Fig. 6.6
**Program interference—both programs are ready
to resume at the same instant.**

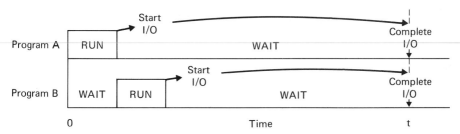

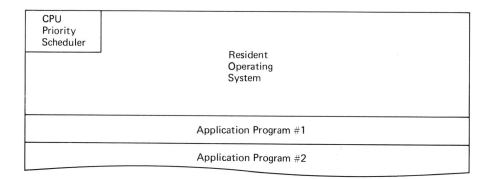

Fig. 6.7
Core layout for multiprogramming, with an
operating system.

and the possible location of the CPU allocation program described above is shown. Whenever conflicts occur, this program is called and executed, resulting in a decision at computer speeds.

Some form of *priority* scheme is often used in making this decision. A job's priority might be indicated on the job card and, once in core, the job with the top priority goes first whenever conflicts occur. Almost any conceivable priority rule can be implemented in this operating system module, with the only restriction being programmability. There are, of course, some practical limits—why spend ten seconds determining which three second program should go first? The important point to remember is that the decision is made by a program, a program written using the same instruction set available to any assembly-language application programmer.

Time-sharing uses a timer to force a sort of pseudo-I/O operation on a lengthy program, thus causing the program to surrender the CPU to some other user. Most modern computers have a built-in hardware timer that can be set by an operating system program. If time runs out on an application program the timer, much like an alarm clock, sends a signal—an interrupt, to the CPU. A program must be provided to handle the timer interrupt. This program is another operating system module (Fig. 6.8).

The timer, in addition to its use in time-sharing, plays an important role in minimizing the impact of the "infinite loop." Consider the following trivial case in FORTRAN.

```
5    GO TO 5
```

The result of coding this instruction should be obvious (so obvious that very few programmers actually make this particular error); statement number five

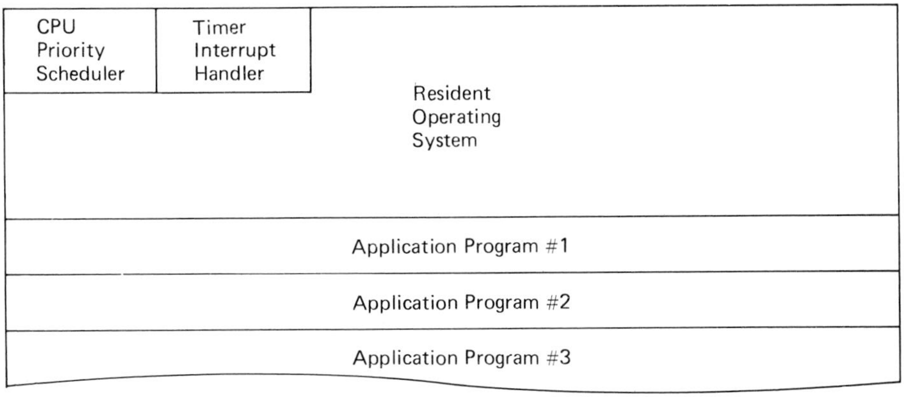

CPU Priority Scheduler	Timer Interrupt Handler	Resident Operating System
Application Program #1		
Application Program #2		
Application Program #3		

Fig. 6.8
The time interrupt handler as an operating
system module.

executes over and over and over again, without end—unless, of course, the program is given a time limit after which the program is interrupted and cancelled.

Priorities and the timer can be used to improve either throughput or turnaround or, in some cases, both. The exact nature of the operating system modules used to control CPU time allocation will depend on the weight given each of these measures by a particular installation.

Main
Memory Allocation _____

Most programmers are at least familiar with the accidental destruction of data where, often due to a program bug, a constant is destroyed or a counter reset to zero. Program overlay structures, as described in the last chapter, are a good example of the intentional destruction of portions of a program. The programmer knows that the computer can "forget" just as efficiently as it "remembers."

This is a serious problem on a multiprogramming system. Imagine the effect on your program if some "mad mover" were to sort your instructions into alphabetical order while you were waiting for the completion of an input or output operation. The accidental or intentional destruction of data *within* a program is one thing; the potential for unpredictable *inter*program effects is something else. If core is to contain more than one program, these programs must be protected from each other. *Memory protection* is another operating system function. No human operator could possibly react rapidly enough to prevent the destruction of one program by another. Memory protection must be implemented at computer speeds; thus the core-protect module is an extremely important resident operating system module.

Memory Allocation— Job Scheduling

Simply getting programs into main memory is a problem on a multiprogramming system. On the serial batch systems described in Chapter 5, this was an operator function; job classes and, perhaps, priorities helped, but the task of scheduling jobs for initial core introduction was essentially a manual process. Is it reasonable, however, to expect a human operator to keep track of ten or fifteen different concurrent programs? Could a human being be expected to watch the changing status of all these programs and, at exactly the right moment, introduce a new program into the proper position in memory? A really sharp operator might be able to keep track of such a complex problem, but certainly not at microsecond speeds. On most large multiprogramming systems, the scheduling problem is handled by operating system software.

One commonly used technique involves *job queueing*. Each job is assigned to a *job class*. Class A might be restricted to ten-second jobs using the card reader and printer only; Class B might be for jobs needing up to 30 seconds of CPU time and up to two tape drives, and so on. The class of each job is indicated on the job card. The jobs are read by an operating system module and spooled to one of a number of job queues; Class A jobs go to the A queue, B jobs to the B queue, and so on (Fig. 6.9). In this way, similar jobs can be grouped together.

Later, these jobs can be retrieved from the on-line device (often disk) to which they were spooled and loaded into main memory for execution by a *job-initiation* operating system module. Since similar jobs are grouped together, this job initiator program can be designed to load programs in a sequence that maximizes system efficiency. Often, one part of the computer's memory is set aside to hold the simple card-reader/printer jobs which, since input card data was read along with the job deck and is thus also on-line, require little or no additional operator intervention. Tape jobs can be run in parallel in another section of core (Fig. 6.10). Once a job completes, another module, a *job terminator,* clears all references to the job and returns control to the job initiator, which repeats the cycle. All this happens, of course, at computer speeds.

We have already discussed the problems associated with the scheduling of the use of the CPU among jobs already in core; in this section, our discussion centers on the problem of getting those programs into memory in the first place. The problems are not unrelated; a good job initialization routine can minimize the problems of internal scheduling.

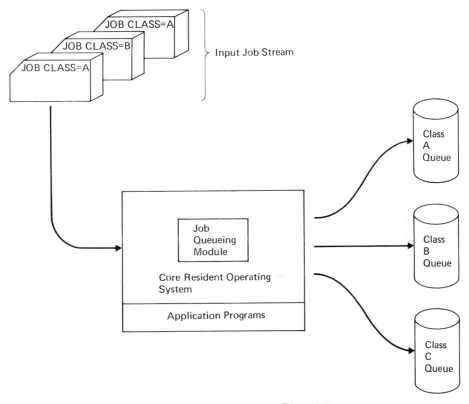

Fig. 6.9
Building job queues.

Scheduling on a time-shared system is just a bit more complex. Often, a large number of users are attempting to communicate with the computer via (often remote) terminals. The sheer number of programs creates a serious problem—main memory is a limited resource. The problem is often solved by some form of *roll-in/roll-out* procedure. In its simplest form, once a program completes a burst of activity, it is copied to disk, making room in core for another program. When the program in question is about ready for another crack at the CPU, it is copied back into main memory. Human reaction speeds of a few seconds or more make all this input and output activity pretty much transparent to the user. See Fig. 6.11 for an example.

Roll-in/roll-out logic is not restricted to time-sharing applications, being a long-time tool of the professional programmer. The basic concept has evolved into the *virtual memory* systems described in a later chapter.

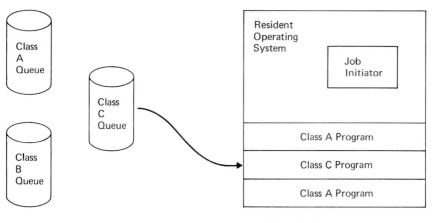

Fig. 6.10
Job initiation.

Job scheduling has a rather obvious impact on system efficiency. Certain job classes might be taken first, improving the turnaround of programs in these classes. Alternatively, jobs might be scheduled so as to increase throughput at the expense of turnaround—longest running jobs first. Software to queue and initiate jobs must be carefully balanced to maximize whatever a given computer installation considers to be its measure or measures of efficiency.

Fig. 6.11
Roll-in/roll-out logic.

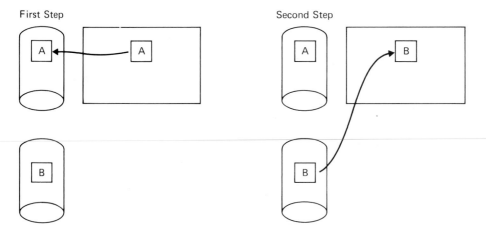

Registers ———————————————————

Contrary to popular belief, the registers used by programmers are not their exclusive property; every program must make use of the same set. Since register contents can change as a program executes, this can cause a problem.

Register conventions provide at least a partial answer. Just before a program is placed in a wait state, the contents of all the registers are copied into a save area in main storage. When the program is ready to resume, the registers are reloaded from this save area. Assembly language programmers are familiar with register conventions, at least in the form of a macro. Compiler language programmers don't see the conventions, but they are still present. The functions of saving and restoring registers are a part of many operating system modules. To avoid excessive duplication of this code, register conventions are often included in the resident operating system in the form of a common subprogram.

I/O Device Allocation ———————————————————

Consider the outcome of two different programs attempting to use the same tape drive, one for input and one for output. Chaos! What happens when a program needs a tape or disk drive that, for some reason, is not available? The program sits in core wasting resources, until the device is free. These are but two of the many problems multiprogramming creates in the area of I/O device allocation. In a serial batch system, each program has control of the CPU and *all* the I/O devices while running; in multiprogramming, these devices must be shared with a number of other programs. It is possible for several different programs to seek or write data on the same direct access device, but tape, cards, the printer, and many other devices do not share this flexibility. Some form of I/O control is essential.

The first control involves program loading. Put simply, if all the I/O devices needed to support a given program are not available, why bother to load and initiate the program? Load some other program and try again at a later time. To achieve this objective, a table of all the I/O devices available on the system is normally maintained somewhere in the region of main memory assigned to the operating system. Before a program is loaded, its I/O device requirements are checked against this table, and any reserved units are noted. When other programs are being similarly prepared for loading at some later time, the fact that all must go through this same table minimizes the danger of multiple programs trying to access the same device or of a program sitting in main memory because a device is not available. Programs that might suffer these problems are simply kept out of main storage until the desired device is free. This checking is normally a part of the program-initialization module described above. The actual details of implementation vary from operating system to operating system, but the idea of checking a table for device availability is pretty common.

If I/O device requirements are to be checked by a program, they must be communicated to the system in machine readable form; the old second generation run book just won't do. Command language or *job control language* statements provide a common solution. We have already discussed two control cards

```
//   JOB   CLASS=A
```

and

```
//   EXEC   COBOL
```

that, respectively, separate jobs and identify the program to be executed. To cite one example of I/O device specification through a command language, IBM uses a third type of control card, a DD card, to define I/O requirements. A typical DD card, such as

```
//TAPE   DD   UNIT=2400,...
```

describes, using a series of parameters, the details of a particular (in this case, tape) data set. We'll be discussing IBM's Job Control Language in greater detail in Part III.

We can make certain that all requested I/O devices are available and thus that all expected input and output operations are possible *before* loading a program into main memory, but that's not the end of our problems. How do we prevent the accidental or intentional destruction of existing data? How do we avoid the interference resulting from two or more programs attempting to, legitimately, access the same disk pack? A common solution is to force all input and output operations to go through the resident operating system. The instructions that actually perform input and output are made *privileged*; i.e., they can be executed *only* by an operating-system module. Application programs cannot communicate directly with an I/O device but, after setting up a number of control fields, must transfer control to the operating system to get things started. In this way, all input and output is forced to pass through the same module, where extensive checks and controls are implemented.

I/O Device
Allocation—Spooling

Off-line spooling was, as you may recall, a second generation concept. In the third generation, *spooling* becomes an on-line operation. The job queueing function described above is essentially a form of spooling, moving card data from a card reader to some faster, on-line device. Program data in card form is, of course, included in the card deck image and can be read, when needed, directly from the on-line device. Many systems include output spooling as well as input spooling, with printer output going first to disk or tape and later to paper.

On-line spooling takes advantage of the high speeds of a modern computer; essentially, it represents one more level of multiprogramming. When all the programs on a system are in a wait state, a common occurrence even with ten or fifteen programs on a fast computer, the input and output spooling routines take over, starting the operations of physically reading a card and printing a line. These slow operations take place when the system has nothing else to do anyway.

Control of Data Resources

Second generation data management has been largely carried over into the current generation with a few important improvements and modifications. The old file organization techniques, access methods, label creation and label checking routines, libraries, compilers, and macros are still around. One major advance is the use of on-line spooling as described above.

Largely because of the multiple program nature of a modern system, the OPEN and CLOSE macros are more complex than they were in the second generation. In addition to checking labels and issuing mount messages, the OPEN macro is the ideal spot for building the tables needed to support an input or output operation. The CLOSE macro destroys these pointers as soon as the program is finished with them; in this way, a device is tied up only when the program is actually using it. Since these two macros are almost certain to be used by every program in core, they are frequently made a part of the resident operating system (Fig. 6.12), with the individual programs simply linking with these modules.

Libraries

A library is a very special form of file. Third generation systems normally support the same types of libraries we discussed in the last chapter—one for compilers and utility programs, another for user programs, and a third for macros. A few additional types of libraries are needed to support some of the special requirements of the third generation and multiprogramming. One is a supervisor library, containing operating system modules whose use does not justify core residency. Another stores job control statements for certain common appli-

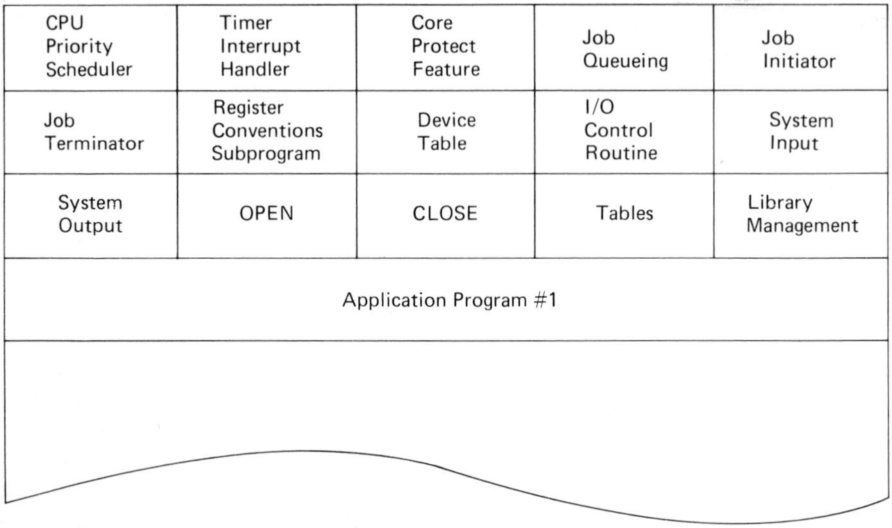

CPU Priority Scheduler	Timer Interrupt Handler	Core Protect Feature	Job Queueing	Job Initiator
Job Terminator	Register Conventions Subprogram	Device Table	I/O Control Routine	System Input
System Output	OPEN	CLOSE	Tables	Library Management

Application Program #1

Fig. 6.12
The resident operating system.

cations; one member of this library might, for example, contain all the JCL statements needed to compile a COBOL program.

A library differs from other data. The old concepts of fields, records, and files are not really relevant; the basic unit on a library is a complete program or a complete macro. Library members are often stored using something called a *partitioned organization*. Visualize, for a moment, a library of object modules on cards. Each program deck is carefully marked and placed on a table (Fig. 6.13). To run a given program, the operator need only select the proper deck and feed it into a card reader. In a partitioned organization, these object or load modules are copied to disk, with the start and end address of each member noted in an index. To load a program, the start address is found in the index and the member simply copied into main memory.

Library management is an operating system function. The programs to support this function are often a part of the resident operating system. (Fig. 6.12, again).

Secondary Storage
Space Management

Key data files and libraries are generally kept for a period of time; in fact, it is reasonable to label these system components as *permanent*. Unfortunately, secondary storage space is limited. If programmers keep adding data and library

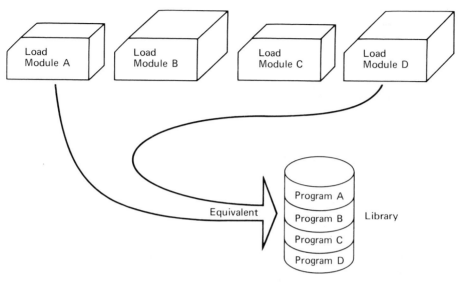

Fig. 6.13
A partitioned library.

members, eventually all the space will be used up, and future growth will be restricted.

Thus secondary space management is necessary. On some systems, space allocation is a manual function, with the computer operations group allocating space and maintaining careful records off-line. On more sophisticated systems, an operating system module maintains a pool of *free space* on secondary storage, and allocates it on request. Often, the application programmer is allowed to request *temporary*, life-of-the-job space without restriction, but only a system programmer is allowed to make permanent allocations.

Data
Base Management

Increasingly, more and more organizations are turning to *data base management* as the solution to their space allocation and data accessibility problems. Under data base management (to be discussed in detail in Chapter 20), all the organization's data are grouped in a single, large central data base, integrating what may have once been hundreds of separate files. Special data base management software is added to the system software, often as an extension of the operating system, to manage this resource. A new computer professional, the *data base administrator*, is often assigned complete technical responsibility for the control of the data base.

The
Operating System

An operating system is a collection of programs or program modules. The purpose of this software is to improve the efficiency of the system. Individual modules are designed to improve the utilization of each of the major system resources—CPU time, core space, registers, input and output devices, and data. Ideally, because of their heavy use, operating system modules are tight, well-written routines. They must be reentrant—capable of supporting a number of concurrent executions—and reusable. Often, they must be recursive—able to be entered over and over again. But they are still programs. With the exception of a few privileged instructions, the instruction set is the same as that used by any assembly language programmer.

Not all operating system modules are core resident. Many computer installations use a disk operating system, with individual routines being moved from disk to main memory on an as-required basis. This saves space but takes time—even high-speed direct access I/O is slow compared with internal processing speeds. Disk operating systems are normally used on smaller, slower computers, where space is at a premium and the disparity between I/O and processing speeds is at a minimum.

At the other extreme is an all-resident operating system. In terms of processing speed this is an optimum configuration, but all those operating system modules take up space that might better be used for application programs. Most systems compromise, with the more heavily used modules being core resident while other less critical routines are stored on a direct-access library and read into main memory as required (Fig. 6.14). Often, one library holds the

Fig. 6.14
**An operating system in core and disk resident
parts.**

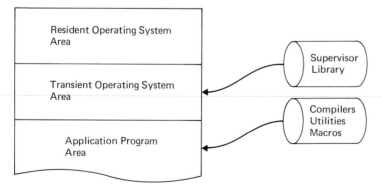

actual operating system routines while such programmer aids as compilers, utilities, and macros are maintained on another system library.

The programs of an operating system are pure overhead; their purpose is to improve the efficiency of the system but, by themselves, they perform no useful work. Like any program, operating system modules consume processing time. They take up space. But without the resource management provided by these routines, modern high-speed computers would represent a marginal economic investment.

Summary

This chapter covered the development of software to support multiprogramming and time-sharing Multiprogramming, the concurrent processing of a number of programs, evolved in response to the extreme disparity between input/output and processing times; essentially, it allows the system to switch its attention to another job during the relatively lengthy input and output wait times. The existence of multiple programs in core creates a number of problems in the allocation and control of central processor time, core space, register utilization, input and output device allocation, and data management. The operating system is a collection of programs designed to deal with these problems.

When the CPU must switch its attention among several programs, conflicts are inevitable. One key operating system module is concerned with making this essential "who goes first" internal priority decision. With multiple programs in main memory, it is possible for one program to destroy the contents of space belonging to another program; thus memory protection is another common operating system feature.

In a serial batch system, it is relatively easy for the operator to determine which program should be loaded onto the computer next. With multiprogramming, determining a job's external priority becomes very difficult; thus job queueing is often part of the resident system. Under time-sharing, roll-in/roll-out adds yet another dimension.

Conflicts on the use of I/O devices are also possible, calling for system-based I/O device allocation decisions. A job control or command language is often used to communicate a user's I/O device requirements to the system. Another common I/O feature on a multiprogrammed system is on-line spooling.

Finally, data resources must be carefully monitored and controlled on a multiprogrammed system. We discussed libraries, secondary space management, and the growing trend toward data base management.

An operating system is a collection of software modules designed to manage all the system resources in as efficient a manner as possible. See Fig. 6.15 for a visual summary of operating system components.

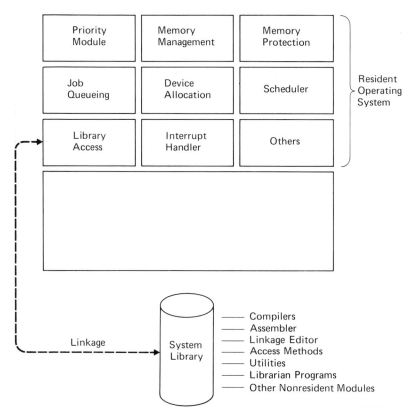

Fig. 6.15
The functions of an operating system.

Key Words ─────────────────────────────────

core resident	operating system
data base management	partitioned organization
internal priority	priority
job class	roll-in/roll-out
job control language	spooling
job initiation	supervisor
job queueing	throughput
job terminator	time-sharing
memory protection	turnaround time
multiprogramming	virtual memory

Exercises ————————————————————

1. Define throughput. Define turnaround time.
2. Why was something like multiprogramming necessary on a modern, high-speed computer system?
3. Explain multiprogramming. Why is the distinction between concurrent and simultaneous operation important?
4. What is time-sharing?
5. Why is it important that a software module be developed to handle the internal priority decision on a multiprogramming system? Why can't the human operator assume this responsibility?
6. What does the term "core resident" mean?
7. Why is memory protection important on a multiprogrammed machine?
8. Explain how job queueing works.
9. Explain roll-in/roll-out on a time-shared machine. Why is roll-in/roll-out necessary?
10. Differentiate between a program's internal (within the computer) and external priority.
11. Why must I/O device allocation be controlled on a multiprogramming system?
12. Explain how on-line spooling works.
13. Briefly explain how a partitioned organization might be used to store a library.
14. Why must secondary space allocation be carefully controlled?
15. Sketch a diagram showing all the components of a typical multiprogramming operating system.

Part

III

Communicating with the Operating System

7

Command Languages and
Job Control Languages

Overview

Part I of this text was a review of the basic hardware, software, and data resources that are managed by an operating system. In Part II, a broad overview of operating systems was developed. We are now ready to begin studying system software in more detail. We begin, here in Part III, with those portions of an operating system that most directly have an impact upon the typical application programmer—command languages, job control languages, linkage editors, and libraries.

This chapter is concerned with the general topic of command and job control languages. We will briefly consider the function of a command language, and then discuss the various sources of commands. Several different types of command languages are in common use today. We'll cite some examples of command languages from a microcomputer operating system (CP/M) and a large time-shared system.

Chapter 8 deals with IBM DOS job control. Chapters 9 and 10 discuss IBM OS job control language. Part III ends (Chapter 11) with a discussion of linkage editors, loaders, and libraries.

The Functions of a Command Language

What exactly is the purpose of a *command language*? Basically, a command language is designed to allow a human being to communicate with the operating system. Computer operators, programmers, data base administrators, and other key technical and management personnel are ultimately responsible for determining the operating procedures under which a computer system functions. The operating system is responsible for coordinating and managing resources on the computer, in real-time. The people use the command language to guide or direct the operating system. On most systems, a single *control module* (Fig. 7.1) is assigned the responsibility for reading, interpreting, and acting on the commands.

To be a bit more specific, one operating system responsibility is that of allocating main memory space to application programs. In part, this consists of loading a selected program from a library into main memory, and giving it control. How does the operating system know which program to load? The operator, programmer, or user must specify the program through the command language. What if a "hot" job requiring immediate action suddenly enters the computer center? The operator must have the ability to override the external priority scheme; once again, the command language is the mechanism for changing standard operating procedures. What if a program falls into an "endless loop"? The operator must be able to cancel the job. Once again the command language provides a means.

Another major operating system responsibility is allocating I/O devices. Before the system can allocate devices to a given program, it must know what device support that program requires. The only way the system can possibly know what devices are required is if a human being tells it. Most command languages contain provisions for defining I/O device requirements.

Fig. 7.1

An operating system control module accepts and interprets system commands.

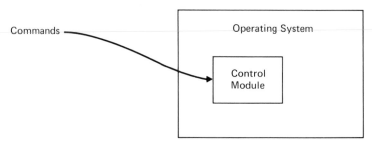

The Sources of the Commands

The command language is the mechanism whereby the human beings who are ultimately responsible for the system communicate their requirements to the system. How is this communication achieved? What is the source of the commands?

One key source of commands is the *operator's console* (Fig. 7.2). It is through the console that the operator exerts real-time control over the operation of the system. At the start of the day, the operator will normally "bring the system up" by using a set of commands that allows such key variables as default main memory space allocations, the internal priority rules, system device assignments, the system date and time, and others to be set or modified. As the system runs, other commands allow the operator to stop a job, terminate a job, load a selected program, check the status of the system, identify a user and, in general, control the flow of work. At the end of the day, other commands allow the operator to "bring the system down."

Through the console, the operator communicates directly with the control module of the operating system. This control module reads and interprets the operator's commands, perhaps involving other operating system modules in response. Often, the control module prints or displays a running log of system activity on the operator's console.

Not all commands are entered through the operator's console; another key source of commands on many systems is the *job stream* (Fig. 7.3). Command statements or *job control language* statements are included with the programs and data as they are submitted to the computer, thus providing a form of as-required control. Typically, there are three different kinds of job stream commands. The first, often called a JOB card or *JOB statement,* serves to identify the job. A typical job stream may contain programs or other work submitted by dozens of different programmers. The system must be able to tell where one job

Fig. 7.2
The operator's console is a key source of commands.

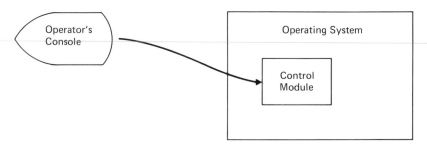

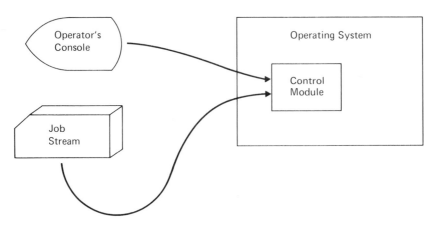

Fig. 7.3
The job stream is another source of system
commands.

ends and another begins. The usual rule is that a JOB statement or command must be the very first card in a job deck. As the control module scans an input job stream, a JOB statement clearly marks the beginning of a new set of work.

Another major job control language function is that of program identification. Before the system can possibly load and execute a program, it must know which program is required. Who knows this better than the programmer? Thus program specification commands are often included in the job stream.

Finally, input and output device requirements are normally specified as part of the job stream. Earlier, we argued that the programmer was the best source of program identification. A similar argument might well be advanced for specifying the I/O devices needed to support that program.

The concept of a job stream seems to imply the use of punched cards. Increasingly, program development is moving from a punched card environment to a terminal environment, with program statements and data entering the system through a CRT screen. Each line entered through the screen is functionally equivalent to a single punched card; thus it is possible to have a perfectly reasonable job stream without any punched cards being involved.

The idea of a job stream is a little different on a time-shared system. The job stream is a batch concept, with a full set of commands, source programs, and data being prepared before the fact and submitted as a single *job* to the computer system. Time-sharing is more interactive. Commands, source statements, and data are simply typed into the system as the occasion demands, often with limited presession planning. There are, however, commands on a time-sharing system. Typically, the user begins a session by signing on, often providing a user number and a password: this is the equivalent of job identification. The user must specify, by name, the program to be run (RUN BASIC, for example), and this is the equivalent of program identification in the job stream. Most terminal users are content with certain standard or *default* I/O device assignments, and thus rarely encounter a need to specify device needs. However, have you ever wanted a printed copy of the contents of your CRT screen, or have you ever wanted to save a permanent copy of a program or data file that you developed? Such tasks often call for the use of special system commands.

Note that the set of commands that can be issued by the user through the job stream or through a terminal is quite limited. The user can identify a job, request a specific program, or request an I/O device, and that's about it. The operator, working through the console, can issue these three general types of commands, as well as many others: cancel a job, give a job higher priority, postpone a job, and so on. Why? Imagine how chaotic it would be if every system user were given access to a complete set of system commands. Be honest: wouldn't you be tempted to cancel a friend's job as a "joke" if you had the opportunity?

We begin to see a touch of complexity in that system control operating system module (Fig. 7.3, again); this module must be written to check the source of a command before executing it. *Any* command coming from the operator's console would be legal, but only selected commands would be accepted from the job stream. This is a key security provision on most modern computer systems. The operator's console, after all, can be placed in a controlled-access room, while the individual jobs might be submitted from anywhere.

Generally speaking, software is the responsibility of the programmer, and hardware is the responsibility of the operator. Where do the data fit? Operations might claim responsibility for the data simply because they are stored on the hardware. The programmers might make a similar claim, based on the argument that the software creates and manipulates the data. Increasingly, more and more large organizations are solving this traditional jurisdictional puzzle by assigning the responsibility for the data to a new professional, the data base administrator or DBA.

In such installations, the data base administrator is responsible for data maintenance, backup, security, and accessibility. In this general area of responsibility, we often find the task of assigning direct access space to the various applications. Many computer manufacturers, recognizing the growing trend toward this new field of specialization, have designed their command language in such a way that selected commands can be split away from operator's console control and made available only from a third, independent source, the data base administrator's console (Fig. 7.4). Commands concerned with allocating secondary space or establishing or changing security procedures would fall into this general category.

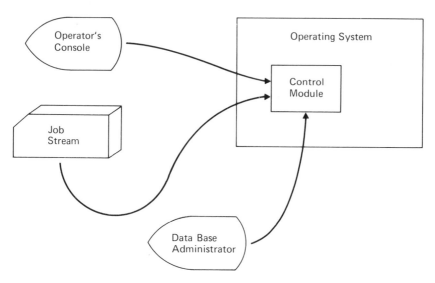

Fig. 7.4
The data base administrator often represents a
third source of system commands.

Perhaps the best way to visualize how a command language works would be to look at a few typical examples. Over the next several pages, we'll consider the command language on a microcomputer system and on a large time-shared system; the job control language for a large IBM system will be covered in Chapters 8 through 11.

A Microcomputer Command Language: CP/M

Let's begin with a microcomputer system. Consider first the characteristics of such a system. It is probably small, almost certainly operating in the serial batch mode. Normally, the operator, the programmer, and the data base administrator are one and the same. On such a system, it would be reasonable to expect that all commands would be entered through the operator's console.

A very popular operating system for microcomputers is *CP/M*, which stands for control program/microcomputers. CP/M was developed by Digital Research of Pacific Grove, California, specifically for use on some of the more popular microprocessor-based systems. A key element of CP/M is an easy-to-use command language.

Let's assume that the user wants to write, test, and execute an assembler language program. The system is running, and thus the problems associated with initial startup can be ignored. (We'll return to this problem in Chapter 12.) How could the user take advantage of the facilities of CP/M to achieve this objective?

One of the features of CP/M is an editor that allows the user to enter new text or modify existing text. To get the editor, the user would simply type

```
ED GAME.ASM
```

through the system console (Fig. 7.5). The "ED" identifies the text editor. "GAME" is the name of the program; ".ASM" indicates that, eventually, this text will be submitted to the assembler. In response to this command, CP/M searches the disk directories or indexes, looking for a file named GAME.ASM. If such a file exists, the system assumes that the user wants to modify the text; thus the file is copied into main memory. If no such file exists, an entry is made in the system directory—the assumption is that this is new text. At any rate, control is given to the editor, and the user can begin to enter or modify the program source statements.

Eventually, the complete program has been entered. Before the code can be tested, however, translation to machine-level code is necessary; this is a function of the assembler program. Thus (Fig. 7.5) the user types

```
ASM GAME
```

In response, CP/M loads the assembler program, which reads the text file GAME, and assembles it. The output consists of two files: GAME.HEX, an object module, and GAME.PRN, a source listing complete with error messages.

The user will probably want to look at the source listing before trying to execute the program, and thus (Fig. 7.5, again) types

```
TYPE GAME.PRN
```

As a result, CP/M causes the source listing to be printed or displayed on the console. If errors were detected during the assembly process, the user would return to the editor step, correct the source code, and recompile. When a

Fig. 7.5
The commands needed to support an assembly and test under CP/M. The symbol > is the system prompt.

```
> ED GAME.ASM
> ASM GAME
> TYPE GAME.PRN
> LOAD GAME
> GAME.COM
```

"clean" compliation is finally achieved, the user is ready to proceed to the next step. The command

    LOAD GAME

invokes a CP/M module that reads a file named GAME.HEX, the object module, and prepares it for execution (in other words, translates it to load module form). The resulting "ready-to-execute" file is named GAME.COM, where the "COM" stands for command form. Finally (Fig. 7.5), the command

    GAME.COM

causes the machine-level version of the program to be loaded and executed.

The intent of this discussion is not to teach you the CP/M command language; rather its objective was simply to illustrate how a typical command language works. Note how each specific step in the process of assembling and testing a program must be specified through a console command. The structure of the commands will change from system to system, but the general concept of directing or controlling the system through such commands remains constant.

A Large Time-Shared System

At the opposite extreme, at least in terms of system complexity, are the large time-shared systems. It is not unusual for such systems to be concurrently supporting 100 or more user terminals—100 or more *different* jobs. This creates very serious problems in job tracking, device allocation, and security. Thus it is not surprising to discover that system access via the command language is divided into different levels.

The Hewlett-Packard 3000 minicomputer series provides a good example. The first level of system commands enters through the job stream—more accurately, through the user terminals. The system is designed to be as "friendly" as possible; keep this in mind as we consider the commands. The first thing the user must do is to provide the system with identification parameters. This is done by typing a HELLO command, followed by a user number and (usually) a password. Programs are executed by typing the word RUN followed by the program name. Compilers and other system-level programs are accessed by simply typing the name of the module: for example, EDITOR or BASIC. When finished, the user simply types: BYE. What could be more friendly?

Look beyond those nice commands, however. The user is essentially restricted to personal identification, program identification, and file identification. With very few exceptions (such as transmitting a message to another terminal), the user can do nothing that impacts any part of the system beyond the user's own work area.

The system operator, on the other hand, has a much larger set of commands. Any user command can be entered through the system console. In addition, the operator has commands to cancel a user's job, investigate what a given user is doing at a given point in time, change a user's priority, send a message to any user (or to all users) and, in general, become involved in the real-time control of the system at almost any level.

On the Hewlett-Packard 3000 series, a third level of system commands is provided. The commands on the third level control such functions as the allocation of work space on disk and the assignment of user numbers, passwords, and other security parameters. In smaller installations, they might be assigned to the operator's console. In other cases, these commands are limited to the data base administrator or system manager, and are recognized only if entered through a separate, specific terminal or terminals.

Job Control Languages

To the typical programmer, however, the most common type of command language encountered is the in-stream job control language. In Chapter 8, we'll consider such a job control language, concentrating on IBM's DOS-level systems. In Chapters 9 and 10, we'll consider the job control language for IBM's larger operating systems.

Summary

This chapter discussed the general topic of command or job control languages. It is through the command language that the computer operator, user, programmer, or data base administrator communicates with the operating system—often with a control module in the operating system. We considered the types of commands that might be expected from each of the major sources and then, to illustrate, cited examples from a microcomputer operating system and a large, time-sharing system. This chapter serves as a lead-in to Chapters 8 through 10.

Key Words

command language	job
control module	job control language
CP/M	job stream

Exercises _____

1. What is the function of a command language?
2. What does an operating system's control module do?
3. What are the primary sources of system commands?
4. What is a job stream? What is a job control language?
5. What is a job? The term has not yet been "officially" defined; what do you think it means?
6. Why can't the user be allowed to submit, through the job stream, all commands that are available to the system operator?
7. What is a data base administrator?

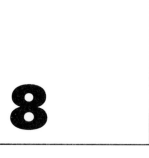

Job Control under IBM's Disk Operating System

8

Overview

Back in the computer's second generation, detailed instructions for running a job were communicated to the system operator via the programmer's run book; on a modern multiprogrammed system, many of the functions previously performed by a human operator are handled by operating system modules—programs—instead. Old Bob, the third-shift operator, may have been able to figure out the meaning of "MONT TAP NMBR AB1253," but most programs are not quite so flexible or forgiving. The old handwritten or typed run book is no longer adequate; modern programmer/system communications have to be carefully structured.

IBM has developed what is, for all practical purposes, a new language—Job Control Language—to achieve this objective; in the next three chapters, we'll take a look at some of the features of this language. In this chapter we'll be concentrating on job control for IBM's Disk Operating System (DOS). Chapters 9 and 10 will cover the considerably more complex job control language developed in support of Operating System/360 and System/370. It is *not* our objective to cover these job control languages fully or in depth. (Entire books have been written on just that subject.) Rather, we will concentrate on a number of the more commonly used features of job control, those features encountered by typical programmers as part of their everyday work.

127

IBM's Disk Operating System (DOS) is a good example of an operating system written to support application programs on small- and medium-scale computer systems. DOS supports multiprogramming, with recent releases supporting up to six concurrent programs, including the resident operating system, in core. The Job Control Language for DOS is straightforward and fairly easy to follow; thus it provides a good starting point for our study of structured programmer/system communication.

A few points must be made before we begin our discussion of job control. First, even though they are called languages, no programs are actually written in pure job control language; job control serves in a support role, describing the real programs to be executed and the input and output devices to be used in the processing of a job. Second, a language designed for such a support function literally must be all things to all people; thus every possible technique for using an I/O device must be supported, even those more esoteric techniques of interest to only a few professional system programmers. Much of the confusion surrounding job control arises from an attempt to teach every programmer all possible language parameters, even the little known or rarely used ones. Normal, everyday job control is not difficult to understand. It's exacting and it can be frustrating, but it is *not* difficult.

The DOS
JOB Statement

Two key functions performed by job control are job separation and job identification; under DOS, these functions are performed by the *JOB statement*. The general form of the DOS JOB statement is

```
//   JOB   jobname   accounting-information
```

The two slashes (//) identify this as a control card; they *must* appear in columns 1 and 2. One or more blanks separate the slashes from the keyword "JOB," which identifies this as a job. The "jobname" consists of from one to eight alphanumeric characters chosen by the programmer to identify the job. Accounting information is optional; if a given installation chooses to require this field, the accounting information is separated from the job name by one or more blanks.

Note the use of blanks on the JOB statement; blanks are used to separate fields. For this reason, blanks may not be embedded in the middle of a job name.

Any combination of from 1 to 8 alphanumeric characters makes up a valid job name; thus

```
//   JOB   DAVIS
```

is perfectly acceptable. If a programmer wishes to identify individual programs with different names, he or she might code

```
//   JOB   DAVIS1
```

for the first job, and

```
//   JOB   DAVIS2
```

for the second.

A few seconds spent looking in almost any telephone book should convince anyone that such a technique for selecting job names can lead to an occasional problem of duplicate job names. To avoid this problem, most firms have developed a standard procedure for naming jobs. In some cases, a job might be assigned a prefix identifying a particular department followed by a sequence number.

```
// JOB   PC0015
```

might, for example, identify the fifteenth job written for the production-control department. Other job names might identify the function of a program, with

```
//   JOB   PAYROLL
```

identifying one of the more popular programs run in any installation.

The JOB *must be* the first card or card image in the programmer's job. It marks the start of a new job.

The DOS
EXEC Statement _____

An *EXEC* (execute) statement identifies the particular program that is to be loaded onto the computer and run or executed. The general form is

```
//   EXEC  program-name
```

Once again, the two slashes (//) must be punched in columns 1 and 2. One or more blanks serve to separate the slashes from the key word "EXEC" which identifies this as an execute statement. One or more additional blanks are needed to separate "EXEC" from the program name; the program name serves to identify a specific module stored in a library. It should be noted that the program name bears absolutely no relationship to the job name; the program name, like the job name, consists of from one to eight alphanumeric characters, but there the similarity ends. A job name serves to identify "this" particular job being run on the computer "right now"; when the job ends, the job name ceases to exist, as far as the computer system is concerned, until the job is rerun. A *program* name, on the other hand, serves to identify a particular program on a system library; when the "current" job terminates, the program still exists on the library ready, perhaps, to be used by another job. The job name, to cite another important difference, might identify a job consisting of several separate programs, *each* having a program name.

Consider, for example, the typical data processing job illustrated in Fig. 8.1. In the first "job step," labor cards are read into an edit program that eliminates certain keypunching errors. The "good" data are then sorted by a second program or "job step." Sorted data are next read, along with a master year-to-date-earnings file, into a payroll-preparation program. The final job step (note that the words job step are no longer in quotes, a job step is nothing more than a single program run as part of a job) is an audit program that prepares reports for the accounting department. The job control statements for this job might be as follows.

```
//   JOB   PAYROLL

//   EXEC   PAYEDIT

//   EXEC   SORT

//   EXEC   PAYROLL

//   EXEC   PAYAUDIT

/&
```

Each individual program in this job (in other words, each job step) requires an EXEC statement; each of the four named programs exist, in load module form, on a system library. When the DOS system control module hits the

```
//   EXEC   PAYEDIT
```

statement, it loads a copy of the program with this name into core and turns control of the CPU over to the first instruction in the program.

You may have noticed that the job name is PAYROLL and the name of the third program is also PAYROLL. There is nothing wrong with this. It's perfectly legal. But it's pure coincidence, the job name and a program name within that job bear no relationship to each other unless the programmer chooses to use consistent names. The operating system doesn't care; we could have called this job "MELVIN" as in

```
//   JOB   MELVIN
```

and still have used the same programs.

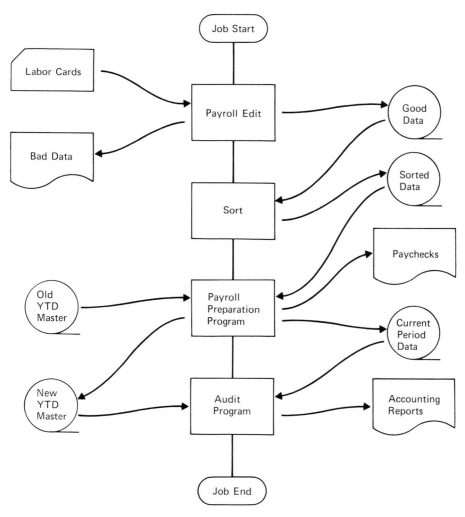

Fig. 8.1
A typical four-step job.

Compiling and
Link Editing

Most programmers are interested in getting their programs onto a library and not simply in using programs already there. The first step in this process is usually compilation. A compiler is a program written to convert input data in the form of programmer source statements into an object module. Like any other program, compilers are stored on a library and loaded into core by the operating system when an EXEC statement names the compiler. To compile a COBOL program, a programmer might code

```
//   JOB   TEST1

//   EXEC   COBOL


        ⎫
        ⎬ source deck
        ⎭


/*

/&
```

Incidentally, this is the second time we've seen a "/&" statement; it marks the end of a job.

The job shown above will produce a listing, compiler error messages, and an object module, and that's all. Once a clean assembly or compilation is obtained, the programmer will almost certainly want to test the program; in order to do this, a new job control statement, *OPTION*, must be used. The general form of this statement is as follows.

```
//   OPTION   option1,option2,option3, . . .
```

To cite one easy-to-understand OPTION, a programmer might wish, during the first few compilations, to bypass the punching of an object module (no sense punching an object module when a program still has compiler errors). This can be done by coding

```
//   OPTION   NODECK

//   EXEC   ASSEMBLY
```

There are many options available to the DOS programmer—we won't attempt to cover all of them. The option we are primarily interested in is the "LINK" option.

```
//   OPTION   LINK

//   EXEC   FORTRAN
```

The LINK option causes the object module to be written to a file where it can be accessed by the LINKAGE EDITOR program and converted to a load module.

The following set of job control statements allows a program to be compiled (COBOL is shown, but it could have been any compiler), link edited, and run.

```
//   JOB   DAVIS1

//   OPTION   LINK

//   EXEC   COBOL


        ⎫
        ⎬ source deck
        ⎭


/*

//   EXEC   LNKEDT

//   EXEC


        ⎫
        ⎬ data cards
        ⎭


/*

/&
```

The last EXEC statement doesn't name a specific program; when the program name field is blank, the system assumes that the load module just created by the linkage editor is to be loaded and executed.

Another new statement, "/*", appears in the example above. This is an end-of-data marker; it follows the last card in the source module and the last data card (if any) and tells the processing program that the last record has been encountered. Some programmers use "/*" statements to separate job steps.

The latest version of the DOS operating system, DOS/VSE (Disk Operating System/Virtual Storage Extended), has incorporated an interesting new feature on the EXEC statement. For the typical programmer, the compile, link edit, and execute sequence is, without question, the most commonly used series of job control commands. Under DOS/VSE, the programmer can simply code

```
// JOB SAMPLE
// EXEC  COBOL.GO

        ⎫
        ⎬ source deck
        ⎭

/*
/&
```

The "GO" option on the EXEC statement *implies* an automatic link edit and execute after the job has been compiled. Serious compiler or linkage editor errors will terminate the job, of course.

Cataloging Programs

Under IBM's Disk Operating System, load modules cataloged on the "core image" library are called *phases*. In order to catalog a new program to this library, the programmer must give the linkage editor a name for the program; under DOS, it's called a phase name and is provided through a PHASE control statement. To assemble a program and have the resulting object module link edited into a load module which is then cataloged to the core image library, the programmer codes

```
//  JOB   PGM14
//  OPTION  CATAL
       PHASE   MYPGM,*
//  EXEC  ASSEMBLY

        ⎫
        ⎬ source deck
        ⎭

/*
//  EXEC  LNKEDT
//  EXEC

        ⎫
        ⎬ data cards
        ⎭

/*
/&
```

If, at a later time, the programmer wishes to use this program again, only the following code is needed.

```
//   JOB   WHATEVER

//   EXEC   MYPGM



      }
      } data cards
      }



   /*


   /&
```

The program has been cataloged to the core image library in load module (i.e., executable) form. This library is called the "core image" library because individual load modules or phases are stored in executable form: i.e., all one must do to execute a phase is copy it into core.

The second operand in the PHASE statement shown above is an asterisk(*). This operand indicates the address within the DOS core partition where the phase it to be loaded for execution; the asterisk indicates that the phase is to be loaded at the first available location in the partition. This load address can be specified in a number of different ways which will not be discussed here. Note that column 1 of the PHASE statement is blank. This isn't a standard job control statement. Instead, its an input *parameter* to the linkage editor program. We'll discuss this program in more detail in Chapter 11.

Programmers often find it necessary to include subprograms, standard headers, and other modules written by other programmers as part of their own program. Under DOS, this can be done by using an INCLUDE statement. These subroutines are stored on a "relocatable library" in object module form and can be added to a cataloged phase or load module by the linkage editor by coding statements such as

```
//   JOB   NAME

//   OPTION   CATAL

     PHASE   PGMA.*

//   EXEC   ASSEMBLY
```

```
⎫
⎬ source deck
⎭

/*

      INCLUDE   SUBR1

      INCLUDE   SUBR2

//   EXEC   LNKEDT

//   EXEC

⎫
⎬ data cards
⎭

/*

/&
```

The cataloged phase will include the main program and the two indicated sub-routines. The INCLUDE is another linkage editor statement; thus column 1 (at least) is blank.

DOS I/O Control

Under DOS, every physical I/O device attached to a system is given a fixed symbolic name. Programmers read their input cards through SYSIPT, send lines to be printed to SYSLST, handle tapes through (perhaps) SYS006, and so on. The exact meaning of a particular symbolic name may vary from installation to installation, but within a particular computer center, symbolic names have consistent meanings. Unless a programmer wishes to change the meaning of a symbolic name from the standard to some other physical device, no job control is needed.

The key element in DOS I/O control, as far as the programmer is concerned, is the DTF or *Define The File Macro*; the programmer is required to code a DTF (Define The File) for each file accessed by program (often, the actual DTF's are stored in a relocatable library and added to a load module through the use of INCLUDE statements as described above, but the programmer still has one DTF for each file). The function of the DTF is to define key parameters of a given file and to indicate the access method needed to process the file. Each general type of I/O has its own DTF. The DTFCD defines parameters for a card file; the DTFPR defines a print file; the DTFMT defines a magnetic tape file; the DTFSD defines a sequential disk or other sequential direct access file; the DTFDA defines a direct access file on a direct access device. Other combinations of device and access method are also represented. The DTFCD provides a good example of the type of parameters included in this macro; a sample assembler language program with a DTFCD is shown in Fig. 8.2.

Three parameters are shown in the sample DTF: the DEVADDR is the symbolic name of the physical I/O device, the IOAREA1 is the label of an 80-character region of main memory set aside to hold an input record, and EOFADDR is the address (label) of the instruction to be executed when the end of file marker (/*) is sensed. In this example, the device address (DEVADDR) is SYSIPT, which just happens to be the symbolic name of the physical device normally used to provide card input to application programs; this program could be run with no job control reference to the I/O device.

Other parameters which might be coded in a DTF include: blocksize, the name of a second I/O area for dual-buffer overlapped I/O, label types, the file type (input or output), record form on devices where this can be a variable (blocking, fixed length, variable length), logical record length, information identifying a direct access or indexed sequential key, and many others.

Changing Standard Assignments—the ASSGN Statement

There are times when a programmer may wish to change a standard device assignment. Assume, for example, that a DTFMT (magnetic tape) refers to DEVADDR=SYS010 and that SYS010 is assigned to a particular tape drive. As the programmer enters the computer center, the tape drive is tied up on a two-hour job, but two other drives are free. By using an *ASSGN* statement, the programmer can change SYS010 from its standard device assignment to one of the available devices *for this program only*.

To understand the way the ASSGN statement works, it is first useful to have an understanding of how devices are addressed on an IBM computer system. All I/O takes place through a channel; devices are attached to the computer through the channel. Each channel has a number—the multiplexer channel is number 0 while selectors are numbered 1, 2, 3, and so on, up to a maximum of 7.

Each device is given a two-digit hexadecimal number ranging from a minimum of 00 to a maximum of FF (255 in decimal); thus up to 256 devices can be attached to any one channel. The system address or device address of any

```
PGMA      START  0

GO        BALR   12,0     INITIALIZE BASE REGISTER

          USING  *,12

          OPEN   CARDS

RUN       GET    CARDS

          ⎫
          ⎬  other instructions
          ⎭

          B      RUN

QUIT      CLOSE  CARDS

          EOJ

*

*      * * * * * * * * * * * * * * * * * *

*      *   THE DTFCD MACRO DEFINITION        *

*      * * * * * * * * * * * * * * * * * *

*

CARDS     DTFCD  DVADDR=SYSIPT,IOAREA1=INPUT,EOFADDR=QUIT

          ⎫
          ⎬  other data definitions
          ⎭

INPUT     DS     CL80     CARD READER INPUT AREA

          END GO
```

Fig. 8.2
A program segment containing a DTFCD macro.

physical I/O unit attached to the system is simply the device number preceded by the number of the channel to which it is attached. Device 008 is found on channel 0 and has a device number of 8; device 00E is also on channel 0 (the multiplexer) but has a device number of 14 (0E in hex). Device 181 is found on channel 1, while device 281 is found on channel 2. Look around any computer center, and you'll find each and every physical device has a permanent number attached; these numbers look much like the kind of numbers we've been discussing in this paragraph. The first digit identifies the channel; the second and third digits identify the device.

If SYS010 has a standard assignment of device 180 and device 181 is free, the programmer can change the device by coding

```
// ASSGN SYS010,X'181'
```

and placing this statement in front of the EXEC for the job step using the device. The change in assignment holds for *this job only*; after the program completes processing, the standard assignment once again takes over. The standard assignment of other core partitions is not changed by an ASSGN statement.

What happens if the programmer is not allowed physical access to the computer center? In many installations, this is the rule. How is the programmer to know which tape drive, disk drive, printer, or card reader is free? Perhaps more to the point, does the programmer really care which specific tape drive is used to support a program? Although different drives (or different printers, etc.) might have different features, generally, all the programmer wants is a device to read input or write output, and one tape drive is pretty much like any other tape drive.

Newer versions of the DOS operating system give the programmer the ability to specify a device class on the ASSGN statement. For example, if *any* tape drive would do, the programmer might code

```
// ASSGN SYS005,TAPE
```

The system would simply assign logical device SYS005 to the first available tape drive. Likewise,

```
// ASSGN SYS014,DISK
```

would represent a request for the first available disk drive. Other valid device classes include: READER, PRINTER, PUNCH, DISKETTE, CKD (cylinder/track addressed disk devices), and FBA (for the newer fixed-block architecture disk devices).

It is not unusual for a computer center to have several different models of tape drives, disk drives, card readers, or printers attached to the system. The programmer can, of course, always go back to specific channel/device address assignments, but there is a middle road—the device type can be specified. For example

```
//  ASSGN  SYSLST,1403
```

will assign the logical device SYSLST to the first available 1403 printer, but will not consider using a 3211 printer, while

```
//  ASSGN  SYS008,2400T9
```

will assign the first nine-track 2400 tape drive, and will avoid the seven-track 2400 tape drive. Using device class or device type assignments can save the programmer a fair amount of work.

Device type and device class assignments are fully supported under DOS/VSE. Some of the earlier versions of DOS include similar features. Be careful, however, as many active DOS installations do not support such assignments.

Other DOS Job
Control Functions

Most DOS programmers use very little job control beyond the few statements we've already discussed. The JOB statement is, of course, essential, and EXEC statements are needed to describe the specific programs to be run. On compile and test runs, an OPTION statement is required. Once testing is completed, load modules are often cataloged to a core image library, meaning that OPTION, PHASE, and possibly one or more INCLUDE statements must be part of the job. Occasionally, an ASSGN statement is used to change a standard device assignment. That's about all the average DOS programmer really needs. Other job control functions are usually left to one or more "experts" within the computing center.

Since the purpose of this chapter is to cover some of the more commonly used features of DOS Job Control, we won't spend much time discussing the details of the "lesser used" job control statements; we will, however, briefly describe some of those which the average programmer may occasionally encounter.

Most magnetic tape and direct access files are created with labels. The DLBL statement provides information for writing and/or checking direct access labels; the TLBL statement performs the same functions for magnetic tape labels. The LBLTYP statement tells the linkage editor how much main storage space is to be set aside for label processing.

A single direct access volume (one disk pack, for example) can hold several different files; to prevent the accidental destruction of data, the physical location of a new file on a disk or other direct access volume must be carefully controlled. This control is implemented through the use of the EXTENT statement which passes such information as the symbolic unit name (SYSnnn); the file serial number; the file type (index, main data area, overflow area); the number of the track on which the new file is to start; and the number of tracks to be assigned to the file. DASD file creation usually involves the use of both the EXTENT and the DLBL statements. Often, a specialist within the data processing function is responsible for maintaining a "book" showing the location of each file on each physical volume; new files must be authorized by this individual.

Under DOS, the programmer has access to a set of "user program switch indicators." These are often used to indicate certain key conditions at the start of a program run—they can be tested using standard assembly language statements. These switch indicators can be set to a particular configuration by the UPSI job control statement.

Cataloged Procedures

Once a program has been successfully compiled and tested, it is ready to be placed into *production*. A final execution of the compilation and link edit steps produces a load module which is given a name and placed on a library. From this point on, the program will be executed without the need for the compilation and link edit steps; the load module or phase is simply loaded into main memory and given control.

A production program is often part of a system. Earlier in the chapter, for example, we considered a set of programs that formed the payroll system (see Fig. 8.1).

```
//   JOB  PAYROLL

//   EXEC  PAYEDIT

//   EXEC  SORT

//   EXEC  PAYROLL

//   EXEC  PAYAUDIT

/&
```

The first program in the system edits input labor data. The good data are then sorted into employee number sequence. In the third job step, the actual payroll is computed. Finally, an audit program is run. Although we have not illustrated additional job control statements in this example, you can probably imagine a need for several ASSGNs, and perhaps other control statements. Although no source statements are needed, the list of job control commands can *easily* climb to 25 or 30 for such a job.

Rather than submit scores of control commands every time the production job is run, a programmer can create a *cataloged procedure,* a special type of library entry consisting of nothing but control statements. Let's assume that the name PAYSYS has been chosen for this application. By coding

```
//  EXEC  PROC=PAYSYS
```

```
/&
```

the programmer will cause *all* the job control statements stored under the name PAYSYS on the procedure library to be, in effect, "inserted" into the job stream. Thus the one EXEC statement, referencing a cataloged procedure, might be equivalent to dozens of individual job control language statements.

Cataloged procedures have been supported under DOS for quite some time; thus it is reasonable to expect that this feature will be generally available. Once again, however, a caution is necessary. Not all DOS systems are completely up to date. Failure to support cataloged procedures or other advanced features is not necessarily an indication that a system is behind the times, or obsolete; often there are very compelling technical arguments for *not* implementing a new feature. The point is to check before using a newer feature.

The System Command Language

DOS has a system command language that is supported through the operator's console. In fact, the job control language described above is nothing more than a subset of the system command language. Any job control statement can be entered through the operator's console. In addition, the operator has a set of system initialization and job control commands that *cannot* be submitted through the job stream. The "application programmer subset" approach is very common; it is found in most system command languages.

Summary

In this chapter, we've covered some of the basic features of the job control language for IBM's Disk Operating System. The two key job control statements, at least as far as the average DOS programmer is concerned, are the JOB statement which separates and identifies individual jobs and the EXEC statement which identifies the specific load module to be run or executed. A single JOB statement may be followed by more than one EXEC; each EXEC statement marks a single job step.

On a compile and test run, the programmer must inform the system that the load module produced by the linkage editor is to be loaded and executed. This is done through the OPTION statement. When the programmer codes

```
//  OPTION  LINK
```

the object module is written to a system file (usually a direct access file) and, following an EXEC with no program name, is loaded into core and started. Under the newer versions of DOS, the programmer can code a GO option on the EXEC statement for the compiler; GO implies that the program will be automatically link edited and tested.

In a production environment, programs are usually run by loading and executing a load module directly from a library, bypassing the lengthy assemble (or compile) and link edit steps. Under DOS, these library load modules are known as phases. To catalog a phase to the core image library, the programmer first codes

```
//  OPTION  CATAL
```

This OPTION statement performs two distinct functions: first, like the LINK option, it causes the load module to be written to a system file; and, second, the CATAL option informs the linkage editor that the load module (or phase) is to be catalogued to the core image library.

Each cataloged phase must be given a unique name; this is provided through a PHASE statement. Additional subroutines and other precoded modules can be added to the phase with an INCLUDE statement. The PHASE and INCLUDE statements provide information to the linkage editor; the first column (at least) of these two statements is blank. The other job control statements we've discussed in this chapter—JOB, EXEC, and OPTION—must begin with two slashes (//) in columns 1 and 2, with column 3 (at least) blank.

Each physical I/O device on a DOS system is assigned a symbolic name. A programmer who wishes to change the physical device indicated by a given symbolic name for the current run of a job can make the change by using an ASSGN statement. Like the JOB, EXEC, and OPTION statements, the ASSGN statement card starts with (//) in columns 1 and 2. Another new DOS feature allows the programmer to specify a device type or a device class rather than a specific physical device on an ASSGN statement.

The key element in DOS I/O control is the DTF macro coded within the problem program. Each combination of a physical device and an access method has its own DTF (Define The File); the DTFCD defines a card file, the DTFPR defines a printer file, the DTFMT defines a magnetic tape file, and so on. This macro indicates the specific input or output device, the access method to be used on this device, and detailed data descriptions.

For the average programmer, these few relatively simple control statements are enough. In most DOS installations, the other less commonly used features of DOS job control are generally left to a few specialists.

One additional feature described in the text was the cataloged procedure. A cataloged procedure is essentially a set of precoded job control language statements stored on a library and accessed by name through a single EXEC statement. Cataloged procedures are commonly used on production systems.

A detailed summary of DOS JCL can be found in Appendix B.

Key Words _____

ASSGN statement	JOB statement
cataloged procedure	OPTION statement
DTF (Define The File)	parameter
EXEC statement	phase

Exercises _____

1. What are the functions of a JOB statement?

2. What are the functions of an EXEC statement?

3. Explain the difference between a job name and a program name?

4. What is implied when the program name field on an EXEC statement is blank?

5. What is the function of the GO option on an EXEC statement (DOS/VSE)?

6. Explain the process of cataloging a program to the core image library, starting with a source module.

7. What functions are performed by the DTF macro?

8. What does the ASSGN statement do?

9. What are some of the advantages associated with device type or device class assignments?

10. What is a cataloged procedure?

Job Control Language for the IBM Operating System/360 and System/370 — JOB and EXEC Statements

Overview

IBM's Disk Operating System was designed to control operations on smaller computers; DOS can handle, depending on computer size and the release level, from one to five application programs in addition to the operating system itself. On a system of this size, techniques such as assigning each I/O device to a specific symbolic name or requiring a file specialist to keep track of the location of each and every file on each and every DASD (direct access storage device) volume do not cause too great a problem.

IBM's Operating System/360 and Operating System/370, including the virtual memory operating systems designed for more current versions of System/370, allow for the control of many more concurrent application programs. On such large systems, the relatively simple approaches of standard device assignments and single source DASD file control just won't do. Additional software support is essential. If a program is to perform the function of allocating disk space, for example, the job control language for such a system must be capable of communicating considerable information to the responsible operating system module; thus a job control language for this larger system will probably be considerably more complex than that of a DOS level system. The job control language for IBM's larger operating systems *is* considerably more complex than that of DOS.

As with DOS, most programmers need only a limited subset of the full job control language in their everyday work. We'll concentrate on those job control statements and parameters that are likely to be used by "average" programmers. Since the job control language for the full operating system is a bit more complex than that of DOS, we'll divide our analysis into two parts. Here in Chapter 9, the JOB and EXEC statements will be discussed; in Chapter 10, the DD or data definition statement will be covered. We will not attempt to cover all the features of IBM's System/360 and System/370 Job Control Language (JCL), only the more commonly used features. We hope that by using this approach we'll be able to avoid the "total confusion" so often felt by the beginning programmer encountering JCL for the first time.

Job Control Language Statements

There are three basic JCL statements.

1. The *JOB* statement serves to separate and identify jobs. Secondary functions include passing accounting and priority information to the system.
2. The *EXEC* or execute statement serves to identify the specific program or load module to be run or executed.
3. The *DD* or data definition statement is used to define, in detail, the characteristics of each and every input and output device used by the job.

In this chapter, we'll concentrate on the first two types and a few general concepts, leaving DD statements for the next chapter.

Jobs and Job Steps

Consider the job diagrammed in Fig. 9.1. This job involves three distinct steps—a compilation, the link edit step, and the final execution of the load module. To the programmer, all these steps constitute a single job producing a single set of output data. To the system, three distinct programs must be executed. The programmer sees a *job;* the computer sees a series of *job steps.* The job consists of all the code needed to complete a given data processing objective. A job may consist of a number of separate programs—compilers, linkage editors, sorts, application programs—all sequenced to obtain this objective: each of these programs is a separate job step.

One JOB statement must be provided for each job. It must be the first statement in the job. One EXEC statement must be provided for each job *step.* There may be almost any number of EXECs in a single job.

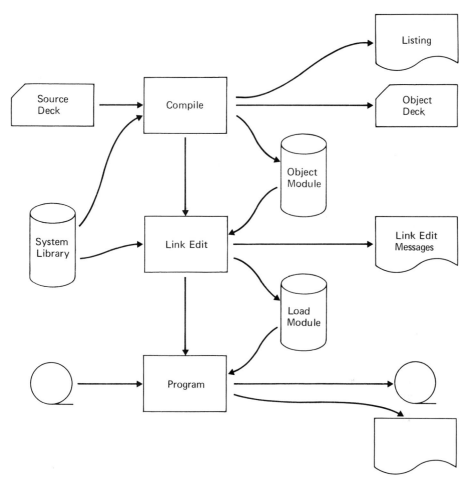

Fig. 9.1
A three-step job—compile/link edit/execute.

As an example, let's consider the simple compile, link edit, and execute program of Fig. 9.1. We have already noted the need for three distinct job steps; let's add the input and output device requirements to our discussion and attempt to list the job control language needed to support this application. In the first job step, compilation, input comes from the card reader and a macro library, and output goes to the printer or the card punch for an (often optional) object deck, and to disk, where a copy of the object module is saved for future job steps. The linkage editor gets its input from the disk file created by the first job step and, perhaps from a subroutine library. Output goes to the printer and to a disk file where a copy of the load module is stored. Input to the final job step starts with this load module and includes any input and output devices specified by the programmer. In this example, input comes from tape and output goes to the printer and to another tape.

Now, let's consider the job control language needed to support this job. Before listing the control statements, we must remember two points: first, the computer treats each job step as a separate entity, and second, one DD statement must be provided for each and every input and output device. To support this job, we need the following statements.

1. a JOB statement;

2. an EXEC statement for the compilation step;

3. a DD statement for the disk object module file;

4. a DD statement for the printer output;

5. a DD statement for card output;

6. a DD statement for card input;

7. an EXEC statement for the link edit step;

8. a DD statement for the object module input from disk—this is the same object module file described in number three but because this is a different job step a separate DD statement is needed;

9. a DD statement for the load module output to disk;

10. a DD statement for printer output;

11. an EXEC statement for the load module;

12. a DD statement for the input tape;

13. a DD statement for the output tape;

14. a DD statement for printer output;

15. a DD statement for the program-load module—this is the same file created in (or by) statement number nine, but, once again, this is a new step.

The first statement identifies the job; statements 2, 7, and 11, the three EXEC statements, mark the start of each of the three job steps, respectively. Note carefully that, within a given job step, *all* the DD statements actually needed by the job step are listed.

Cataloged Procedures

That's a lot of JCL for a simple compile/link edit/execute job! And with the exception of a few DD statements describing the actual input and output requirements of the final job step—12, 13, and 14 in our example—the statements are meaningless to the typical programmer. Also, every job involving a compile/link edit/execute is just about like any other job with the same three steps. Who cares about the exact nature of a temporary file created strictly to hold the results of a compile operation and having little or no direct bearing on the final results? For years, programming languages have handled such repetitious activities with macros. The job control language equivalent of a macro is a *cataloged procedure.*

A cataloged procedure is a set of precoded JCL statements. This macrolike module is normally stored on a library and added to the job stream as it enters the system; the function of grafting cataloged procedures into a job stream is performed by the job reader or job-queueing operating system module described in Chapter 6. Using cataloged procedures, our JCL for the compilation program we've been discussing becomes

1. a JOB statement;
2. an EXEC COBOL or EXEC FORTRAN statement describing, in programmer terms, the cataloged procedure desired;
3. a DD statement for tape input;
4. a DD statement for tape output;
5. a DD statement for printer output.

Upon reading the EXEC statement, the job reader goes to the cataloged procedure library, obtains a copy of the JCL included in the requested procedure, and adds this JCL to the programmer's deck, which is about to become a series of card images on a class queue anyway. The programmer need be concerned only with the JCL that is unique to the job; all of the repetitious code is contained in the procedure. The programmer need not be concerned with the actual names of the compiler programs or the linkage editor, and can ignore the details of the temporary work data sets of these routines.

A bit later, after we've looked at a few actual JCL statements, we'll analyze some typical cataloged procedures.

The Language—
Basic Parameters

Let's get down to specifics. A traditional place to begin the discussion of any language is with the basic format of a statement; job control language is no exception. The basic format of an IBM Job Control Language statement is

```
//NAME    OPERATION    OPERANDS    COMMENTS
```

Verbally, the individual fields can be described as follows.

1. Columns 1 and 2 *must* contain the "slash" character (/). This is the same character used to denote division in FORTRAN.
2. The NAME field (essentially a label) begins in column 3. This field serves to identify a particular job, job step, or data set; as we shall see, the NAME field allows the programmer and the operating system to identify or refer to a particular JCL statement.
3. The NAME field is followed by at least one blank. If column number three is blank, the system assumes that there is *no* NAME; the blank character serves as a field separator.
4. Following the first set of blank characters is the OPERATION field which describes the type of JCL statement. The three basic operations are JOB, EXEC, and DD.
5. The operation field is followed by one or more blanks.
6. Following this second set of blank characters come the OPERANDS, a series of parameters providing detailed information about the job, job step, or data set.
7. Again, one or more blanks separate the operands from the next field.
8. Optional comments.
9. Except for comments, the JCL code cannot go beyond column 71.

The name, chosen by the programmer, is limited to no more than eight alphanumeric (letters and digits) or national (@,$ #) characters. The first character may not be a digit. The operation and operands fields must be coded according to some very exacting standards: only the three operations mentioned above are legal, and we'll be discussing some of the rules for coding operands in this and the next chapter. Comments are, of course, up to the programmer.

Note very carefully the use of blanks on a JCL statement; *blanks are used to separate fields.* Stray blanks are the most common cause of JCL errors among beginners. Stray blanks *will* be interpreted as field separators. Coding

```
//   STEP1   EXEC   COBOL
```

will result in a strange error message—there is no such operation as STEP1; only JOB, EXEC, and DD are valid. You know what you mean, but the computer doesn't. Try

```
//STEP1   EXEC   COBOL
```

with no blanks between the // and the name field.

The JOB
Statement

The basic function of the JOB statement is to mark the beginning of a job and thus separate it from all other jobs coming into the computer. The name field serves to give each job the unique identification required in a multiprogramming system and thus must normally be coded. Any combination of eight or fewer characters, as long as the first is alphabetic and only letters and numbers are used, is a legal job name, although many computer centers place their own restrictions on job names. Often, a computer center will issue job cards with prepunched and prenumbered job name fields; frequently, the cards are numbered in sequence, thus practically eliminating the problem of two or more jobs with identical job names.

In some computer centers, only the job name and operation fields are used.

```
//JOB396    JOB
```

Other centers require additional information, which gets us into the operand field of the JOB card.

The JOB Statement—
Accounting
Information

One important secondary function of the JOB statement is passing accounting information to an accounting module in the operating system. This information is coded as the first *parameter* in the operands field.

```
//JOB396    JOB    1234
```

might, for example, indicate that the cost of running the job named JOB396 is to be charged against account number 1234. Often, multiple accounting subparameters must be provided, as in

```
//JOB435    JOB    (1234,875)
```

which might mean that job JOB435 is to be charged against account number 1234, user number 875. The exact content of the accounting field is up to the individual installation; that is each computer center can define its own requirements.

Note the use of parentheses; when more than one subparameter is coded, parentheses are required. Note also the position of the accounting information—the first set of information in the operands field. Accounting information is a good example of a *positional parameter*; the meaning of the accounting field and the meaning of the individual subparameters within the accounting-information parameter is determined by position.

We've been using the terms "parameter" and "subparameter" throughout our discussion of the accounting-information field; what do these terms mean? A parameter is simply a single, logically related set of information in the operand field of a JCL statement—a collection of accounting information is a logical entity. A subparameter is a single piece of data within a parameter. A subparameter would, for instance, be analogous to an individual's name, with the parameter being the individual's complete mailing address.

The JOB Statement—
Programmer Name

To simplify programmer identification, the programmer's name is often placed on the JOB statement. A second positional parameter is provided for this purpose, as in

```
//JOB098    JOB    (2987,235),DAVIS
```

A slightly different format is sometimes used.

```
//JOB098    JOB    (2987,235),'   DAVIS '
```

The use of apostrophes is required only when special characters—a comma, blanks, etc.—are desired as a part of the name field. As long as the programmer stays with letters of the alphabet, digits, and no more than one period, the apostrophes are optional. Your computer center probably has a standard format for the programmer-name parameter.

The JOB Statement—
The CLASS Parameter

A few chapters back when the concept of a JOB statement was first introduced, the use of this statement to indicate a job's class (priority) was mentioned. In IBM's Job Control Language, this function is performed by the *CLASS* parameter. Adding this to our existing parameters, we get

```
//JOB760    JOB    (3984,444),' W.S. DAVIS ',CLASS=A
```

The JOB Statement—
The TIME Parameter

Remember the computer's timer and the way the timer routines in the operating system can be used to cancel a program caught in an endless loop? The data for setting the timer must come from somewhere; the source is often a *TIME* parameter coded on the JOB statement. The TIME parameter has two possible subparameters.

```
TIME=(minutes,seconds)
```

The TIME parameter

    TIME=(5,30)

asks for five minutes and thirty seconds of CPU time, while

    TIME=5 or TIME=(5) or TIME=(5,0)

asks for exactly five minutes, and

    TIME=(,30)

requests thirty seconds. Note the use of parentheses. When the first subparameter *alone* is coded, they can be skipped if desired; when more than one parameter is coded, however, parentheses *must* be used. The values coded for minutes and seconds are positional subparameters; i.e., they are defined by their position in the TIME parameter. In the "seconds only" form, a comma was coded to indicate the *absence* of the "minutes" positional subparameter.

The CLASS and TIME parameters are themselves *keyword parameters*; i.e., the word CLASS and the word TIME give these parameters a meaning *independent* of their position on the JOB statement. Once the accounting and programmer name *positional* parameters have been coded in their proper position, the keyword parameters can be coded in any order. Here are a few examples.

    //XY1   JOB   (345,86),JONES,CLASS=C,TIME=3

    //XY2   JOB   (296,25),'A.SMITH',TIME=(,45),CLASS=A

    //XY3   JOB   (111,22),DAVIS,CLASS=D,TIME=(3,30)

The REGION Parameter

On some systems, a job's priority is determined, in part, by the amount of space it requires. The programmer can indicate the amount of space needed by a program by coding a *REGION* parameter; this is another keyword parameter, with core being allocated in blocks of 2048 (2K) bytes, as in

    REGION=34K

or

    REGION=124K.

The MSGLEVEL Parameter

Programmer-coded JCL statements, the JCL statements included in a cataloged procedure, and messages indicating what action the system has actually taken with respect to various data sets and devices are valuable to the programmer during program debug, but once this stage is completed this information becomes excessive and is usually meaningless to a nonprogramming user of a report. The *MSGLEVEL* or (message level) parameter allows the programmer to select which JCL and device allocation messages are to be printed. The general form of this parameter is

MSGLEVEL=(JCL-statements,messages)

The two subparameters have the following values and meanings.

JCL	MEANING
0	Print only the JOB statement.
1	Print all JCL statements, including programamer-coded statements and those added by a cataloged procedure.
2	Print only programmer coded JCL.

MESSAGES	MEANING
0	Don't print any allocation messages unless the job ends abnormally.
1	Print all messages.

The parameter

MSGLEVEL=(1,1)

means to print everything, while the parameter

MSGLEVEL=(0,0)

means print only the JOB statement unless the job fails. The parameter

MSGLEVEL=(1,0)

instructs the system to print all JCL statements but to skip allocation messages.

Default Options

Rather than insisting that each and every JOB parameter be coded by the programmer, many computer centers use *default* values. Stated very simply, if the programmer fails, for any reason, to code a particular parameter, the system assumes a value. Often, a number of key parameters—accounting information, the programmer's name, and the job class—must be coded; defaults are based on the job class with, for example, all CLASS=A jobs being assigned a REGION of 90K and a TIME limit of 30 seconds while CLASS=B jobs get 120K and a two-minute time limit. If the programmer is not satisfied with the default value, the desired parameter can be coded, thus overriding the default.

Other JOB Parameters

Other parameters, all keyword in nature, allow the programmer to specify such things as job priority, run type, condition code limits, roll-in/roll-out options, and restart options. We won't attempt to cover these parameters except to mention the fact of their existence; when a need arises, check these parameters with a system programmer or look them up in a JCL manual.

Some JOB Statements

```
//JOBA     JOB (2938,24),ADAMS,CLASS=B

//C1234567    JOB   (3998,659),'A.B. JONES',CLASS=A,

//              TIME=(5,30),REGION=128K
```

Continuing a JCL Statement

The second sample JOB statement shown above won't fit on a single card; thus this is as good a place as any to introduce the rules for continuing a JCL statement. The rules are quite simple.

1. Interrupt the field after a complete parameter or subparameter, including the trailing comma, has been coded; i.e., stop after a comma (which you must admit is a natural break point).
2. *Optionally* code any nonblank character in column 72. Column 72 may be left blank; the use of a continuation character is optional.
3. Code slashes (//) in columns 1 and 2 of the continuation line.
4. Continue your coding in any column from 4 through 16–column 3 must be blank and code must be resumed no later than column 16.

In other words, just break after a comma and resume coding on the next line.

The EXEC Statement

An EXEC statement marks the beginning of each job *step*; its purpose is to provide the system with the identification of the program (or cataloged procedure) to be executed. Thus it is only fitting that the first parameter on an EXEC statement be the one that identifies the program or procedure,

```
//  EXEC   PGM=SORT6
```

or

```
//  EXEC   PROC=COBOL
```

When indicating a cataloged procedure, as in

```
//  EXEC   COBOL
```

the keyword *PROC* may be skipped. When executing a *program,* the keyword *PGM must* be used.

A good example of what the EXEC statement does can be found in a typical cataloged procedure—let's look at the FORTRAN procedure. Coding

```
//   EXEC  FORTRAN
```

identifies a cataloged procedure, causing the following code to be read from the procedure library and added to the programmer's job stream

```
//FORT   EXEC   PGM=IEYFORT
//SYSPRINT  DD   parameters  (printed output)
//SYSLIN    DD   parameters  (object module output)
//LKED   EXEC   PGM=IEWL
//SYSLIB    DD   parameters  (system library)
//SYSLMOD   DD   parameters  (load module output)
//SYSPRINT  DD   parameters  (printed output)
//SYSUT1    DD   parameters  (work space)
//SYSLIN    DD   parameters  (object module input)
//GO     EXEC   PGM=*.LKED.SYSLMOD
```

That final statement is just a bit confusing. What it says is "execute the program created in the job step named LKED and stored on a data set named SYSLMOD." The name field of a JCL statement serves much the same purpose as a label, allowing a given step to be referred to by another statement; the particular format used for the reference in question

```
*.LKED.SYSLMOD
```

is called qualification. To cite another example of qualification, there are two data sets named SYSLIN in this procedure, one in each of the first two job steps; the first one would be referred to as *.FORT.SYSLIN, while the second becomes *.LKED.SYSLIN—the asterisk denotes a reference to another job step.

The programmer coded a cataloged procedure. The procedure itself contained, in this case, three EXEC statements, each calling for the execution of a specific program. All references to a specific program contained the keyword "PGM=."

Often, the program or cataloged procedure identification is all the programmer need code on the EXEC card. Some applications, however, require more information, and a number of additional parameters do exist.

The COND or
Condition Parameter

Most programmers have, at one time or another, submitted a job with one or more compiler errors. The result is usually a compilation with a listing of errors followed by a message indicating that, because of the compiler errors, the link edit and go steps were not executed. This makes a great deal of sense—why bother with subsequent steps if the first one is wrong? You've probably never thought about it before, but just how does the computer system know enough to skip a job step, particularly when a catalogued procedure tells it to execute the link edit and go steps?

You may have noticed something called a severity code on your compiler errors—warnings are worth 4, simple errors might be worth 8, severe errors might be worth 12 points; a program containing severe errors will almost certainly not run. The compiler reports the value of the highest encountered severity code to the system by placing a condition code in one of the registers—assembler language programmers are probably familiar with the idea of a condition code as part of normal register conventions. The operating system's job initiator module can check this condition code prior to loading and executing a job step, bypassing the step if the actual condition code returned by a prior job step is not acceptable; the programmer passes along the limits for this comparison via the *COND* or condition parameter.

The general form of the COND parameter is

```
COND=(value,comparison,stepname)
```

The parameter

```
COND=(12,LE,FORT)
```

attached to the EXEC statement for the link edit step tells the initiator program that if 12 is less than or equal to the actual condition code returned by the FORT step (an EXEC statement with a step name of "FORT"), the link edit step is to be skipped. Let's run through that logic again. The COND parameter on the following EXEC statement

```
//LKED   EXEC   PGM=IEWL,COND=(12,LE, FORT)
```

means that the step named LKED is to be *bypassed* if 12 is less than or equal to the actual condition code returned by the step named FORT. The logic is a bit unusual, so be careful. Most programmers when comparing a variable and a constant in an IF statement or a logical comparison will code the variable first—it's pretty much a standard programming procedure. On the COND parameter, the *constant* is coded first, making the logic seem to read backwards. The fact that the comparison is made to implement a negative decision, skipping a step, adds to the confusion. The safest way to handle COND logic is to read it as it's coded, from left to right—the step is skipped if some constant meets a certain condition with respect to the actual condition code returned by a prior job step. Incidentally, the third positional subparameter (the step name of the prior job step whose condition code is to participate in the comparison) can be skipped; if the step name is not coded, the most recently completed step in the job is assumed.

A number of comparisons can be coded, including greater than (GT), equal to (EQ), less than (LT), greater than or equal to (GE), less than or equal to (LE), and not equal to (NE). In the FORTRAN cataloged procedure described above, COND parameters are found on the EXEC statements for the link edit and go steps; they were left off simply because we had not yet covered the parameter. By coding

```
//LKED   EXEC   PGM=IEWL,COND=(4,LT,FORT)
```

we are instructing the operating system to skip the LKED step if 4 is less than the actual condition code returned by the FORT job step. The JCL statement

```
//GO   EXEC   PGM=*LKED.SYSLMOD,COND=(4,LT,FORT)
```

places the same restriction on the go step. In some cases, multiple conditions are coded, as in

```
COND=((4,LT, FORT),(4,LT,LKED))
```

that causes "this" job step to be skipped if 4 is less than the actual condition code returned by the FORT step *or* if 4 is less than the actual condition code returned by the LKED step. Note the use of parentheses; punctuation can become tedious in coding JCL, and accounts for the bulk of programmer errors and difficulties.

The logic of the COND parameter seems a bit cockeyed to many people, perhaps because the test is performed in order to implement a negative decision—skipping a job step. So be careful when using or interpreting this parameter; read it exactly as coded, and you shouldn't go too far wrong.

Other EXEC
Parameters

Other EXEC parameters allow the programmer to pass parameters to a job step, provide *job step* accounting information, set a dispatching priority for the step, set a time limit for the job step, specify the region size, and handle roll-in/roll-out and restart options. Several of these parameters could have been coded on the JOB statement; the programmer has the option of specifying such things as a time limit, core limit, roll-in/roll-out options, restart options, and conditions for the complete job or for each job step independently.

Programmers often encounter the *PARM* option in the form

```
//   EXEC   FORTRAN,PARM.FORT='NODECK,LIST'
```

that informs the FORT job step, the compiler, that no object deck is to be punched and that a list is to be printed. Detailed information on the meaning of parameters for any compiler language can be found in the programmer's guide to that language.

Summary ————————————————————————————

In this chapter, we've studied some general ideas of IBM's Job Control Language and covered specific parameters of the JOB and EXEC statements. A detailed summary of these parameters in reference form is found in Appendix C. These ideas will be carried into Chapter 10.

Key Words ————————————————————————————

cataloged procedure	keyword parameter
CLASS parameter	MSGLEVEL parameter
COND parameter	parameter
DD statement	PGM parameter
default	positional parameter
EXEC statement	PROC parameter
job	REGION parameter
JOB statement	TIME parameter
job step	

Exercises ————————————————————————————

1. Differentiate between a job and a job step. Relate the JOB and EXEC statements to these two concepts.
2. What is a positional parameter? Give some examples.
3. What is a keyword parameter? Give some examples.
4. What does "MSGLEVEL=(1,1)" mean when coded on a JOB statement?
5. What is a cataloged procedure? Why are cataloged procedures used?
6. Explain default options.
7. Code a JOB statement using the job name of your choice, your course number as an accounting field, and your own name, requesting 90K of core for one minute and thirty seconds in the Q job class. Don't bother printing allocation messages. Print only the JCL that you code.
8. Code an EXEC statement to execute a cataloged procedure named COBOL (compile, link edit, and go). Skip this step if STEP1 returned a condition code of 100.

The DD Statement

Overview

In this chapter, we continue the discussion of IBM's Job Control Language, concentrating on the data definition or DD statement. The DD statement allows the programmer to pass to the system a detailed description of each data set used by a program. There is one JOB statement per job, one EXEC statement for each job step, and one DD statement for each and every file accessed by the individual programs in each job step.

There are many different types of input and output devices. Each type has its own characteristics, strengths, and weaknesses. Job control language must be capable of handling even the most esoteric of applications on even the least often used devices; thus the number and complexity of DD statement parameters is mind-boggling. In this chapter, we'll concentrate only on the most common of the DD statement parameters—those used by most programmers in their everyday work. Coverage of the more advanced topics and lesser used parameters is left to a more advanced course in job control. Seeking expert advice from your local systems programmer or a consultant is a good idea when you're planning for an application involving some of the trickier aspects of job control language.

Many JCL texts present the parameters of a DD statement as a series of independent entities; this can be confusing. In this text, we'll take a somewhat different approach, concentrating on the input and output devices and describing the JCL needed to define data on a given device type. Essentially, we'll be following a three-step approach.

1. Discuss the characteristics of a particular input and/or output device.
2. Identify those characteristics that must be communicated to the operating system.
3. Introduce and discuss the specific DD statement parameters needed to communicate this information.

Unit record equipment, direct access devices, tape, and the system input and system output devices (spooling) will be covered.

One more point before we start. JCL is an independent entity, attached to a program in order to communicate information to an operating system; it is *not* a part of the actual program but serves in a support role. This creates no problem with JOB and EXEC statements, but the DD statement defines a data set that must be accessed by the program; the program and its DD statements must therefore be linked in some way. Under the IBM operating systems we are currently studying, this link is achieved by the name field of the DD statement and a program macro called a data control block or DCB. This link is the subject of the next several paragraphs.

The DD
Statements
and Data
Control Blocks

Back in the second generation, the decision to change from, say, card to tape input on a program was a potentially expensive one, often involving an almost complete rewrite of the old program to allow for blocking, multiple buffering, and a new set of input and output macros. Operating system modules, in particular the access methods discussed previously, helped, but did not eliminate the problem. This expense made many firms hesitant to change to a new technology. The continued use of something less than the best technology was wasteful and, from the manufacturer's point of view, often meant the loss of a potential sale; thus the concept of device-independent programs became an important part of IBM's System/360–370 design philosophy.

Device independence means that a programmer should be able to change one or more input and/or output devices with a minimum of effort and a minimum of program rewrite. The IBM System/360–370 solution to this problem involves the input and output macros, a new macro called a *data control block,* and the *DD statement.*

Let's start inside the program. The data control block or DCB macro, coded in assembler language as

```
INPUT   DCB   MACRF=GM,DSORG=PS,DDNAME=CARDS,     C
              other-parameters
```

sets up a series of constants and addresses describing the characteristics of the physical and logical records to be manipulated. Three parameters are coded above. The MACRF or macro-form parameter and the DSORG or data-set organization parameter, taken together, describe the access method to be used. The DDNAME parameter is the link to a DD statement; more about this parameter later. Other parameters that might be coded describe the logical record length, blocksize, record form, buffering technique, density (tape), and numerous other physical characteristics of the record. The three parameters coded above represent the minimum that must be coded within the program; other parameters, as we shall see, can be coded on the DD statement and incorporated into the data control block at OPEN time.

The actual input or output macro is a pretty simple affair. The basic macro for input from a sequential file is

```
label   GET   dcbaddress,areaaddress
```

The output macro for sequential files is

```
label   PUT   dcbaddress,areaaddress
```

Consider the simple "read a card and print it" program of Fig. 10.1. The DCB macros are coded in among the constants and work spaces; this macro contains no executable code but consists of constants and addresses. The DSORG and MACRF parameters define the access method. The EODAD or end-of-data address parameter is a new one; it gives the program an address to branch to when an end-of-data marker is encountered in the input data.

The EXEC statement specifies a cataloged procedure—ASMFCLG; this is a procedure for compile, link edit, and go, using the assembler program in the first step. The assembler creates an object module, containing the skeleton of a data control block. The access method identified in the DCB is grafted onto the load module by the linkage editor. The GET and PUT macros contain a DCB address and an address for storing input data or finding output data; these macros generate into two constants and a branch to the actual access method. The load module for this program is pictured in Fig. 10.2.

The input operation works in the following manner. A GET macro is encountered as part of the program's normal cycle. This results in a branch to the access method. The access method knows the detailed specifications of the data from the data control block (address of the DCB is part of the GET macro) and also knows, again from the GET macro, where to put the data once it enters

```
//JOB33   JOB   (2398,34),DAVIS,CLASS=A

//    EXEC   ASMFCLG

//SYSIN   DD   *

          STARTUP    macro to handle register conventions

          B     GO        branch around constants and work area

CARDOUT  DC    CL1' '

CARD     DS    CL80

         DC    CL51' '

INPUT    DCB   MACRF=GM,DSORG=PS,DDNAME=CARDS,EODAD=QUIT

OUTPUT   DCB   MACRF=PM,DSORG=PS,DDNAME=LINES

GO       OPEN  (INPUT,INPUT)

         OPEN  (OUTPUT,OUTPUT)

RUN      GET   INPUT,CARD

         PUT   OUTPUT,CARDOUT

         B     RUN

QUIT     CLOSE (INPUT,OUTPUT)

QUIT2    CLOSEOUT    macro to handle end of job housekeeping

/*

//LINES  DD   parameters

//CARDS  DD   parameters

/*
```

Fig. 10.1
An assembly language program using device-independent input and output macros.

(a)

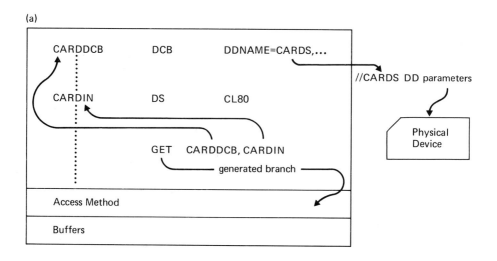

(b)

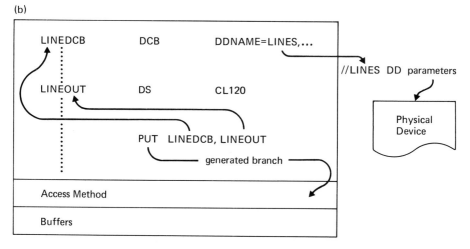

Fig. 10.2
System/360-370 I/O.

core. In short, everything is here except for the identification of the physical
input device. This is the function of the DD statement. The DCB contains a
parameter—the DDNAME parameter—that points to the DD statement associated with the file in question. The parameters on the DD statement identify
the physical input device.

Let's review these steps by looking at what happens on output. The data
control block, output macro, and access method are all part of the program load

module (Fig. 10.2b). The access method to be used has been defined by the programmer through DCB parameters; the linkage editor has simply grafted the proper one to the load module. The PUT macro causes a branch to the access method. Using the addresses provided by the PUT macro, the access method can locate the DCB and the data address, giving it the detailed record information needed to control output. The DCB contains a pointer to the associated DD statement which identifies, via a series of parameters, the physical output device.

A switch from tape to disk can be accomplished by changing a job control statement. Most production programs, once past the compiler debug stage, are stored on a library in load module form and run without additional compilation. Since the JCL statements are not a part of the program load module, the change from tape to disk doesn't even involve recompilation! Even if a recompilation is needed to allow a new blocking factor or a new access method to be used, a modification of a single DCB macro may be all that is needed.

How about a higher-level language like COBOL or FORTRAN? The source of the GET or PUT macro is obvious—the READ and WRITE instructions—but where do the data control blocks come from? In COBOL, a data control block is build from a SELECT . . . ASSIGN clause in the ENVIRON-MENT DIVISION and a number of DATA DIVISION clauses such as BLOCK CONTAINS, LABELS ARE, and others. In FORTRAN, the DCB is built as soon as a READ or WRITE statement is encountered by the compiler, and is assumed to call for sequential access unless a FILE statement specifies otherwise. In COBOL, the DDNAME parameter is part of the SELECT . . . ASSIGN clause, with

```
SELECT DATAIN ASSIGN TO UT-S-CARDS.
```

pointing to

```
//CARDS   DD   parameters.
```

In FORTRAN, the DDNAME is built from the device number of the input or output instruction, with

```
WRITE (6.15) A.B.C
```

pointing to a data control block containing

```
label   DCB   DDNAME=FT06F001,...
```

which leads to a JCL statement like

```
//FT06F001   DD   parameters
```

Let us now turn our attention to the DD statements themselves.

Unit Record Equipment

Very few programmers read data *directly* from a card reader or send data directly to a printer on a modern, high-speed computer; for reasons of economy, such data are normally spooled to tape or disk by an operating system module. Unit record equipment is, however, the least complicated class of input and output devices and, thus, gives a convenient starting point for our discussion of the DD statement.

What are the characteristics of unit record data? First, and perhaps obviously, we are discussing "unit" records; there is no blocking, all records are the same length, and the logical and physical record lengths are identical. Labels are not normally present. The cards and paper containing this data are not reusable except as recycled scrap; thus standard operating procedures—"Give the stuff back to the programmer"—are adequate for unit record data. Printers can handle lines of different lengths and not all card readers are restricted to the "standard" 80-column card, but, aside from this possible need to specify the record length, the only thing the programmer must give to the system is the identity of the specific input or output device. This is done via the UNIT parameter.

The UNIT Parameter—Unit Record Equipment

The *UNIT parameter* allows the programmer to specify a particular input or output device. This parameter can be coded in any one of three forms.

1. UNIT=unit address
2. UNIT=device-type
3. UNIT=group-name

The first form, UNIT=unit address, permits the coding of an actual device address. Every piece of equipment attached to an IBM system is assigned a specific, three-digit address; if, for example, a particular printer is device number 8 on channel 0, its unit address is 008, and a DD statement to permit a program to access this device and only this device would be coded as

```
//PRINTR   DD   UNIT=008
```

If the requested device is busy, or for some other reason not available, the program must wait to be loaded. This is a very specific request—*no* other printer will do. As a consequence, this form of the unit parameter is rarely used.

The second form of the UNIT parameter, UNIT=device-type, is a bit more general. If the programmer wants a 3211 printer, and *any* 3211 printer will do, the DD statement might be

```
//OUTS   DD   UNIT=3211
```

Assuming that the system has a number of 3211 printers, the job can be loaded and run as soon as any one of these devices is free; it's a much less restrictive form and thus more heavily used. A 2501 card reader can be requested by coding UNIT=2501; a 2520 card-read punch is requested by coding UNIT=2520. Any unit of the specified device type can be used by the requesting program.

UNIT=group-name is the final form of the UNIT parameter. The DD statement

```
//XYZ   DD   UNIT=READER
```

might be a request for any available card reader, be it a 2501, a 2520, or a 3505; it's the most general form of the UNIT parameter. Each computer installation can define its own group names; there are no universal standards, although UNIT=PUNCH is a *typical* way of defining a request for a card punch and UNIT=PRINTER is an obvious group name for the printers attached to a system. In using this form of the UNIT parameter, the programmer is asking for any card reader or any punch or any printer, regardless of its device type, physical address, manufacturer, or other characteristics.

Note that there are *no* blanks in "UNIT=READER." Blanks, remember, are used as field separators on a JCL statement.

The Data Control Block (DCB) Parameter— Unit Record

The programmer must code within a program a Data Control Block macro for each file accessed by that program; this is the obvious place to indicate the logical record length of a unit record. This approach presents one small problem—a decision to switch from 80-column cards to the 96-column cards, to cite one example, means a recompilation of the program.

There is an alternative: DCB parameters can be coded on the DD statement. This is done via the *DCB parameter*. In the example cited above, the old DD statement might have been

```
//CARDIN   DD   UNIT=READER,DCB=LRECL=80
```

Replacing this JCL statement with

```
//CARDIN   DD   UNIT=READER,DCB=LRECL=96
```

changes the logical record length without recompilation. The LRECL subparameter specifies logical record length. DCB subparameters can be specified either within the program data control block or on the DD statement. The use of DD subparameters is a bit more flexible, allowing for changes in record characteristics without a need for recompilation.

Data control block subparameters† are moved into the *program DCB* at OPEN time, a procedure to be described in detail at a later time. Any record information coded in the *program* DCB will *not* be modified even if the DD information is different; i.e., "hard-coded" information takes precedence. If a programmer anticipates any change in the basic record format, the volatile parameters should not be coded in the program but passed to the system via the DD statement. Many assembly language shops code only the absolute minimum—DSORG, MACRF, DDNAME—parameters in the program DCB and consider this to be a normal coding standard.

There are no blanks within the DCB field. No blanks separate the two parameters we've looked at thus far; if a stray blank were to fall between the UNIT and DCB fields, the entire DCB parameter would be treated as comments and ignored.

Both the UNIT and DCB parameters are keyword parameters; i.e., they can be coded in any order.

Magnetic Disk

Perhaps the most commonly used of the secondary storage devices is magnetic disk. Disk data can be much more complex than unit record data. Logical records are not restricted in format: they can be almost any length, and the logical record length can vary within a file. Blocking is legal; thus the programmer must be able to deal with blocked, unblocked, fixed, and variable length records.

Complicating the problem is the fact that the data on a disk surface are not human-readable. Visual checking is impossible. A human operator is unlikely to load already-punched cards into a card punch, or used paper onto a printer, but it's quite possible that a disk pack containing important data might be loaded on a drive and reused, thus destroying the old data. Simple "give it back to the programmer" operating procedures are not adequate with disk. Instead, the operator must be given very specific instructions as to what to do with the disk.

---

† Within a program, we refer to DCB *parameters,* but the DCB is *itself* a parameter on a DD statement; thus LRECL is a DCB *parameter* when it occurs within a program DCB, but it is a DCB *sub*parameter when coded as part of a DD statement's DCB parameter.

Disk is also a shared resource—typically, numerous data files and libraries are stored on a single disk pack (or volume). Since human beings cannot directly read disk, catalog entries are used to identify the individual files by name.

In many computer centers, disk packs can be dismounted and stored off-line. It is not unusual to have perhaps eight disk drives supporting 15 or 20 packs, with a few system packs being permanently mounted, and the other volumes mounted by the operator as required. How does the operator know which pack to mount? Again, the programmer must provide this information through the DD statement.

Disk space is a limited resource in most computer installations. To ensure the availability of sufficient space before a program that creates a disk file is executed, the programmer must give the system an estimate of the amount of space needed.

One disk file is not necessarily just like any other disk file. The programmer must provide the system with enough information to clearly define all these sources of potential variability. Specification of the physical input/output device is, of course, essential. The serial number(s) of the volume(s) to be mounted must be clearly established. The operator must be told what to do with the disk pack at the conclusion of the job step. If the file is to be cataloged and stored in a library, a catalog name must be provided. Detailed record information must be communicated through the data control block, either within the program or in the DD parameter. Job control language provides a formal structure for communicating these facts to the operating system.

In the discussion that follows, the various DD parameters needed for disk will be introduced from the point of view of creating a new file. After the key parameters have been described, the problem of retrieving an existing file will be covered.

The UNIT Parameter

The UNIT parameter for disk and the UNIT parameter for unit-record equipment are identical, with only the specific unit designator changing. UNIT = 181 is an example of the "unit-address" option, instructing an operator to mount a volume on the unit numbered 181 (channel 1, device 81). In most computer centers, the device number of each piece of hardware is clearly indicated on each device. The device-address form of the UNIT parameter is, however, rarely used when accessing disk or drum.

Direct access devices are often requested by device type, with the 2311, 2314, 3330, and 3340 being common disk device types and the 2301, 2302, and 2303 being drum units. Coding

```
UNIT=3330
```

represents a request for space on any 3330 disk unit.

Disk and drum are frequently used for storing the intermediate results of a data processing job. To simplify a request for such work files, many installations have defined various group names for one or more direct access volumes—typical group names include SYSDA and WORK1.

The DCB Parameter

A disk data control block is just like a unit-record data control block, only a bit more complex. The purpose of a data control block is to define, for the system, the characteristics of individual records. On disk, records can be fixed or variable in length and blocked or unblocked; thus additional DCB subparameters are needed to fully define the data. Commonly used DCB subparameters include

Subparameter	Meaning
BLKSIZE=	blocksize in bytes
LRECL=	logical redord length in bytes
RECFM=	record format

The blocksize and logical record length subparameters are pretty much self-explanatory; the RECFM subparameter defines the record format, with F meaning fixed-length records, B meaning blocked records, FB meaning fixed-length blocked data, V meaning variable-length records, and so on.

The Disposition Parameter

What does the operator (or the system) do with a given disk file following job completion? The answer to this question is coded in the disposition (*DISP*) *parameter*. The general form of the disposition parameter is

```
DISP=(a,b,c)
```

where

    a = the status of the data set at the start of the job,
    b = the status following successful job step completion,
    c = the status following abnormal completion.

All three are positional subparameters.

If a file is to be created within a job step, its "start of job" status is NEW. An existing file is OLD. Some data sets, a library for example, might be accessed by more than one of the programs in core at any time. The prejob status for data sets of this type is SHR, which means share—this status is not used by a job that intends to modify data on the file. When SHR is used, the file can be accessed by two or more programs. A disposition of MOD indicates that the programmer wishes to add more data to an existing file; the system thus position the read/write heads at the old end-of-file marker at OPEN time.

Following normal completion of a job step, the second disposition subparameter takes over. If there is no further need for the data, the programmer can code DELETE; a KEEP subparameter means that the file will be retained. If the data are needed by a subsequent step within the same job, the programmer can PASS the data set. The file can be entered on a catalog (CATLG) and retained, or removed from a catalog (UNCATLG) and made available for reuse.

The desired disposition might be different following abnormal job termination; any of the normal job termination options except for PASS can be coded as the third DISP subparameter. If the third subparameter is not coded, the "normal termination" disposition is assumed to hold for abnormal termination as well.

To create a file, pass it to another job step, and delete it in the event of serious error, code

```
DISP=(NEW,PASS,DELETE)
```

If a file is to be created and, normally, cataloged but in the event of an error simply kept for study or possible restart, code

```
DISP=(NEW,CATLG,KEEP)
```

A temporary work file that is, in any event, needed only for the life of the job step would have, as part of its DD statement, the following disposition parameter

```
DISP=(NEW,DELETE)
```

Since no abnormal termination disposition is coded, the second subparameter, DELETE, is assumed.

The Data Set
Name Parameter

To simplify the task of retrieving cataloged or passed data sets, the programmer can give a file a unique name by coding the *DSNAME parameter* (DSN is an acceptable abbreviation). A valid data set name consists of from one to eight characters (letters, numbers, or one of the national symbols), starting with a letter or a national symbol. Data set names can be qualified; for example,

```
DSNAME=MU.USERDATA.SAN1
```

indicates that a data set named SAN1 can be located by referring to an index named USERDATA and that this index can be located by referring to a master index named MU. Each level of qualification must exist as an index in the system catalog.

Temporary, life of the job data sets are assigned a data set name beginning with the ampersand (&) character, as in

```
DSNAME=&&TEMP
```

Normally, to avoid possible confusion with certain system parameters, a double ampersand is used at the beginning of the temporary data set name.

You may have noticed that we seem to be using the terms "file" and "data set" as synonyms. This usage is not quite accurate, but it's close enough for most situations. A file contains data. A library, while it does contain electronic pulses that are just like the elementary pulses held in a file, does not, technically, contain data. Some time ago, IBM coined the term "data set" to encompass both traditional files and libraries. It's a more general term than file, but data set is not an industry standard. When discussing IBM-specific material such as JCL, we'll use data set; when discussing more general material, we won't.

The VOLUME
Parameter

The *VOLUME parameter*, often shortened to VOL, allows the programmer to request the mounting of a specific disk volume (a volume is simply a single, physical disk pack). Individual volumes are normally given a unique serial number. To request the mounting of a pack with a serial number MU 1234, the programmer would code

```
VOL=SER=MU1234
```

where "SER=volume-serial-number" is a subparameter of the VOLUME or VOL parameter. To request the mounting of this particular volume on a 3330-series drive, code

```
//NAME    DD    UNIT=3330,VOL=SER=MU1234,...
```

along with other needed parameters. Note once again the absence of blanks.

The VOLUME parameter is used to define a specific direct access volume. On a temporary data set where the precise location of a file prior to its creation is not too important, the VOLUME parameter is not normally coded; on a permanent file, a data set is probably restricted to one and only one volume, so the parameter is needed. If a VOLUME parameter is coded, it means that the file may be stored "on this volume and only on this volume."

The SPACE
Parameter

On most computer systems, space on a direct access device is a limited commodity. If a program requiring ten cylinders were to be loaded and allowed to start processing at a time when only five cylinders were available, the program would either sit in core until direct access space became available or be terminated and rerun, in both cases wasting valuable system resources. To prevent, or at least minimize this problem, the programmer is required to provide the system with an estimate of direct access space requirements through the *SPACE parameter.*

Space can be requested in tracks, cylinders, or blocks of data. The type of space-unit and the number of units are defined by two positional subparameters; coding

```
SPACE=(TRK,20)
```

means a request for 20 tracks, while

```
SPACE=(CYL,14)
```

asks for 14 cylinders, and

```
SPACE=(200,10)
```

asks for ten 200-byte blocks. The type of space allocation, cylinders, tracks, or blocks is the first positional subparameter; the number of units of space comes second.

Estimating space requirements is not always easy. To ensure the availability of sufficient space, the programmer might be tempted to request a bit more space than the program could possibly need, thus tying up a limited resource—direct access space—and, possibly, lowering the priority of the program. Fortunately, another option is available. Coding

```
SPACE=(TRK,(10,5))
```

means that ten tracks will be set aside for the use of this program; should this space be consumed, an additional five tracks will be allocated if available. The first positional subparameter, as before, represents the type of storage unit desired; the second subparameter states the number of units requested. The third subparameter is a secondary allocation, to be made available only if the program exceeds its primary space allocation. It is important to remember that the primary space allocation is made before the program begins executing, in fact, before the program is even loaded into core. The secondary allocation is filled on an as-needed, if-available basis after the job step begins executing. A job step may be cancelled for insufficient direct space, even though the primary and secondary requests are more than adequate, if space is not available at the time of the secondary request. It is to the programmer's advantage to make the primary space estimate as accurate as possible. A secondary space allocation can be repeated as many as 15 times. For example, the SPACE parameter

```
SPACE=(CYL,(5,2))
```

represents a request for, at most, 35 cylinders—five primary cylinders plus two cylinders on each of a maximum 15 secondary allocations.

The punctuation of this parameter, with nested parentheses, is a bit unusual. The use of parentheses is easy to remember if you consider the fact that both the second and third positional subparameters deal with the number of units of direct access space to be allocated and thus should be treated as a single entity.

A request for too much space can tie up a limited system resource and possibly cause the execution of another program to be postponed. The programmer can give all unused space back to the system at the end of a job step by coding the RLSE or release subparameter, as in

```
SPACE=(CYL,(5.1),RLSE)
```

This is a positional subparameter which must follow the "quantity of allocation" subparameters.

To obtain optimum disk input and output, space is sometimes requested in contiguous units, thus minimizing the amount of disk seek time needed to move from cylinder to cylinder. The parameter

```
SPACE=(TRK,(5,2),RLSE,CONTIG)
```

asks for five *contiguous* tracks with a secondary allocation of an additional two contiguous tracks, releasing any unused space back to the system at the conclusion of the job step. Without the RLSE subparameter, this parameter would be coded

```
SPACE=(TRK,(5,2),,CONTIG)
```

Note the extra comma indicating the absence of a positional subparameter.

Retrieving an
Existing File

If a data set has been cataloged or passed by a prior step of the same job, it can normally be retrieved by coding only the DDNAME and DISP parameters

```
//DISK   DD    DSNAME=&&WORK,DISP=(OLD,DELETE)

//MAGS   DD    DSN=MASTO1,DISP=(OLD,KEEP)

//FILE   DD    DSNAME=MU.USERDATA.SAN1,DISP=SHR
```

Other parameters, including the data control block parameters, are part of the catalog entry for cataloged data sets and part of the operating system tables for a passed data set; thus they need not be recoded. On many systems, however, if one of these other parameters is coded, they all must be coded.

In the second example cited above, a previously cataloged data set was kept following job completion; the result is to simply retain the data set and all index entries. If a *non*cataloged data set is kept, the programmer must code DSNAME,DISP,UNIT, and VOLUME parameters to retrieve it; for example:

```
//DATA   DD   DSNAME=KEEPIT,DISP=(OLD,KEEP),
//              UNIT=3330,VOL=SER=X12
```

DCB information is optional, and can usually be obtained from the label at OPEN time.

Examples—Creating a Data Set on a Direct Access Device

1. A temporary data set on the system work pack

```
//DISK   DD   DSNAME=&&TEMP,UNIT=SYSDA,
//              DISP=(NEW,PASS),SPACE=(CYL,5),
//              DCB=(LRECL=120,BLKSIZE=2400,
//              RECFM=FB)
```

2. A cataloged data set on a specific volume

```
//RECS   DD   DSN=MU.USERDATA.SAN4,UNIT=3330,
//              VOL=SER=MIAMI3,DISP=(NEW,CATLG),
//              SPACE=(TRK,(20,5),RLSE,CONTIG),
//              DCB=(LRECL=155,RECFM=FB,BLKSIZE=1550)
```

3. A kept data set

```
//KEEPIT  DD   SPACE=(CYL,(10,2),RLSE),
//              DCB=(RECFM=FB,LRECL=72,BLKSIZE=720),
//              VOL=SER=MYPACK,DISP=(NEW,KEEP),
//              DSNAME=MYDATA,UNIT=3330
```

Examples—Retrieving a Data Set from a Direct Access Device

1. A passed data set

```
//DATA   DD   DSNAME=&&TEMP,DISP=(OLD,DELETE)
```

2. A cataloged data set

```
//STUFF  DD   DSN=MU.USERDATA.SAN4,DISP=OLD
```

3. A kept data set, existing on no catalog or index, requires the UNIT and VOLUME parameters in addition to the DSNAME and DISP

```
//DDNAME DD DSNAME=MYDATA,UNIT=3330,
//              VOL=SER=MYPACK,DISP=(OLD,KEEP)
```

Magnetic Tape

Magnetic tape was once the most commonly used secondary storage device. It is no longer, but most computer centers continue to support several tape drives. One current application for magnetic tape is to back up the on-line disk files. Older applications, particularly cyclic accounting applications, continue to use tape. Finally, magnetic tape is an excellent medium for transmitting data or programs between computer centers.

Tape and disk have a great deal in common. Both support a variety of record lengths and record formats. Neither is human-readable; thus both require careful labeling, cataloging, and careful attention to postjob disposition.

There are also some important differences. On disk, a typical volume holds a number of files or data sets. On tape, one volume per file is the general rule, but it is not unusual for a large file to spill over onto a second or third tape reel—the multivolume file. The programmer must be able to request multiple volumes *and* (perhaps) multiple drives to mount those volumes. While this situation can occur on disk, it is so rare that we can ignore it.

Disk is almost entirely an "internal" medium in that all the drives are under the complete control of the computer center. Tape, on the other hand, is often used to transfer data between centers. This "foreign interface" can create additional problems because not all magnetic tapes are the same. Some record data on seven tracks; some use nine tracks; others use ten. The recording density can vary as well. Finally, different manufacturers and even different installations can have incompatible standards for tape labels.

Once again, the programmer must be able to communicate all the unique characteristics of a given tape file to the system before the system can access that tape. DD parameters will be used to describe the tape files to the system.

The UNIT
Parameter—
Magnetic Tape

The UNIT parameter is used to define the physical device, in this case, a specific tape drive. As was the case with disk, the programmer can choose to specify the channel/device address of the desired drive, but this is rarely done. Often, an installation will define one or more device classes, such as TAPE, TAPE9, or TAPE7. The parameter

```
UNIT=TAPE9
```

might, for example, represent a request for a tape drive that is able to handle nine-track tapes, while

```
UNIT=TAPE7
```

might be a request for a drive that can work with seven-track tapes.

The UNIT=device type is the most commonly used form for magnetic tape. For example, the following device types have been defined for IBM's 2400-series tape drives.

Device Type	Description
2400	nine track, 800 bpi (bytes per inch) density
2400–1	seven track, no data conversion
2400–2	seven track with data conversion
2400–3	seven track, 1600 bpi density
2400–4	seven track, 800 and 1600 bpi density
2400–5	2420 model five unit, 1600 bpi

Other tape units have similar device-type designations. Using this form of the UNIT parameter, the programmer who wishes to read a nine-track 800-bpi tape would code

```
UNIT=2400-4
```

Let's pause for a moment and clear up a possible point of confusion. The parameter cited above, UNIT=2400-4, refers to a device with 800 *and* 1600 bpi density; how can that be? Very simply, that particular device can read or write at either density; the operator sets the density as a tape is mounted. Remember that the UNIT parameter is a request for a physical drive; it says nothing about the tape that might be mounted on that drive. Later we'll encounter a density DCB subparameter, and you'll be tempted to ask yourself, "Didn't we already specify the density in the UNIT parameter?" The answer is no! You requested a drive that was *capable* of handling tape recorded at a certain density. The UNIT parameter is concerned *only* with the physical device, and *not* with the volume that might be mounted on that device. It seems like a trivial point but if you grasp it, some of the JCL parameters we're about to discuss will seem less arbitrary.

Occasionally, when handling a multiple volume data set, a programmer may wish to request more than one tape drive. The "unit count" subparameter is provided for this purpose. Coding

```
UNIT=(2400-3,3)
```

means that a total of three nine-track 1600-bpi drives are needed by this program. Both the device-type and the unit-count subparameters are positional in nature; i.e., the device type *must* be coded first and the unit count *must* be coded second. If a programmer were to code

```
UNIT=(3,2400)
```

which is incorrect, the system would probably interpret this parameter as a request for 2400 tape drives of device type 3. Positional parameters derive their meaning from their relative position.

Note that, once again, the coding of more than one subparameter means that parentheses must be used. If the unit-count subparameter is not coded, a request for a single unit is assumed.

To save system time and eliminate lengthy waits by a program already in core, (a waste of valuable system resources) tape mount messages are normally given to the system operator by the job initiator program just as the job is about to enter the system. Occasionally, when probable errors or other special processing characteristics make the tape's use questionable, it makes sense to postpone the tape mount operation until the actual time of file OPEN when use is assured. Coding

```
UNIT=(2400,2,DEFER)
```

requests two nine-track, 800-bpi tape drives and postpones mounting; the DEFER option is a third positional subparameter. To postpone the mounting of a single 1600-bpi tape, the parameter

```
UNIT=(2400-3,,DEFER)
```

could be coded; the extra comma indicates the absense of a positional subparameter. Positional subparameters, to belabor a point, derive their meaning from their relative position. DEFER is the *third* positional subparameter.

The DCB
Parameter—Tape

The DCB parameter on magnetic tape is much like the DCB parameter on disk; LRECL, BLKSIZE, and RECFM subparameters are commonly used. Once again, the DCB parameter is optional; it can be coded either on the DD card or within the program data control block. One commonly used subparameter that is simply not needed on disk is the DEN or density subparameter. The density subparameter specifies the tape recording density with a code 0 for seven-track, 200 bpi; 1 for seven-track, 556 bpi; 2 for seven- or nine-track, 800 bpi; and 3 for nine-track, 1600 bpi. Why bother with a density code when density seems to be a part of the UNIT parameter? The UNIT parameter is concerned *only* with the physical device.

The DCB parameter

```
DCB=(BLKSIZE=750,DEN=3,LRECL=75,RECFM=FB)
```

defines fixed-length blocked records, 75 bytes in length, stored in blocks of 750 bytes (ten logical records) on 1600-bpi tape.

The DISP
and DSNAME
Parameters—Tape

Direct access dispositions and tape dispositions are, for all practical purposes, identical. Since disk packs are not dismounted as frequently as tapes, the operator action may be different. From the programmer's point of view, however, the dispositions are identical. As before, the data set name or DSNAME or DSN parameter provides a convenient mechanism for retrieving a cataloged or passed data set.

The VOLUME
Parameter—Tape

Many computer centers try to minimize the number of disk mounts performed during at least the prime shifts. Changing a disk pack is time-consuming, and the drive can be out of use for five minutes or more. The result is a tendency to view the disk resources as almost permanently mounted; the programmer as a result tends to use standard packs. Thus the VOLUME parameter is frequently not used in accessing a disk file.

Magnetic tape is different. A tape is normally mounted on a drive when a program requests it; "permanently" mounted tape volumes are almost unheard of. As a result, the programmer will almost always use the VOLUME parameter when requesting access to a file on magnetic tape. (The only exception to this general rule occurs in an installation that catalogs tapes by data set name.) The VOLUME or VOL parameter is no different from what it was on disk. For example,

```
VOL=SER-MIAMI5
```

Note that SER is a keyword *sub*parameter of the VOLUME parameter.

This same set of parameters and subparameters can handle multiple volume files, as in

```
VOL=SER=(M01,M02,M03,M04)
```

where a request is made to mount four different volumes. Perhaps we should comment on the relationship between the VOL and the UNIT parameters. A request for four volumes *might* be accompanied by a request for four drives

```
UNIT=(TAPE,4)
```

one per volume. On the other hand, if the tape volumes are to be accessed one after another, a single drive might do.

The programmer can request the mounting of a scratch or work tape by simply omitting the VOLUME parameter. Some installations prefer that this option not be used, insisting that a scratch tape be requested by coding something like

```
//TAPE   DD   UNIT=2400-3,VOL=SER=SCRTCH,...
```

The VOLUME parameter is used to generate tape-mount messages. A message like

```
MOUNT TAPE SCRTCH ON DEVICE 182
```

is a pretty obvious indication that a scratch tape is desired. (Just don't assign a real tape a similar serial number—SCRATCH, for example.)

The LABEL
Parameter—Tape

The *LABEL parameter* is used to define the type of labels on the selected volume; the OPEN macro uses this information to create labels for a new data set and to check the labels of an existing file. In addition to defining the label type, this parameter is used to specify the relative position of the desired file on a multiple-file volume—a single reel of tape containing more than one file. Other subparameters do exist, but we'll skip them for now. For our purposes, the basic form of the LABEL parameter is

```
LABEL=(sequence-number,label-type)
```

The file sequence number is simply the relative position of the desired file on the volume—for the first file, the sequence number is 1; for the third file, it's 3. Valid label type subparameters include

Label Type	Meaning
SL	Standard Labels
SUL	Both Standard and User Labels
NL	No Labels Present
NSL	Nonstandard Labels
BLP	Bypass Label Processing

Standard labels can be created or checked by the operating system; user labels and nonstandard labels must be checked by a programmer routine (if they are checked at all). The "bypass label processing" option implies that labels are present but, for some reason, they are not to be processed.

Normally, a single file is placed on each tape volume; to request the creation of a new tape volume with standard labels, the programmer codes

```
LABEL=(1,SL)
```

or

```
LABEL=(,SL)
```

with the lone comma indicating the absence of the first positional parameter which is assumed to be 1. On a new tape data set, the OPEN macro creates a label; on an existing data set, the OPEN macro checks the label to determine if the proper file has been mounted.

In many installations, the use of standard labels is treated as a default, and the LABEL parameter is not coded for any internal tape files. If the programmer does not code a label parameter, the programmer will not (accidentally or intentionally) create tapes with nonstandard labels. Remember, however, the "foreign interface" application of tape. Some "other company" may have created a tape, and they may not use the same standard. The programmer should be at least familiar with the LABEL parameter.

The DUMMY Parameter—Tape

Loading tapes is not the typical operator's favorite job, and tape jobs frequently have a very low priority. In testing code, the programmer may wish to bypass the generation of tape load messages (and, hence, the mounting of tape). This can be done by coding the *DUMMY parameter*

```
//DATA    DD   DUMMY,UNIT=2400,...
```

The word DUMMY is a positional parameter and must be the first parameter in the operands field. Later, when the programmer wishes to process the tapes, the job can be resubmitted without the DUMMY parameter.

Creating a Tape Data Set—Sample DD Statements

1. Create a temporary data set and pass it to a subsequent job step.

```
//TAPE    DD   UNIT=2400-3,VOL=SER=WX2453,
//              DCB=(LRECL=145,BLKSIZE=2900,RECFM=FB),
//              LABEL=(,SL),DISP=(NEW,PASS),DSN=&&T
```

2. Create and catalog a permanent data set.

```
//MAG1    DD   UNIT=2400-4,LABEL=(,SL),DNS=TT,
//              VOL=SER=A572,DCB=(RECFM=FB,
//              BLKSIZE=1200,LRECL=120,DEN=3),
//              DISP=(NEW,CATLG)
```

3. Use a scratch tape.

```
//SCRATCH   DD   DISP=(NEW,DELETE),DSNAME=&&WORK,
//               DCB=(BLKSIZE=104,LRECL=52,RECFM=FB),
//               LABEL=(,SL),UNIT=2400-3,
//               VOL=SER=SCRTCH.
```

All of the DD parameters are key word parameters; i.e., they can be coded in any order. (Many of the *subparameters* are positional.) Also, note the way the JCL statements are continued onto a second, third, and fourth line—we simply break coding after *any* comma and resume on the next line. Continuation lines must begin with the // in the first two columns—this defines it as a control statement—and coding must be resumed prior to column sixteen.

The System Input and System Output Devices

Spooling creates two new data sets, with a *system input device* replacing the physical reading of cards and a *system output device* replacing direct communication with a printer. On many systems, a third system device is provided for spooling punched card output. Disk is often used in such spooling operations; tape is another possibility. Spooling might be done on-line or off-line. The physical volume might change from day to day or even within the same day. Because these devices are in such common use, most of the DD parameters are predefined within the operating system, leaving only token coding for the programmer.

Most programmers who have worked on IBM equipment are familiar with the statement

```
//SYSIN   DD   *
```

SYSIN is obviously a DDNAME, but what does the asterisk mean? As you may remember, a job is submitted to the system in the form of a card deck (or card deck image) including JCL statements, perhaps one or more source modules, and data. The asterisk indicates that the data follows "this" DD statement and is part of the same job stream. The entire job stream is spooled to some device; if the system is capable of finding this DD statement, it can find the associated data by looking in the same place. There is, by the way, nothing sacred about SYSIN; it's a DDNAME and nothing more. The programmer may use any DDNAME for the system input device, as long as the DDNAME parameter of the program's internal data control block matches the chosen name. Many compilers and utilities, (programs not normally modified by the programmer) use SYSIN as the DDNAME of a card (or card image) file coming from the system input device; such use probably accounts for the popularity of this particular name.

Spooling data for eventual printer output is normally done by coding

```
//SYSOUT   DD   SYSOUT=A
```

Punched card output will be the final result from

```
//SYSPUNCH  DD   SYSOUT=B
```

SYSOUT and SYSPUNCH, like SYSIN, are simply commonly used DDNAMEs; they have no other real significance. Programmers who code their own data control blocks within a program can use any DDNAME for system input and system output devices, although there is something to be said for the documentation benefits of following standard or accepted practices.

In the examples cited above, the letter A designated eventual printer output, while B meant punched cards. These designators are commonly used, but they are hardly universal; an installation can choose any set of symbols to indicate the various system devices.

Many installations limit the amount of disk space available to a single program on the system output device. When large amounts of output data are expected, this limit may be overridden by coding a space parameter.

```
//SYSPRINT  DD   SYSOUT=A,SPACE=(CYL,(5,2))
```

Job Step Qualifiers on a DD Statement

Often, two or more DD statements, each in a different job step but still within the same job, are assigned the same DDNAME. This frequently happens when using a cataloged procedure for a compile, link edit, and go. The compiler program gets its input from the system input device, so the source module usually follows a //SYSIN DD * statement. The GO step, assuming job stream input to the program, also uses the system input device for data, and the data, unless the programmer codes customized program data control blocks, is also preceded by a "SYSIN DD *" statement. To differentiate between these two statements, the following JCL is often coded.

```
//JOBNAME   JOB   (9824,18),DAVIS,CLASS=A
//    EXEC   FORTRAN
//FORT.SYSIN  DD   *
```

⎫
⎬ FORTRAN source module
⎭

```
/*
//GO.SYSIN   DD   *
```

⎫
⎬ Data
⎭

```
/*
```

The execute statement calls for a cataloged procedure named FORTRAN; this procedure contains three job steps named FORT (the compiler), LKED (the linkage editor), and GO (the program load module). FORT.SYSIN is the name of a DD statement attached to the first job step. FORT is the step-name of the first job step. GO.SYSIN is attached to the GO step. Note: Qualified DDNAMES can be used *only* within a cataloged procedure.

Incidentally, the delimiter statement, the /*, marks the end of data submitted through the job stream. Comments may be coded beginning in column four. Some programmers use a /* statement to mark the end of each step in a multistep job.

Libraries _____

Program libraries and data files are a bit different. We'll consider the creation of a library in some detail in Chapter 11. Here in Chapter 10, our concern will be with accessing an already existing library. As is the case with most files, an existing library can be accessed by its DSNAME and a DISP parameter.

A typical library contains a number of different programs. While a file does contain a number of different records, these records are closely related; the programs on a library may well have absolutely nothing to do with each other. Each program on a library is called a *member* of that library. In general, to access a given member, it is necessary to provide a member-name as part of the DSNAME parameter.

```
DSNAME=library-name(member-name)
```

For example, to access a program named EDIT from the PAYROLL system program library, the programmer might code

```
DSNAME=PAYROLL(EDIT),DISP=SHR
```

The programmer's main concern with libraries is that of locating and executing a given program. For system software such as compilers, the linkage editor, and utility programs, no library reference is needed; the system knows where to find its own libraries. A private library, however, does call for more explicit identification. Assume, for example, that the programmer wants to load and execute a program named MYPGM. The JCL statement

```
//  EXEC  PGM=MYPGM
```

would cause the system trouble, as it simply could not hope to find MYPGM. Let's assume further that MYPGM is stored on a private library named MYLIB. It is the programmer's responsibility to give the system this critical bit of information. By coding

```
//   EXEC  PGM=MYPGM
//STEPLIB  DD  DSNAME=MYLIB,DISP=SHR
```

the programmer has, in effect, said, "Load and execute MYPGM; you'll find the program on MYLIB."

The DDNAME *STEPLIB must* be used. The STEPLIB DD statement must be the *first* JCL statement after the EXEC. Two parameters are coded—DSNAME, which defines the library name, and DISP. Why is DISP = SHR coded? The programmer will not be modifying the contents of the library, and it is possible that several other concurrent users may have a need to access the same library. Note that the member name has not been specified; the EXEC statement has essentially defined the member name.

Each time the programmer wishes to execute a program that is stored on a private library, a STEPLIB statement must be coded following the EXEC statement. There is one exception to this rule. Let's assume that, in a multistep job, several programs are to be executed, and that all are stored on the *same* library. Rather than repeating the same STEPLIB statement several times, a single *JOBLIB* statement can be coded. The JOBLIB statement is virtually identical to a STEPLIB statement. It follows the JOB card, and precedes the *first* EXEC statement; it is the *only* JCL statement that can precede the first EXEC. A JOBLIB statement defines a library for *all* steps in the job.

The PROC Statement

The JOB, EXEC, and DD statements are far and away the most commonly used job control statements, but other statements do exist. The PROC statement, for example, is used to assign default values to symbolic parameters in a cataloged procedure. Another, the null statement, is coded by simply placing slashes (//) in the first two columns. This statement is sometimes used to mark the end of a job. A comment has //* punched in the first three columns and anything at all punched in the remainder of the statement. Comments may be inserted at any point in the JCL job stream.

A Complete Example

One of the best ways to gain an understanding of any language is by looking at and studying an actual example of its use; job control language is no exception. Our example (see Fig. 10.3) is a fairly typical multistep job. The first job step reads and edits card data through the system input device, spooling the output to disk; the edit program is stored on a private library. Step two sorts this data, using a cataloged procedure sort routine; the output goes to tape. In the third job step, this tape file is merged with a master file on disk; errors are written to

Fig. 10.3
Our JCL-example job—flowchart.

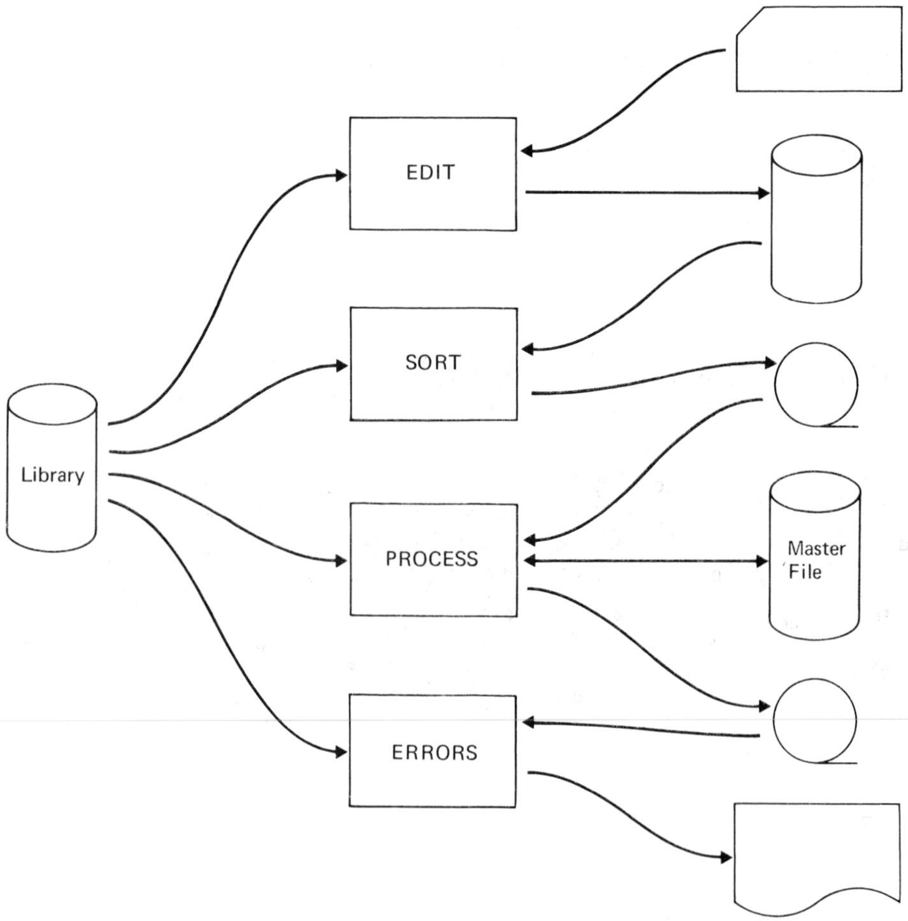

```
//MYJOB    JOB    (9182,222),'W.S. DAVIS',CLASS=A
//STEP1    EXEC   PGM=EDIT
//STEPLIB    DD    DSN=MU.USERPGM.SAN,DISP=SHR
//OUTS  DD    DSNAME=&&TEMP,UNIT=SYSDA,DISP=(NEW,PASS),
//             SPACE=(TRK,(10,2),RLSE),DCB=(LRECL=80,
//             BLKSIZE=800,RECFM=FB)
//SYSIN    DD    *
                [Data cards]
/*
//SECOND    EXEC   SORTPC
//SORTIN    DD    DSN=&&TEMP,DISP=(OLD,DELETE)
//SORTOUT    DD    DSNAME=MYOUTS,UNIT=2400-3,VOL=SER=R712,
//             LABEL=(,SL),DISP=NEW,PASS),DCB=(LRECL=80,
//             BLKSIZE=800,RECFM=FB)
//* THE NEXT TWO CARDS GIVE THE SORT ROUTINE ITS FIELDS.
//SYSIN    DD    *
    SORT  FIELDS=(1,5,CH,A)
/*     THE FIELD STARTS IN COLUMN 1, CONSUMES 5 COLUMNS,
//*    AND HOLDS CHARACTER DATA WHICH ARE TO BE SORTED
//*    INTO ASCENDING ORDER.
//THIRD    EXEC   PGM=PROCESS
//STEPLIB    DD    DSN=MU.USERPGM.SAN,DISP=SHR
//TAPEIN    DD    DSN=MYOUTS,DISP=(OLD,CATLG)
//MASTER    DD    DSN=MU.USERDATA.SAN5,DISP=(OLD,KEEP)
//TAPEOUT    DD    DSN=MYERRS,UNIT=2400-3,VOL=SER=E712,
//             LABEL=(,SL),DISP=(NEW,CATLG),
//             DISP=(LRECL=80,BLKSIZE=1200,RECFM=FB)
//LAST    EXEC   COBOL
//COB.SYSIN    DD    *
)
|
}[COBOL source module]
|
)
/*
//TAPEIN    DD    DSN=MYERRS,DISP=(OLD,KEEP)
//
```

Fig. 10.4
An example of the JCL for a complete job.

another tape, and, at the end of the job step, both tapes are cataloged. The final step is a new one for this job—it is still in the form of a COBOL source deck. This step reads the errors tape and prepares an error report which is sent to the printer. The JCL to support this job is shown in Fig. 10.4.

   Incidentally, all of the //STEPLIB cards of Fig. 10.4 could have been replaced by a single statement

```
//JOBLIB    DD    DSN=MU.USERPGM.SAN,DISP=SHR
```

coded immediately after the JOB statement. With the exception of this JOB-LIB statement, no other DD statement may precede the first EXEC. Also, you may have noticed an absence of library identification statements for our cataloged procedures; the mechanism for accessing the cataloged procedure library and certain other system libraries is a part of the operating system.

Summary _____

In this chapter, we've covered the parameters of the DD statement for unit record, direct access, tape, and system data sets. A detailed summary of these parameters, in convenient reference form, is found in Appendix C. By far the best summary of the material in Chapters 9 and 10 is the complete JCL example shown in Fig. 10.4.

Key Words _____

data control block	SPACE parameter
DCB parameter	STEPLIB statement
DD statement	subparameter
DISP parameter	system input device
DSNAME parameter	system output device
DUMMY parameter	UNIT parameter
JOBLIB statement	VOLUME parameter
LABEL parameter	

Exercises _____

1. Explain how a program is linked to a physical I/O device under operating system/360-370.

2. Explain the relationship between a program DCB and the DCB parameter on a DD statement.

3. Code a UNIT parameter to reserve three 2400-series tape drives with 800-bpi capacity. Don't mount the tapes until open time.

4. Code a DD statement DCB parameter for a magnetic tape file holding fixed-length, blocked records—logical records are 50 characters in length and the blocking factor is 50. It's a 1600-bpi tape.

5. Code a space parameter to reserve 20 contiguous cylinders. Allow for additional cylinders, requesting two at a time. Return unused cylinders to the system at the end of the job step.

6. Code a DD statement for creating a 1600-bpi tape, serial number MY-TAPE. Catalog the tape if the job step ends normally; otherwise, keep the tape for analysis. For simplicity, the tape serial number and the catalog name should be the same. Records are 125 characters each blocked in groups of 20; all records are the same length. Use standard labels.

7. Code a DD statement for a temporary, work data set on the system direct access device (SYSDA). Get ten tracks. Request secondary tracks in a group of two. They do not have to be contiguous, but do return unused tracks to the system at the end of the job step. Logical records are 100 bytes each and should be blocked in groups of 30. The data set is to be passed to a subsequent job step.

8. Explain why a JOBLIB or STEPLIB statement is necessary when executing a program stored on a private library.

Your instructor may assign additional JCL exercises.

11

Libraries and the
Linkage Editor

Overview

Once the programmer has learned the essentials of the job control or command language, the next major point of interface with the operating system often involves the use of libraries. During program development, the code may be maintained on a source statement library. Commonly used subroutines are found on an object module library. Completed programs are stored on a load module library. The intelligent use of source, object, and load module libraries can be of tremendous benefit, and the programmer who knows how to use them enjoys a distinct advantage. The intent of this chapter is to explain the differences between source, object, and load modules, and to show how they can be placed on an appropriate library. The key is understanding *what* happens: Given a basic sense of the underlying concepts, it is relatively easy to determine how to create and access libraries on a given system. Examples (based on the IBM System/360-370 series of computers) will be cited to illustrate these concepts.

We begin with the compile/link edit/execute sequence, recalling the normal program flow from an earlier chapter. In this context, we'll develop a rough idea of the structure of source, object, and load modules.

Next, source modules will be considered in greater detail. Examples from assembler, COBOL, and other languages will be used to illustrate source code,

190

and we'll show how the compiler can combine source modules from several different libraries. Job control language for the IBM System/360–370 will be used to illustrate the creation of a library, and a utility program will be used to add a member to that library.

The output of the assembler or compiler program is an object module. We'll discuss the structure of an object module, and show how compiler output can be placed on a library.

The linkage editor creates a load module by combining a number of object modules. We'll consider the structure of a typical load module in general terms. Then we'll turn our attention to a specific example of load module creation using the IBM System/360–370 linkage editor program.

Much of the material in this chapter is quite general, and, with a few minor changes in terminology, can be applied to almost any computer system. Other material is very IBM-specific. For the benefit of those who do not use an IBM computer, the vendor-specific material will be clearly identified.

The Compile/ Link Edit/ Execute Sequence _____

Earlier, in Chapter 3, the compile/link edit/ execute sequence was described (Fig. 11.1). The vast majority of programs submitted to a computer go through this sequence. All too often, the programmer views the compile/link edit/ execute control statements as a sort of "magic bullet" that "must be there or my program won't work." Why is this sequence necessary? What exactly is a source module? an object module? a load module? The programmer who knows the answers to these questions has a significant advantage over the programmer who basically follows the rules, by rote.

In general, a *source module* is a set of program statements written in a source language such as FORTRAN, COBOL, PL/1, or assembler. No computer can directly execute source statements; they must first be translated to machine-level code by a compiler or interpreter program. A *compiler* accepts a complete source-level program, and generates a complete object-level module in a batchlike mode. An *interpreter* accepts a single source statement, translates it to machine level, and executes the resulting code, before turning to the next source statement. Interpreters are commonly used on microcomputers and time-shared systems, often by a "casual" programmer; the professional programmer is more likely to use a compiler.

An *object module* is pure binary, machine-level code. A computer can execute object-level code, but a typical object module is incomplete, containing references to other object modules such as access methods or subroutines. Be-

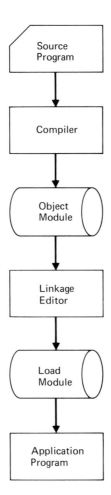

Fig. 11.1
The compile/link
edit/execute sequence.

cause the object module is often incomplete, it cannot normally be loaded on a computer and executed. Instead, a number of object modules must first be linked to form a *load module,* a complete, machine-level program that *can* be loaded and executed. The process of linking object modules to form a load module is performed by a system program called (at least by IBM) the *linkage editor.*

The program flow illustrated in Fig. 11.1 is not quite accurate; it is an oversimplification of reality. In fact, a variety of libraries are involved in the process of compiling and link editing a program (Fig. 11.2). Let's analyze the compile, link edit, and execute steps one at a time, and consider the nature of each of these libraries.

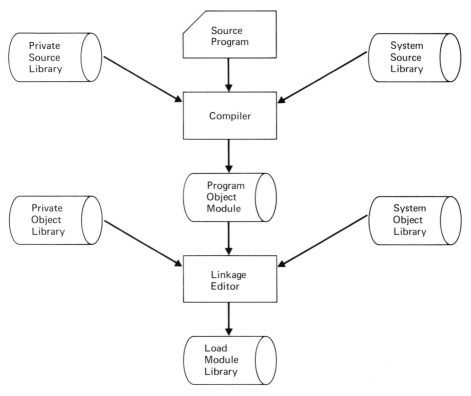

Fig. 11.2
System and private libraries in the compile/
link edit/execute sequence

Compilers and
Source Statement
Libraries ⎯⎯⎯⎯⎯⎯⎯⎯⎯⎯⎯⎯⎯⎯⎯

A source module is written, normally by a programmer, in assembler, COBOL, FORTRAN, or any other source language. The statements may be keypunched, thus creating a source deck. Increasingly, students and professional programmers enter source code through a terminal under control of a text editor program that stores the statements on disk—an electronic source module.

The source code as prepared by the programmer is normally incomplete. For example, consider a program written in assembler language. Most assembler language programmers use *macro instructions*. Before a program can be assembled, each macro must be expanded into several source statements. Look

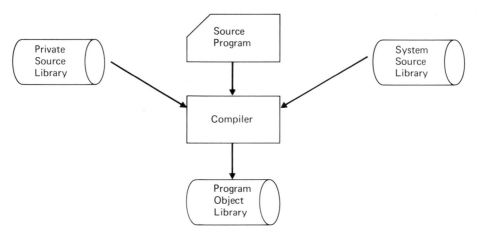

Fig. 11.3
The libraries involved in the compilation process.

at an assembler listing, and you can see the source statements generated by a macro. Some are *system* macros, and are stored on a system *source statement library* (Fig. 11.3): for example, GET, PUT, OPEN, and CLOSE. Others are *private,* written by a programmer or by a given installation for local use. These are stored on a private source statement library. The COBOL programmer can code a COPY statement to introduce prewritten source code into a program. A PL/1 programmer might use an INCLUDE to achieve the same objective. The compiler program combines the programmer's source module with precoded source modules from system and/or private source statement libraries, thus building a *complete* source module before compiling the code.

Perhaps the best way to visualize this process is through an example. Let's imagine that the systems analyst working on a payroll application has carefully defined the structure of each of the required data files. One of these files, containing labor time records, has been defined as a COBOL data structure (Fig. 11.4). We'll assume further that the analyst has had the source code of Fig. 11.4 keypunched and, by using a utility file-copy program, has copied it to a disk library (Fig. 11.5).

Some time later, a programmer is assigned to the payroll system. Rather than recoding the file structures from scratch, the programmer simply includes a COPY statement at the appropriate spot in the source program (Fig. 11.6). Following compilation, the COPY library statements will appear in the source listing, as though the programmer actually coded them. How does this happen?

```
01  LABOR-TIME-RECORD.
   05 EMPLOYEE-NUMBER  PICTURE 9(9).
   05 EMPLOYEE-NAME    PICTURE X(20).
   05 HOURS-WORKED     PICTURE 99V9.
   05 HOURLY-PAY-RATE  PICTURE 99V99.
   05 FILLER           PICTURE X(44).
```

Fig. 11.4
A source module to be placed on a source statement library.

Fig. 11.5
Creating the source statement library entry.

The Source Module

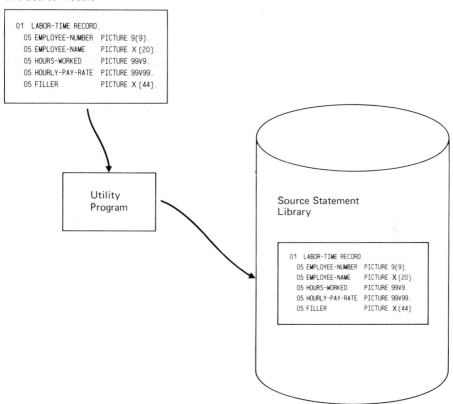

```
                           .
                           .
                           .
                       DATA DIVISION.
                        FILE SECTION.
                         FD LABOR-TIME-FILE
                               LABEL RECORDS OMITTED.
                           COPY TIMECARD.
           Fig. 11.6            .
       The COBOL source
       program as coded.        .
                               .
```

Fig. 11.6 The COBOL source program as coded.

The answer is really quite simple. As the compiler program (in this example, the COBOL compiler) scans the source code, it looks for COPY statements. Whenever a COPY is encountered, the compiler reads the specified COPY library entry from disk and inserts the code where it belongs (Fig. 11.7). Once all the COPY statements have been expanded, the source module is complete, and the final compilation process can begin. An assembler program expands macros in precisely the same way.

Thus we have source statement libraries. A *private* source statement library contains "home-grown" macros and customized source code. A *system* source statement library contains more widely used source code (I/O macros, for example). The compiler combines source statement library entries with the programmer's source code to produce a source module, which is translated to machine-level object code.

Creating a Library (IBM)

A *library* is really nothing more than a special type of file with the individual library members, the programs and program segments, being roughly analogous to records.

A typical library is divided into two primary regions (Fig. 11.8). At the beginning of the library is a *directory*. The *members* of the library, source, object, or load modules, follow the directory area. In the directory is an entry for each member, listing the member name and its absolute (cylinder/track) address on disk. If, for example, the programmer asks for member TAX on a library named PAYROLL, the operating system will find the library, search the

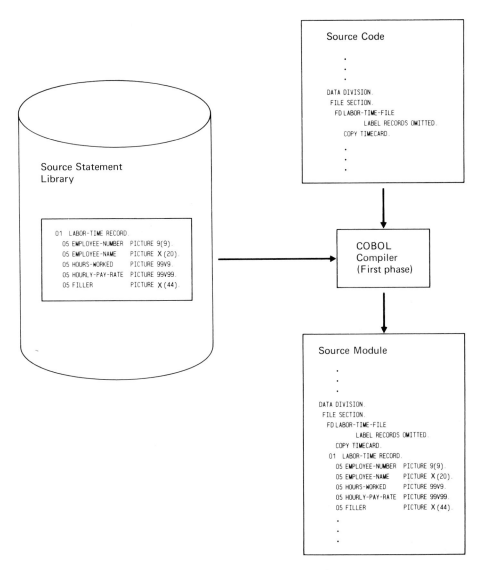

Fig. 11.7
The compiler completes the source module.

directory for a member named TAX, and read in the requested module. IBM
calls this library structure a *partitioned data set* or *PDS*.

The basic difference between a regular data set (a file) and a partitioned
data set is the directory that is found at the beginning of the PDS. In creating a
library, the programmer must tell the system how much space is to be allocated
to the directory. Using OS JCL, this is done through a positional subparameter

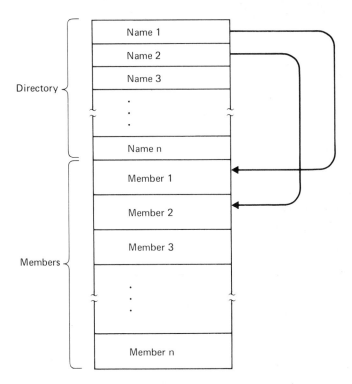

Fig. 11.8
An IBM partitioned data set (PDS) as an
example of the structure of a typical library.

of the SPACE parameter.

```
SPACE=(type,(primary, secondary, directory))
```

The type of space parameter (from Chapter 10) may be cylinders (CYL), tracks (TRK), or blocks. The primary allocation identifies the amount of space that must be available before the program can begin, while the secondary allocation indicates the amount of space that will be allocated in real time if the primary allocation is used up during execution. The *directory* subparameter defines the number of 256-byte blocks that are allocated to the directory; each block can hold enough information to identify five (at most six) members.

For example, assume that we are about to create a library. We have estimated a need for ten cylinders of space. About 60 programs will be stored on this library. Because each directory block can hold, conservatively, five program identifications, we'll need 12 blocks. The following JCL statement might

```
                              //    JOB   ....
                              //    EXEC  PGM=IEFBR14
                              //PDS  DD    DSNAME=MYLIB,DISP-(NEW,CATLG),UNIT=3330,
        Fig. 11.9            //          VOL=SER=MYPACK,SPACE=(CYL,(10,,12)),
   Creating an empty        //          DCB=(LRECL=80,RECFM=FM,BLKSIZE=400)
 partitioned data set.      /*
```

be used to create the partitioned data set.

```
//PDS   DD   DSNAME=MYLIB,DISP=(NEW,CATLG),UNIT=3330,
//           VOL=SER=MYPACK,SPACE=(CYL,(10,,12)),
//           DCB=(LRECL=80,BLKSIZE=400,RECFM=FB)
```

Note that 12 directory blocks are specified; space for these blocks is taken from within the ten primary cylinders. There is no secondary space allocation in this example.

Incidentally, the logical record length (LRECL) is set to 80 bytes simply because many installations continue to use punched cards as a source of library members or as a library backup. Because disk can support any logical record length, it makes sense to accommodate the less flexible medium.

On an IBM computer, a job control language statement cannot stand on its own; JCL statements are used strictly to support application programs. Thus you *cannot* create a library by simply submitting a DD statement to the system. As a minimum, a JOB statement and a single EXEC statement must accompany the DD that defines the library. One way to create an empty library is to run a dummy program that literally doesn't do anything. Believe it or not, such a program exists. It resides on the system's utility program library under the name IEFBR14. It consists of a single instruction, a branch to register 14. (In COBOL terms, that branch is roughly equivalent to a STOP RUN; in FORTRAN, it's a STOP; in BASIC, it's an END). A job to create an empty partitioned data set using this dummy program is illustrated in Fig. 11.9. When the "program" is executed, the operating system will allocate space for the PDS; in effect, we are "fooling" the system to get it to do some work for us.

Adding Members
to the Library _____

How does the programmer place a source module on a source statement library? Once the library exists, it's really quite simple. On some systems, source statements are entered through a text editor, and the output is simply placed on a designated source statement library. On other systems, the programmer must first prepare a source deck (or an "electronic" source deck on disk or tape), and then use a file-copy utility program to copy the source code to the library.

The utility program most often used for adding members to a source statement library on an IBM System/360-370 computer is named IEBGENER. It's a simple program that reads the content of one file (or data set) and copies it to another. IEBGENER can be used to copy disk files to magnetic tape for system backup, or to display the contents of a file as an aid to programmer debugging; it has many uses. The utility also has several options that allow the programmer to selectively copy records, or to reformat the output. We won't concern ourselves with the options at this time.

Let's assume that the programmer wants to add a source module named MASTFILE to the library created by the JCL of Fig. 11.9. Using the IEBGENER utility, the JCL of Fig. 11.10 might be coded. The utility program *requires* that certain DDNAMEs be used. The input data set *must be* called SYSUT1, while the output must go to SYSUT2. A SYSPRINT DD statement

Fig. 11.10
Using a utility program to add a member to a
source statement library.

```
//          JOB   ....

//          EXEC  PGM=IEBGENER

//SYSUT1    DD    *
        ⎫
        ⎬ source module
        ⎭
/*

//SYSUT2    DD    DSNAME=MYLIB(MASTFILE),DISP=(OLD,KEEP),
//                DCB=(LRECL=80,RECFM=FM,BLKSIZE=400)

//SYSPRINT DD     SYSOUT=A

//SYSIN     DD    DUMMY

/*
```

must be provided so that the program can write messages to the printer. Finally, SYSIN is used to allow parameters defining optional features to be passed to the program; in this case we are not using the optional features, so we code the DUMMY parameter.

Look carefully at the SYSUT2 DD statement (Fig. 11.10). Note the DSNAME parameter. We have coded

```
DSNAME=MYLIB(MASTFILE)
```

Clearly, MYLIB is the name of a partitioned data set, but what is MASTFILE? It is a *member name*. Remember the directory at the beginning of the PDS? An entry under the name MASTFILE is made in the directory; in the future, the source module will be retrieved by this name. The member name must be enclosed in parentheses, and immediately follow the DSNAME. The rules for defining a member name are the same as the rules for defining a data set name.

Note: Assuming that DCB parameters were defined when the library was created, the DCB on the SYSUT2 statement of Fig. 11.10 would not be needed.

Using a Private Source Statement Library

Now that we have created and added members to a private source statement library, how would we go about using these members? If an assembler or compiler is to add our private macros or COPY members to our source code, it must be able to find the library. It is the programmer's responsibility to identify clearly any private libraries that are referenced in the code. How can this be done?

Compiling or assembling a program involves a number of input and output data sets; normally, the programmer will use a cataloged procedure to define them. Consider, as an example, the statements generated by the cataloged procedure ASMFC (Fig. 11.11), a compile-only procedure. One statement is of particular importance.

```
XXSYSLIB   DD   DSNAME=SYS1.MACLIB,DISP=SHR
```

It defines the system macro library, SYS1.MACLIB; this is how the assembler knows where to find the standard system macros such as GET, PUT, OPEN, CLOSE, DCB, and so on. The programmer who wants to use a private library can simply change this statement by coding

```
//     EXEC  ASMFC
//ASM.SYSLIB  DD  DSN=MYLIB,DISP=SHR
```

```
//          JOB   ...

//          EXEC  ASMFC

XXASM       EXEC  PGM=IEUASM

XXSYSLIB    DD    DSNAME=SYS1.MACLIB,DISP=SHR

XXSYSUT1    DD    ...

XXSYSUT2    DD    ...

XXSYSUT3    DD    ...

XXSYSPRINT DD     SYSOUT=A

XXSYSPUNCH DD     SYSOUT=B

XXSYSGO     DD    DSNAME=&&LOADSET,SPACE=(400,(100,20)),

XX                DISP=(OLD,PASS),UNIT=SYSDA,

XX                DCB=(LRECL=80,BLKSIZE=400,RECFM=FB)

//ASM.SYSIN  DD  *

      source code

/*
```

Fig. 11.11
The cataloged procedure for the assembler
program, ASMFC. Statements preceded by // are
coded by the programmer. Those beginning with
XX are part of the cataloged procedure.

Coding an explicit SYSLIB statement *overrides* the cataloged procedure, replacing the standard SYSLIB statement with the one provided by the
programmer.

What if *both* system *and* private macros are referenced? To identify *two*
(or more) source statement libraries, the programmer can code

```
//    EXEC  ASMFC
//ASM.SYSLIB  DD  DSN=SYS1.MACLIB,DISP=SHR
//            DD  DSN=MYLIB,DISP=SHR
```

Note that the second DD statement has *no* DDNAME. The last name encountered, SYSLIB, still holds; the two libraries are said to be *concatenated*. When a macro is encountered, the assembler will search the directory for SYS1.MACLIB. If the macro is not found, the assembler will search MYLIB. Additional libraries can be concatenated by attaching additional unnamed DD statements; the order of the DD statements determines the order in which the libraries will be searched.

Object Modules

The output from a compiler or assembler program is an object module. The object module contains machine-level code, but it is normally incomplete, and thus cannot be loaded directly onto a computer and executed.

For example, consider the code generated by a typical input macro such as a READ or a GET. Once expanded, such macros usually include a call to an access method (or its equivalent). The access method contains a great deal of relatively complex logic. Many different programs will use the same access method. It makes little sense to store the access method in a source statement library and recompile it every time a programmer needs it. Instead, the access method is compiled and stored in *object module* form. Thus the access method is added *after* compilation is complete.

To cite another example, consider a standard subroutine such as the FORTRAN SQRT function. The programmer codes

```
X = SQRT(Y)
```

and expects the square root of Y to be stored in the field called X after the instruction is executed. It isn't quite that simple; the square root must be estimated using an iterative technique. The subroutine is fairly large. It would be possible to store this logic in the form of FORTRAN code, copy it into the source module each time the programmer references SQRT, and recompile the function over and over again, but this would be very inefficient. Instead, the SQRT function is compiled once and stored on an object module library.

The problem is simply this. A compiler is designed to work with source code. Certain key logical elements such as access methods and standard subroutines *do not exist* at the source level; hence there is *no way* for the compiler program to incorporate this essential logic in an object module it creates. As a result, the object module will refer to logic that simply is not there. Can you see why this incomplete machine-level program cannot be loaded and executed?

IBM uses the term *unresolved external reference* to designate any reference from within an object module to a location that is not part of that object module. In building an object module, the compiler program generates a table

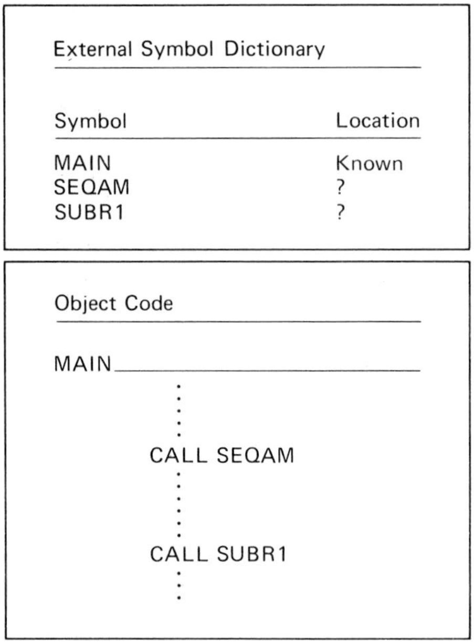

```
┌─────────────────────────────────────────────┐
│                                             │
│   External Symbol Dictionary                │
│   ──────────────────────────                │
│                                             │
│   Symbol                     Location       │
│   ─────────────────────      ────────       │
│   MAIN                       Known          │
│   SEQAM                      ?              │
│   SUBR1                      ?              │
│                                             │
└─────────────────────────────────────────────┘
┌─────────────────────────────────────────────┐
│                                             │
│   Object Code                               │
│   ──────────────────────────────────        │
│                                             │
│   MAIN_____        │
│                       ⋮                     │
│                                             │
│               CALL SEQAM                    │
│                       ⋮                     │
│                                             │
│               CALL SUBR1                    │
│                       ⋮                     │
│                                             │
└─────────────────────────────────────────────┘
```

Fig. 11.12
An object module.

of such unresolved external references and places this table at the beginning of
the object module (Fig. 11.12). This table is called the *external symbol dictionary*. This dictionary (the ESD) is used by the linkage editor in building a load
module, a process we will discuss shortly.

Creating an Object
Module Library

Physically, there is no difference between a source statement library and an
object module library; both are stored on a partitioned data set. In fact, at least
on the larger IBM systems, it is possible to mix source and object modules on
the same library.

Under DOS, the object module library is called the *relocatable library*.
The term *linkage library* is sometimes used on an OS system. As before, it is
possible to have both private and system object module libraries (Fig. 11.13),
with the "most recently compiled" object module perhaps being viewed as a
special case.

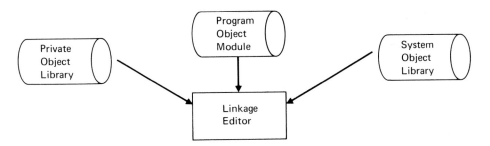

Fig. 11.13
Object level libraries on a typical system.

Adding a Member
to an Object
Module Library

Object modules are generated by compiler programs. Thus it follows that the way to add an object module to a library is to control the destination of the output from the compiler. The chances are that you have never really worried about the output from the assembler or compiler program (except, of course, for the listing). Most programmers have never looked seriously at the DD statement that creates the temporary data set to hold the program object module; it is, after all, buried in the cataloged procedure. Let's consider the JCL code generated by a typical cataloged procedure, ASMFC (see Fig. 11.11) and then discuss how the object module might be placed on a private library.

ASMFC is a procedure that generates the JCL needed to support only the assembly step; it uses IBM's level F assembler. The first generated statement is an EXEC; IEUASM is simply the name of the assembler program. The SYS-LIB DD statement identifies the source statement macro library, which is one of the inputs to the assembler. We'll ignore SYSUT1, SYSUT2, and SYSUT3; they are assembler work files. The compiler listing is printed through SYS-PRINT, and an object deck, should we need one, is generated through SYSPUNCH.

The statement we are really interested in is

```
XXSYSGO    DD    DSNAME=&&LOADSET,SPACE=(400,(100,20)),
XX               DISP=(OLD,PASS),UNIT=SYSDA,
XX               DCB=(LRECL=80,BLKSIZE=400,RECFM=FB)
```

It defines a temporary data set named &&LOADSET; the object module produced by the assembler program will be the only resident of this data set. The secret to placing an object module on a private library is very simple: change this statement.

For example, assume that the program being assembled is known as MYPGM. We have already created a library named MYLIB. The following JCL would assemble the program and place the object module on the library.

```
//      EXEC  ASMFC
//ASM.SYSGO  DD  DSNAME=MYLIB(MYPGM),DISP=(OLD,KEEP),
//                DCB=(RECFM=FB,LRECL=80,BLKSIZE=400)
//ASM.SYSIN  DD  *

     } source program

/*
```

As we did earlier with the source statement library definition, we have overridden the cataloged procedure; the SYSGO statement *as coded in the job stream* takes precedence over the SYSGO statement in the cataloged procedure. The object module will no longer go to a temporary data set named &&LOADSET; instead it will go to MYLIB, under the name MYPGM. Although this example was based on the assembler, you will find parallel job control statements for any standard compiler or assembler program on an IBM computer.

Note: Once again, given an existing library, we could skip the DCB parameter. If coded, the logical record length, blocksize, and record format must match that of the library.

Building a
Load Module

An object module contains unresolved external references. Before the program can be loaded and executed, the external references must be resolved; this is the job of a program that IBM calls the *linkage editor.*

Assume that we have just finished compiling the program whose object module was pictured in Fig. 11.12. The program is named MAIN. It references two other object modules, calling a sequential access method (probably through a READ instruction) and a private subroutine named SUBR1. As we begin the process of link editing the program, we face the situation pictured in Fig. 11.14. The access method SEQAM, resides on a system object module library. The subroutine, SUBR1, is on a private subroutine library. The just compiled object module, MAIN, is on another private library (or, perhaps, on a temporary data set).

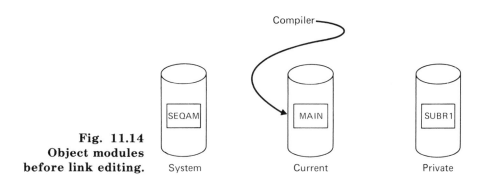

Fig. 11.14
Object modules
before link editing.   System   Current   Private

How does the linkage editor go about the process of building a load module from this input? The starting point is MAIN, the just compiled object module. It is read into main memory, the external symbol dictionary is separated from the object code, and the beginning of MAIN is established as the base address or reference point for the load module.

Now the linkage editor begins to scan the external symbol dictionary. Reference is made to an object module named SEQAM. The system library is searched, and SEQAM is found. The access method is read into main memory, the ESD and the object code are separated, and the object module is placed just after MAIN (Fig. 11.15).

Fig. 11.15
The load module.

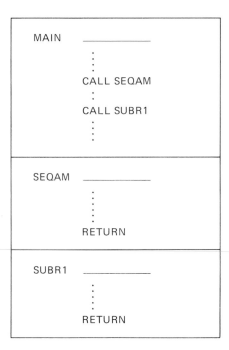

The next step is to scan SEQAM's external symbol dictionary; it is certainly legal for one subroutine to call another. To simplify this first example, we'll assume that SEQAM does not call a lower-level subroutine. The reference to SEQAM has now been fully resolved, and we can return to the external symbol dictionary for the main program.

MAIN also calls SUBR1. The system library is searched, but SUBR1 is not found. Thus the private subroutine library is searched; SUBR1 is there. The object module is read into memory, the ESD and the object code are separated, and the code is placed after SEQAM in the load module (Fig. 11.15). Now the external symbol dictionary for SUBR1 is scanned for unresolved external references; once again we'll assume that there are none.

Returning to the main program's external symbol dictionary, we find that there are no more unresolved external references. Thus the load module is complete, referring only to locations that are contained within the load module. It is ready to be loaded and executed.

**Fig. 11.16
A more complex
load module.**

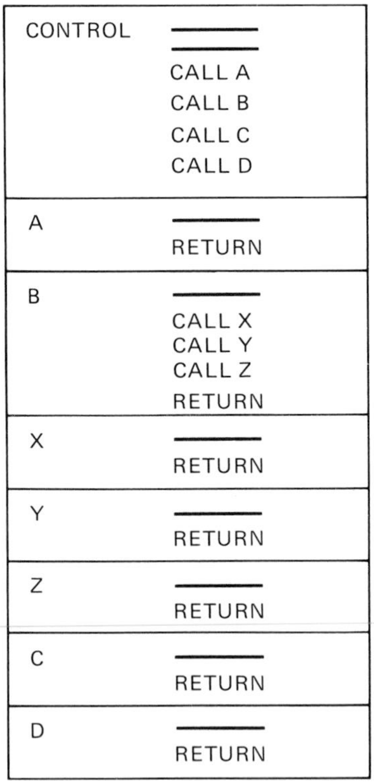

CONTROL	———
	CALL A
	CALL B
	CALL C
	CALL D
A	———
	RETURN
B	———
	CALL X
	CALL Y
	CALL Z
	RETURN
X	———
	RETURN
Y	———
	RETURN
Z	———
	RETURN
C	———
	RETURN
D	———
	RETURN

Let's imagine a somewhat more complex program. The primary module is named CONTROL. It calls four subroutines: A, B, C, and D. Routines A, C, and D are relatively simple, performing a computation and returning directly to CONTROL, but routine B contains subsequent calls to X, Y, and Z (we'll end the chain here). When the linkage editor reads in module B and scans its external symbol dictionary, three lower-level unresolved external references to X, Y, and Z will be encountered. These references must be resolved before the linkage editor returns to the main program; thus subroutines X, Y, and Z will follow B in the load module (Fig. 11.16).

Using the Linkage Editor (IBM)

The linkage editor is a program. Its input consists of one or more object modules. It produces a load module. As is the case with any program run on an IBM computer (under OS), a DD statement must be provided for each input and each output file. If you have ever used an IBM System/360-370 computer, you have almost certainly used the linkage editor, but you have probably never looked at the JCL that supports it; once again the control statements are buried in the cataloged procedure. An expansion of the cataloged procedure ASMFCL is shown in Fig. 11.17; the linkage editor step is highlighted.

The first statement in the linkage editor step is an EXEC; the program name is IEWL. The SYSLIN DD statement defines the input data set for the linkage editor. Note the DSNAME, &&LOADSET. Where have you seen that before? It's the same name the assembler used to store the object module—look at the SYSGO DD statement.

A few lines below SYSLIN is a rather strange-looking JCL statement.

```
//      DD    DDNAME=SYSIN
```

It has no DDNAME! Since there is no DDNAME, the last name encountered still holds; this is another data set that goes by the name SYSLIN—another input to the linkage editor. The two files are concatenated.

The parameter, DDNAME=SYSIN, is a bit unusual, too. It represents a postponement of the data definition. Essentially, the DDNAME parameter implies two things.

1. We are not going to provide a detailed description of this data set just yet.
2. Look ahead in the job stream for a DD statement with the specified DDNAME (in this example, SYSIN). You will find a detailed description of the data set in that statement.

```
//          JOB    ...

//          EXEC   ASMFCL

XXASM       EXEC   PGM=IEUASM
XXSYSLIB    DD     ...
XXSYSUT1    DD     ...
XXSYSUT2    DD     ...
XXSYSUT3    DD     ...
XXSYSPRINT  DD     ...
XXSYSPUNCH  DD     ...
XXSYSGO     DD     DSNAME=&&LOADSET,...

//ASM.SYSIN DD     *

      ⎫
      ⎬ source program
      ⎭

/*
```

```
XXLKED      EXEC   PGM=IEWL
XXSYSLIN    DD     DSNAME=&&LOADSET,DISP=(OLD,DELETE),
XX                 DCB=(LRECL=80,BLKSIZE=400,RECFM=FB)
XX          DD     DDNAME=SYSIN
XXSYSLMOD   DD     DSNAME=&&GOSET(GO),SPACE=(1024,(50,20,1)),
XX                 DISP=(NEW,PASS),UNIT=SYSDA
XXSYSUT1    DD     ...
XXSYSPRINT  DD     SYSOUT=A

/*
```

Fig. 11.17
The ASMFCL cataloged procedure. Statements
that begin with // are coded by the programmer.
Those that begin with XX are part of the
procedure.

The programmer uses SYSIN to pass object modules and control statements to the linkage editor; we'll consider an example shortly.

The SYSLMOD (for *system load module*) statement defines the data set on which the output load module will be placed (Fig. 11.17, again). The data set name is &&GOSET(GO). It defines a temporary partitioned data set on the system direct access device (SYSDA); this particular load module is given the member name GO. Note the SPACE parameter. Space is requested in 1024-

byte blocks. The primary request is for 50 blocks, with a secondary request for 20 more; a single 256-byte block is set aside to hold the directory.

The Primary
Object Module

If the linkage editor is to produce a valid load module, it must start somewhere. One of the object modules must be designated as the primary object module, and must be input to the linkage editor through the DD statement named SYS-LIN (*system linkage editor input*). Typically, this is the most recently compiled object module; in the compile/ link edit/ execute sequence, it's the module that started as source code. Figure 11.17 shows the output from the assembler going to SYSGO, where it is stored under the data set name &&LOADSET. This DSNAME also appears on the SYSLIN statement as input to the linkage editor.

What if the object module is placed on a private library? The programmer will find it necessary to override *both* the SYSGO and SYSLIN statements (Fig. 11.18).

Another important consideration is the timing of the compile and link edit steps. The programmer is used to working with "compilelinkeditgo", almost viewing the process as a single operation. In reality, three distinct programs are involved. When a single job such as ASMFCLG or COBVCLG is run, these three steps may be separated by a few seconds or even microseconds as they run in sequence. However, it is certainly possible to run the compile on Monday, the link edit on Tuesday, and the execute step on Wednesday (substitute January, February, and March, if you wish). Once a source, object, or load module is written to a file, it is captured for "later" use, and can be used at virtually any time.

System Libraries

There are actually several different levels of "system" libraries. One, a true system library, contains such object-level modules as the standard access methods. These are used by almost every program on the system; the original source language is not a factor. The system "knows" where to find these modules.

Other system libraries are more language-dependent. FORTRAN, for example, supports a number of scientific subroutines. The programmer who wants to use one of these scientific subroutines must clearly specify to the linkage editor where the subroutine library can be found. Thus one additional DD

```
//     EXEC    ASMFCL
XXASM          EXEC  PGM=IEUASM
XXSYSLIB       DD   ...
XXSYSUT1       DD   ...
XXSYSUT2       DD   ...
XXSYSUT3       DD   ...
XXSYSPRINT     DD   ...
XXSYSPUNCH     DD   ...
```

```
//ASM.SYSGO    DD   DSNAME=MYLIB(MYPGM),DISP=(OLD,KEEP),

//                  DCB=(RECFM=FB,LRECL=80,BLKSIZE=400)
```

```
//ASM.SYSIN    DD   *
```

> source program

```
/*
```

```
XXLKED        EXEC   PGM=IEWL
```

```
//SYSLIN       DD   DSNAME=MYLIB(MYPGM),DISP=(OLD,KEEP)

//             DD   DDNAME=SYSIN
```

```
XXSYSLMOD     DD   ...
XXSYSUT1      DD   ...
XXSYSPRINT    DD   ...
```

Fig. 11.18
Link editing an object module from a private
library.

statement is normally found in the cataloged procedure for a FORTRAN/link edit sequence.

```
XXSYSLIB  DD  DSNAME=SYS1.FORTLIB,DISP=SHR
```

Often, other subroutine libraries are identified by concatenating additional DD statements to the SYSLIB. Similar language-dependent functions are supported in COBOL, PL/1, and most other languages.

Note the difference between these two levels of system libraries. The first, containing such modules as the standard access methods, is language-independent—almost every program created by the linkage editor will require one or more of these object modules. System pointers allow the linkage editor to locate this library; no programmer-generated DD statement is required. The other libraries *are* language-related: FORTRAN programs access the FORTLIB, and COBOL programs request object modules from the COBLIB. They are system libraries because they are not written locally, but they are not quite as general as the true *system* library we have just been discussing. The programmer (or cataloged procedure) must clearly identify such language-dependent libraries through a SYSLIB DD statement.

Private Libraries

Unless the programmer provides a complete description of a private library, the linkage editor (or any other system program) will simply be unable to find it. Most programmers use the cataloged procedures to access compiler programs or the linkage editor. As we have seen (Fig. 11.17), the cataloged procedure for the link edit step normally contains an unnamed DD statement concatenated to SYSLIN. This statement, in turn, points to DDNAME-SYSIN. The application programmer can take advantage of the SYSIN statement to pass private library information to the linkage editor.

Assume, for example, that a subroutine named SUBR1 resides on a private library named MYLIB. We have just compiled a program that references SUBR1. We can tell the linkage editor to INCLUDE the subroutine in the load module by passing a control statement to the editor via SYSIN (Fig. 11.19).

Fig. 11.19
**Identifying private library modules to the
linkage editor by using an INCLUDE statement.**

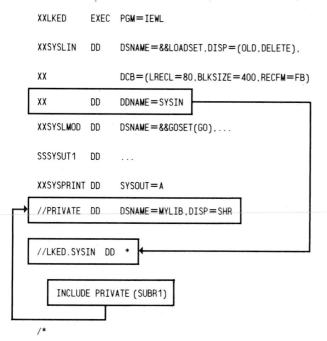

```
XXLKED      EXEC  PGM=IEWL

XXSYSLIN    DD    DSNAME=&&LOADSET,DISP=(OLD,DELETE),

XX                DCB=(LRECL=80,BLKSIZE=400,RECFM=FB)

XX          DD    DDNAME=SYSIN

XXSYSLMOD   DD    DSNAME=&&GOSET(GO),....

SSSYSUT1    DD    ...

XXSYSPRINT  DD    SYSOUT=A

//PRIVATE   DD    DSNAME=MYLIB,DISP=SHR

//LKED.SYSIN  DD  *

      INCLUDE PRIVATE (SUBR1)

/*
```

Follow the code very carefully. First, we have the "normal" JCL as it exists in the cataloged procedure, with the SYSLIN DD statement and its associated unnamed DD statement in place. Following SYSPRINT comes a new statement—the // in the first two positions shows that it was coded by the programmer. This statement, named PRIVATE, describes our private library. The SYSIN statement follows (the LKED, is a step qualifier), and precedes one or more linkage editor control statements. In this example, only one control statement has been coded.

```
INCLUDE PRIVATE
```

It tells the linkage editor to look for a DD statement named PRIVATE to find a detailed description of one or more object modules that are to be included in the load module.

Look through the process one more time. The SYSIN statement makes a series of control statements available to the linkage editor. One control statement, an INCLUDE, identifies one or more DD statements. Each of those DD statements defines, in turn, one or more object modules that are to be included in the load module. The skeleton of another, more complex, example is shown in Fig. 11.20.

Fig. 11.20

A link edit step with more than one private library.

```
//          EXEC  ASMFCL

//ASM.SYSIN  DD  *

  ⎫
  ⎬ source program
  ⎭

/*

//LIBRA      DD  DSNAME=ALIBRARY,DISP=SHR

//LIBRX      DD  DSNAME=XLIBRARY,DISP=SHR

//LKED.SYSIN DD  *

   INCLUDE LIBRA(A,B,C,D)      Note: The INCLUDE references

   INCLUDE LIBRX(X,Y,Z)             multiple members.

/*
```

This is simply one example of how the programmer might use the linkage editor. There are several ways to identify private object modules to the linkage editor, and numerous other commands can be coded. It is not our intent to cover all the features of this most useful program.

Creating a Load Module Library

A load module library is simply a partitioned data set. It is created just like the PDS that we earlier used for a source statement library and an object module library. Under DOS, a load module library is known as a *core image library.*

Placing a Load Module on a Library

A load module is the output of the linkage editor. Specifically, when using a cataloged procedure such as ASMFCL (Fig. 11.17), the load module is output to the partitioned data set defined by the DD statement

```
XXSYSLMOD  DD  DSNAME=&&GOSET(GO),SPACE=(1024,(50,20,1)),
XX             DISP=(NEW,PASS),UNIT=SYSDA
```

To place the load module on a private library, all you must do is change this DD statement (Fig. 11.21).

Fig. 11.21
Placing a load module on a private library. Note: While it is *legal* to use the same logical record length and blocksize for source module, object module, and load module libraries, this is unusual. In a production environment, load modules are often written to a library using full-track blocking.

```
//             EXEC  ASMFCL

//ASM.SYSIN    DD    *

       } source program

/*

//LKED.SYSLMOD DD     DSNAME=MYLIB(LOADMOD),DISP=(OLD,KEEP)

/*
```

Executing a Load Module from a Private Library

Once a program is in load module form, it can simply be loaded and executed by the system in response to an EXEC command. The system can find load modules that are stored on a system program library. When a private library is used, the programmer must identify it through a JOBLIB or STEPLIB statement; for example

```
//        EXEC  PGM=LOADMOD
//STEPLIB DD    DSNAME=MYLIB,DISP=SHR
```

The Loader (IBM)

The linkage editor produces a load module that it places on a library. The library may be temporary, but the linkage editor still outputs a complete load module that could be permanently stored. The programmer does not always need a permanent load module. Often, particularly in the earlier stages of program development, all that is needed is a temporary load module. In such cases, the programmer can use the *loader* instead of the linkage editor.

The loader does everything the linkage editor does, except that it does not output a load module. Instead, it builds a load module in main memory and, when complete, simply gives this load module control. With the linkage editor, the load module is written to disk and then read back in. With the loader, these two I/O operations are dropped, a considerable savings for a one-time execution.

Because there is no load module output from the loader, there is no SYSL-MOD DD statement. To access the loader, the programmer codes cataloged procedures such as ASMF<u>CG</u> or COBV<u>CG</u>; the CG stands for compile and go.

We should mention that there are some advanced linkage editor functions that are not supported in the loader program—generating overlay structures, for example. Still, for the compile and test activities common to program development, the loader is usually more than adequate, and it does represent a considerable savings in computer time and, hence, in computer cost.

Summary

The chapter began with a brief discussion of the compile/link edit/execute sequence. We defined, in general terms, source modules, object modules, and load modules, and briefly described the functions of a compiler, an interpreter, and the linkage editor. Libraries can be maintained at the source, object, or load level.

We then turned our attention to compilers and source statement libraries. Macro instructions in assembler and COPY statements in COBOL were cited as references to a source statement library. The difference between private and system libraries was explored, and an example illustrating the expansion of source code into a source module prior to compilation was developed using the COBOL language.

On an IBM computer, a library is called a partitioned data set or PDS. The creation of a PDS was illustrated, and a utility program named IEBGENER was used to add members to a source statement library. We then briefly considered the nature of an object module, pointing out that most contain unresolved external references, and thus must be link edited before execution. A member is placed on an object module library by controlling the destination of the compiler output.

Load modules are built by the linkage editor from a series of object modules. The linkage editor process was discussed in general terms, and then a specific example using the IBM linkage editor was developed. Because a load module is output by the linkage editor, the secret to placing a load module on a library is to control the destination of the linkage editor output.

The chapter ended with a brief discussion of the loader program.

Key Words

compiler	member
concatenated data set	member name
core image library	object module
directory	partitioned data set (PDS)
external symbol dictionary (ESD)	
	private library
interpreter	relocatable library
library	source module
linkage editor	source statement library
linkage library	system library
load module	unresolved external reference
loader	
macro	

Exercises _____

1. What are the differences among a source module, an object module, and a load module? Don't simply say that a source module is produced by a programmer, an object module is produced by a compiler, and so on; it is assumed that you know where the modules come from and, besides, giving the sources doesn't answer the question. How do these modules differ from each other?

2. Briefly explain how a compiler or assembler program incorporates source statement library members into a source module.

3. Explain the difference between a system library and a private library.

4. Describe the structure of a typical library.

5. Explain how a partitioned data set can be created on an IBM System/360-370.

6. How can a programmer add a member to a source statement library?

7. Why does a typical object module contain unresolved external references?

8. What is an external symbol dictionary?

9. Explain how a member can be added to an object module library.

10. What does the linkage editor program do?

11. What is a concatenated data set?

12. Explain how the linkage editor follows a chain of unresolved external references in building a load module.

13. How is a load module placed on a private library? How is this load module eventually executed?

14. What is the loader program?

The following exercises are directed at readers who have access to an IBM System 360-370 computer. Users of other systems might consider parallel assignments.

15. Submit a program (any program) using a cataloged procedure such as ASMFCLG, COBVCLG, or one you have used in class. Include MSGLE-VEL=(1,1) on the EXEC statement. Read and explain each generated job control statement.

16. For this exercise you will need a main program and a main program and a subroutine written in any language (or even in two different languages). Use source code from a previous class. If you don't have such source code, write a main program to read two values, call a subroutine, and write their sum; the subroutine should do nothing but add the values. (In other words, don't waste time on the code—this is a library manipulation exercise.) Do the following.

a) Compile the subroutine and store it on a private library.
b) Independently compile the main program and store it on a private library.
c) Link edit the two object modules and store the load module on a private library.
d) Execute the load module.

Part

IV

Operating System Concepts

Basic Operating
System Concepts

Overview

The typical programmer will almost certainly use a command or job control language. This same programmer will probably use the linkage editor or a similar program, and will probably do a considerable amount of work with libraries. The operating system functions that support these features represent the front line in the programmer/operating system interface.

We are about to drop below the front line and turn our attention to the internals of the operating system itself. Here in Part IV, we'll analyze a number of operating system concepts in considerable detail, citing a variety of examples. This chapter is concerned with several basic operating system concepts.

We begin in a very general way by discussing the functions of an operating system—essentially, resource management. A number of measures of effectiveness can be applied to an operating system; unfortunately, the fact that these measures are often in conflict with each other tends to make the job of the operating system designer much more difficult. As a result, most operating systems are designed with a particular class of applications in mind.

Microcomputer systems are growing in importance and, being relatively simple, represent an excellent starting point for an in-depth study of this software. We'll consider the nature of a typical "basic" microcomputer system, and then develop a reasonable list of the software support features we would hope to find on such a system. Using this list, the skeleton of a basic operating system will be designed. The problems associated with system generation and initial program load will then be discussed. Finally, a specific example of a popular microcomputer operating system, CP/M,® will be presented.

The Functions
of an
Operating System

It is sometimes useful to view a computer as a series of levels (Fig. 12.1). The programmer tends to approach the machine from an application program level. We have just finished several chapters that took us closer to the actual hardware; we might call it the command language level. At the bottom is the hardware, and on top of the hardware is the computer's microcode (in this text, we will view the hardware and its microcode as a single level). In between is the operating system. This level-by-level view of a computer clearly establishes the position of the operating system and thus its primary function—it serves as a hardware/software interface.

Looking beyond the simple interface function, it would seem reasonable to argue that ideally, we would like to design an *efficient* interface. Since the operating system lies between the hardware and the software, this would seem an ideal position from which to manage these system resources. Thus, on most

Fig. 12.1
The levels of a
computer system.

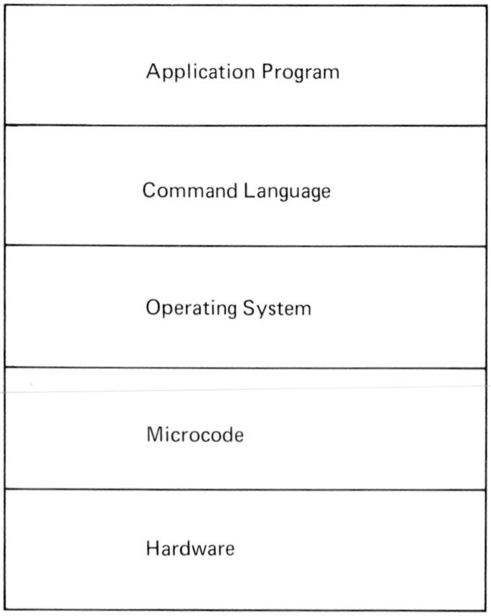

Application Program
Command Language
Operating System
Microcode
Hardware

modern computers, the operating system serves as the primary resource manager.

The software needed to support multiprogramming is an almost perfect example of this premise; multiprogramming, as we've seen, significantly improves the utilization of the CPU by making use of otherwise wasted time. Other system resources include main memory space, registers, the input and output devices, secondary storage space, various data resources including program libraries and, to a lesser extent, human resources including programmers, operators, and the eventual user of the results of a data processing operation; a well-designed operating system must be concerned with most if not all of these factors. A popular word in science and engineering circles is optimization. The word *optimum* means "the best or most favorable degree, condition, amount, etc." (at least according to Webster). To optimize means to achieve the best possible result. The function of an operating system, simply stated, is to optimize the utilization of all the system resources.

Measures of Effectiveness

That definition sounds pretty easy, but it isn't. Let's consider an analogy. What's the optimum engine for an automobile? What is your idea of effective performance? Are you primarily interested in speed? or safety? or gasoline consumption? or internal space and truck space? or a comfortable ride? or cost? or status? or some combination? In other words, what are your measures of effectiveness, and how heavily do you weight them? Different people tend to answer these questions in different ways. Tell me what characteristics you consider to be important in an automobile. Then we can *begin* to discuss the precise meaning of the word optimum as used in conjunction with an automobile or an automobile engine. "Best" is a relative term.

A number of different factors can be used to measure the performance of a computer system, including

1. *Throughput,* a measure of the amount of work going through a computer. Throughput is often expressed as a percentage, measuring actual run time as a fraction of total available system time.

2. *Turnaround,* a measure of the elapsed time between job submission and job completion.

3. *Response time* is an important characteristic on time-shared systems; it's a measure of the elapsed time between a request for the computer's attention and the actual response to that request.

4. *Availability* is a measure of system accessibility.

5. *Security,* which is becoming an increasingly important consideration.

6. *Reliability.*

7. *Cost.*

8. *Ease of use.*

The perfect operating system would allow us to maximize throughput while minimizing both turnaround and response time. The system would be available to any programmer on a few moments notice. Security would, of course, be absolute, and system reliability would approach 100 percent. All this would be accomplished at a very low cost. Good luck.

Conflicting Objectives

Our ways of measuring computer effectiveness are, in many cases, in conflict. Throughput can be increased by overloading a system, perhaps by purchasing too small a machine—like the supermarket working with only a single checkout counter. But what does overloading do to turnaround or response time? Conversely, turnaround and response time can be helped by underloading a system—buying considerably more computer than is needed. This, of course, clobbers throughput, since an underloaded system is bound to be idle at times.

Does this imply that turnaround and response time are always compatible? Not really. Consider a time-shared system designed to minimize response time. To achieve this objective, each program is restricted to a brief shot of CPU time, returning to the end of the job queue if this time slice isn't enough to allow the program to reach a natural break point. A ten-second program, restricted to one-tenth of a second each second, would need a total of 100 seconds of elapsed time to complete. The quest for response time can have a negative impact on turnaround.

System availability and throughput are in obvious conflict. How can a busy system be considered available?

Security is another measure of effectiveness that is in conflict with many others. The controls and checks necessitated by a concern for security take up time—both computer time and operator time. Time spent on security is time *not* spent on production. Many security procedures tend to contract rather than expand system availability. Security checks can add to run time, thus increasing turnaround. Response time can also be slowed by security arrangements.

The equipment used in our space program is among the most reliable hardware ever developed. In this program, reliability is often gained by duplicating all or part of a particular hardware subsystem—everything has its backup; this is expensive. System reliability and system cost are conflicting objectives.

In a business environment, cost often becomes an overriding objective—design a system to do the job at the lowest possible cost. A system enjoying high throughput is probably doing quite well in terms of *equipment* or hardware cost, but there are other cost factors that must also be considered. In an airline reservation application, for example, slow response time can lead to the loss of a customer, a substantial cost.

Constraints

As if conflicting objectives were not enough, the designer of an operating system faces a number of factors that severely limit his or her flexibility. Perhaps the most obvious constraint is technology itself; an instantaneous response is physically impossible. The limits of the electronics used in a particular machine are a constraining influence; multiprogramming software is hardly needed for an electronic tube machine but becomes almost essential with integrated circuits.

Another technology problem arises from the fact that computers are rarely planned around an operating system; instead, the operating system is planned and designed to fit on existing hardware. Throughput might be significantly improved by keeping 25 or 30 programs in main memory and multiprogramming; if, however, hardware design limits the equipment to a maximum core address of one million or so, there may not be enough room to hold all those programs.

Economic factors represent another valid constraint on the designer of an operating system. People simply will not buy a system that costs too much.

Strangely, perhaps, political factors represent another common constraint. An operating system might be designed to give priority to the type of program normally submitted by a certain department simply because of the influence wielded by its manager; other departments or functions with less political clout might find jobs typical of their department suffering from a poor priority. A strong computer operations group might succeed in pushing hated tape and disk-mount jobs to the third shift by controlling the priority decision. Every system will tend to favor the pet project of the general manager. This is an often overlooked or ignored problem, but it is an important one.

Stating System Objectives

Different applications call for different objectives. When stated explicitly, computer system and operating system objectives often take the form of target figures as in "Maintain a minimum of 75 percent throughput while keeping turnaround under one hour." Other targets might call for maintaining response time at a maximum of three seconds for at least 95 percent of system requests, or keeping average response time below two seconds. The availability parameter often takes the form of a certain level of excess capacity, (perhaps not included in throughput figures) which is made available to programmers or engineers on a demand basis. Security specifications are often written and enforcement is guaranteed by planned audits. Cost limits represent the most common type of objective—don't spend more than X dollars.

To be most effective, planning should be done for a complete system and not just the operating system. Ideally, hardware and software planning should be done together. Usually, they are not. Usually, the operating system is planned and implemented after the hardware is in place; the software objective becomes one of optimizing the utilization of system resources, *given the restriction* of the existing hardware.

Evaluating an Operating System

A *good* operating system is one that does an efficient job of managing the system resources. It performs its management functions in the context of a particular hardware system; the hardware both limits and shapes the operating system. Looking beyond the hardware, the effectiveness of an operating system can be measured only with respect to the effectiveness criteria that are considered relevant on a particular system. A large time-shared computer that is concurrently used by hundreds of users will probably stress response time, security, and reliability. An equally large business system might be more concerned with generating massive, end-of-period accounting reports in a timely fashion and at reasonable cost; throughput and turnaround time thus become this system's key measures of effectiveness. The operating systems for these two machines will be quite different.

When studying an operating system, it is useful to begin by answering two questions.

1. What hardware is the operating system designed to support?
2. What "typical" or assumed application mix is the operating system designed to support?

A reasonable understanding of the hardware and the application mix is essential if you are to understand *why* a particular operating system was designed the way it was. In this section, we'll be studying a variety of operating systems. In each case, our analysis will begin with a description of the hardware environment and the assumed application mix. We start with an analysis of microcomputer operating systems.

The Microcomputer System Environment

A microcomputer is a small computer. Typically, although 16- and 32-bit micros are commercially available, it's an 8-bit word machine. Such systems are relatively slow, contain a limited amount of main memory (usually no more than 64K), and support a limited number of peripheral devices (perhaps a CRT, a printer, and two diskette drives). A basic system might cost less than $1000; system cost rarely exceeds $10,000.

One potential user of a microcomputer system is the computer "jock," a person who simply enjoys "fooling around" with a computer. Such people require (and probably desire) very little support. A reasonable decision might be to provide almost no system software support on such a system.

A much larger market, however, is composed of people who are interested in using a microcomputer for a specific purpose such as tracking inventory, playing games, or supporting research. Such people are rarely interested in the subtle nuances of I/O device control or diskette track configurations. Their concern is with ease of use. In general, they want to get on with their application, and they don't want the hardware to get in the way.

This application-oriented microcomputer user will probably be a one-person computer center—the analyst, programmer, operator, data entry clerk, and manager rolled into one. On such a small system, multiprogramming is simply out of the question. Basically, the environment includes a small machine, a limited number of peripheral devices, single program execution, and a single user/programmer/operator.

How would this user tend to measure system effectiveness? What is the user's application mix? Knowing the kinds of programs that the user is likely to execute provides a clear insight into the parameters that this user is likely to consider important. On a small system, the programs will probably be small. Each program will process a limited amount of data. In a given day, relatively few programs will be run; in fact, with the possible exception of a micro that is dedicated to the task of collecting data from a piece of laboratory or production equipment, the computer will be unused most of the time. These are of course assumptions but given the environment described above (in particular, the single user), the assumptions seem reasonable.

On a machine that is used perhaps two to three hours per day, throughout is not a relevant concern. Given small programs processing a limited amount of data, turnaround is not a problem. On a single user computer, the hardware is the only component that really affects response time, and even a slow computer is much faster than any human operator. Forget availability. The machine is used only a few hours a day, so it's usually available. Security is achieved simply because of the very limited number of users; it is not a major concern.

What, then, are the microcomputer user's criteria for measuring effectiveness? Basically, there are three—cost, reliability, and ease of use. Cost is the big one. People are drawn to microcomputer systems because they are inexpensive; the designer of a microcomputer operating system must be aware of this fact. Each function added to an operating system increases the development cost, and hence the selling price. An operating system occupies main memory, and the larger the operating system, the more memory it occupies. Memory tends to be one of the more expensive components of a computer system. Thus the operating system for a microcomputer must be tightly written, and must contain only the essential functions; cost considerations demand that a stripped-down model be developed.

Reliability and ease of use vie closely for second place. Reliability, unfortunately, is very difficult to measure, and tends to be viewed from a system perspective, often in a negative light: the ABC model 50 is always going down. From an operating system point of view, reliability is largely a function of the complexity of the code. Put simply, on a micro it is better to do a few things well then many things badly. Once again, the argument favors simplicity.

Finally, we consider ease of use. Most micros are programmed in easy-to-use languages such as BASIC, FORTRAN, Pascal, or APL. Translation to machine level is necessary, so compilers and interpreters are needed. What other problems does the microcomputer user face? Simply communicating with the machine can be difficult, so an elementary command language will probably be needed. A command language implies that there will be an operating system module to read and interpret the commands; we must have a command processor. Communicating with the peripheral hardware is another problem area. Before a record can be read or written, some very precise signals must pass between the computer and a peripheral device. While coding at this level is certainly not difficult, it can be tedious, and it is error prone. Thus it is not uncommon to find an input/output control system in a microcomputer operating system. Data management—locating files, allocating space, and locating records—is another problem area; thus data management routines and librarian modules are often included. All these features are directly concerned with the ease-of-use factor.

What about some of the other operating system functions? Many of the functions described in Chapter 6 were concerned with multiprogramming; we won't be doing multiprogramming on a micro, so we don't need memory management, priority routines, memory protection, I/O device allocation, or job queueing modules. Is there any need for spooling? On a system that processes relatively little data, why bother? Scheduling is the responsibility of the operator; the command language is all the support we need. Given the microcomputer's effectiveness criteria, the more sophisticated operating system elements are simply not necessary.

The Geography of a Microcomputer Operating System

An operating system designed for a microcomputer is going to be small, and will perform a limited number of functions. A typical system (Fig. 12.2) is probably composed of a microprocessor, 16K to 64K of main memory (RAM), a

Fig. 12.2
The geography of a typical microcomputer operating system

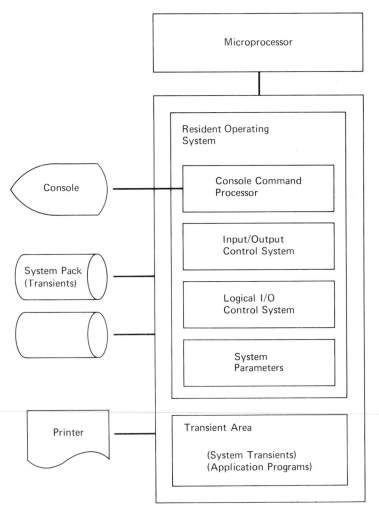

CRT that acts both as the primary data entry device *and* the operator's console, a printer, and two to four diskette drives.

Typically, main memory is divided into a number of regions (Fig. 12.2, again). At the top we see the *resident operating system,* sometimes called the nucleus or the supervisor. Inside the resident operating system is a module to handle operator commands (the console *command processor*), a module to handle communications with the I/O devices (the *input/output control system* or *IOCS*), and (often) a module to handle a number of data management functions (the *logical input/output control system* or LIOCS). These modules are *resident*; they are stored in main memory and provide real-time support to the application programs.

Why are these particular modules made resident? Remember the two primary criteria for a microcomputer system: low cost and ease of use. The low-cost criterion suggests that the operating system be kept simple; thus a minimum number of functions will be resident. The command processor, IOCS, and LIOCS modules are essential if ease of use is really important.

Perhaps the most difficult single function to perform on a computer is I/O. The apparently simple task of reading a record from a peripheral device is, in reality, quite complex. It involves two different physical devices, and before these devices can begin to communicate, they must be synchronized. Thus a series of very precise electronic signals must be exchanged. Rather than have the programmer code the logic needed to generate and test these signals, most computer manufacturers provide customers with an input/output control system (IOCS).

Few casual programmers are interested in the details of disk storage. With only IOCS in place, the programmer must specify files and records by actual physical disk address. By adding a logical input/output control system (LIOCS), the user can reference files by name, with the operating system converting this name to a specific physical location, and then accessing the file via IOCS. The command processor, of course, provides a convenient mechanism to allow the user to issue commands to the system.

Not all operating system modules must be core resident. Consider, for example, the task of loading a program from a library into main memory. The logic that responds to the operator's command must, of course, be in the computer, but what about the logic that locates and transfers the program? This second module is needed for a brief time only, during the actual program transfer. It is stored on disk. Once the command processor receives a load command, the loader logic is transferred into memory and given control. It loads the program, and is no longer needed. Now, the command processor can reuse the space occupied by the loader logic for some other *transient* function. The free area or *transient area* of main memory (Fig. 12.2), containing all the space not allocated to the resident operating system, can hold one of these transient modules or an application program.

The final region of the resident operating system holds key system constants, parameters, and control fields. This is where the operating system stores its constants and control information.

Where in main memory is the operating system found? That depends on the system. The architecture of many computers requires that key control information be stored at specific main memory locations, thus defining the address of at least the system parameters. Other systems assume a standard load address for a primary control program. On other systems, subtle differences in the access time for various regions of memory shape the operating system's geography. Often, the placement of modules is based on an argument no more substantial than "That's the way we've always done it." Module placement is rarely arbitrary, but it can vary from system to system. Figure 12.2 shows the regions of an operating system in a general sense, without regard for their placement.

Few microcomputers operate 24 hours a day—usually they are frequently turned off and then restarted later. Most main memory, RAM, is *volatile*; in other words, it loses its contents when power is removed. Thus the resident operating system is *not* permanent; it must be reloaded each time the system is restarted. Normally, a copy of the operating system is kept on diskette, the system pack. How is the system pack created, and how is the resident operating system copied from this diskette into main memory?

Creating the Operating System—System Generation

An operating system is a collection of software modules. Obviously, someone must write the operating system. The starting point is usually a bare computer, pure hardware, the raw iron. Working initially in binary, and using Boolean logic at the microcode level, an instruction set is built. An assembler language is then developed to execute the microcode. Given an assembler, the operating system can be coded at a reasonably high level. Once all the code has been written, it is stored on diskette or (more likely) on a hard disk—the master pack. Numerous copies of this master pack can then be made.

When a customer purchases the operating system, the master is copied to cassette, tape, diskette, or another magnetic medium. Perhaps a selective copy is made, with only certain features being transmitted to the customer, but the key point is still that of copying the master pack. This process is known as *system generation* or *SYSGEN*. Once the customer has a copy of the operating system, the copy can be loaded onto his or her system diskette drive. It is now available to the customer's computer.

Initial Program Loading— Cold Start

Operating system modules on diskette do little good; the logic must be copied into main memory before it can be used. The process of copying the operating system from the system diskette into main memory is called *initial program load (IPL)*, or *cold start*.

How is the operating system read into main memory? Remember that the operating system software, before cold start, exists as a series of bits on disk. The input/output control system is part of the operating system; it isn't in main memory yet, so we can't use the facilities of IOCS to help read the operating system. We are literally starting from scratch.

The process of IPL or cold start normally involves *bootstrapping*. Basically, a tiny kernel of the operating system is read into memory under direct operator control; this kernel is sometimes called a *boot*. The boot contains a small amount of program logic—just enough to read a sector or two from the system disk drive. This new information, in turn, contains the logic needed to read in the rest of the resident operating system, and begin communications with the operator. A small module brings in a larger module, which brings in a still larger module, and so on; the system is literally "pulled in by its bootstraps."

For example, imagine the operator's control panel pictured in Fig. 12.3. The control panel contains eight switches, a bank of eight lights, dials, and a few push buttons. The dials allow the operator to address a specific main memory location when the computer is stopped; by setting the dials, the programmer can select an address and display the contents of that address in the bank of lights. The switches allow the operator to change the contents of that memory word; a switch in the up position might represent a 1-bit, while a switch in the down position might be a 0.

The boot program in this elementary example is written in pure binary, and consists of perhaps ten words. In order to cold start the machine, the operator must follow a very precise initial-program-loading procedure. First, the dial is set at memory location 000. Next, the eight switches are set to match the first eight bits in the boot program. A button is pushed, and the eight bits in main memory word 000 are changed to match the switch settings. Looking at the bank of lights, the operator can visually verify the contents of the first word before moving on.

The first word of the boot program is now in memory. The operator resets the dials to 001, the address of the second word. The switches are set to match the second word in the boot, a button is pushed, and the second word is stored in main memory. This process continues, bit by bit and word by word, until the entire boot is entered. Once the boot is in, the operator resets the address dials to 000, and pushes the start button. The boot begins to execute, reading the

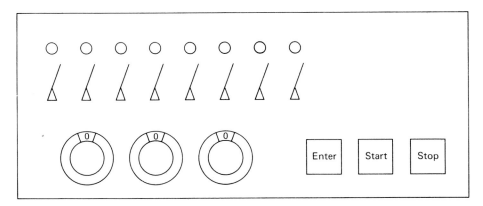

Fig. 12.3
A microprocessor control panel.

kernel of the operating system from the system pack. The kernel, in turn, reads the rest of the operating system. Now, the operator can communicate with the system through the command language.

This cold start example is very primitive; the process is much easier on most modern computers. Often, the boot is stored on the first sector or two of the system pack. A special hardware module is designed to read these first few sectors when a button is pushed (often when the computer is turned on). Once the boot is in, the step-by-step building of the operating system in core can proceed, without direct operator intervention.

On many computers, the boot is stored on a read-only memory (ROM) chip inside the computer. When the IPL button is pushed or the system is turned on, the contents of this ROM chip are simply copied into main memory, and the boot begins to execute. It is a fairly inexpensive way to make the system easier to use, and that is a key objective on a micro.

Warm Start

A cold start occurs when the machine is first turned on; main memory contains nothing but garbage, so we must start from the very beginning. Ideally, a cold start is done only once a day, but a restart (re-IPL) may be necessary if the system encounters problems. A sure sign of system problems is a need for frequent cold starts.

Not all errors are so serious as to cause us to go all the way back to the beginning. Often, much of the operating system will be unaffected, with at least the kernel still intact. *Warm start* procedures allow the operator to bring the machine back "up" by starting the IPL at a point well after the boot is introduced. In the event of minor errors, a warm start saves time.

An Example— CP/M

One of the most popular of the microcomputer operating systems is *CP/M,* the control program for microprocessors, developed by Digital Research, Pacific Grove, California. CP/M is designed to run on a popular 8-bit microprocessor, the Intel 8080; it can also run on a Zilog Z-80. A minimum of 16K words of main memory is required. A typical system will have about 48K of RAM, a console, a printer, and two diskettes; a maximum of four diskette drives can be supported.

Under CP/M, main memory space is divided into five regions (Fig. 12.4). Beginning at memory location 0000 (low core) are the *System Parameters,* the

**Fig. 12.4
CP/M Operating
System Geography.**

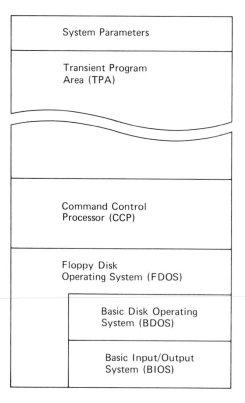

Command	Purpose
DIR	Displays a directory of all the files on a given diskette.
ERA	Erases a specified file on a specified diskette.
REN	Renames a file.
TYPE	Displays the contents of a specified file on the console.
SAVE	Stores the contents of the transient program area on a specified diskette under a specified name.
X:	Log-on a disk drive. With two or more drives on a system, the drives are identified as A, B, C, and (at most) D. The command B: would log-on drive B.

Fig. 12.5
CP/M resident commands.

control constants and variables required by the operating system. Next comes the *Transient Program Area* (the TPA), which holds the application programs; the TPA is the largest region of memory. Following the TPA is the *Console Command Processor* (the CCP), a module that contains the logic to respond to operator commands. BDOS is the *Basic Disk Operating System*; BIOS is the *Basic Input Output System*; together, these two components form the *Floppy Disk Operating System* (FDOS).

The Command Control Processor is the basic control module of a CP/M system. It accepts and interprets operator commands. Through the commands, the operator can tell the CCP to load and execute a program, create a file, and perform a variety of other functions. Some of the commands are *resident* (Fig. 12.5); in other words, they are kept within the CCP in main memory. Other commands are *transient* (Fig. 12.6). They are stored on diskette and, under control of the command control processor, are read into the transient program area on demand. The SAVE function is a good example of a resident routine. It copies the contents of the transient program area to a specific diskette drive. If the SAVE routine were transient, it would be read and stored in the transient program area, thus destroying the logic or data that it is expected to save. Can you see why this module must be resident?

The floppy disk operating system, FDOS, controls access to the input and output devices. The basic disk operating system (BDOS) portion of FDOS contains the primitive commands needed to access the disk drives; the command control processor or a transient program must call BDOS whenever disk access is required. The basic input/output system (BIOS) performs the same functions for the other I/O devices—the console, the printer, and so on. On a CP/M system, BDOS and BIOS, contain the instructions needed to translate logical I/O requests to physical I/O requests.

Command	Purpose	Command	Purpose
ASM	Assemble a program	DDT	Load dynamic debug routine
DUMP	Display file in hex	ED	Load and start editor
LOAD	Create executable pgm	STAT	Display diskette status
SYSGEN	Copy CP/M	BASCOM	Run Microsoft BASIC compiler

Fig. 12.6
Selected CP/M transient commands.

One of the key features of CP/M is a very easy-to-use data management scheme implemented as part of BDOS. The user simply provides a name for a file. CP/M, in turn, allocates space to the file and maintains an index. The file can subsequently be retrieved by name.

The rule for defining a file name is simple—use from one to eight characters. It is recommended that you stay with uppercase characters (capital letters). Different files can be used to hold different kinds of information—data, source statements, object modules, and load modules, for example. To clearly identify the function of a given file, CP/M allows the user to extend the file name with a three-character suffix

    filename.EXT

For example, the source statements going into an assembler program might be stored on

    MYPGM.ASM

while the object module for this program might be

    MYPGM.HEX

A list of some of the more commonly used file name extensions is shown in Fig. 12.7. Some programs *require* that a particular suffix be used; for example, input to the assembler must come from a ".ASM" file, while input to the loader must be from filename .HEX. The user is not limited to the standard extensions. For example, many programmers use .001 to identify a first version of a program, .002 for the second version, and so on.

How would a programmer go about running an assemble/link edit/execute sequence under CP/M? Let's follow the process, step by step (Fig. 12.8). As we begin, diskette drive A is the active device; in other words, unless the program-

Extension	Meaning
.ASM	Assembly language source file.
.BAK	Backup file.
.BAS	BASIC source file.
.COB	COBOL source file.
.COM	Load module (Command file).
.DAT	Data file.
.HEX	Object module (Hexadecimal file).
.PRN	Assembly language listing file.
.TXT	Text file.
.$$$	Temporary file.

Fig. 12.7 Commonly used CP/M file name extensions.

mer specifies otherwise, all input files will be read from diskette A, and all output files will go to diskette A.

The first step is to enter the source code. This is done under control of the CP/M text editor program. The system prompt, A>, is a request by the command control processor for the operator/programmer to enter a command; the A preceding the actual prompt is simply a reminder that the active diskette is on drive A. The command to load and execute the text editor is ED. The second part of the command tells the system to store the source code on diskette A (by implication, since A is the active device) under the file name MYPGM.ASM. Once the code is entered, the programmer may want to verify it visually. This can be done by entering a TYPE command referencing MYPGM.ASM; the TYPE command causes the contents of the specified file to be displayed on the system console. Errors can be corrected by issuing another ED command and modifying the source code.

Eventually, the programmer will be satisfied with the source code and will want to assemble it. An ASM command causes the Intel 8080 assembler program to be loaded and executed; the source module comes from the file named MYPGM.ASM in this example (Fig. 12.8, again). Note that the assembler might have been run right after the source code was entered, or run some time later. MYPGM.ASM is, in effect, a source statement library file. It is on diskette, and thus can be accessed at any time.

The assembler produces two output files, an object module named (in our example) MYPGM.HEX and an assembler listing named MYPGM.PRN, a print file; the file name is chosen by the programmer, while the extension (.ASM, .HEX, .PRN) is fixed by the system. To display the assembler listing, the programmer enters another TYPE command (Fig. 12.8). To correct errors, it's back to the editor program.

Command	Meaning
	As we begin, diskette drive A has been logged-on as the active device.
A>ED MYPGM.ASM	The "A>" is a system prompt, with A identified as the active diskette. The ED command brings in the text editor and gives it control. Edited source statements will be stored on drive A under the name MYPGM.ASM.
A>TYPE MYPGM.ASM	Display the source code on the console for visual verification.
A>ASM MYPGM.ASM	Load and execute the Intel 8080 assembler using MYPGM.ASM as the source file. Two outputs are produced: an object module named MYPGM.HEX and a listing named MYPGM.PRN.
A>TYPE MYPGM.PRN	Display the assembler listing on the console. At this point, the programmer may want to return to the editor to make corrections.
A>LOAD MYPGM.HEX	Link edit the object (HEX) code. The output, a load module, goes to a file named MYPGM.COM, which contains commands.
A>MYPGM	Load and execute the load module, MYPGM.COM, from diskette A.

Fig. 12.8
The compile/link edit/execute sequence
under CP/M.

Finally, a clean compilation is obtained, and it's time to test the program. First, a load module must be generated from the object level .HEX (for hexadecimal) code; this is done through the LOAD command. The output load module is written to drive A and stored under the name MYPGM.COM (for command). Once a load module has been stored, the program can be loaded and executed by simply entering the file name as though it were a command (Fig. 12.8).

Look beyond the commands, and try to picture what is happening under CP/M. Following initial program load or cold start, the console command processor gets control, displays a prompt, and waits for a command. The operator enters a command, the CCP interprets it, and either gives control to a resident function or brings in and gives control to a transient function. The operator is now communicating with the lower-level function—the text editor or an application program, for example. Eventually, the lower-level function completes its processing; in BASIC, for example, an END statement is encountered. The result is a branch back to the command control processor, which displays a prompt and waits for the next user command.

The system is *command driven*. The pace is controlled by the operator. Each discrete step in the process requires a discrete command. There are extensions to CP/M that allow a series of commands to be entered ahead of time and then executed in something like a job stream approach, but this is an added feature that is not available under the standard version of the operating system. In CP/M's normal, microcomputer system environment, this approach makes a great deal of sense.

CP/M contains a cold start loader program stored on the first few sectors of the system pack. As the system is "brought up," this cold start loader is read into memory. It, in turn, reads the rest of the CP/M resident modules from diskette, and gives control to the console command processor.

Another interesting feature of CP/M is a transient module called SYSGEN. When the SYSGEN command is issued, the contents of CP/M on the master pack are copied to another diskette, thus providing a backup copy. Unfortunately, SYSGEN can also be used to generate a "pirate" copy of CP/M. Copying an operating system (or any software, for that matter) to avoid paying normal lease or use fees is illegal; it violates either the copyright laws or any of a number of privacy laws. It is a difficult crime to detect, however, and software piracy is a *major* problem of the computer industry.

CP/M has become an industry standard. Many microcomputer suppliers, under license from Digital Research, sell a version of CP/M as the primary operating system for their computers. Other manufacturers have developed their own operating systems using CP/M as a model. A great deal of commercially available software—application programs, games, and utilities, for example—has been written to run under CP/M. As we shall see, CP/M provides an excellent base for starting our analysis of larger operating systems as well.

Summary ————————————————————————————————

An operating system provides an interface between the computer's hardware and its software. A key objective is to make this interface efficient; the value of an operating system is a function of how well it manages the system resources. Several measures of efficiency can be used, and they are often in conflict with each other. An operating system can be termed "good" to the extent that it manages system resources within the constraints imposed by the system and according to the measures of effectiveness that are relevant within a particular installation. Before studying a given operating system, it is a good idea to define the hardware environment and the application mix (which, in turn, defines the system's measures of effectiveness).

We then turned our attention to a typical microcomputer system. The environment and application mix were described. Against this background, the key elements of a microcomputer operating system were defined and placed in the context of a system geography. In the resident portion of the operating system we placed a command processor and an input/output control system. Other operating system modules were seen to be transient. The system generation process was described, and initial program load (IPL) or cold start was illustrated through an example.

CP/M was then introduced as an example of a microcomputer operating system. We traced its geography, identifying the console command processor (CCP), the Basic Disk Operating System (BDOS), the Basic Input Output System (BIOS), the Floppy Disk Operating System (FDOS), and the Transient Program Area (TPA). The difference between resident and transient commands was explained through an example. We discussed CP/M data management; in particular, the idea of named files. A specific example of the assemble/link edit/execute sequence on CP/M was presented as an illustration of how the microcomputer operating system works; basically, it's a command driven system. The chapter ended with a brief comment on the computer industry's growing problem—software piracy.

Key Words

boot	response time
bootstrapping	system generation
cold start	(SYSGEN)
command processor	throughput
initial program load (IPL)	transient module
input/output control system	transient area
(IOCS)	turnaround
optimum	warm start

Key Words Relevant to CP/M

Basic Disk Operating System (BDOS)

Basic Input/Output System (BIOS)

Console Command Processor (CCP)

Floppy Disk Operating System (FDOS)

System Parameters

Transient Program Area (TPA)

Exercises

1. What (basically) are the functions of an operating system?
2. What does the term optimum mean?
3. Explain how throughput and turnaround objectives can be in conflict.
4. Explain how throughput and response time objectives can be in conflict.
5. Explain how a security requirement can be in conflict with almost every other measure of system effectiveness.
6. "Best" is a relative term. Explain.
7. Discuss some of the constraints that are placed on the designer of an operating system.
8. Why should the student have a reasonable grasp of the hardware environment and an installation's typical application mix before evaluating an operating system?
9. Describe the environment and application mix of a typical microcomputer system. Are these assumptions reasonable? Why or why not?
10. How does the typical microcomputer user measure system effectiveness?
11. Describe the geography of a typical microcomputer operating system. What does each component of the operating system do? Why is each component needed?
12. Distinguish between resident and transient operating system modules.
13. What happens during system generation?
14. What happens during IPL or cold start? When does IPL occur? Why?
15. Describe the geography of CP/M. Explain what each component of the operating system does.
16. What is a command driven system?

13

Multiuser Systems

Overview

In this chapter, we turn our attention to the large multiprogrammed and time-shared computers, concentrating on the operating system logic needed to support multiple, concurrent users. The basic operating systems of Chapter 12 represent our starting point. The key idea is to place several different programs into the transient program area, and let them share the facilities of the CPU. This creates a number of problems. The approach of this chapter is to select several of the more significant problem areas, one at a time, and then to investigate some typical operating system solutions.

Memory allocation and memory management are considered first. Fixed partition systems, dynamic memory management, time-sharing, segmentation, paging, and virtual memory will be discussed. Following memory management, we turn our attention to processor management and the internal priority problem. Both batch-oriented and time-sharing priority schemes will be investigated. I/O device allocation comes next; once again, multiprogramming and time-shared device allocation techniques will be covered. Finally, we'll consider the problems associated with scheduling and external priorities.

The chapter ends with a brief discussion of the various structures that might be used to link the elements of an operating system.

Multiprogramming and Time-Sharing

A basic operating system contains several predictable components (Fig. 13.1). There will almost certainly be a console command processor to support system/ operator communication. Most contain an input/output control system (IOCS) to simplify communication with the peripheral devices. Many contain librarian or data management functions in a logical input/output control system (LIOCS) that allows the user to create, access, and modify files without paying attention to the physical details of disk storage. Because an operating system is a collection of program modules, there must be space set aside for control fields, constants, variables, tables, and the like; thus a parameters area is usually included. Finally, transient modules and application programs need space in which to execute, so the balance of main memory is set aside as a transient

Fig. 13.1
The components of a basic operating system.

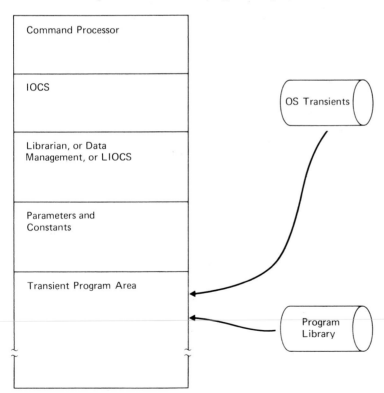

program area. Different systems organize these functions in different ways, but the basic functions are almost always present.

On a larger computer, it is often necessary to support concurrently a number of different users. Rather than placing a single application program into the transient program area, it is possible to subdivide this area of memory and load several programs. With a number of programs in memory, the CPU can switch its attention from one to another, thus sharing the processor's resources. Clearly, we are going to attempt such a multiple-user mode of operation only on a large computer with significant main memory space, a number of I/O devices, and (almost certainly) I/O channels.

Introducing a number of programs into main memory does create several new problems. Although we are discussing a large computer system, the resources are still limited. When multiple programs compete for limited resources, conflicts are bound to occur. Some of the key problems are concerned with memory management (allocating main memory space), processor management (allocating the processor's time), I/O device allocation, and program scheduling. We'll consider each of these problems one at a time, and investigate some common operating system solutions.

Before we begin, however, we should consider the typical application mix to be run on these large computer systems. One classification might be the large, general business system. The primary application is probably the generation of regular business reports, although many other types of applications might be supported as well. A typical program will be large, will process a great deal of data, and will be I/O bound—payroll, accounts receivable, accounts payable, and the ledger are good examples. A variety of front-end devices will be used to provide source data, but most of the input and output will involve high-speed secondary storage devices such as magnetic tape or disk. The key measures of effectiveness on such a system will probably be throughput and turnaround time; other measures are, of course, important, but the designer of an operating system for this environment will tend to favor these two.

As an alternative, consider a large time-shared system. On a general business system, programs are written to process a file, reading record after record from a predefined batch. A time-sharing system is different. Time-shared applications tend to be less predefined and more conversational or reactive. Users enter *transactions,* single lines or single screens; the system's response to transaction A often suggests transaction B. The programs are usually small, processing relatively little data. As in multiprogramming, a time-shared system must support a number of concurrent users, but these users are communicating with the system over slow, manually operated keyboard terminals. Small programs, slow I/O, relatively little data, and an inability to anticipate the next program cycle (due to the transaction nature of the typical application) make time-sharing very different from general business applications. The logical control structure of a time-sharing operating system will be very different from the structure of a general operating system. As we consider the problems of a multiuser system, both multiprogramming and time-sharing solutions will be discussed in detail.

Memory Allocation and Memory Management

If several programs are to occupy main memory at the same time, there must be a mechanism for allocating space to those programs. A number of different techniques can be used. Some involve allocating space before it is actually needed; other techniques are more dynamic.

Multiprogramming: Fixed-Partition Memory Management

One approach is to divide the transient program area into fixed-length *partitions* at either SYSGEN or IPL time (Fig. 13.2). Each of these partitions might be a different length. The key point is that once a partition size is set, it can't

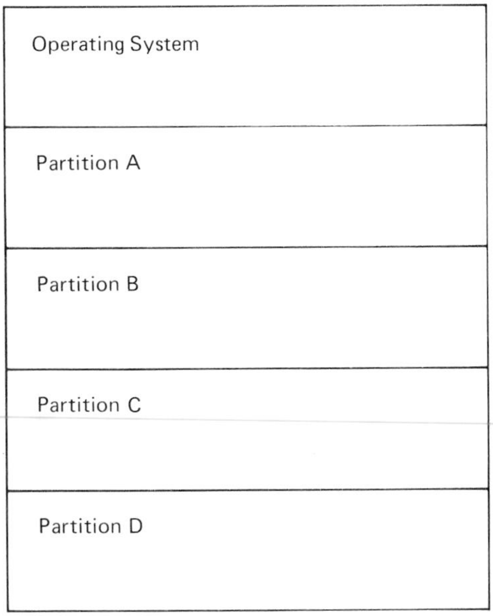

Fig. 13.2 Fixed partition memory management.

| Operating System |
| Partition A |
| Partition B |
| Partition C |
| Partition D |

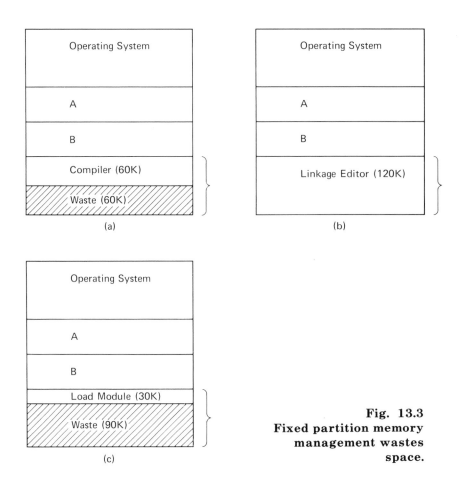

**Fig. 13.3
Fixed partition memory
management wastes
space.**

be changed without stopping the machine and repeating the initial program load (or at least warm start) procedures.

Fixed-partition memory management involves making the memory allocation decision before the fact—in other words, before the actual amount of space needed to load a specific program is known. It is a relatively simple technique. *Memory protection,* another key element of memory management, is a function of the fixed partition organization; if the program in partition A attempts to modify the contents of partition B, a protection exception occurs, and the offending program is usually cancelled.

Fixed-partition memory management is a good choice if the installation's job mix is well known and fairly consistent; ideally, if every program were exactly the same size, fixed-partition memory management would be the perfect approach. This rarely happens, however. Most of the time, fixed-partition memory management wastes space.

Consider, for example, the assemble/link edit/execute sequence. Three different programs are involved: the assembler, the linkage editor, and a load module. A typical assembler program might need 60K of main memory. The linkage editor might need 120K. It is quite possible that the load module, the application program, will be small, needing perhaps 30K of memory. If the entire compile/link edit/execute sequence is to be run in a single partition, the partition must be large enough to hold the biggest program—a 30K program can run in 120K, but a 120K program cannot run in 30K of memory. Thus the partition size would have to be *at least* 120K.

During compilation (Fig. 13.3), fully half the partition space would be unused. During the link edit step, the entire partition would be needed. During execution, 90K of the 120K partition, fully 75 percent of the assigned space, would be wasted. There is simply no way to avoid the problem of waste space on a fixed-partition system.

The key advantage of fixed-partition memory management is its simplicity. Partitions are set by intializing address constants at SYSGEN or IPL time; the operating system's memory management logic (Fig. 13.4) would consist of a very limited amount of executable code and a few tables. Memory protection would also be very easy. The memory tables would certainly contain the start

Fig. 13.4
Memory management and memory protection
modules are added to the operating system.

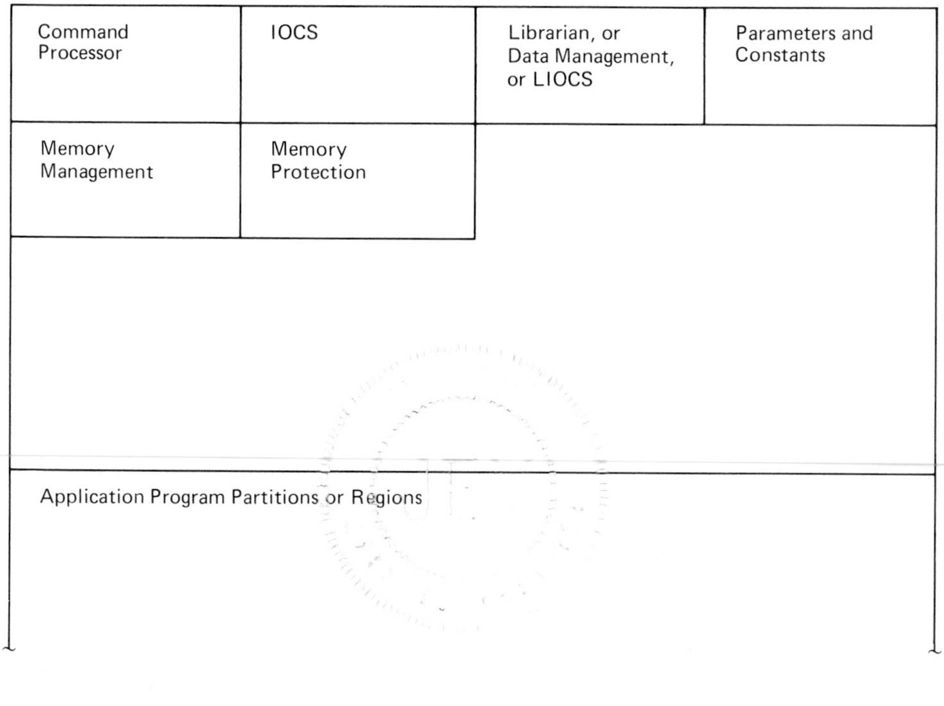

Command Processor	IOCS	Librarian, or Data Management, or LIOCS	Parameters and Constants
Memory Management	Memory Protection		
Application Program Partitions or Regions			

and end addresses of each partition, thus defining a range of legal references. Anything outside this range would be a protection exception. Several examples of fixed partition operating systems are in common use today, including IBM DOS, IBM OS/MFT, and other systems provided by a variety of suppliers.

Multiprogramming: Dynamic Memory Management

Fixed-partition memory management wastes space simply because the partition size is set ahead of time and must reflect the largest program that might be loaded and executed. Under *dynamic memory management,* space is allocated to a program as that program is being loaded. Such systems treat the transient program area as unstructured free space. When the system decides that a particular program is to be loaded, a *region* of memory just sufficient to hold the program is allocated from the pool of free space. Dynamic memory management implies that space is allocated in *real-time,* in response to specific program needs. Because the space allocation is customized to the program, very little space is wasted (Fig. 13.5)—the 60K assembler gets 60K, and the space that would have been wasted under a fixed-partition system is available for another program. Thus one or two more programs might be loaded into the same main memory space. With more programs in main memory, more of the CPU's time can be utilized. (See the discussion of multiprogramming in Chapter 6.)

Dynamic memory management is more complex than fixed-partition memory management. Making decisions and searching a table requires more code than simply initializing a few constants; thus the memory allocation operating system module will be larger. The tables themselves will be more complex. Memory protection could still be based on the memory allocation scheme, but it too would be more complex. Thus it follows that a dynamic memory operating system will be bigger, more complex, and require more memory space than a fixed-partition operating system. Except on a relatively small system, the benefits gained from dynamic memory management probably outweigh the costs, but there are costs. Perhaps the best known of the dynamic memory management operating systems is IBM OS/MVT (for *m*ultiprogramming *w*ith a *v*ariable number of *t*asks); many other manufacturers supply a similar product.

Dynamic memory management does not, however, completely solve the "wasted space" problem. Assume, for example, that one of the regions of memory has just held a 120K program. As that program terminates, there are no 120K programs available. Perhaps the system can load a 60K assembler into some of the space. A 50K application program might be loaded as well, but we

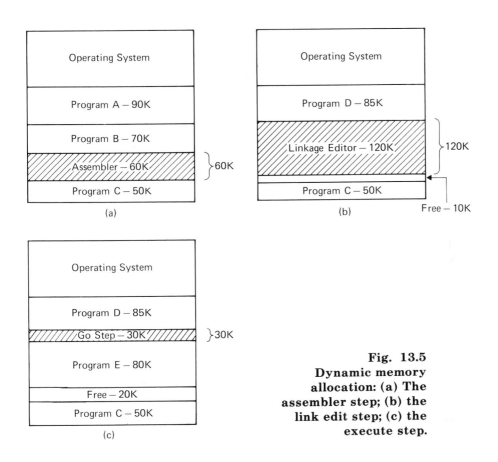

Fig. 13.5
Dynamic memory
allocation: (a) The
assembler step; (b) the
link edit step; (c) the
execute step.

still have 10K unallocated. If there are no 10K or smaller programs on the system, the space will simply not be used (Fig. 13.6). Over a period of time, this situation is going to occur again and again until, eventually, there are little chunks of unused space spread throughout main memory. The problem is known as *fragmentation*.

The fragmentation problem arises from a rather unobvious aspect of program loading and execution. On most systems, the linkage editor (or its equivalent) is designed to produce load modules that are addressed relative to the beginning of the load module; in other words, the address of an access method might be defined as "so many" bytes away from the main program's entry point. Although the load module itself can be placed anywhere in main memory, it must be loaded into *contiguous* space. The word contiguous means "in physical contact, or adjoining." The need for contiguous loading means that a 100K program must be loaded into 100K consecutive memory locations, with

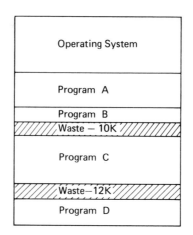

**Fig. 13.6
The fragmentation
problem.**

no other programs intervening. Although the unused fragments of main memory might represent enough to hold a complete program, the fact that they are noncontiguous means that they cannot be used.

If the empty fragments of memory could be compacted into a single, contiguous region, another program could be loaded. This is the basic idea behind *dynamic memory relocation*. Why not simply shift application programs toward the beginning of core to fill in any dead spaces (Fig. 13.7)? The result would be the concentration of the fragments at the end of main memory, thus providing enough space for another program.

Although the idea seems simple, it is very difficult to implement on many computers. For example, registers on an IBM System/360 or System/370 are available for general-purpose use; i.e., a given register can be used for arith-

**Fig. 13.7
Dynamic memory
relocation.**

```
┌─────────────────────────┐
│                         │
│    Operating System     │
│                         │
├─────────────────────────┤
│                         │
│      Program  A         │
│                         │
├─────────────────────────┤
│      Program  B         │
├─────────────────────────┤
│                         │
│      Program  C         │
│                         │
├─────────────────────────┤
│                         │
│      Program  D         │
├─────────────────────────┤
│//////  Free — 22K //////│
└─────────────────────────┘
```

metic at one time and for addressing at another. When a program is relocated, every memory location in the program is shifted by a constant relocation factor (moving a program from core location 152K to core location 148K means subtracting 4K from every address in the program); every register used for addressing must be modified by this factor, but arithmetic registers may *not* be modified (imagine the impact of a decision to subtract 4096 from the contents of a register used as a counter in a statistical analysis program). The problem can be overcome by the imposition of tight register conventions or by restricting the programming department to compiler languages which (normally) store register contents immediately following arithmetic computations. Undoubtedly, there are installations which have done this, but dynamic program relocation is not a standard feature on IBM machines.

Other manufacturers have an easier time of it. Many firms have designed their computers around separate addressing and arithmetic registers, often with only limited programmer access to the addressing registers. Given this hardware design, dynamic program relocation can be achieved by simply incrementing or decrementing the addressing registers. Still, dynamic memory relocation is not commonly used today, simply because other techniques have proven more efficient.

Multiprogramming: Segmentation and Paging

In discussing fragmentation, we mentioned that because the free space is not contiguous (in other words, gathered in one place) we cannot use it. Why not? Why must an entire program be loaded into contiguous memory before it can run? Good question. It doesn't have to be.

As an alternative, a program can be broken into logical segments, locations within each segment can be addressed relative to the start of the segment, and the segments can be loaded into noncontiguous memory locations (Fig. 13.8). No dynamic memory relocation is needed, and we can still take advantage of the small pieces of available memory.

Programmers tend to segment their programs anyway, with key functions viewed as separate problems to be solved and linked together, so *segmentation* makes sense. In a payroll program, for example, one segment might hold the instructions that compute gross pay and prepare a check for output, while the computation of income tax, a fairly complex activity, might be performed in a separate segment.

Closely related to segmentation is the concept of paging. Using this technique, a program is divided into a number of fixed-length pieces called *pages*. The memory locations within a page are addressed relative to the start of the page. Under *paging*, a program can be loaded, page by page, into noncontigu-

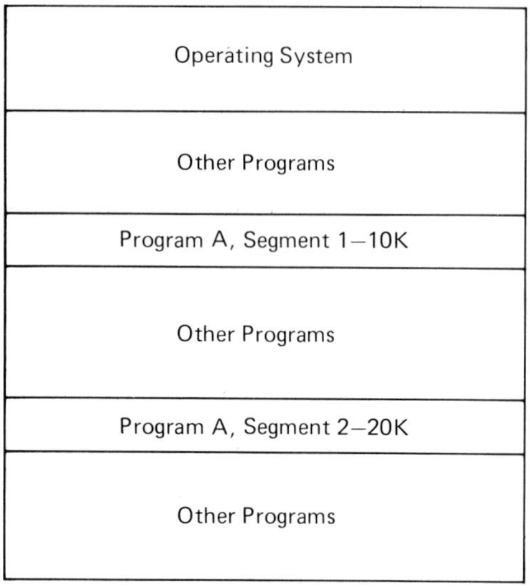

Operating System
Other Programs
Program A, Segment 1—10K
Other Programs
Program A, Segment 2—20K
Other Programs

**Fig. 13.8
Program segmentation.**

ous memory and executed. The basic difference between segmentation and paging is that under segmentation a program is broken into pieces that follow the logic of the program, while under paging a program is divided into fixed-sized pieces with the page size being selected for the computer's convenience. Common page sizes are 2K and 4K.

Note that the programmer does not directly control paging. A page is "so many" memory locations, period. Wherever a page break occurs, it occurs without regard for the logic of the program. Paging is imposed by the compiler or by the operating system. The size of a segment, on the other hand, is variable, and a good programmer can designate where a segment is to begin and end, thus matching the physical loading of a program into memory with the actual logic of that program. This is the essential difference between segmentation and paging.

Under segmentation or paging, the memory management function of the operating system becomes even more complex. Not only do we have to keep track of the dynamic start and end points of a program but we now must control the dynamic locations of the *parts* of a program. The operating system must be bigger, and its logic more complex.

Multiprogramming:
Virtual Memory

Now that we have successfully questioned the need for continguous memory before a program can run, let's ask another question. Why must the entire program be in main memory before execution can begin? You know that a computer, more specifically the central processing unit, can execute only one instruction at a time. Why should it be necessary for the entire program to be present if the computer can execute only one instruction at a time?

It isn't necessary. Under a memory management technique known as *virtual memory,* an entire program is stored on a secondary storage device such as disk or drum. The program is divided into pages or segments and moved into main memory (called *real memory*) a piece at a time.

Consider, for example, the computer system sketched in Fig. 13.9(a). Real memory is large enough to hold four pages. A total of three programs has been loaded into virtual memory, representing four times the available real memory.

As we begin, the first page in program A (page A-0) is copied into real memory page 0 and starts to execute. Soon it requests an I/O operation and drops into a wait state; thus the first page in program B (page B-0) can be loaded into real page 1 and started. In this way, we'll eventually reach the point illustrated in Fig. 13.9(b), with all four real pages filled.

Let's assume that we are executing instructions on page A-1 (Fig. 13.9b). We reach a break point. Program B would like to take over, but its next instructions are on page B-1, which has not yet been copied into real memory. The CPU cannot access instructions residing on virtual memory—they must be in real. What should we do?

The answer is really quite simple. Program A has moved on to the instructions on its second page, no longer needing page A-0. Thus we can copy page A-0 back out to virtual memory (Fig. 13.9c), and copy page B-1 into the vacated real page 0 (Fig. 13.9d). Once this has been done, execution can proceed to the instructions on the new page. By swapping pages between virtual and real memory, it is possible to execute many concurrent programs in a very limited amount of space.

The computer's main memory is called real memory. Since the secondary device that holds the major part of the program isn't "real" memory (at least not in this context), we need another name for it. The term used to describe this bulk memory is virtual memory. The word virtual means "being in essence but not in fact." Virtual memory is "in essence" just like real memory, but "in fact" it is not real memory.

The idea of keeping something less than the full program in main memory has been around for quite some time. In the second generation, tight core limitations sometimes forced a programmer to literally write a 16K program on an 8K machine. This could be done only by breaking the program into segments. Through very careful planning, the programmer determined the most crucial 8K of the program and arranged to have this portion in main memory, with the rest of the program remaining on disk. When a need for one of these less-used modules occurred, the module was read into core, overlaying (and thus destroying) a part of the program that was in core. Later, when this new module had finished, the program was restored to its initial condition.

Real Memory

Virtual Memory

0	1
2	3

0 A-0	1 A-1	2 A-2	3 A-3
4 A-4	5 B-0	6 B-1	7 B-2
8 B-3	9 B-4	10 B-5	11 B-6
12 C-0	13 C-1	14 C-2	15 C-3

(a)

Real Memory

Virtual Memory

0 A-0	1 B-0
2 C-0	3 A-1

0 A-0	1 A-1	2 A-2	3 A-3
4 A-4	5 B-0	6 B-1	7 B-2
8 B-3	9 B-4	10 B-5	11 B-6
12 C-0	13 C-1	14 C-2	15 C-3

(b)

Fig. 13.9
A virtual memory system (a) as we begin our
example; (b) as real memory is filled.

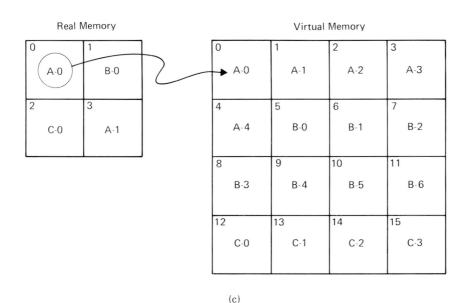

(c)

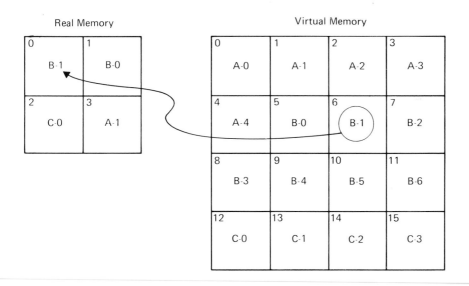

(d)

Fig. 13.9 (cont.)
A virtual memory system (c) as an unneeded
page is copied back to virtual memory; (d) as a
new page is copied from virtual to real memory.

Operating systems incorporating many of the concepts of virtual memory have existed since the mid-1960s. The term "virtual" came into common use in the early 1970s when IBM announced a new series of operating systems incorporating this concept to support their System/370 computers.

What is the advantage of the virtual memory approach? Since only part of any given program must be in main memory at any one time, it is possible to get more different programs into the same amount of main memory. More programs mean greater efficiency, greater throughput.

What is the cost? Because programs are located partly in real memory and partly in virtual memory, keeping track of the location of a program is much more difficult than it is in the simpler operating systems. Thus a virtual operating system is more complex, larger, and more expensive than an operating system designed to keep track of programs stored in contiguous memory. Also it takes time to transfer pages between virtual and real memory.

We'll return to the topic of virtual memory in Chapter 14.

Time-Sharing and Memory Management

The characteristics of a time-sharing environment create several unique memory management problems. Perhaps the best way to visualize these problems is through an example.

Let's assume a rather small time-shared system capable of supporting up to 50 terminals at the same time. Two problems stand out in trying to analyze such a system. First, we are dealing with 50 different users, and our operating system must be capable of keeping track of all 50. Imagine the amount of core needed to support 50 independent programs—a mere 25K per user (a pretty small partition) would mean that we would need 750K of core for programs alone, not counting the operating system! The second key factor is the I/O speed and transaction rate we can expect from each of these users. They are going to be using keyboard terminals, which are slow. If this group of users is at all typical, there will be considerable "head scratching" time. In other words, we might expect 30 seconds, a minute, even more to transpire between a computer-generated message and the human response; on a computer capable of executing over one million instructions per second, that's an awfully long time.

Roll-in/roll-out logic is an obvious fit in such an environment. For starters, let's assign five different users to each of ten 25K partitions (a total of only 250K of core); we'll concentrate on users A through F who are sharing our first partition. User A has control first and, after a brief flurry of activity, finds it necessary to provide additional data and so issues a read instruction. The computer "knows" that it will take user A at best 30 seconds or so to figure out exactly what is needed next, type a response, and send it to the computer; this is more than enough time to roll user A's program out to disk and roll-in user B's program. In fact, the computer is *so* fast that, in all likelihood, all five users will have had a shot at core before the first one is ready with a response—a computer can easily keep up with five human beings working at human speeds.

An even better approach involves relocation of user programs as they come back from disk or drum. Very few time-sharing users are interested in programming at the assembly language level, with most working in BASIC, FORTRAN, APL, Pascal, PL/I or some other compiler language. Few compiler languages use registers as accumulators or counters, thus eliminating one of the major problems of dynamic relocation. The basic idea is simple: When a user is ready to resume processing, the program is rolled into any available partition, and not necessarily into the partition it occupied before. Using this dynamic approach, the possibility of drawing an unlucky "busy" partition would disappear. Assuming that the average user would require the computer for one full second (a pretty long shot of time) between I/O operations, it would be theoretically possible to support up to 30 users in a *single* partition and still be able to respond to each and every user's normal 30-second cycle (we're probably overestimating our user's capabilities here) without any delays. Responses, of course, are not regular (this is a good queueing theory problem), but four or five regions should be more than adequate for our 50-user system.

Processor Management and Internal Priorities

Whenever two or more programs are concurrently sharing the resources of a single CPU, it is inevitable that conflicts over CPU access will occur. The processor can support only one program at any given instant of time. When more than one program is ready to use the CPU, a decision must be made: who goes first? Dealing with this internal priority question is a key element of a multiuser operating system.

Multiprogramming and Processor Management

A common approach on a multiprogramming system is to link the priority decision to the memory allocation scheme. For example, consider a simple fixed-partition system with two application program partitions (Fig. 13.10). One of these partitions can be designated as the *foreground,* while the other is known as the *background.* When the system is ready to give control to an application

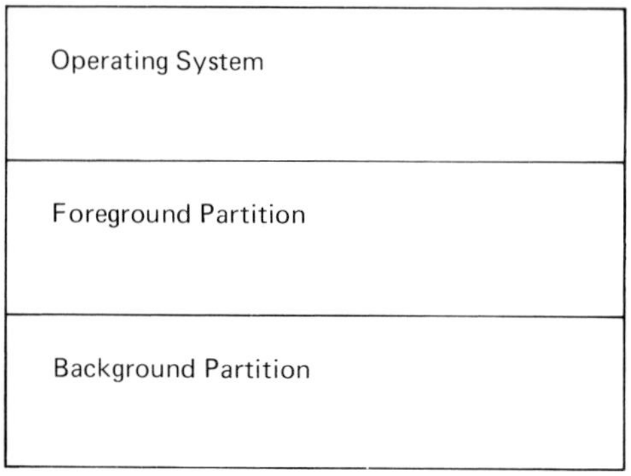

| Operating System |
| Foreground Partition |
| Background Partition |

**Fig. 13.10
Foreground and
background partitions.**

program, it first checks the control fields for the foreground partition. If the foreground program is ready, it gets control; only if the foreground program is still waiting do the control fields for the background partition get checked. The foreground has high priority; the background has low priority.

This basic idea can easily be extended to larger system. With, for example, twelve application program partitions or regions, the *internal priority* module can be written to check partition A first, then partition B, and so on. The first partition checked has highest priority; the last has lowest priority. In fact, the only way the low-priority partition can get control is if *all* the higher-priority partitions are waiting for something.

How might such a priority scheme be implemented? One technique is to link the priority decision to the memory allocation tables described earlier in the chapter. It is necessary to keep track of the starting and ending address of each partition or region. Why not add a field to keep track of the status of the program in that partition? If you view the memory allocation table as an array, the priority decision would be implemented by starting with array element 1, checking the status bits, incrementing the subscript by 1, checking the next element's status bits, and continuing the search until a ready program is found.

Actually, there are a number of control fields that must be maintained in support of each main memory partition. Often, a single *control block* is created to hold these flags, constants, and variables (Fig. 13.11), with one control block for each partition (or region). A common approach is to maintain, in the system parameters region, a pointer to the high-priority partition's control block. The first control block points, in turn, to the second, which points to the third, and so on (Fig. 13.11, again). The priority module determines which program is to be given control by following this chain until a ready program is located. As you can see, under such a system, the priority of a program is fixed by its partition or region assignment.

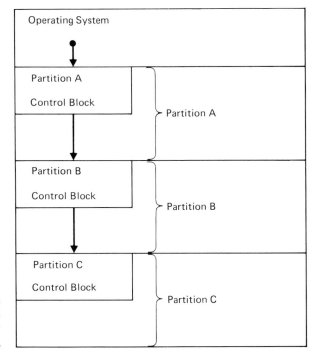

Fig. 13.11
Often, each partition
or region has a control
block to hold key
control information.

It is, of course, possible to implement more complex priority schemes. On some systems, for example, rather than always beginning the priority search with the same partition control block, the priority routine, often called the *scheduler* or *dispatcher,* can be designed to resume its search where it left off—this would tend to give all partitions roughly equal priority. Another alternative is to assign each program a priority through the command language, with this priority determining the order in which the control blocks are searched. Such factors as program size, time in memory, I/O device requirements, and other measures of the program's impact on system resources can be used to *compute* dynamically an internal priority, thus determining the search order. The more complex the scheduling algorithm, however, the more complex the scheduler operating system module (Fig. 13.12).

Interrupts and the
Flow of Control

Throughout our discussion of the internal priority problem, we've been making an implicit assumption. The operating system, more particularly, the scheduler

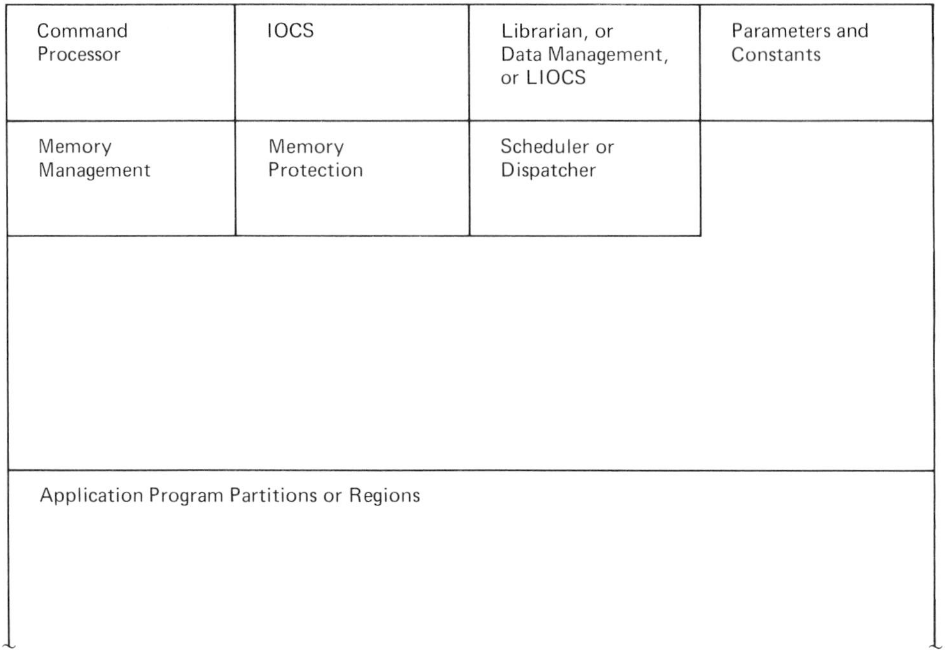

Command Processor	IOCS	Librarian, or Data Management, or LIOCS	Parameters and Constants
Memory Management	Memory Protection	Scheduler or Dispatcher	
Application Program Partitions or Regions			

Fig. 13.12
Another key operating system component is the
scheduler or dispatcher.

"decides" in some way that the time has come to give control to an application program. How does the scheduler know that "it's time"? There must be some mechanism, some signal, that alerts the operating system to a need to transfer control of the processor to some other program. On many multiprogramming systems, that mechanism is the *interrupt*.

What is an interrupt? Basically, it is an electronic signal to the CPU. For example, when a channel senses that an I/O operation is complete, it signals the CPU by sending an interrupt. In response, the CPU stops what it is doing, transfers control to the interrupt handling logic, and (later) resumes what it was doing at the time of the interrupt.

The external channel is not the only possible source of interrupts: programs can generate them too. On many systems, the instructions that actually start an I/O operation are made *privileged*; in other words, they can be executed only by the operating system. Whenever an application program wants to start an I/O operation, it must transfer control to the operating system. A simple branch would violate the memory protection rules—you can't branch to a location outside your own partition. By generating an interrupt signal, however,

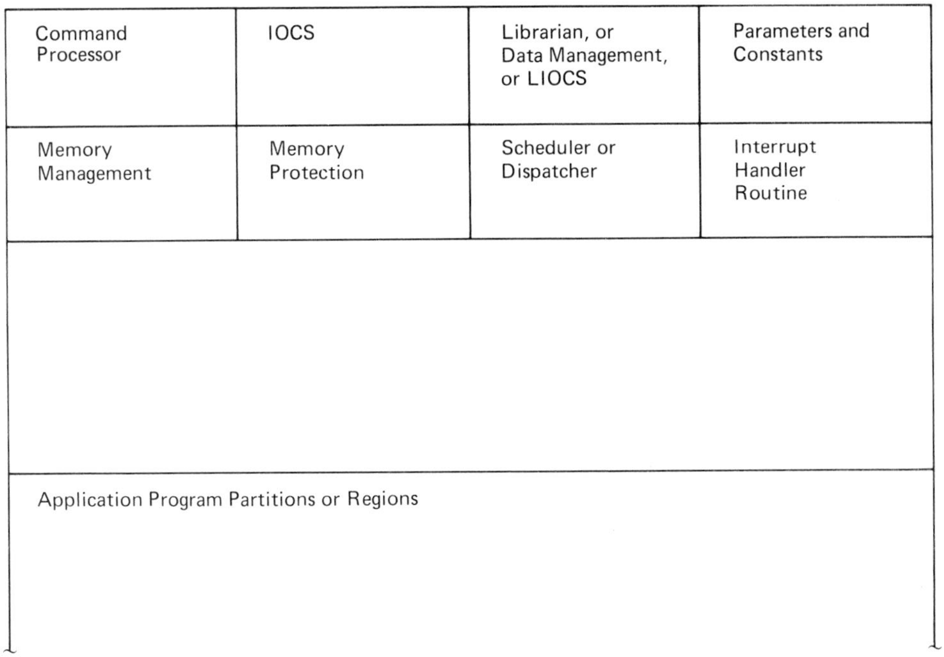

Command Processor	IOCS	Librarian, or Data Management, or LIOCS	Parameters and Constants
Memory Management	Memory Protection	Scheduler or Dispatcher	Interrupt Handler Routine
Application Program Partitions or Regions			

Fig. 13.13
The interrupt handler routine is another
important operating system module.

the program can achieve a hardware branch directly to a specified location in the operating system.

Once the I/O operation has been started, the program that requested it can be placed in a *wait state* by the operating system's interrupt handler routine (Fig. 13.13). Control can then be passed to the scheduler, and another program can be given control of the CPU. Later, the I/O interrupt coming from the channel serves to signal the operating system that it is time to remove the program from a wait state, and place it in a *ready state.*

Perhaps an example would help to illustrate this concept. Assume that our system is as pictured in Fig. 13.14(a). We are concerned only with the operating system and the first two program partitions, A and B. Each partition has a control block, and in that control block is a "state" bit: 0 means ready, and 1 means wait. As we begin, both programs A and B are in a ready state, and the scheduler has control.

The scheduler begins by checking the control block for partition A. It's ready, so partition A gets control (Fig. 13.14b). Eventually, the program in partition A requires input data, and issues an interrupt; the operating system's

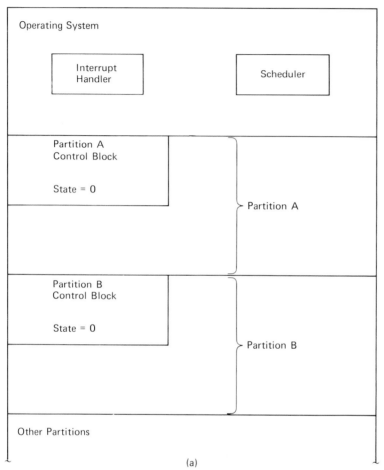

Fig. 13.14
Interrupt and program states. (a) As we begin,
programs A and B are both ready.

interrupt handler logic is now in control (Fig. 13.14c). The I/O operation is started, program A is placed in a wait state, and the scheduler is given control. It begins by checking the control block for partition A. The program is in a wait state, so control block B is checked. It's ready, so program B gets control (Fig. 13.14d).

Eventually, B will need input data, and issue an interrupt. The interrupt handler will start the I/O operation, place B in a wait state (Fig. 13.14e) and give control to the scheduler. The scheduler will find A in a wait state, B in a wait state, and move on to program C.

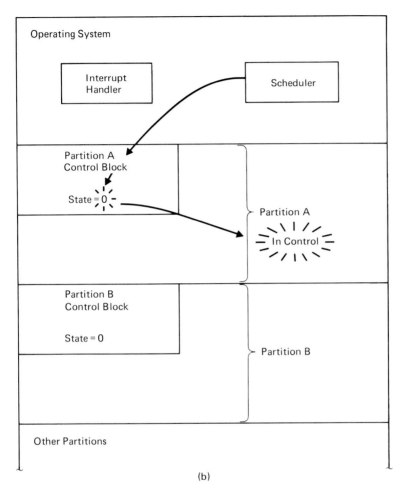

(b)

Fig. 13.14
(b) Program A gets control first.

It is only a matter of time, milliseconds probably, before the I/O operation started for program A is finished. When this happens, the channel sends an interrupt to the CPU. Let's assume that as the interrupt arrives, the CPU is executing instructions in program E. When the interrupt occurs, control is given, through hardware, to the interrupt handler routine in the operating system. This module saves status information for program E, and then turns its attention to the interrupt. The I/O operation for A is finished, so the state bit for control block A is reset to a ready condition (Fig. 13.14f); control is then given to the scheduler. Following its normal pattern, the scheduler searches the con-

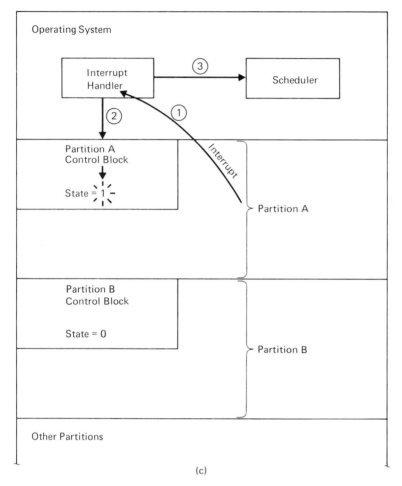

Fig. 13.14
(c) Program A issues an interrupt.

trol block chain, starting with the high-priority partition, A. Because program A is ready, it gets control.

Basically, that's how the internal priority scheme works. A program is given control until it needs input or output support. At this time it must surrender control to the operating system, which places the program in a wait state and gives control to a different program. When the I/O operation is completed, the channel signals the CPU through another interrupt; in response, the interrupt handler routine places the program in a ready state, making it eligible for another crack at the processor. The specific algorithm used to determine "who

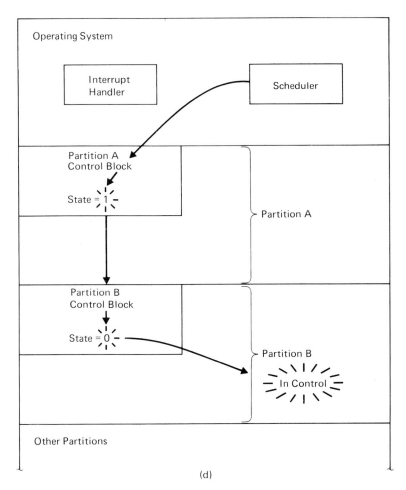

Fig. 13.14
(d) The scheduler gives control to program B.

goes first" can vary significantly from system to system, but the basic control structure remains fairly constant. Such systems are said to be *interrupt driven*.

Let's return to an earlier question: what is an interrupt? We should be able to define the term more clearly now. First, an interrupt is an *electronic signal*. Electronic signals are handled by *hardware*, so an interrupt is really a hardware concept. In effect, the interrupt is an electronic branch instruction that always transfers control to the interrupt handler routine. Be careful to distinguish between the interrupt itself (the electronic signal) and the logic that handles the interrupt; it's much like the difference between a CALL instruction and the subroutine it calls.

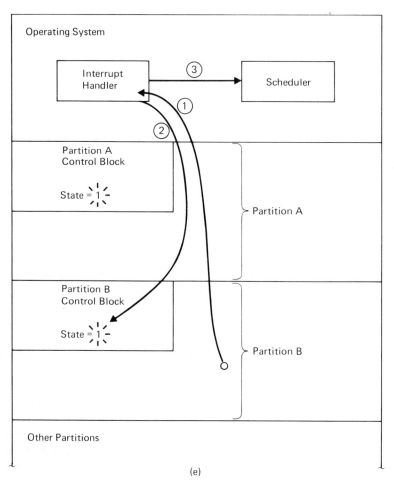

Operating System

Interrupt Handler   ③   Scheduler

①
②

Partition A Control Block

State = 1

Partition A

Partition B Control Block

State = 1

Partition B

Other Partitions

(e)

Fig. 13.14
(e) Program B drops into a wait state.

When an interrupt occurs, the CPU stops what it is doing, and is forced to turn its attention to a particular software module, the interrupt handler routine. A second key element to the interrupt concept is the ability to resume processing where we left off. When a programmer calls a subroutine, control will return to the instruction following the CALL after the subroutine logic is executed. Similarly, the system must be able (at some time) to return to the instructions that were executing at the time of the interrupt. Normally, the key control fields of a partition are saved or stored, electronically, when an interrupt occurs. Thus an interrupt can be defined as an electronic signal that

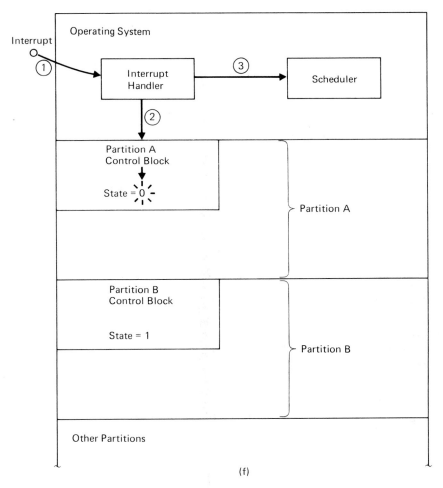

Operating System

Interrupt

① Interrupt Handler ③ Scheduler

②

Partition A Control Block

State = 0

Partition A

Partition B Control Block

State = 1

Partition B

Other Partitions

(f)

Fig. 13.14
(f) Eventually, the channel sends an interrupt.

causes the computer to stop what it is doing, take action, and then (eventually) to resume what it was doing at the time of the interrupt.

We won't get into specific techniques for stacking, queueing, or otherwise handling interrupts just yet; such details will be left for subsequent chapters. The important idea at this stage is the interrupt *concept*. You should be able to visualize an electronic signal like an interrupt as a mechanism for causing a computer to change directions, or to shift control from partition to partition. The interrupt, please note, is merely a signal that the time has come to change; considerable operating system logic is needed to actually *implement* that change. Distinguish between the interrupt itself and the logic that handles the interrupt.

We have viewed two different kinds of interrupts in this chapter: one coming from within the computer, and the other coming from outside. Most interrupts fall into one of these two general categories, but there are many different sources of interrupt signals. The interrupt structure supported by a given machine is a critical part of its basic architecture and design philosophy; thus it is not surprising to learn that different computers support different types of interrupts. We'll be investigating this problem in Chapter 18. View the material of this chapter as a generalized example of the interrupt concept.

Processor Control and Time-Sharing

Under multiprogramming, a program is given control until it issues an interrupt requesting I/O. (For the moment, we'll ignore the fact that a program can exceed its time limit.) It is possible for a compute-bound job to gain control of the system and force every other program to wait. On a batch-oriented system, this is not really a major problem; placing compute-bound jobs in a background partition is often an acceptable solution. A time-shared system, however, is different. The key measure of time-sharing effectiveness is response time. Given this response time orientation, the idea of forcing all users to wait for one compute-bound job is simply unacceptable.

Note the difference between the multiprogrammed system and the time-shared system because it is important. The multiprogramming system stresses throughput and turnaround as its measures of effectiveness. The compute-bound job certainly helps throughput. A good multiprogramming system will provide reasonable turnaround on all jobs, including that compute-bound job; if every other program has to wait an extra minute or two so that one big program can run, so be it. The time-shared system, on the other hand, stresses response time. If 50 users are currently logged on, the 49 will not be forced to wait so that the one can get good turnaround. Instead, the one will be forced to wait so that the 49 can get good response time.

Time-shared systems are often controlled through a process known as *time slicing*. A program is given a fixed amount of time to access the CPU—perhaps one one-hundredth of a second. If, during this period of time, the program is able to complete its processing and request its next I/O operation, fine; the program is placed in a wait state and another program is given control. If not, the time slice expires, and control is taken from the program and given to another.

Often a technique known as *polling* is used to determine which program gets control. Imagine that information to access all of the programs or regions on a system is stored in an operating system array (Fig. 13.15); such an array is

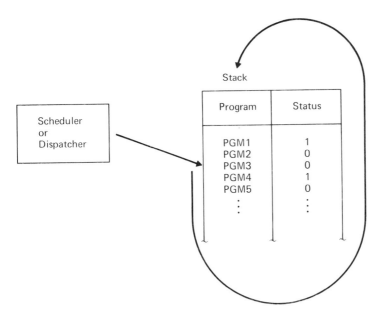

Fig. 13.15
Polling by scanning a stack.

sometimes called a *stack*. The scheduler begins at the top of the stack, checking the status of the program in the first region. Assume that it's in a wait state. The scheduler thus moves on (by simply incrementing a counter) to the control information for the second region. If this program is ready, it gets control. Assume that the program uses its entire time slice. A timer interrupt occurs, the scheduler gets control again, and moves on to the third region's control area. Note that the scheduler has passed the control information for region two; program two is now at the end of the waiting line. Eventually, the scheduler works its way through the entire stack, the stack counter is reset to one, and the process is repeated. Program two will get another shot at the CPU only after every other program on the system has a chance.

   There are a number of variations to this "round robin" polling technique. High-priority programs can be assigned several slots in the stack, thus getting multiple shots at the CPU on each scheduler cycle. Different priority levels can be implemented by using several stacks. On a Hewlett-Packard 3000 system, for example, two different priority levels are recognized. High-priority programs are placed on a primary stack (Fig. 13.16), while low-priority programs are placed on a secondary stack. The secondary, low-priority stack is assigned a single slot on the high-priority stack. The scheduler goes through the primary stack, giving control to the programs in turn. When the slot assigned to the

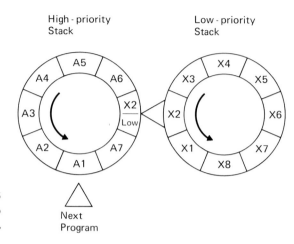

High - priority
Stack

Low - priority
Stack

**Fig. 13.16
Polling with two
priority levels.**

Next
Program

low-priority stack is encountered, the "current" low-priority program is given control, as though it were a regular, high-priority program. When this program finishes, however, the next low-priority program is moved into the primary slot. The scheduler goes all the way through the primary stack before getting to the second low-priority program, and may go through the stack dozens of times before the first-low priority program gets another shot.

Such systems are said to be *poll driven.* A command driven microcomputer operating system reacts or changes states in response to an operator command. An interrupt driven multiprogramming system reacts or changes states in response to an interrupt. A poll driven system reacts to a polling signal. The functions performed by the operating systems are similar; what differs is the control structure of the system software. Basically, the driving mechanism represents the system's main control module. More about this later.

I/O Device
Allocation

Another key resource of any computer system is its I/O devices. The number of peripherals on a system is always limited. If several programs are going to execute concurrently, contention for the limited I/O resources is inevitable. The operating system is normally responsible for this function; thus we can add other modules to our system (Fig. 13.17).

Multiprogramming
and Device Allocation

Multiprogramming operating systems are (for the most part) designed around a batch processing assumption. Batch processing implies significant levels of I/O:

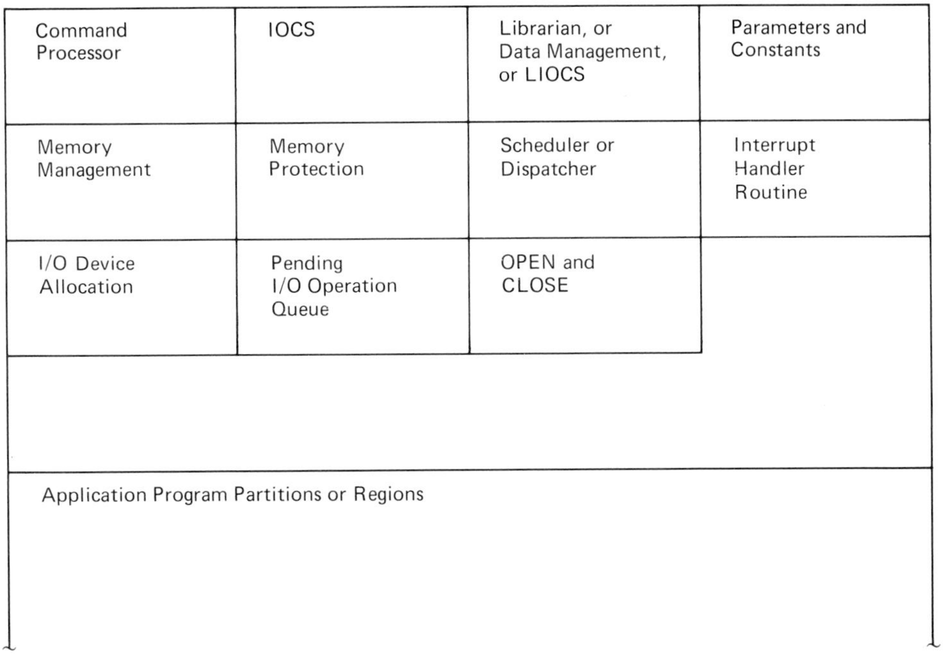

Command Processor	IOCS	Librarian, or Data Management, or LIOCS	Parameters and Constants
Memory Management	Memory Protection	Scheduler or Dispatcher	Interrupt Handler Routine
I/O Device Allocation	Pending I/O Operation Queue	OPEN and CLOSE	
Application Program Partitions or Regions			

Fig. 13.17
Other operating system modules are concerned
with the I/O device allocation decision.

secondary storage will almost certainly be required. The programmer on such a system will probably require a great deal of I/O support, and will probably need flexible access to secondary storage.

On most multiprogramming systems, a table listing all system I/O devices is maintained in the system parameters area. When a program is loaded and given control, it is normally expected to *OPEN* its files before beginning I/O. An OPEN command is really an interrupt; control is given to the operating system which scans its list of I/O devices and allocates available peripherals to the program. Because access to a given device *must* pass through the operating system, controls to make certain that the same device or space is *not* allocated to two different programs can be implemented. A *CLOSE* command, normally coded at the end of a program, frees the device in question so that the operating system can assign it to another program. OPEN and CLOSE logic is normally a part of the resident operating system (Fig. 13.17, again).

What if the requested device is not available? What if, for example, two programs want the same printer? If the printer has already been allocated to program A, then program B must wait. The chances of this problem occurring increase as the number of partitions increases. On many large systems, rather than tying up main memory with programs that cannot run because a requested I/O device is not available, device allocations are made *before* the program is even loaded. The programmer specifies, through a command language or job control language, all needed I/O devices (except, perhaps, for the standard system input and output devices). The operating system checks this list of requirements against its device tables and, if a device is not available, does not even load the program. Better to have the program wait on disk than to allow it to tie up main memory.

Several unique problems occur when dealing with disk. Disk is designed to be shared—multifile volumes are the rule rather than the exception. It is not at all unusual for program A to access one area of a disk, while program B is dealing with the data stored on another.

The system cannot, however, simply allow two or more programs to share a disk drive without controls. Consider, for example, the following "horror story." Program A issues a command to the disk drive to locate the read/write mechanism over cylinder 50. During the time the channel and the I/O control unit are moving the access mechanism, program B gets control and tells the same disk controller to move the access mechanism to cylinder 175. Since B is now waiting for I/O, A gets control once again, and issues a read command. The only problem is that B has moved the read/write mechanism. A, once again, tells the disk controller to move the access mechanism back to cylinder 50, and gives up control. B gets control, issues its read, and discovers that the access mechanism has moved. Try to picture the access mechanism moving back and forth between cylinder 50 and cylinder 175 in response to competing commands, and you'll have a good sense of what can happen.

This can't be allowed. It's a good example of a *deadlock*. More generally, a deadlock occurs when two programs each control a resource needed by the other, and neither is willing to give up that control. Neither can continue until the other "gives in," and neither is willing to give in. One common solution to the problem is prevention: do not allow two programs that access the same disk drive or require the same device support to be loaded at the same time.

It is possible to load two or more programs that access the same disk if a *locking* facility is implemented on the system. When program A requests the start of an I/O operation on a given disk drive, the operating system can "lock" the device. Subsequent requests for I/O against the same device can be postponed until program A is finished. Locking can be achieved by simply setting a switch in the I/O device control table entry for the device. On many systems, more complex track locking or even record locking can be implemented.

With locking, it is possible to have several I/O operations pending against a single device. Where are these "pending" I/O requests kept? More generally, remember that a selector channel operates in burst mode, linking a single device at a time to the computer. For example, if a disk drive and a tape drive are attached to the same selector channel, an active I/O operation in support of the disk means that any I/O against the tape must wait. Once again, we have pending I/O operations. On most operating systems, these pending I/O requests are kept on a queue and issued as a device becomes available (Fig. 13.17, again).

Time-Sharing and
Device Allocation

The time-sharing environment is different from the multiprogramming environment. Most time-sharing users are more-casual programmers. The programs are smaller; less data are processed; fewer I/O devices are needed. Terminal allocation is easy—either there is an available terminal or dial-up port, or there isn't. Users are normally assigned a fixed amount of disk work space; requests for additional space must go through the operations department or the data base administrator. Large output can be spooled to the printer. Basically, that's it. Users who require more support must request such support before the fact, so that extra space or a special device can be allocated. For standard applications, the time-shared system seems much simpler, because device assignments are all made by *default*. Nonstandard applications require special support.

Scheduling and
External Priorities ───────────────────────────────

Most of the problems we've discussed thus far are concerned with supporting the programs *in core*. How do those programs get into main memory to begin with? In the second generation, and on a small system, the operator schedules programs, loading one at a time. Direct operator intervention becomes impossible when a system is concurrently executing dozens of programs; a human operator simply cannot keep up the demand. Scheduling, according to a set of *external priority* rules, is another operating system function.

Scheduling and
Multiprogramming

How can programs be scheduled for execution on a multiprogramming system? One common technique is to set up a series of external queues. Remember the discussion (in Chapter 5) of second generation scheduling techniques? One early system required the programmer to drop a job into one of several baskets. Basket A might be limited to small programs; basket B might be for tape jobs; basket C might hold the multipart paper jobs, and so on. The basic idea was to group jobs with similar support needs so that the operator could schedule them.

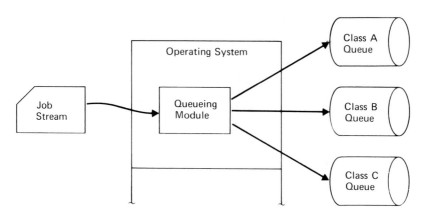

Fig. 13.18
The function of the queueing module.

This discussion led to the concept of a job class and the need for a JOB statement.

We don't use baskets today, but it's still a good analogy. On a modern system, the concept is known as job *queueing*. The programmer's job is first read by a queueing module (Fig. 13.18) and, based on the job class, placed on one of several queues. This is a continuing process; all the queueing module does is read the job stream, separate the individual jobs, and enqueue them. Normally, as a job is read it is placed at the end of its queue. Command language parameters can be used to override this default, allowing a high-priority job to move to the beginning of its class queue.

Meanwhile, the operating system is concurrently supporting a number of programs in main memory. Eventually, one of those programs will terminate (normally or abnormally), and control will go back to the operating system. Sensing that this partition is now available, the scheduler routine will start the process of bringing in another program. Usually, control will be given to yet another operating system module, the *initiator* (Fig. 13.19), which loads the first job from the queue.

If there are several class queues, which one is given priority? Several answers are possible. The various classes can be assigned priorities, with the programs from the high-priority queue being loaded first. Another option is to assign the external queues to specific internal memory partitions or regions. For example, class A programs might be assigned to partition 1, while class B jobs are assigned to partition 2. When partition 1 becomes free, the next program on the class A queue will be loaded.

Often, the initiator is a transient program; it is, after all, needed only during the process of loading a program. When the scheduler encounters a free

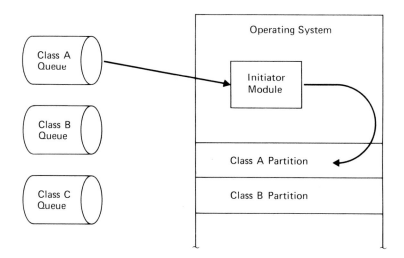

Fig. 13.19
The initiator loads a program from a class queue
into a main memory partition or region.

partition or region, the initiator is read into that partition. When the initiator is in and gets control, it begins the process of reading in the application program, often destroying itself (overlaying itself) in the process; a copy of the initiator still exists on disk, of course, so nothing is lost. Many systems use multiple initiators, one for each partition or region.

The basic idea of job queueing is to first enqueue the jobs to an on-line secondary storage device such as disk, and then to load the programs from the queues. It is a sophisticated form of on-line spooling, with the task of reading the job stream being one more module in a multiprogramming system. The queueing module and the initiator have been added to our functional view of an operating system in Fig. 13.20.

Clearly distinguish between a program's internal priority and its external priority. Once a program is in main memory, its internal priority determines its right to access the CPU. An external priority is concerned with getting the program into main memory in the first place. Until the program is in core, it has no internal priority. Once in memory, its external priority is no longer relevant.

Scheduling and
Time-Sharing

Scheduling is a batch concept. Time-sharing, almost by definition, is an unscheduled form of data processing. A programmer who decides to work on a time-shared system either walks to the computer center or dials the computer's

Command Processor	IOCS	Librarian, or Data Management, or LIOCS	Paramenters and Constants
Memory Management	Memory Protection	Scheduler or Dispatcher	Interrupt Handler Routine
I/O Device Allocation	Pending I/O Operation Queue	OPEN and CLOSE	Queueing Module
Initiator			
Application Program Partitions or Regions			

Fig. 13.20
Many operating systems contain job queueing and indicator modules.

telephone number. If no terminal is available or the line is busy, programming is postponed. On a time-shared system, equipment availability is the real determinant of external priority.

The truly high-priority user can be assigned a personal terminal. To ensure fast response, this terminal can be polled several times in a single internal polling cycle. Except for these few special cases, however, scheduling and external priorities are not factors on a time-shared system.

Operating System Structures

Figure 13.20 shows the basic functional components of a large, multiprogramming operating system. These functions are not independent; they are elements of an operating system. The individual functions must be invoked or called in response to specific situations that occur dynamically. If the functions are to be called, they must be called by some other module.

We might cite the basic ideas of structured programming as a reference point in evaluating the structure of an operating system. Structured programming suggests that program logic be broken into functionally complete modules—we've already done that for an operating system. These functional modules are the low-level or detailed routines; in a payroll program, for example, one might compute regular pay, another overtime pay, another federal income tax, and so on. A control structure is used to link these functional modules (Fig. 13.21). In a similar fashion, we need a control structure to link the functional components of an operating system.

A key factor in determining a program's control structure is the driving mechanism of that program. For example, a simple program is driven by the input/process/output sequence, while a business report generator might be driven by control breaks. The program's main control module is defined by this driving mechanism.

How can we drive an operating system? A small system might be *command driven*. On such a system, everything waits for the operator to submit a command. The operating system displays a prompt, the operator types a command, the command is executed, the operating system prints the next command prompt, and so on. The main control module of a command driven system is the console command processor (Fig. 13.22). Other operating system modules and application programs run under the command processor.

Many large multiprogramming systems are *interrupt driven*. This means that the basic control module of the system is the interrupt handler (Fig. 13.23); all other operating system modules and application programs are subject to this main control. Earlier in the chapter, we considered an example of how a large multiprogrammed system is driven by interrupts. It is through an interrupt that such a system changes its state or status; on a command driven system, only an operator command can bring about a similar change. What if a command driven system is sitting idle? How can it begin doing useful work again? By accepting an operator command. How can an idle interrupt driven system resume processing? By accepting an interrupt. (Note: the operator's console may well be the source of an interrupt.)

Many time-shared systems are *poll driven*. On such systems, the basic control module is the polling routine. The polling routine gives control to a program, which keeps control until I/O is required or until a time slice is used up. Then, it's back to the polling routine to determine the next program to get control. The system changes its status through the polling mechanism. If the system is idle, it remains idle until the polling routine finds a ready program.

In several subsequent chapters, we'll become quite specific about the internals of a particular operating system. It is easy to get lost in the details of a control block or a logical module. Try to keep the basic idea of an operating system's structure in mind. If you have a sense of how a function fits into the overall picture, you'll find it much easier to comprehend the details.

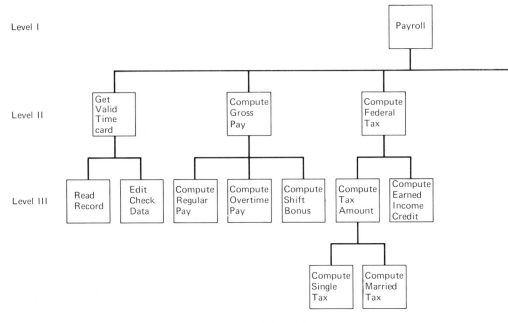

Fig. 13.21
An example of a program control structure.

Fig. 13.22
The control structure of a command-driven operating system.

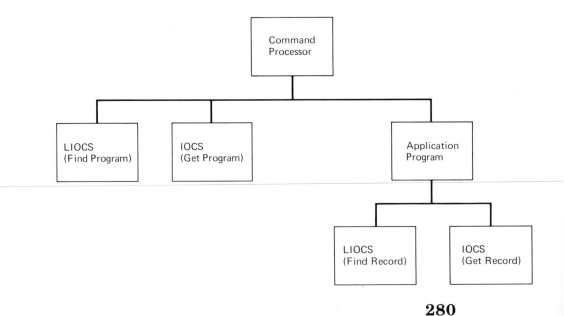

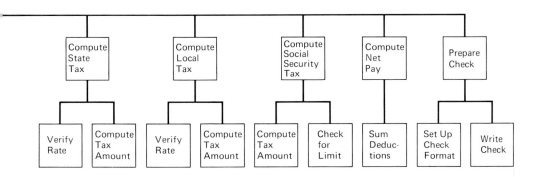

**Fig. 13.23
The control structure of an interrupt-driven
operating system.**

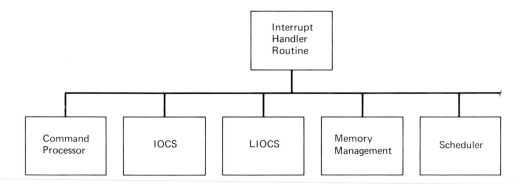

Summary _____

This chapter was concerned with multiuser computer systems. We began with a view of several basic operating system functions (from Chapter 12). On a multiuser system, a number of programs are introduced into the transient program area, and share the CPU. We then considered the major problems caused by this arrangement, one at a time.

If multiple programs are to occupy the transient program area, memory space must be managed. On some systems, main memory is broken into a number of fixed-length partitions, each of which can hold one program. Fixed partition memory management wastes space; often the solution is to allocate space dynamically, as a program is loaded. Even dynamic memory management can waste space, leaving small pieces of unused memory throughout the machine—fragmentation. Dynamic memory relocation is the solution to the fragmentation problem on some systems. A more common solution is program segmentation or paging, a concept to be discussed in more detail in Chapter 14. Virtual memory techniques are used on many current systems.

On a time-sharing system, the memory allocation technique often involves program roll-in and roll-out, taking advantage of the long time delays between transactions. Throughout our discussion of memory management, the idea of memory protection was mentioned; most memory protection schemes are linked to the memory allocation techniques.

A second major multiuser problem is processor management—when two or more programs are ready, who goes first? On some systems, the partitions are designated as foreground and background, with the foreground having higher internal priority. The idea of control blocks was introduced, and we discussed how a scheduler or dispatcher module can make the internal priority decision by scanning these control blocks in either fixed or priority order. Often, the act of switching control of the processor from one program to another is set in motion by an interrupt; such systems are said to be interrupt driven. On a time-shared system, a polling mechanism is often used to determine internal priorities.

I/O device allocation is another major multiuser problem. Normally, every I/O device on the system is listed in a device table. Before allocating a device to a program, the operating system can check this table, and thus avoid conflicts. Under certain conditions, two programs may encounter a deadlock, with each requiring a resource controlled by the other. The operating system must either prevent, or detect and correct, such situations. I/O device allocation is not quite as big a problem on a time-shared system, with most user needs being met by default device allocations.

The final problem discussed in the chapter was external priority and scheduling—which program is loaded onto the computer next? Often, programs are placed on queues based on the job class to await future processing. When the scheduler discovers that a partition or region is empty, it gives control to an initiator module, which loads the next program from the queue. Once again, external priority is not a major problem on a time-shared system.

The chapter ended with a brief discussion of the structure of an operating system. Some are command driven, others are interrupt driven, and most time-shared systems are poll driven. The driving mechanism serves as the main control module for the operating system.

Key Words

background
CLOSE
command driven system
contiguous
control block
deadlock
default
dispatcher
dynamic memory management
dynamic memory relocation
external priority
fixed partition memory management
foreground
fragmentation
initiator
internal priority
interrupt
interrupt driven system
locking
memory management

memory protection
multiprogramming
OPEN
paging
partition
poll driven system
polling
privileged instruction
queueing
ready state
real memory
region
roll-in/roll-out
scheduler
segmentation
stack
time-sharing
time-slicing
transaction
virtual memory
wait state

Exercises _____

1. Describe the key components of a basic operating system.

2. Multiprogramming creates a number of problems arising from possible interprogram conflict. Name some of the problems.

3. Describe the typical application mix of a large, business-oriented multiprogramming system.

4. Describe the typical application mix of a time-shared system.

5. Explain fixed partition memory management. What is the major disadvantage of this approach? Why?

6. Explain dynamic memory management.

7. What is fragmentation? How can this problem be solved?

8. What do we mean when we say that a program must be loaded into contiguous space?

9. Explain segmentation. Explain paging. Explain virtual memory.

10. How is memory managed on a time-shared system? Why couldn't we use this approach on a multiprogramming system?

11. Explain how a program's internal priority is determined.

12. What is an interrupt?

13. Explain how interrupts can be used to control a multiprogramming system.

14. Distinguish between a wait state and a ready state.

15. What is time-slicing? How does a time-sliced, time-sharing system differ from a multiprogramming system with respect to the internal priority decision? How are they similar?

16. Explain polling.

17. Explain how a multiprogramming system allocates its I/O devices. Why is this a potential problem area?

18. What is deadlock?

19. Distinguish between a program's internal priority and its external priority.

20. Explain queueing. What does the initiator program do? Why can the initiator program be transient?

21. Distinguish between a command driven system, an interrupt driven system, and a poll driven system.

14

Segmentation, Paging, and Virtual Memory

Overview

Multiprogramming, as we should certainly know by now, involves placing several programs in core at the same time and allowing them to share the resources of the CPU in an effort to improve the degree of system utilization. The limiting factor on this process is usually main memory space and not CPU time, a problem which becomes more and more acute as computers become faster and faster. In this chapter, we'll take a look at program segmentation and paging, two techniques that tend to improve the utilization of core. Using these two concepts as a base, we'll develop the key ideas of virtual memory.

Multiprogramming and Processor Efficiency

As we've already seen in our discussion of multiprogramming, the more programs we can load into main memory, the greater is our utilization of the central processing unit's time. There is a limit, of course—eventually program interference begins to overwhelm any gain in efficiency—but this point, except in the case of a relatively few well-planned and well-run systems, is rarely

285

reached. In general, adding another program to core means improving system efficiency; i.e., throughput.

This was the whole point of dynamic memory management—improve the utilization of core so that additional programs might be added. It did represent an improvement over fixed-partition operating systems but, as you may remember, had a nasty habit of leaving small chunks of storage spread here and there throughout memory—the fragmentation problem. Dynamic program relocation helps, but creates problems of its own, particularly when hardware has not been designed with this facility in mind. First, we have the problem of address translation—addressing, but not arithmetic registers, must be relocated. A second problem, perhaps of even greater impact, is the fact that the computer must literally stop doing useful work during the relocation process. Some machines are designed to handle dynamic program relocation through hardware; these can do the job quickly and with a minimum of lost time. Other machines do not have this feature and must implement dynamic relocation through software. At best, variable partitions or regions, even with dynamic relocation, will leave an occasional 2K or 4K or 10K chunk of unused main memory.

As electronic technology advances, computers become faster and faster; this ever-increasing speed makes the problem of core efficiency even more crucial—to cite a fairly simple example, a ten-program system, which previously was able to utilize only 50 percent of available CPU time, suddenly drops to a mere 25 percent utilization on a machine which is twice as fast. Is it any wonder, then, that so many manufacturers are offering hardware and software packages designed to improve memory utilization along with their solid logic and integrated circuit computers?

Segmentation

Why must a program always occupy contiguous regions in main memory? Why not break it into pieces and place individual segments wherever they fit in core (Fig. 14.1)? Many programs are composed of individual modules and subroutines anyway, with relative addressing being of a critical nature only *within* a given *segment* and not across segments. Individual segments would certainly be smaller than complete programs without *segmentation*, and these smaller pieces would be better able to fit into small openings in memory, yielding the advantages of dynamic program relocation without the disadvantages. The extra 10K chunk (or two or three) of unutilized core left behind by even the best dynamic memory management schemes can be used to hold an extra program or two with no increase in total main memory, thus improving system efficiency at a relatively low cost.

There are, however, some costs—mostly in the area of addressing. In a program written as a contiguous whole by some programmer, or created as a

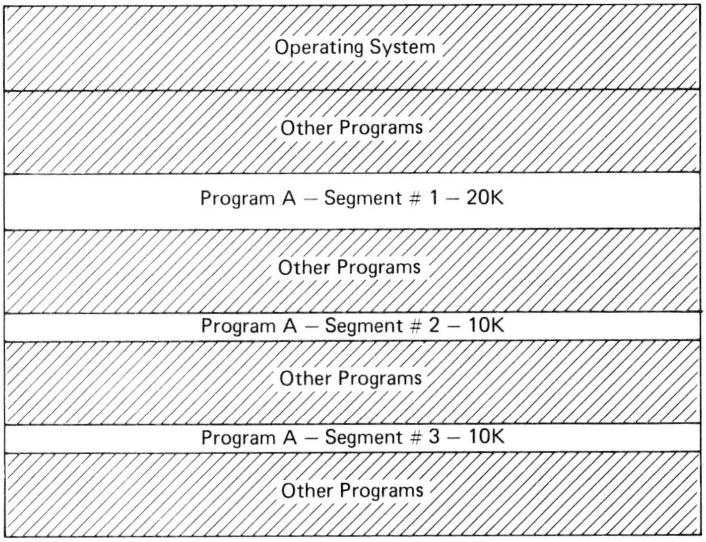

Fig. 14.1
Program segmentation.

contiguous whole by a linkage editor, how are the addressing problems caused by noncontiguous program loading handled?

One approach is to simply leave it to the programmer. Most programs have a number of separate and obvious (to the programmer) logical functions to perform; a good programmer, or one writing under a set of good program standards, can break these functions into segments that make sense. Each segment can be assigned a different base-addressing register to be initialized at program load time. Since all addresses can be computed relative to the base register, addressing within a segment is not a problem. In assembly-level languages, setting up a separate base register and a control section for each of several segments is common practice. Some higher-level languages either have this facility or can easily implement it through the compiler; subroutines, for example, can be defined in almost any language. Looking beyond the application program, the object modules that are assembled by the linkage editor form rather obvious independent segments.

Addressing under segmentation is different. One addressing scheme involves breaking an address into two pieces (Fig. 14.2), a segment number occupying the high-order bit positions and the displacement within the segment

Fig. 14.2
Program segmentation
addressing.

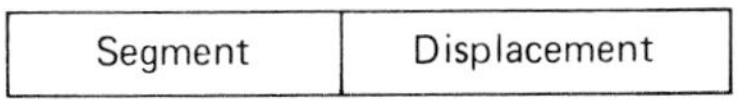

| Segment | Displacement |

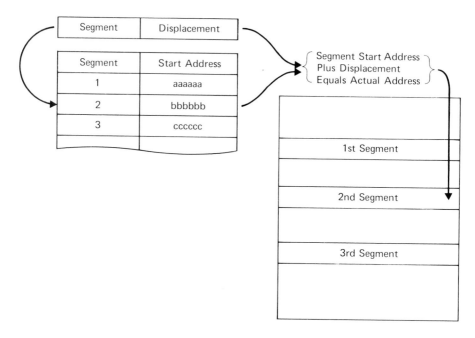

Fig. 14.3
Dynamic address translation.

filling the low-order bits. As a program is loaded, a *segment table* (Fig. 14.3) is built, containing the segment number and the actual address of the first memory location in each segment. During program execution, addresses are dynamically translated, with the segment number being converted to a base address through a table look-up operation and the actual, absolute address being computed by adding the displacement portion of the address to the base address. (Fig. 14.3).

Sometimes it's easier to see exactly what is going on by following an example. To keep things as simple as possible, let's use a 16-bit mini-computer as our model—on this machine, all addresses are 16 bits long. We'll assign the following meanings to these 16 bits.

1. the high-order 4 bits hold the segment number.

2. the low-order 12 bits hold the displacement.

A 4-bit segment number means that we have room for at most 16 segments (0000 through 1111). The 12-bit displacement allows for 4096 (0000 through 4095) storage locations in each segment. Before going any further, it is important that we take note of the arbitrary nature of this addressing scheme—we might just as well have chosen a 2-bit segment number and a 14-bit displacement or a 3-bit segment number and a 13-bit displacement or any other combination that strikes our fancy. Ideally, the segment size should be small enough to actually utilize random pieces of free core, large enough to hold a full complement of program logic, and flexible. It should be a reflection of the kinds of programs (the job mix) actually run in a given installation—which is easier to say than to do.

At any rate, we've chosen an addressing scheme involving a 4-bit segment number and a 12-bit displacement for our installation; once the decision has been made, all we must do is follow it consistently. In Fig. 14.4, we'll be tracking the segmentation process on our minicomputer.

Fig. 14.4
Program segmentation. An example (a) of
program loading; (b) Program A's segment table;
(c) Address translation.

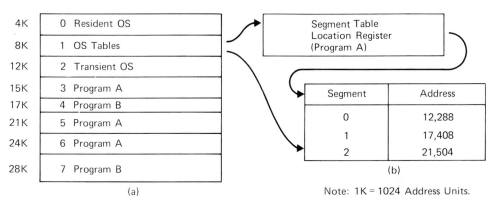

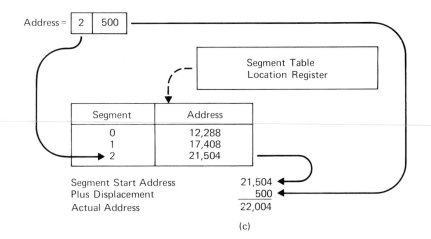

The first program in memory is, as you might expect, the operating system. This software has been broken into three segments (Fig. 14.4a) holding, respectively; a resident portion, some tables and pointers, and a region to hold transient modules that will be read in from disk when needed. Each segment is a full 4096 memory locations long; hence, the segment table for this "program" has a rather unusual property. Consider the following table.

Address Seg.	Disp.	Absolute Address	Binary Address Seg.	Disp.	Absolute Binary Address
0	000	0	0000	000000000000	0000000000000000
0	FFF	4095	0000	111111111111	0000111111111111
1	000	4096	0001	000000000000	0001000000000000
1	FFF	8191	0001	111111111111	0001111111111111
2	000	8192	0010	000000000000	0010000000000000
2	FFF	12,287	0010	111111111111	0010111111111111

The address as expressed in segment terms and the address as expressed in absolute terms are identical! This happens, except by chance, only in the operating system. It makes sense when you think about it. The operating system is the one place where machine-dependent programs must be written and the only place where absolute addressing must be used. When the operating system is running, no address translation is needed, but all addresses in all other programs must be "translated" through the program's segment table.

There is one other property that might be noted from the address table shown above. Note the relationship between the last address in segment 0— (0FFF)$_{16}$ or 4095 in decimal terms—and the first address in segment 1— (1000)$_{16}$ or 4096. In hexadecimal, 0FFF plus 1 is 1000. All we are doing is counting, which is really all there is to addressing memory. Segment/displacement addressing is not a *new* addressing scheme; it is simply a new way to look at an *old* addressing scheme.

Let's assume that a program consisting of three segments has been loaded into memory as described in Fig. 14.4(a). The segment table holds the start address of each segment in the program (Fig. 14.4b); the segment table is located in the table region of the operating system and is found through a special register called, predictably, the *segment table location register.*

At some point in the program, the address shown in Fig. 14.4(c) is referenced by the program. Using the high-order 4 bits of this address, the program's segment table, located through the segment table location register, is searched, yielding the address of the start of this segment. The contents of the last 12 bits in the address are added to this base address, giving the actual address in main memory.

In a multiprogramming system, each program will have its own segment table. Several different approaches might be used for linking to this table through the segment table location register. The use of stacks or queues of segment table addresses might be an excellent choice, with a hardware or software pointer indicating the location of the register pointing to the "active" program's segmentation table. Since dynamic address translation is not essential in the operating system, the contents of this special register might be loaded by a scheduler or initiator. This "register" need not even be a register; any known and consistent location would suffice.

Once again, please note that our 16-bit address example is only an example and not an industry standard; address sizes vary from manufacturer to manufacturer, and the exact rule for breaking an address into segment and displacement portions can vary even among the installations of a single manufacturer.

Memory management is a little tougher under this kind of system than it is under fixed or even dynamic memory management. The operating system must keep track of all free spaces no matter how small. A table something like the one pictured in Fig. 14.5 is probably maintained by such an operating system; the table simply lists regions of memory that are in use and regions that are free. This table has nothing to do with programs that are in core and executing; it exists only for the convenience of the operating system's scheduler and initiator programs (or their equivalents).

The use of segments does allow for fairly efficient program loading simply because segments are smaller than complete programs and will therefore fit into smaller chunks of memory. Segmentation is somewhat programmer oriented in that it allows for variable-length segments attuned to actual program logic; using a 24 bit address, for example, the high-order 8 bits might be as-

Fig. 14.5
Memory allocation table—segmentation system.
Lengths, of course, would be in actual binary
form rather than in the shorthand form shown in
the figure. The status would probably be
represented by a simple bit flag.

Start Address	Length	Status
0K	16K	In Use
16K	8K	Free
24K	16K	In Use
40K	4K	Free
44K	12K	In Use
66K	10K	Free

signed to the segment number while the low-order 16 hold the displacement, yielding a total of 256 segments ranging in size from a few to as many as 64K storage locations.

Address Translation

Using segmentation, the programmer can visualize a load module as a contiguous set of instructions and storage areas, with each object module beginning as a new segment. The first object module is seen as segment 0, with locations within the segment expressed as displacements from the beginning of the segment. The second object module can be viewed as segment 1; the third is segment 2, and so on. These addresses make sense to the programmer, but do not represent where a program is really stored in main memory. As a result, the address translation process described above must be performed.

When does this address translation take place? What hardware component of the computer performs this function? Address translation is a function of the control unit portion of the central processing unit. During instruction time or I-time, the control unit fetches one instruction from main memory and decodes it. During this decoding phase, the instruction control unit first verifies that the operation code is valid, and then translates all addresses in the operands from relative or segment/displacement form to absolute main memory addresses. When control is given to the arithmetic and logical unit, it has the real, absolute memory addresses to work with. The process of converting addresses in segment/displacement (or similar) form into absolute memory addresses is called *dynamic address translation.*

Incidentally, address translation is a key function of the instruction control unit even on nonsegmented systems. Addresses in an instruction are often expressed in relative (base plus displacement) form rather than in absolute form. The arithmetic and logical unit is limited to absolute addresses. When programs are loaded contiguously, the process of address translation is a bit easier, but the process is still there. Very simply, the instruction control unit of the CPU translates all addresses in an instruction to absolute form during I-time.

Paging _____

Segmentation breaks a program into pieces in a manner related to the logic of the program—individual segments can vary significantly in length. The number of bits in the displacement portion of the address does set an upper limit on segment size, but the "convenience of the program's logic" is the key factor involved in breaking down the program. Some fragmentation is still possible; if no segment is small enough to fit into an available piece of core, that memory space will be wasted.

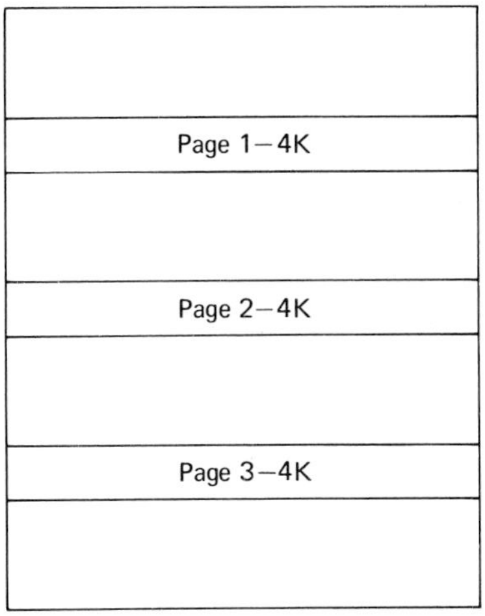

Fig. 14.6
Program loading
under a paging system.

Paging breaks a program into fixed-sized pieces called *pages*; page length is usually determined by hardware and other system factors. IBM, for example, uses two different page sizes in its paging systems: 2K and 4K. Given such small pages, the risk of unusable regions of memory is significantly reduced. Also, given the fixed-length nature of the pages, memory management is somewhat easier to implement than it was on the more variable segmentation systems. Memory management under segmentation involves keeping track of dynamically changing small regions of free memory space. Memory management under paging is more static: simply divide the available memory space into fixed-length pages at SYSGEN or IPL time.

Beyond the fixed-length page approach, the implementation of a paging system is almost identical to that of a segmentation system. Programs are loaded into memory in noncontiguous pages (Fig. 14.6). An address is broken into two parts (Fig. 14.7), a page number in the high-order positions and a displacement within the page in the low-order bits; addresses are dynamically translated as the program is executing through a program *page table* (Fig. 14.8). What was called a segment table location register will now be called a *page table location register*.

Memory allocation is a little easier to track under a paging system; core is simply divided into a series of fixed-length pages (Fig. 14.9), with a *page frame table* (Fig. 14.10) indicating the status (free or in use) of each page via a simple

Fig. 14.7
Addressing under
a paging system.

Page Number	Displacement

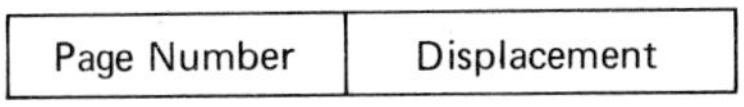

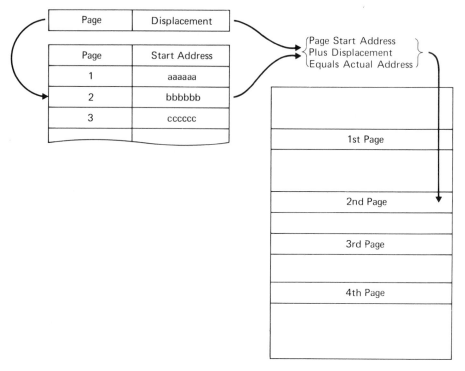

Fig. 14.8
Dynamic address translation under paging.

Fig. 14.9
Memory divided into pages.

1	2	3	4	5	6	7	8	9
10	11	12	13	14	15	16	17	18
19	20	21	22	23	24	25	26	27
28	29	30	31	32	33	34	35	36

Page Frame Number	Program ID	Page Number	Status
1	Operating System	1	1
2	Operating System	2	1
3	Operating System	3	1
4	Operating System	4	1
5	Program A	1	1
6	Program B	1	1
7	Program A	2	1
8	Program C	1	1
9			0
10			0
11	Program A	3	1
12	Program C	2	1
			0

Fig. 14.10
The page frame table.

one-bit flag. In trying to locate a free spot in core, the scheduler or initiator program (or their equivalents) need only search the page frame table for a "0" bit, assign that page to the program, and change the bit to a "1." It should be noted that there is a significant difference between this page frame table and the program page table described above. The page frame table is for the use of the operating system in allocating main memory space, while the program page table supports dynamic address translation for executing programs that are already in core.

As we've seen, some wasted space is inevitable with any memory allocation scheme; paging, even with its fixed size modules, shares the same problem, though not quite in the same way. To state the paging problem as simply as possible, *any* fixed-size page is bound to be the wrong length. Perhaps a bit of additional explanation is in order. Programmers just do not write their programs in fixed-length increments; almost every program will have at least one page that is only partially used. Even if this averages only 1K per program, a multiprogramming system working with ten programs in memory will waste a full 10K.

Segmentation and Paging

Both segmentation and paging allow the system to utilize noncontiguous, small pieces of storage for active programs. We've considered the possibility of occasional waste due to the existence of a region smaller than the smallest segment or the fact that program length and page length may not be perfectly matched. Segmentation tends to be program oriented, dividing a program into pieces that complement actual program logic. Paging is a more hardware-oriented technique, with page sizes being geared to a system's memory allocation scheme.

Fig. 14.11	Segment Number	Page Number	Displacement
Segmentation and			
paging addresses.			

Combining *segmentation and paging* on the same system might be expected to give us the best of both worlds. Under such a system, a program could be broken into logical segments and the segments then subdivided into fixed-length pages—the programmer could plan a segment structure while the system loads pages. How is this an improvement on a standard segmentation system? If a program need not occupy contiguous memory, why must a segment? Under segmentation *and* paging, it doesn't, meaning that chunks of memory smaller than the smallest segment can now be utilized.

Of course, this technique is not without its cost. Dynamic address translation now involves two tables, with an address being divided into three pieces—the segment number, page number, and displacement (Fig. 14.11). First, the program's segment table must be found via the segment table location register (Fig. 14.12) and searched for the proper segment number. This table, in turn,

Fig. 14.12
Dynamic address translation under a
segmentation and paging system.

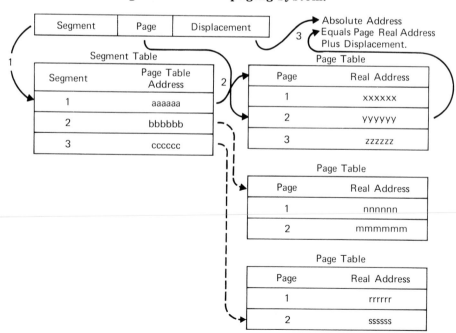

gives the address of the segment's page table that can be searched for the base address of the page. This series of calculations is bound to have a negative impact on system overhead.

To help minimize this cost, many systems using the segmentation and paging approach provide a boost to *dynamic address translation* through a series of special registers called *associative array registers* or *page address registers*. Before delving into a discussion of the implementation of this feature, it might be instructive to digress for a paragraph or two and look into the underlying logic. Back in the late 1800s, an Italian economist named Vilfredo Pareto, following a study of the distribution of wealth in his native land, came to the conclusion that something in excess of 90 percent of the wealth was in the hands of something less than 10 percent of the population. A generalization of this idea became known as Pareto's Law. We see examples of this basic concept every day—a very large percentage of the earth's people lives on a very small portion of the available land; a small percentage of the world's population uses a very large percentage of the world's energy; 80 percent of a company's patents are filed by 20 percent of the firm's employees.

Applying this law to a segmentation and paging system, it might be reasonable to state that a significant percentage of the system's address translation requests is associated with a relatively few pages. This makes sense when you think about it. Programs normally execute in fixed sequence, with numerous instructions lying between branches (deviations from this fixed sequence); once one instruction is executed within a given page, the chances are very good that the next instruction to be executed by the same program will be found on the same page.

Which brings us back to the page address registers. As instructions are executed by the system, the base address of the "last several pages accessed" can be placed in these special registers. Before going through the table look-up process of normal dynamic address translation, these registers can be checked for the desired base address; if it's there, no additional address translation is needed. To save time, these registers are usually searched in parallel.

If the desired address is not in the page address registers, of course, normal address translation through the segment and page tables takes place. In order to avoid clogging these registers with "obsolete" addresses, this actual address translation step is often the point at which these registers are modified, with the newly translated address replacing the contents of the register which has been "least currently" accessed. Consider, for example, a typical page. The first time a program branches to this page, dynamic address translation through the tables is necessary; following this step, the address of the new page is placed in the page address registers. As additional instructions are executed within the page, the base address is in the registers and address translations is taken care of very quickly by hardware. Eventually, a branch to another page is encountered, and dynamic address translation must once again take place, with this new base address replacing the contents of one of the registers. If the program does not return to the original page, eventually all other entries in the registers will be more current than the entry for "this" page, meaning that the reference to "this" page will be the next one to be dropped from the array to make room for a new page address.

The actual implementation of this technique will, of course, vary from manufacturer to manufacturer. The basic concept of hardware-aided address translation for the "most commonly used" pages is, however, common.

Memory allocation is implemented much as it is in a pure paging system, with the operating system maintaining a page frame table. Once again, remember that the page frame table is for the use of the operating system for the purpose of memory allocation, and it has nothing to do with the actual execution of loaded programs.

Segmentation Systems and Paging Systems— Conclusions

The whole point of segmentation and paging, either singularly or in combination, is to divide a program into relatively small pieces so that random segments of noncontiguous storage can be utilized. Some form of dynamic address translation is essential because of the noncontiguous nature of programs on such systems—programmers cannot be expected to foresee the exact location of their pages or segments. The end result is more programs on line within the same amount of main memory; this improves system efficiency.

Some languages—notably, PL/I and assembly-level language—include features that allow the programmer to define segment break points, and other languages will probably contain something analogous to PL/I's BEGIN block in the future but, if a segmentation and/or paging system is to be implemented in such a way as to have a positive impact on system costs, the actual functions of subdividing a program should be system responsibilities pretty much transparent to the programmer; otherwise, any gains in system efficiency might be offset easily by increased programming and debug time.

We've already considered the possibility of wasted space due to chunks of storage too small for even the smallest segment, or logic which does not quite fill a complete fixed-length page. Another source of potential waste arises from the belief that every instruction in a program must be in main memory before that program can begin executing. A 10K block of core might be more than enough to hold a few extra pages or a complete segment, but if no *complete* program needs 10K or less, it makes no sense to load only a portion because if the entire program must be in core before execution is possible it couldn't run anyway. As we'll see in the next few pages, this belief is a myth.

Virtual Memory _____

We've already seen that programs do not have to be loaded into contiguous core in order to execute properly. We also know that the CPU is capable of executing only one instruction at a time. In this section, we'll be attempting to deal with the following question: Why is it necessary for *every* instruction in a program to be in main memory for that program to execute properly?

We've already seen cases where it was not necessary. Remember the overlay structures we discussed in our analysis of second-generation concepts? With overlay structures, complete modules of logic are rolled into core on an as-needed basis.

Segmentation and/or paging concepts provide an almost perfect framework for implementing a system in which only a part of a program is actually in memory at any one time. Taking advantage of the roll-in and roll-out concepts we've already covered, why not load only a page or two of a program at a time, keeping the rest on some direct access device? This is the essence of a *virtual memory* system (Fig. 14.13).

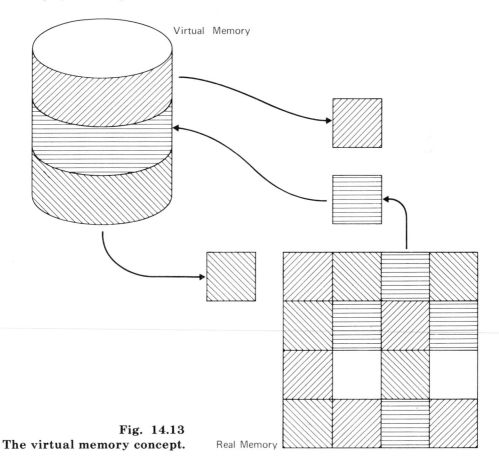

Fig. 14.13
The virtual memory concept.

It's not a new idea. Back in the early 1960s (prehistory as far as computers are concerned), Burroughs had a fully operational virtual system (they didn't call it "virtual") for their 5000 computer series. UNIVAC, CDC, and GE/Honeywell all had it during the 1960s. RCA was the first to use the term "virtual memory" in 1970. The key date in the development of the virtual memory concept was, however, August 2, 1972, when IBM announced its System/370 series of computers; for the first time *the* major computer manufacturer had decided to make the virtual memory concept a key element in a full line of computers.

The word virtual means "not in actual fact"; virtual memory therefore means memory that does "not in actual fact" exist. Basically, the system works something like this. Programs are written as though there were an almost unlimited amount of space, and stored on disk or drum. Addresses on the direct access device are sequential just like main memory addresses, so the disk or drum address of a given program or module is analogous to the address it might occupy if it were really in main storage. Storage on this "virtual memory" device is subdivided into segments or pages or both, and a few pages from each of several programs are moved into "real storage" for execution, with the dynamic address translation features we've already discussed handling the translation from a virtual address to a real address. As the instructions on a particular page are executed and, eventually, completed, this page can be rolled-out to virtual memory again and a new page rolled-in to replace it. In this way, only that portion of a program that is actually being executed need be in main memory, meaning that less real core must sit passively waiting for something to happen to the instructions or the data it holds.

Consider, for example, the program flow illustrated in Fig. 14.14. Previously, programs were loaded from a library into main memory and executed. Now,

Fig. 14.14
The relationship among a program library,
virtual memory, and real memory.

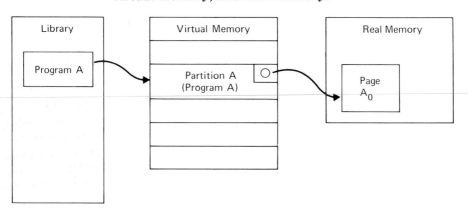

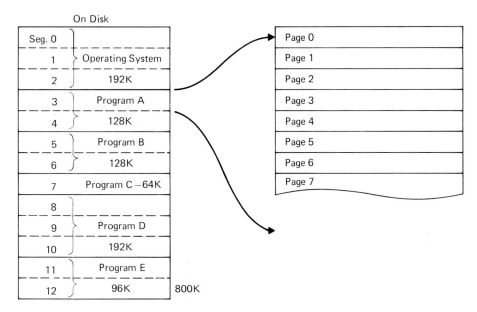

Fig. 14.15
Virtual memory contents in our example.

programs are loaded from a library onto *virtual* memory. Once in virtual, *selected portions* of that program can be paged into real memory for execution. The old idea of fixed-length partitions or variable-length regions still exists, but it is implemented in *virtual* memory. Pages are transferred between virtual and real, and the programmer has no control over the physical paging process.

Let's assume that our virtual system holds the programs shown in Fig. 14.15—an operating system and five application programs. This system is stored, in exactly the given sequence, on disk. The addressing scheme used in this virtual memory is very much like the addressing we studied in the segmentation *and* paging system. Our disk-based virtual memory holds some 800K memory units; program D, to cite on example, actually needs only 150K but has been assigned to a 192K region to simplify segment addressing—after all, it's only virtual memory.

Over in real memory (Fig. 14.16) the operating system has at its disposal a *real* page frame table and a series of segment and page tables describing all of the pages *available* in *virtual* memory (Fig. 14.17). As the system begins the operation of bringing a page from virtual memory into real memory, it first searches the page frame table to locate an available page; once located, this page is changed to a "busy" status in the page frame table and the actual *page-in* operation begins. When the operation is completed, the program page occu-

Page	Program	Program segment	and page	Status
0	OS	0	0	1
1	OS	0	1	1
2	OS	0	2	1
3	OS	0	3	1
4	OS	0	4	1
5	OS	0	5	1
6	OS	0	6	1
7	A	3	5	1
8	B	2	9	0 ← Free page
9	X	1	1	1
10	B	2	1	0
11	D	5	12	1

Fig. 14.16
Real memory—the page frame table.

Fig. 14.17
Real memory—segment and page tables.

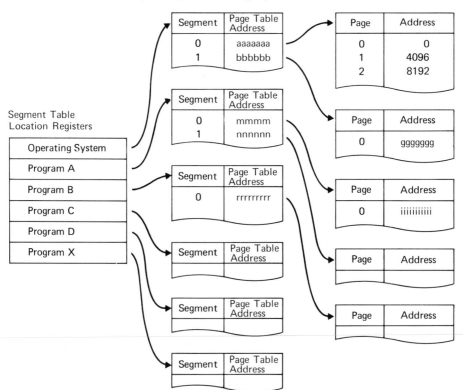

pies the selected page frame, and the address of this page frame is entered into the segment and page tables.

As a page is executing, addresses that are expressed in virtual terms are converted into real addresses by

1. accessing the segment table using the high-order bits of the address as a key,
2. using the pointer in this table to locate the proper page table,
3. accessing this page table using the middle bits as a key and, finally,
4. adding the displacement found in the low-order bits of the virtual address to the base address found in the page table.

On most systems, this rather tedious translation process is streamlined through the use of page address registers.

What happens when a virtual address points to a page that is not in real storage? How does the system "know" if a given page is in real or virtual storage? In the segment and page tables, there is a one-bit flag called (by IBM, at least) the "invalid" bit. If it's "off" (a 0 bit) the page is in real storage; if it's "on" (a 1 bit) the page is in virtual storage. When the dynamic address translation feature of our computer encounters a 1 bit at the end of the translation process a *page fault* is recognized and an interrupt is issued, causing a link to the operating system module responsible for the page-in operation.

What if a survey of the page frame table shows that there is no real core available for the new page? This means that some page must be *paged-out.* Many different schemes and algorithms for choosing the page to be paged-out (in prior chapters, we would have used the term "rolled-out," it's the same concept) have been implemented, ranging from simple LIFO and FIFO rules to more complex techniques designed to identify the least often used pages.

Bringing pages into memory only when a page already in core refers to an address in a virtual-resident page is known as *demand paging.* An alternative technique attempts to predict the demand for a new page and bring it into memory before it is actually needed; this is known as *prepaging*—it's an ideal, and obviously fairly difficult to implement. Strict programming standards, perhaps implemented through a special compiler might help. If segments really do hold logically related elements of a program, the page-in supervisor might be designed to always keep a few pages ahead of the currently executing page within the same segment.

One feature often available on a virtual system allows the programmer to designate certain pages as key routines that are to remain resident for the life of the job step. If the routine really is a key one, any "least often used" page-out rule would probably achieve the same objective, but knowledgeable programmers should have the opportunity to "make sure."

You may note that the operating system as pictured in Figs. 14.16 and 14.17 occupies the same locations in both real and virtual memory. Operating system routines perform such tasks as dynamically modifying channel programs and often refer to an absolute address; because of the unique requirements of operating system modules, it is highly desirable that the operating system be loaded into contiguous storage. Most virtual storage systems have a *"virtual equals real"* feature in which selected modules or pages are loaded into real memory in such a way that the virtual and real addresses are in fact identical.

Segmentation, Paging, and Virtual Memory—Advantages

The biggest practical economic advantage of segmentation, paging, and virtual memory is better utilization of available real memory, meaning that, potentially, more programs can be placed on line yielding greater CPU utilization. Other advantages accrue to the programmer. In a virtual memory system, there is, for all practical purposes, no limit on program size. The programmer is relieved of the burden of planning overlay structures and fitting a program into a partition of limited size; the system assumes these responsibilities. The computer system itself receives some of the benefit—programs occupy only as much space as they actually require.

The big benefit, though, is economic. More programs on-line means that memory space, the major limiting factor on multiprogramming capability, can be minimized as a limiting factor.

Segmentation, Paging, and Virtual Memory—Problems

There are, of course, costs and problems associated with these techniques. Probably the most obvious new cost is increased system overhead—it takes time to do all that paging and it requires space to hold all those segmentation and paging tables. Dynamic address translation isn't instantaneous either; the page address registers help but do not eliminate the overhead loss. The size of these new operating systems with their increased functions creates still another overhead cost; virtual memory operating systems are big.

Of course, central processing units are getting faster all the time. As memory speeds begin to keep pace and cycle times begin to drop into the nanosecond range and below, the time loss for execution of an operating system module will become negligible, approaching the speed of hardware with considerably greater flexibility. This doesn't mean that the overhead cost will disappear; it will just become a bit more difficult to pin down.

A brand new problem on a virtual memory system is *thrashing*. When real memory is full (or close to it), a demand for a new page means that another page must be paged-out before the new one can be paged-in. If during a given period of time this happens frequently, the system finds itself spending so much time paging-in and paging-out that little time is left for useful work. This is called thrashing. Some systems have the ability to recognize this problem when it occurs and take corrective action, perhaps removing one or more programs from real memory until things are running more smoothly, but thrashing can still have a negative impact on system performance.

Program design can also have a negative impact on performance. Consider, for example, the following simple FORTRAN program segment.

```
10    X = X + 1
15    ACCUM = ACCUM + Y
20    If (X − 25) 10,10,30
30    AVG = ACCUM/X
```

Assume that, by pure chance, page 0 ends with statement number 15 and page 1 begins with statement 20. The program will obviously bounce from page to page. This is no problem if both pages are in core, but what if they're not? Expand a bit on this basic idea and try to picture a program that branches madly from routine to routine, often skipping over thousands of storage locations in the process; such a poorly planned program would be a disaster on a virtual memory system. Do such programs exist? Ask any programmer.

How can this be avoided? Special compilers can help, but they don't solve the whole problem—no systems programmer could possibly foresee every dumb move a programmer might make. The answer, instead, would seem to lie in good programming standards, a solution that tends to offset many of the "programmer flexibility" benefits touted by virtual memory marketeers. Top-down or structured-programming concepts could prove to be most helpful here.

Implementing Virtual Memory

How might a virtual memory system be implemented? One possibility is to use the real/virtual relationship as described in Fig. 14.14. The virtual memory space might be viewed as a staging area, with programs being loaded directly into virtual, and then paged, as required, into real. Under such a system, virtual memory would contain everything (including the operating system) that used to be in main memory. The only real problem with this approach is that the operating system is physically stored, in its entirety, twice—once in real memory and once in virtual.

A more common approach is illustrated in Fig. 14.18. Three levels of memory are recognized—virtual memory, the *external paging device,* and real memory. Under such an approach, virtual memory does not *physically* exist anywhere; it is purely imaginary. This imaginary space contains the operating system and all the application programs—this is what we found in main memory on a fixed partition or variable region system.

Fig. 14.18
Implementing a virtual memory system.

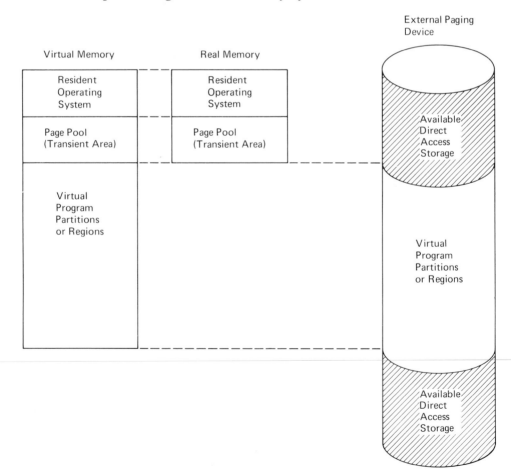

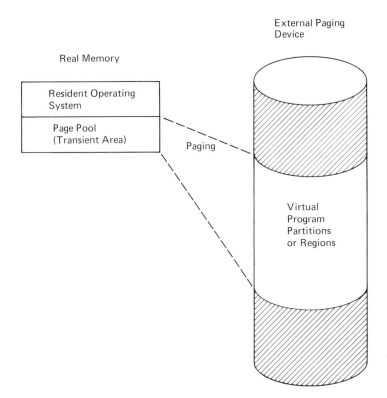

Fig. 14.19
Paging involves the transient area or page pool
in real memory and the external paging device.

The virtual memory contents are physically stored on two devices: real memory and the external paging device. Real memory is good, old-fashioned main memory, directly addressable by the CPU. The paging device is usually disk or drum—secondary storage. It is possible to divide the virtual memory into two distinct components. The first is exactly equal to the amount of real memory on the system (Fig. 14.18, again). The second component of virtual memory holds space that is above and beyond the capacity of real memory.

The first component of virtual memory is physically stored in real; it contains (Fig. 14.18) the resident operating system and the transient program area. The second component of virtual memory is physically stored on the external paging device; it contains the application programs. Paging takes place between the external paging device and the transient area of real memory (the page pool, see Fig. 14.19).

Using such a system, the operating system is loaded into real memory at IPL time. Application programs are then loaded into partitions or regions (just like the partitions or regions described in Chapter 13) on the external paging device. From the external paging device, selected pages are swapped between the transient program area or page pool in real memory and the external paging device.

For example, picture a system with 1000K real memory locations. We might run 4000K of virtual memory on this system—four times as much. The imaginary virtual memory might contain 250K for the operating system and 750K for the page pool (transient area); the remaining 3000K would represent memory over and above the available real storage (Fig. 14.20). The first 1000K would be stored in real memory (Fig. 14.21), and would contain the operating system and page pool; the second 3000K would be stored on the external paging device, and would contain application program partitions or regions. Program pages would be swapped back and forth between the 750K page pool and the 3000K virtual program partition area, under control of the operating system.

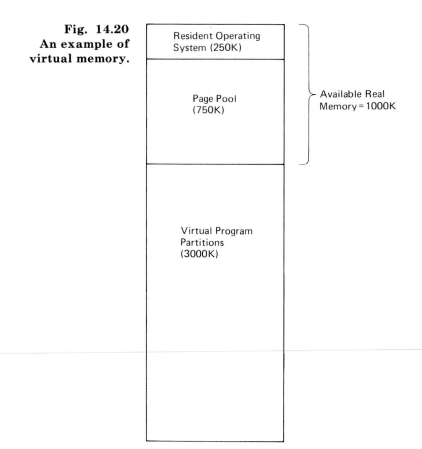

Fig. 14.20 An example of virtual memory.

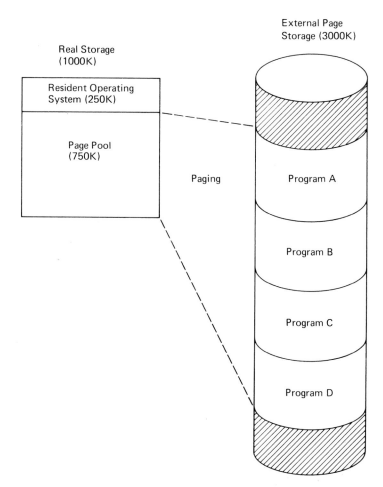

Fig. 14.21
Physical storage of virtual memory.

Traditional memory management would now be concerned with allocating space on the external paging device, but we might visualize, logically, the allocation of *virtual* space. The area that will be stored on the external paging device can be divided into fixed-length partitions, variable-length regions, segments, or pages, as the case may be. The transfer of pages between the paging device and real memory is a system function that happens *below* the operating system—in other words, one level closer to the hardware. In fact, it is not unreasonable to view the act of paging in much the same light that we currently view the transfer of an instruction from main memory into the instruction register for execution. Previously, we viewed a hierarchy of storage, following a program from a library, to main memory, and then into the CPU. We can now expand that view, as the program moves from a library, to virtual memory (or the external paging device), to real memory, and then to the CPU. That is really all that has changed. At the risk of belaboring a point, remember that virtual memory *does not physically exist* anywhere. Virtual memory is nothing but a logical *model* of memory contents.

Exactly how the paging operation takes place is a function of the system. Paging is basically an I/O operation, with the pages being read into real memory or written from real memory just like blocks of data. The key difference between paging and data I/O is the fact that paging *always* involves a fixed-length record. It is relatively easy to design hardware to handle fixed-length blocks of binary patterns. Thus as virtual memory systems develop, we begin to see special hardware devices designed to handle this very special form of I/O. Rather than involving an access method, the operating system, a channel program, and an I/O control unit, it is possible to cram all this logic into a single, special-purpose microcomputer, and control the *entire* paging operation in this device in response to a simple page-in or page-out "instruction." Fixed-block architecture disk devices are an outgrowth of this development. More and more, the paging operation is becoming a hardware function.

How are application programs loaded onto the external paging device? The control will be provided by the scheduler and initiator modules, as before. Some systems are designed simply to load a program directly to the external paging device. Others try to load the program into real memory, and begin paging-out to the external paging device when real memory is full. Once the program is on the system, however, its active pages will be the only ones in real memory. With only a portion of each program in main memory, more different programs can be loaded in the same memory space. The result is higher utilization of the CPU and therefore higher throughput.

The next three chapters investigate two different virtual memory operating systems: IBM DOS/VS (Disk Operating System/ Virtual Storage) and IBM VS-1. First, Chapter 15 defines the hardware environment of these two operating systems by analyzing the principles of operation of an IBM System/370 computer. Both DOS/VS and VS-1 are general-purpose, multiprogramming operating systems; the material of Chapter 13 was a preview.

Summary

This chapter covered many of the basic concepts of segmentation, paging, and virtual memory systems. In segmentation, a program is broken into variable size segments that can be loaded into memory in noncontiguous fashion, thus allowing fragmented pieces of free space to be utilized. Dynamic address translation is implemented through a series of segment tables. Paging is similar to segmentation except that pages are fixed in length and the length is chosen more for the convenience of the machine than for program logic considerations. Memory allocation is a bit more complex in segmentation systems and paging systems; under paging, it's implemented through something called a page frame table.

A segmentation *and* paging system attempts to have the best features of both. Programs are broken into logical segments, but are loaded in page form, meaning that smaller regions of memory can be utilized.

The underlying concept behind virtual memory can best be stated in question form—Why load the entire program into main memory when the CPU can execute only one instruction at a time? Under this system, a program is kept, in segment and/or page form, on a direct access device (virtual memory) and individual pages are paged-in to core as they are needed.

The implementation of virtual memory techniques often involves three distinct levels of storage. Virtual memory itself is an imaginary form of storage that does not physically exist anywhere; it provides a logical model of the system's complete memory contents, and contains everything that is traditionally stored in main memory—the operating system and application programs. Real memory contains the actual operating system and a page pool (the transient area). The virtual memory space over and above the amount of available real memory contains the application programs; physically, this component of virtual memory is stored on an external paging device. This latter component of space is divided into partitions or regions as on earlier, nonvirtual multiprogramming systems. Paging and/or segmentation is superimposed on top of the memory allocation scheme; pages are normally swapped between real memory and the external paging device.

The big advantage of these techniques lies in better utilization of main memory meaning more programs on-line which in turn means better CPU utilization. The big disadvantage is increased overhead cost.

Key Words

associative array registers	page frame table
demand paging	page fault
dynamic address translation	page-in
	page-out
external paging device	page table
page	page table location register
page address registers	

paging
prepaging
segment
segment table
segment table
location register
segmentation

segmentation and
paging
thrashing
virtual equals real
feature
virtual memory

Exercises _____

1. Explain program segmentation.

2. Explain how the various segments of a program can be loaded into noncontiguous main memory and independently addressed. How are the segment table and segment table location register involved?

3. Why is memory management under segmentation more difficult to implement than fixed partition memory management?

4. What is the difference between segmentation and paging?

5. Why is a page-oriented memory management system easier to implement than a segment-oriented memory management system?

6. Explain segmentation *and* paging.

7. Explain dynamic address translation. Why are such things as associative array registers or page address registers necessary?

8. How does a virtual memory system work? Distinguish between virtual memory and real memory.

9. What is a page fault? If a virtual memory system finds it necessary to page-out a page to free some space, how is this page selected?

10. Distinguish between demand paging and prepaging.

11. Why is something like a virtual-equals-real feature needed on a virtual memory system?

12. What are the advantages of virtual memory? What are the disadvantages?

13. Virtual memory does not make a computer faster—just more efficient. Explain.

14. Virtual memory does not physically exist anywhere. Explain.

15. If virtual memory is a *logical* model of a system's memory contents, where are these contents *physically* stored?

Operating Principles of the IBM System/370

Overview

An operating system is designed to perform within a given environment; a key component of that environment is the computer hardware. The electronic design of a computer serves to both limit and support operating system design. In this chapter, we'll take a look at some of the key design concepts of the IBM System/370 series of computers, stressing those factors that have had the greatest impact on software design; in Chapters 16 and 17, two different operating systems designed to work within this environment will be studied. Among the important concepts covered in this chapter are the program status word or PSW, the mechanism for actually controlling an input or output operation, and interrupts.

Addressing Memory on the IBM System/370

Main memory is a collection of electronic components that store bits. These bits are grouped to form bytes (or characters) and, usually, words. Some computers are byte-addressed, meaning that the basic addressable unit of memory is the byte. Others are word-addressed.

The IBM System/370 is a byte-addressed machine. Each byte contains eight bits, and is capable of holding a single EBCDIC coded character. The first byte in memory is address 0, the second byte is address 1, the third is address 2, and so on. Bytes are, in turn, grouped to form halfwords, fullwords, and doublewords; a fullword is four bytes in length (most other computer manufacturers use the term word for this element of memory).

On an IBM System/370, fullwords begin with every fourth byte; bytes 0, 1, 2, and 3 form the first fullword, bytes 4 through 7 form the second, and so on. The address of a fullword is simply the number of the first byte in that fullword: 0, 4, 8, . . . From a programmer's perspective, addressing main memory on an IBM System/370 consists of little more than counting bytes.

The Program
Status Word _____

A programmer takes a great deal for granted when submitting a program, assuming that individual statements *will* be executed in sequence unless, of course, a branch instruction is coded. It seems simple, but just how does the computer, more specifically the CPU, know which instruction to execute next? And, how is this instruction located? The answer to both questions is found in the *Program Status Word* or *PSW*. In more general, non-IBM terms, the PSW is the instruction counter described in an earlier chapter.

Actually, there are two different forms of the program status word on an IBM System/370. On a computer that does *not* have (or is *not* using) the dynamic address translation feature, the *basic control (BC) mode* of the PSW is used. The *extended control (EC) mode* of the PSW is used when the dynamic address translation feature is implemented. We'll look first at the basic control mode of the PSW, pointing out the differences in EC mode near the end of the chapter.

The program status word really isn't a word at all: it's a doubleword, 64-bits in length. It occupies a special system register. To illustrate the key program control function of the PSW, we'll use the brief assembler language program segment on the facing page.

This program segment loads two binary numbers stored at locations X and Y into registers 3 and 4, respectively, adds these two numbers, and stores the sum at Z, eventually coming back to repeat the instructions. The actual addresses shown on the left are expressed in decimal for convenience.

The last three bytes of the PSW (Fig. 15.1) contain the instruction address; this is the address of the instruction that is to be executed next. As the program segment is executed, we'll follow the changing content of this PSW field.

Address	Instruction		
1000	GO	L	3,X
1004		L	4,Y
1008		AR	3,4
1010		ST	3,Z

} several more instructions

| 1050 | | B | GO |

} balance of program

1100	X	DS	F
1104	Y	DS	F
1108	Z	DS	F

and so on.

In executing an instruction, the CPU goes through two distinct steps: the instruction cycle and the execution cycle. During the instruction cycle, the CPU gets one instruction from memory and decodes it; during the execution cycle, the computer executes the instruction. The PSW's instruction address field is the key to the instruction cycle.

As our program segment begins, the instruction address is, we'll assume, the binary equivalent of the decimal number 1000. The CPU simply looks at the PSW (which, you may remember, is *always* found in the same register) and gets the address of the instruction to be executed. In this step, the selected instruction is the first load, which is moved into the CPU for decoding. At some time during the instruction cycle, the central processing unit bumps the instruction address field of the program status word by four (the length of the load instruction) thus causing the PSW to point at address 1004 where the next instruction in sequence is stored. After the first load is executed and the value stored at location X is copied into register 3, the computer is ready for another instruction cycle. CPU's are not very original; the action taken is the same as before.

1. Find the instruction address in the PSW;
2. fetch the instruction stored at that address;

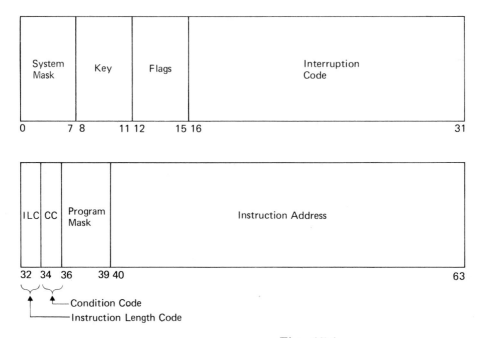

Fig. 15.1
The program status word format (BC mode).

3. bump up or increment the instruction address by the length of the current instruction—it now points at the "next" instruction;

4. decode the instruction;

5. enter the execution cycle;

6. go back to step number 1.

Thus the second load instruction is moved into the CPU (actually, into the instruction register and thus made available to the CPU), decoded, executed, and at some point in the instruction cycle, the instruction address is incremented by four so as to contain the address 1008, the location of the next instruction in sequence.

Following execution of this second instruction, the CPU again consults the PSW, fetches the add instruction from location 1008, adds two to the instruction address, decodes the instruction, and adds the contents of registers 3 and 4 during the execution cycle. Note that the instruction address was incremented by only 2 instead of 4 this time. Instructions can vary in length; the "AR" instruction is only two bytes long. How can the CPU tell the difference between a two-byte and a four-byte instruction? More about this in a few paragraphs.

The PSW now points at the store instruction; thus, during the next instruction cycle, the store instruction is fetched and decoded while the instruction address is bumped up by 4. Continuing in its single-minded fashion, the computer executes a number of other instructions, in sequence, until finally the instruction address points to the branch instruction. As before, the instruction stored at this address (1050) is moved into the CPU and decoded while the instruction length is incremented by 4. The execution cycle of a branch instruction is, however, a bit different. The branch instruction causes the CPU to replace the contents of the instruction address field of the PSW with the address specified in the instruction operand—in this case with address 1000. The next instruction to be executed will be the one labeled GO.

The instruction address is 3 bytes or 24 bits long. The biggest binary number that can be stored in 24 bits is equivalent to the decimal number 16,777,215; this 3-byte format makes it impossible for an IBM System/370 computer to address more than 16 megabytes of main memory.

Variable
Length Instructions

As we saw in the example above, not all instructions need be the same length; the main factor affecting the length of an instruction is the addressing scheme used by IBM. Registers can be addressed in four bits—the 16 general-purpose registers are numbered 0 through 15, which is a hexadecimal "F." Main memory addresses require more information. Back in the second generation when core was occupied by one program at a time, the programmer could assume a start point for a job, usually address zero, and address everything from this reference point. With multiprogramming, this control disappeared; with ten programs in memory at any one time, the programmer cannot assume a constant load point. The solution to this problem involves relative addressing. Programs are written as though they start at location zero, with the actual start address being supplied as the program begins its execution. The actual start address is stored in a register called the base register; byte locations relative to this base are called displacements. The absolute address of a particular byte in main memory can be obtained by adding the displacement to the contents of the base register. Displacements are limited to 4095 bytes (hex FFF) from any base; longer programs require multiple base registers. Note that even without segmentation, paging, or virtual memory, these base-plus-displacement addresses within an instruction must be converted to absolute main memory addresses before the arithmetic and logical unit can execute the instruction; this is part of the instruction control unit's address translation function.

Let's assume, using our sample program from above, that the address of the first instruction, address 1000, has been loaded into register 12 (the digit

"C" in hex). The absolute and relative addresses of the instructions and storage areas in this program segment are

Absolute Address	Relative Address		Instruction
	Base	Displacement	
1000	C	000	L 3,X
1004	C	004	L 4,Y
1008	C	008	AR 3,4
1010	C	010	ST 3,Z

Displacements are once again expressed in decimal to simplify the discussion.

The first instruction, as you may recall, had a label—GO. The address of this label can be expressed in several ways. For one thing, it's at absolute address 1000. If this address has been stored in register twelve, another way of expressing this same location is as a displacement of zero from base register twelve, i.e., the content of a base register plus a displacement. Because a register can always be identified with four bits and the maximum allowable displacement from a single base register is 4095 bytes which in binary is a 12-bit number, the entire, "base register plus displacement" address fits in a 16-bit or two-byte field.

Back again to variable length instructions. Some instructions (for instance, the AR or add registers instruction of our example) involve two registers. Combining a one-byte operation code with the one byte needed to identify two separate registers yields a two-byte (halfword) instruction. Other instructions, the loads and stores for example, involve the movement or processing of data between memory and a register. The one-byte operation code, combined with a half-byte register address and a two-byte memory address, sums to three-and-one-half bytes; the extra half byte is normally used to hold an index register, giving an instruction four bytes (two halfwords) in length. Storage-to-storage operations are also possible; these include an operation code, two memory addresses, and, frequently, a one-byte length field for a total of three halfwords (six bytes).

How does the CPU know the difference? If the first two *bits* of the operation code are $(00)_2$, as in the add register instruction which has as its op code $(00011010)_2$, the instruction is a register-to-register instruction. Instructions involving both a register and a storage location begin with $(01)_2$ or $(10)_2$; those involving two storage locations all start with $(11)_2$. The CPU "knows" how long an instruction is by looking at its operation code.

The PSW contains a field to indicate the length of the instruction currently being executed; this is the "Instruction Length Code" field (predictably) of the PSW and occupies (Fig. 15.1 again) bits 32 and 33. This code is set at the same time the instruction address is incremented; both are hardware functions performed by the CPU. The instruction length code is used to track back to the address of the currently executing instruction should an error occur. Don't forget that the instruction address portion of the program status word points to the *next* instruction to be executed.

When exactly does this updating of the PSW take place? How does the computer know whether to get two, four, or six bytes per instruction without actually getting the instruction and checking the first two bits of the operation code? The answers to these questions depend on the hardware of a given machine. On a smaller machine or on any computer designed to move information into the CPU in 16-bit chunks, the instruction cycle consists of two distinct operations—get the first halfword, check it, and get the rest if necessary. With this system, the time spent waiting for the "rest" of the instruction provides a perfect opportunity for updating the PSW. Other machines might be designed to move more data between memory and the CPU at one time; on such a machine, it might make sense to always fetch the maximum possible instruction, simply ignoring unwanted material. At any rate, updating the PSW is a hardware function that can be performed at very high speed and in parallel with almost any other function.

Condition Codes

Have you ever wondered how the computer knows whether or not it is to branch following a conditional branch instruction? Following a comparison instruction or certain arithmetic instructions, a condition code is set; the conditional branch instruction checks this condition code and, if the condition code matches the condition indicated in the instruction, the branch is executed (the instruction-address portion of the PSW is modified). The condition code is found in bits 34 and 35 of the program status word (Fig. 15.1, again).

Memory Protection—
The Protect Key

On the IBM System/370, memory is allocated to an individual program in 2048 (2K) byte blocks. One problem with multiprogramming that you may recall from a prior chapter is the possibility of interprogram interference, i.e., one program destroying or modifying another. To avoid this problem, IBM has developed a protection feature, the key to which is the *protection key* found in bits 8 through 11 of the PSW. As main memory is assigned to a program, each 2K block is given the same four-bit protection key; later, during execution of the program, access to any 2K block not having the same protect key is grounds for immediate program termination.

Note that a *different* protect key is *not* assigned to each 2048 byte block in the system's memory; instead, the *same* key is assigned to *all* blocks associated with the same program. The resident operating system, to cite one example, is normally assigned the protect key $(0000)_2$; if this operating system needs 50K of memory, the first 25 blocks would *all* have protect key $(0000)_2$. Later, a 100K application program might be assigned 50 consecutive blocks all with protect key $(0011)_2$. Refer to Fig. 15.1 for a diagram of the PSW fields.

Other PSW Fields

Thus far, we've discussed the meaning of the protection key, the ILC or instruction length code, the CC or condition code, and the instruction address portions of the PSW. Several other fields (Fig. 15.1 again) remain. Most of these fields have to do with program interruptions; thus we'll postpone our discussion until a bit later.

Controlling I/O

Input and output devices are very slow when compared with the internal processing speeds of the computer itself; multiprogramming, as you may remember, was essentially a reaction to this problem. Back in the chapter on hardware, we discussed a partial solution to this problem—the channel. A channel is essentially a small, special-purpose computer placed between the I/O device and the computer; among its functions are buffering, counting bytes, and incrementing a memory address. Because the channel is a separate hardware device, these functions can be performed in parallel with other computer operations such as the execution of another program.

How does a channel know what to do? Where does the channel get its instructions (it is a kind of computer)? How does the channel know how many bytes are to be moved between an I/O device and the computer's main memory? Where in core can the data be found (output)? Where are the new data to be placed (input)? This information is given to the channel and the channel communicates with the CPU through three fields called the Channel Address Word (CAW), Channel Status Word (CSW), and Channel Command Word (CCW).

Let's consider the CCW first. Like any computer, the channel needs instructions to operate; a *channel program* consists of a series of *channel command words* or *CCW's*. (Fig. 15.2). A channel command word is really a doubleword; it holds a command code analogous to an operation code in a regular instruction, a data address showing where data can be found (or where they are to be stored) in memory, a byte count field showing the number of bytes to be moved, and a number of flags to hold channel and operation information. An

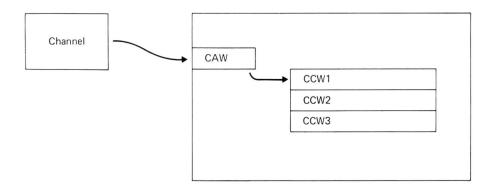

Channel Command Word

Channel Address Word

Fig. 15.2
**The channel address word and the channel
program**

operation might indicate a read, or a write, or a tape rewind, or any other operation. A channel program consists of one or more channel command words; it is written by a programmer to control a specific I/O operation. Like any other program, it is stored in main memory, often as a part of an access method. The relationship of the channel command word to the channel is just like that of the program instruction to the central processing unit.

Much as the computer program has its program status word, the channel has its *channel address word* or *CAW*. The channel address word is found at a fixed location in main memory, byte address 72, and contains the address of the first channel command word to be executed by the channel (Fig. 15.2). The channel program address is placed in the channel address word just prior to the actual beginning of the I/O operation; the channel uses this field to find its first command. Following this initial contact, the channel keeps track of its next command on its own. A computer may have several channels and there is no sense tying up the system's only channel address word to support one channel.

Information relating to the status of a channel is passed to the computer through the *channel status word* or *CSW* (Fig. 15.3). Like the channel command word, it's really a doubleword; the channel address word is the only *word* in this group. The CSW contains, in addition to the address of the channel program being executed, the data address, byte count, and a status field where a binary code is used to indicate such information as device busy, channel-end, device-end, or a program check—in other words, the status of the input or output operation. Both the channel address word and the channel status word contain the program's protection key, allowing for memory protection checks during an input or output operation.

Let's briefly review I/O control on an IBM System/370 (Fig. 15.4). We begin with the application program. The application program transfers control to another part of the load module—the access method. In the access method is a channel program. The access method logic, using the parameters passed to it by the main program, completes the channel program (the CCWs), and issues an interrupt to transfer control to the operating system. The operating system's interrupt handler routine places the address of the first CCW in the channel program into the CAW or channel address word, which is found at main memory address 72, and issues a start I/O (SIO) instruction. The channel, at a later

Fig. 15.3
The channel status word

Channel Status Word

Key		Command Address	Status	Byte Count

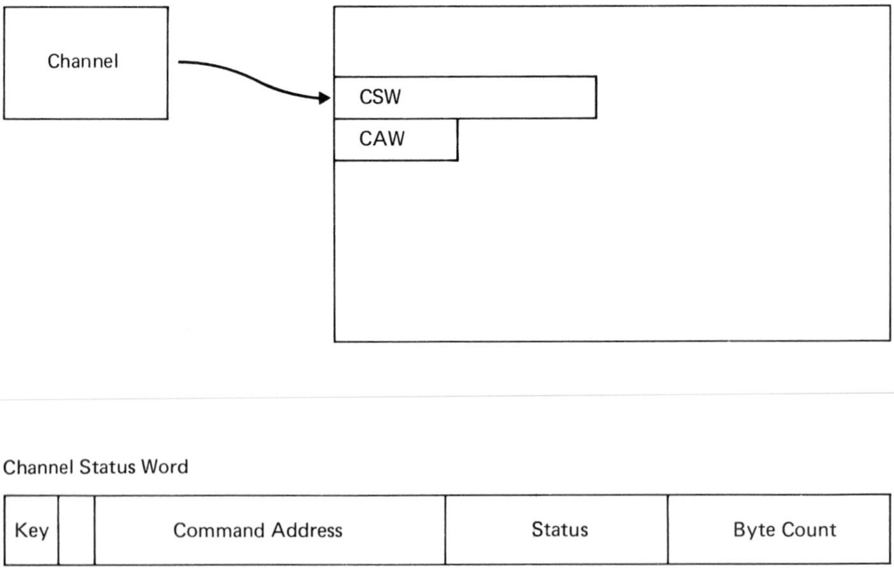

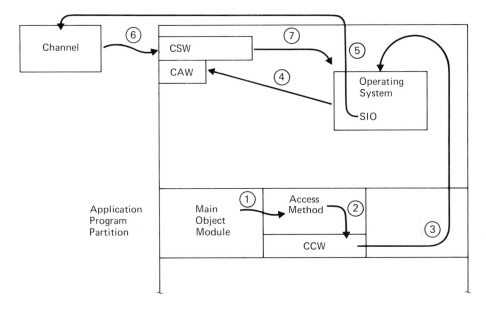

Fig. 15.4
Channel communication. ① The main object
module transfers control to the access method. ②
The access method logic completes the channel
program. ③ The access method transfers control
to the operating system. ④ The operating system
places the address of the first CCW in the CAW
(channel address word). ⑤ The operating system
issues a start I/O instruction. ⑥ The channel
issues an interrupt when the I/O operation is
complete, placing its status in the CSW. ⑦ The
operating system checks the channel status as
part of its interrupt handling routine.

time, issues an interrupt of its own, and reports its status to the operating
system through the channel status word (CSW)—memory address 64. The operating system can now return control to the application program.

Privileged Instructions

On a computer system running multiple programs and several channels at the
same time, the result of a policy allowing each program to completely control
its own I/O could be disastrous; a better approach is to funnel all input and

output operations through a single operating system module. This sounds great in theory, but what about the programmer who "cheats"?

On the IBM System/370, only a limited number of instructions are used to actually communicate with a channel; for example, Halt I/O (HIO), Start I/O (SIO), Test CHannel (TCH), and Test I/O (TIO). These instructions are *privileged;* i.e., they can be executed only by an operating system module. This principle is enforced by the memory protection feature; the operating system is given a protection key of $(0000)_2$ and the privileged instructions can be executed *only* when the protection key field of the PSW is $(0000)_2$.

In order to start an I/O operation, the programmer must first branch or link to an operating system module. This system program can then take over, set up the CAW, issue the privileged Start I/O instruction, and test the channel-status word (CSW) for error or successful start (Fig. 15.4). Since only the operating system can issue a privileged instruction, the programmer *must* surrender control to the operating system in order to start an I/O operation. Even if the programmer chooses not to use the channel programs found in the standard access methods and handles all the details of I/O with original code and original channel programs (a not very common but certainly not illegal choice), control must still be given to the operating system before I/O can begin.

Interrupt Concept

Exactly how does a programmer link to an operating system module? Labels won't work because a label is translated into a relative address by a compiler or an assembler and has meaning only within an object module. A branch to a fixed absolute address isn't practical; for one thing, the operating system has a different protection key. An external reference of some kind might provide a solution, but the *interrupt* concept provides a better one.

On an IBM System/370 computer, interrupts are recognized by switching PSW's. To visualize the workings of an interrupt, let's look at a typical system and highlight a few key components:

1. Our program
2. The operating system module that will start an actual I/O operation
3. The PSW (Fig. 15.5)
4. Two additional doublewords known respectively as the *old PSW* and the *new PSW* (Fig. 15.5)

The CPU is executing the application program by following its usual pattern—look at the PSW to find the address of the next instruction, find that instruction and decode it, execute the instruction, look at the PSW for the address of

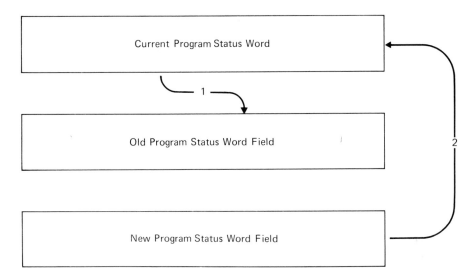

Fig. 15.5
The interrupt concept as implemented on an IBM
System/378.

the next instruction, and so on. At some point in time, the programmer is ready
for an I/O operation, and codes a special instruction: on the IBM computers, a
supervisor call (SVC) instruction. This instruction, like any other instruction, is
found by the CPU through the PSW, moved into the central processing unit,
decoded, and executed. What happens when the instruction is executed is, however, a bit different.

The SVC instruction, when executed, causes an interrupt to occur. An interrupt is implemented by system hardware. It's a two-step operation. First,
the current program status word is copied into the old PSW field. The new
PSW has as its instruction address field the address of the first instruction in
the operating system module; this new PSW is moved into the current PSW
field during the second step of the hardware operation. The central processing
unit now enters its next instruction cycle, looking for the instruction to be executed at the address specified in the current program status word; because of
PSW switching, this next instruction is in the operating system. The new PSW,
since it allows linkage to an operating system module, probably contains $(0000)_2$
in its protection key field thus allowing privileged instructions to be executed.
Later, control is returned to the application program by moving the old PSW
back into the current PSW location.

Let's review this interrupt concept again, step by step, using Fig. 15.6 as a

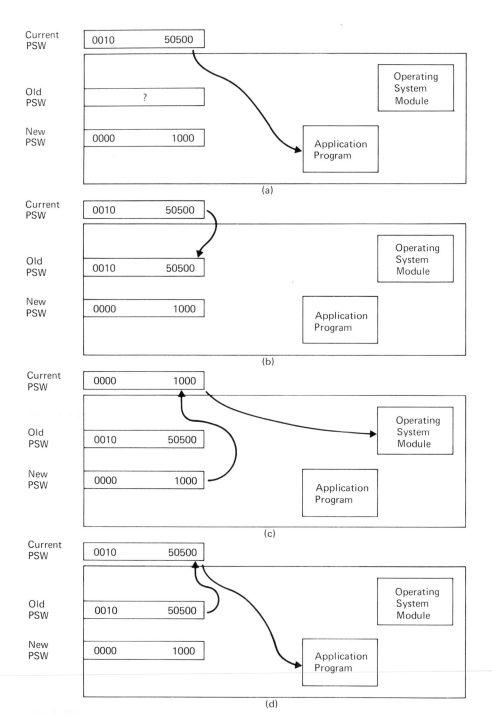

Fig. 15.6
The interrupt concept, step by step.

guide. Our program is loaded beginning with core location 50,000; the operating system module that will eventually handle our I/O is loaded starting with address 1000. The new PSW field, which is found at a fixed location in memory, has zeros as its protect key and 1000 as its instruction address (Fig. 15.6a); the old PSW, as we begin this operation, contains "who knows what." The current PSW, the key to CPU functioning, contains a protect key of $(0010)_2$, the key of our program; the instruction address reads 50,500 which is, let's assume, the address of the instruction immediately following a supervisor call (meaning that the supervisor call is currently executing).

The supervisor call instruction is like any other instruction during instruction time; not until the execution time does the actual interrupt occur. First, the current PSW is copied into the old PSW field which is found in a fixed location in memory (Fig. 15.6b). As soon as this step is completed, the new PSW is electronically copied into the current PSW register (Fig. 15.6c). This completes the interrupt.

The central processing unit is now ready for its next instruction cycle. Not being a particularly original thinker, the CPU looks for its next instruction at the address specified in the last three bytes of the current PSW, which now contains 1000, the address of the desired operating system module. The operating system module thus begins executing; since the protection key is $(0000)_2$, privileged instructions are allowed. Later, after the input or output operation has been started, the old PSW field is moved into the current PSW by the last instruction in the operating system module (Fig. 15.6d); the next CPU cycle will once again fetch an instruction in the application program.

That's really all there is to it, the interrupt concept is that simple. Don't try to look for complicating factors just because you're sure that interrupts "must be confusing"; there aren't any.

Interrupt Types

The IBM System/370 recognizes five distinct types of interrupts; they are

1. external,
2. supervisor call,
3. program,
4. machine-check,
5. input/output.

A sixth type, *restart,* is available on the System/370. It allows the operator or another CPU to start a program. We will not cover restart interrupts in detail.

External Interrupts

An *external interrupt* can come from any of three sources.

1. The operator's console (operator commands),

2. Another CPU or some other control device,

3. The timer.

Of prime importance to the average programmer is the timer interrupt; this is the mechanism for controlling a time-shared system or for terminating a program that has exceeded its time estimate.

An external interrupt is an electronic signal to the central processing unit. As the interrupt signal is received by the central processing unit, hardware takes over, dropping the current program status word into the old external PSW field (memory address 24, the fourth doubleword in main memory) and, shortly thereafter, moving the new external PSW into the current PSW field (Fig. 15.7). Incidentally, if the interrupt should arrive while the CPU is execut-

Fig. 15.7
External interrupts.

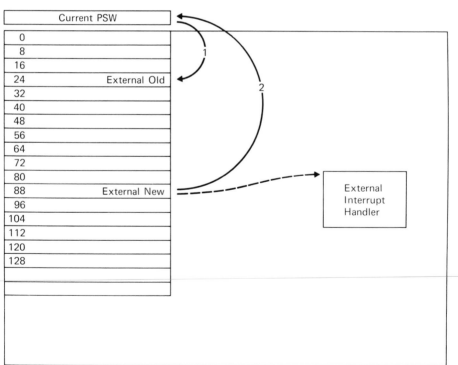

ing an instruction, the interrupt is delayed until the instruction is complete; i.e., external interrupts are recognized between instructions.

Bits 16 through 31 of the PSW contain an interrupt cause code. As part of the interrupt process, this 16-bit field is set in the old PSW, giving the external interrupt handler routine in the operating system the ability to identify the exact cause of the interrupt.

Supervisor Call (SVC) Interrupts

On the System/370, the programmer does not directly control any I/O operations, needing the help of the operating system—the resident portion of the operating system is known as the supervisor. The programmer links to this operating system module through the supervisor call or *SVC interrupt.*

The supervisor call interrupt is a bit different, starting with a program instruction. The SVC instruction is pretty straightforward with, for example,

        SVC   17

representing a request for supervisor module number 17 that might be a read or a write or an OPEN or a CLOSE or any other operating system module. The SVC interrupt handler routine starts with a branch table which gets us to the right module—each individual routine has its own number. Most programmers don't code their own SVC's, this instruction usually being buried in a macro or an access method.

During the execution cycle of an SVC instruction, the interrupt's hardware functions take over, dropping the current program status word into the old SVC PSW doubleword (memory address 32), moving the new SVC PSW (memory address 96) into the current PSW, and moving the operand fields of the SVC instruction, the 17 in our example above, into the interrupt code field of the old SVC PSW (Fig. 15.8). If you're getting tired of reading about PSW switching, that's good—you're learning it.

Program Interrupts

It's a rare programmer who doesn't soon learn about program interrupts—zero divides, invalid data, overflows, addressing, protection exceptions, and so on. A *program interrupt* is brought on by a programming error; the CPU recognizes such errors as they occur and implements hardware functions that copy the current PSW into the old program PSW field (address byte 40), copy the new program PSW (byte 104) into the current PSW, and move the interrupt cause

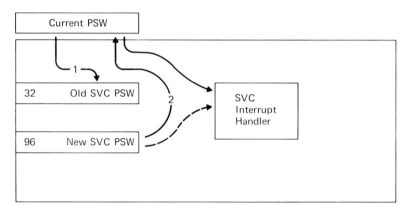

Fig. 15.8
Supervisor call interrupts.

code into the old program status word (Fig. 15.9). There are a total of twenty-one different program interrupt cause codes summarized in Fig. 15.10.

Machine
Check Interrupts

A *machine check interrupt* indicates that the self-checking circuitry of IBM's System/370 series has detected a hardware failure. If an instruction is executing when a machine check occurs, the instruction is terminated—there is no sense

Fig. 15.9
Program interrupts.

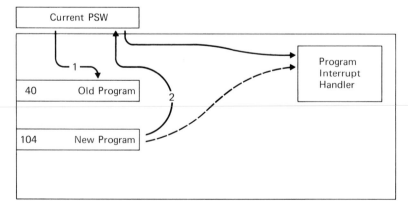

Code

Decimal	Hexidecimal	Meaning
1	0001	Operation—invalid operation code.
2	0002	Privileged operation—programmer attempted to execute a privileged operation outside protect key 0000.
3	0003	Execute—an EXECUTE instruction led to another EXECUTE instruction.
4	0004	Protection.
5	0005	Addressing.
6	0006	Specification—incorrect word boundary or register.
7	0007	Data—invalid data.
8	0008	Fixed-point overflow.
9	0009	Fixed-point divide—often a zero divide.
10	000A	Decimal overflow.
11	000B	Decimal divide.
12	000C	Exponent overflow—floating-point exponent too big.
13	000D	Exponent underflow.
14	000E	Significance—a floating-point addition or subtraction yields an all zero fraction.
15	000F	Floating-point divide.
16	0010	Segment-translation exception.
17	0011	Page-translation exception.
18	0012	Translation specification exception.
19	0013	Special-operation exception.
20	0014	Monitor event.
21	0015	Program event.

Fig. 15.10
Program interrupt cause codes. Note: The last six
codes are associated with dynamic address
translation and virtual memory.

trying to perform any computations or logical operations on a computer known to be malfunctioning. As a result of a machine check interrupt, the current PSW is copied into the doubleword starting at address 48 (the old machine check PSW), the new machine check PSW is copied into the current PSW and, under control of the operating system, the state of internal circuitry is copied into memory. The new machine check PSW is found in the doubleword beginning at address 112; this interrupt is described in graphical form in Fig. 15.11.

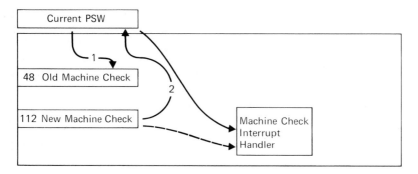

Fig. 15.11
Machine check interrupts.

Input/Output
Interrupts

Channels and the central processing unit work independently—the fact that a channel can free the CPU from the need to directly control an I/O operation is the primary justification for its use. Because the channel is working independently, it must have a mechanism for signaling the CPU when an operation is completed. This mechanism is the *input/output interrupt.*

When a channel completes input or completes output or for some other reason requires the attention of the central processing unit, an interrupt is sent. Note that the input/output interrupt originates in the channel. An *I/O interrupt* causes the current PSW to be copied into the old Input/Output interrupt doubleword (address 56), the new Input/Output PSW to be moved up to the current PSW location, and the channel and device address of the unit causing the interrupt to be dropped into the interrupt-cause-code field (bits 16 through

Fig. 15.12
Input/output interrupts.

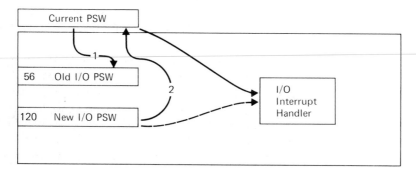

31) of the old program status word. The channel status word is also set by the interrupt hardware. If the central processing unit is executing an instruction at the time of the interrupt, that instruction is completed before the interrupt is recognized. The input/output interrupt is summarized in Fig. 15.12.

Permanent Storage Assignments

Throughout our discussion of the program status word, channel status word, channel address word, and interrupts, we indicated that most of these important fields are found in fixed memory locations; these *permanent storage assignments* are summarized in Fig. 15.13. Since these locations are fixed, the system programmer need not worry about the location of key information.

Masking

The typical data processing system has more than one channel—perhaps one multiplexer and two or three selectors; these channels operate independently and, often, simultaneously. It is possible that two or more I/O interrupts might

Fig. 15.13
Permanent storage assignments.

Address			
Decimal	Hexadecimal	Length	Purpose
0	0	doubleword	Restart new PSW
8	8	doubleword	Restart old PSW
16	10	doubleword	Unused
24	18	doubleword	External old PSW
32	20	doubleword	Supervisor call old PSW
40	28	doubleword	Program old PSW
48	30	doubleword	Machine check old PSW
56	38	doubleword	Input/Output old PSW
65	40	doubleword	Channel status word
72	48	word	Channel address word
76	4C	word	Unused
80	50	word	Timer
84	54	word	Unused
88	58	doubleword	External new PSW
96	60	doubleword	Supervisor call new PSW
104	68	doubleword	Program new PSW
112	70	doubleword	Machine check new PSW
120	78	doubleword	Input/Output new PSW

occur, from different channels, in a very brief span of time, perhaps even at the same instant of time. Let's see what might happen if two I/O interrupts were to arrive at the central processing unit within a few microseconds of each other.

As we begin this exercise, an application program, program A, has control of the CPU. The first of our input/output interrupts arrives at the central processing unit (Fig. 15.14a), dropping the current program status word into the old I/O interrupt slot and moving the new I/O interrupt PSW into the current PSW register. A brief instant later, a second interrupt arrives while the first one is still being processed. Hardware, in its automatic way, drops the current PSW into the old I/O PSW and moves the new I/O PSW to the current position (Fig. 15.14b). What happens to the link back to the program? Eventually, the operating system will return control to the original application program but, as a result of the perfectly normal system action in handling the second interrupt, the PSW showing where to resume the program has been wiped out. We've lost the ability to resume processing where we left off. This cannot be allowed to happen.

**Fig. 15.14
The problem with multiple input/output
interrupts in a brief span of time.**

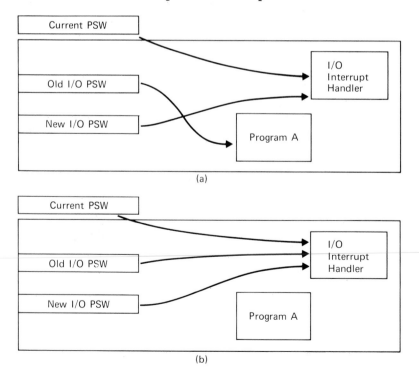

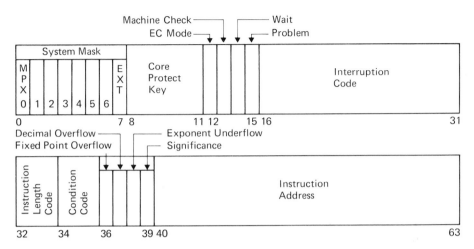

Fig. 15.15
The program status word.

The system mask, the first eight bits of the PSW, provides a mechanism for getting around this problem (Fig. 15.15). The first bit is associated with channel zero, usually the multiplexer; if this bit is a binary 1 the central processing unit can accept an interrupt from this channel, while a binary 0 indicates that the interrupt cannot be accepted and must be kept pending in the channel. Bits 1 through 6 have the same meaning for channels 1 through 6—selectors; a 1 means that an interrupt can be accepted by the CPU and a 0 means that the interrupt must be kept pending. If the new I/O PSW has binary zeros in its first seven bit positions (Fig. 15.16), no additional input/output interrupts can be accepted as long as this PSW is in control; as soon as the operating-

Fig. 15.16
Masking input/output interrupts.

	Mask	Key		
Current PSW	0000 0000	0000		I/O Interrupt Handler Address

	Mask	Key		
Old I/O PSW	1111 1111	0101		Application Program Address

	Mask	Key		
New I/O PSW	0000 0000	0000		I/O Interrupt Handler Address

system module that handles the interrupt finishes processing and, as its last act, moves the old I/O PSW back to the current position, a pending I/O interrupt can be recognized.

The eighth bit (bit number 7 since our count starts with 0) is used to mask external interrupts for much the same reason—one external interrupt might be closely followed by another. Much less likely, but still possible, is the occurrence of an external interrupt closely followed by an input/output interrupt closely followed by another external interrupt (or an I/O, external, I/O sequence), that could destroy a key program status word in the old external field even if external interrupts masked out all other external interrupts. To prevent this, both input/output and external interrupts are normally masked during the handling of *both* external *and* input/output interrupts.

What about the other three interrupt types? What happens if a supervisor call, a program interrupt, or a machine-check were to happen during the processing of some other interrupt? As far as simultaneous interrupts of the same type are concerned, both the SVC and program interrupts arise from a program instruction and because the CPU can only process one instruction at a time, simultaneous interrupts can't occur. If the operating system is handling an interrupt of any kind, it has no need for an SVC interrupt because the machine is already in a supervisor state; thus an "SVC and something" problem can't occur. Conflicts with a program interrupt are unlikely since, ideally, the operating system can't program check. If a machine check occurs, why worry about simultaneous interrupts? A machine check indicates a machine malfunction, and it's senseless to attempt to continue processing on a machine known to be in some way defective.

Incidentally, machine checks can be masked; usually during the processing of another machine check—PSW bit 13 controls this function.

The Program Mask

Following a program interrupt on most systems, normal system action is to terminate the program causing the interrupt, perhaps producing a dump. At times, the programmer may wish to override this standard procedure, providing a special subroutine to handle such potential problems as overflows or underflows—PL/1's ON CONDITION options are a good example. Bits 36 through 39 allow for the suppression of fixed-point overflows, decimal overflows, exponent underflows, and significance exceptions.

Program States

The computer, at any one time, is either executing a problem program or a supervisor program: i.e., it is either in the problem state or the supervisory state. Bit 15 of the PSW (Fig. 15.15) is used to indicate the computer's state—1 means problem and 0 means supervisory. This bit, along with the protection key, provides a double check for privileged instruction execution.

A given program is, additionally, ready to resume processing or waiting for the completion of an input or output operation: i.e., it's either in the ready state or the wait state. Bit 14 of the PSW is used to indicate a program's readiness; 0 means ready, 1 means wait.

The only program status word bit we have yet to mention is bit number 12: this bit is used to indicate whether the system is running in basic or extended control mode. To this point, we have considered the format of the PSW in basic control (BC) mode; later in the chapter, we'll discuss the extended control (EC) mode. For BC mode, this bit would be set to 0; for EC, it would contain 1.

Interrupt Priority

"If it can happen, it will." At some point in the life of a computer system, all types of interrupts will hit the central processing unit at precisely the same instant of time. Which is handled first? When faced with such a pure priority decision, almost any answer will do. The important thing is to have some procedure, *any* procedure, ready.

On the IBM System/370, the machine check will be serviced first—no sense trying to handle a supervisor call on a malfunctioning machine. Once the machine check is out of the way, here's what happens (Fig. 15.17).

1. The *program* interrupt is accepted, dropping the PSW of the application program into the old program PSW doubleword.

2. The *external* interrupt is accepted, dropping the current PSW, which points to the program interrupt handling routine, into the old external PSW.

3. The *input/output* interrupt is accepted, dropping the external interrupt's program status word into the old I/O PSW.

Because no more interrupts are pending (or if pending on a channel can't be accepted because of masking), the input/output interrupt handler, which is pointed to by the current program status word, begins processing. Following completion, the old I/O PSW is moved into the current PSW position, allowing the external interrupt handler to take over. This module, by making its old program status word current, transfers control to the program interrupt handler which, through the same mechanism, gets us back to the original program.

Incidentally, step number one above could have described either the program or the supervisor call interrupt; they can't possibly occur simultaneously. Why?

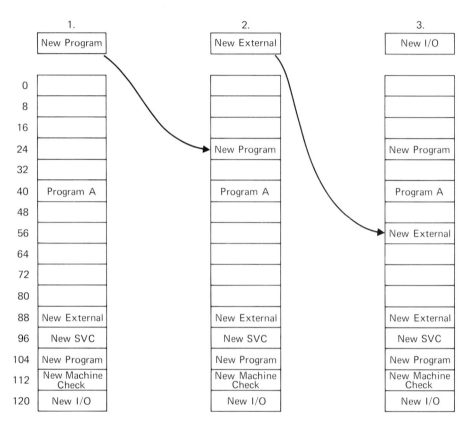

Fig. 15.17
Simultaneous interrupts.

A Typical Example

To illustrate the interrupt concept in a slightly different light, let's consider a simple example. Our program, the only problem program in main memory, is about to issue a supervisor call requesting the start of an input operation; the initial current PSW (Fig. 15.18a) points to the SVC instruction. During the CPU's instruction cycle, this instruction is moved into the central processing unit and decoded, and the instruction address is incremented by two bytes (the length of an SVC instruction).

     The execution of an SVC instruction causes a hardware interrupt, dropping the current program status word into the old SVC PSW and making the new SVC PSW current (Fig. 15.18b). The central processing unit continues to follow its same pattern, entering an instruction cycle by fetching the instruction stored at the address specified in the current program status word; following the interrupt, this instruction is in the supervisor call operating system routine (Fig. 15.18c).

After the supervisor call handling routine gets control, it

1. sets up a start I/O (SIO) instruction;

2. places the address of the first CCW into the channel address word (CAW);

3. issues the SIO, thus starting the physical input operation (Fig. 15.18d).

Before returning control to the initial program, the operating system module repeatedly checks the channel status word (CSW) until the channel reports either a successful or unsuccessful beginning; this is illustrated in Fig. 51.18(e). If unsuccessful, the operating system module either tries again or reports the reason for its failure; if successful, the channel assumes further responsibility for the transfer of data and the operating system module is finished. As its last act, the control program moves the old SVC PSW back into the current position (Fig. 15.18f), making sure to first set bit number 14 to a binary 1 indicating that, since the input operation has not yet been completed, the program is in a wait state.

With the current PSW indicating that the program in control is in a wait state, the CPU does nothing for a while. Finally, at some later time, the channel completes the input operation and sends an input/output interrupt to the CPU, dropping the current PSW into the old I/O PSW location and making the new I/O PSW current (Fig. 11.58g). The new current PSW has bit number 14 set to a binary zero indicating a run state; it points to the first instruction in the input/output interrupt handler routine, so that routine begins executing. The channel status word is checked to make sure that the operation was successfuly completed, while the interrupt cause code portion of the old I/O PSW shows the channel and device address of the interrupt source. After ascertaining that all is well with the requested input operation, the I/O interrupt handler sets bit number 14 in the old I/O PSW to zero (run state) and moves this program status word back to the current position, thus returning control to the original program (Fig. 15.18h).

With multiprogramming, of course, the problem is a bit more complex. During the time our computer spent in the wait state in the above example, a multiprogramming system would have started another program; since there is only one old and one new program status word field for each interrupt type, starting another program means that the latest PSW for the "waiting" program must be saved if a return trail is to be preserved. How this can be done is one of the topics covered in the next two chapters.

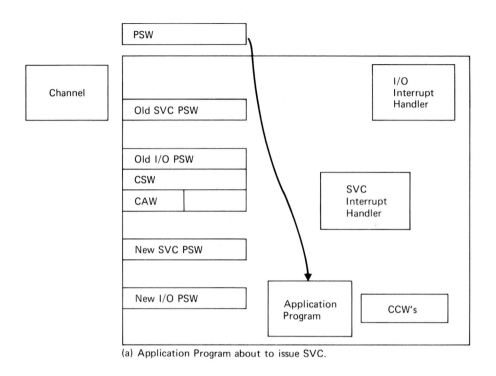

(a) Application Program about to issue SVC.

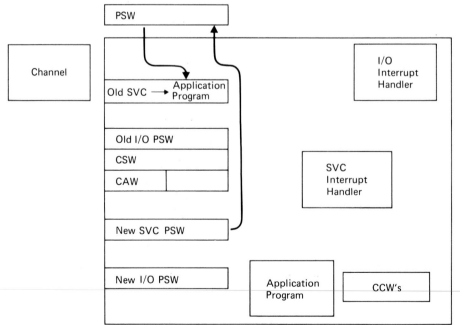

(b) PSWs switched as a result of SVC interrupt.

Fig. 15.18
An example of interrupts and channel
communications.

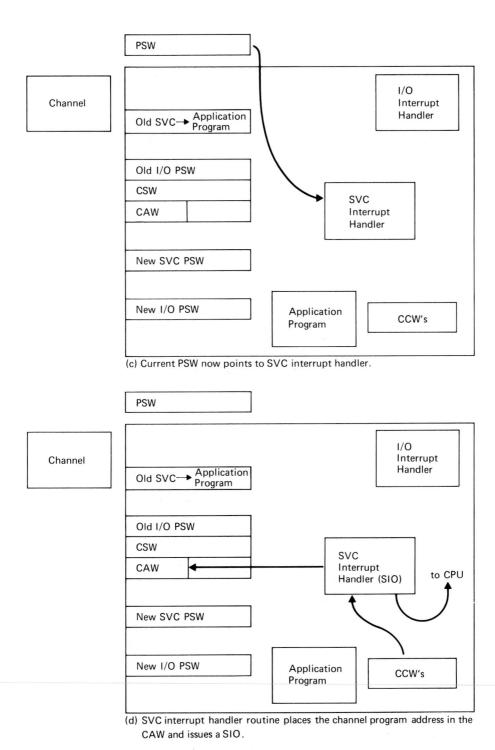

(c) Current PSW now points to SVC interrupt handler.

(d) SVC interrupt handler routine places the channel program address in the CAW and issues a SIO.

Fig. 15.18 (Cont.)

341

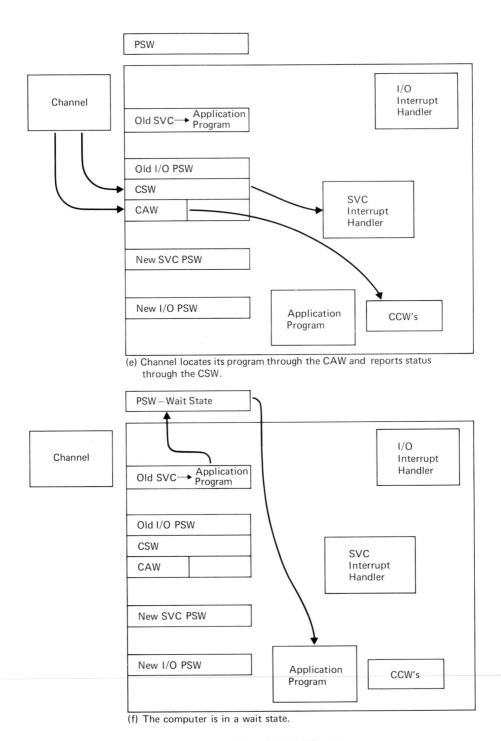

(e) Channel locates its program through the CAW and reports status through the CSW.

(f) The computer is in a wait state.

Fig. 15.18 (Cont.)

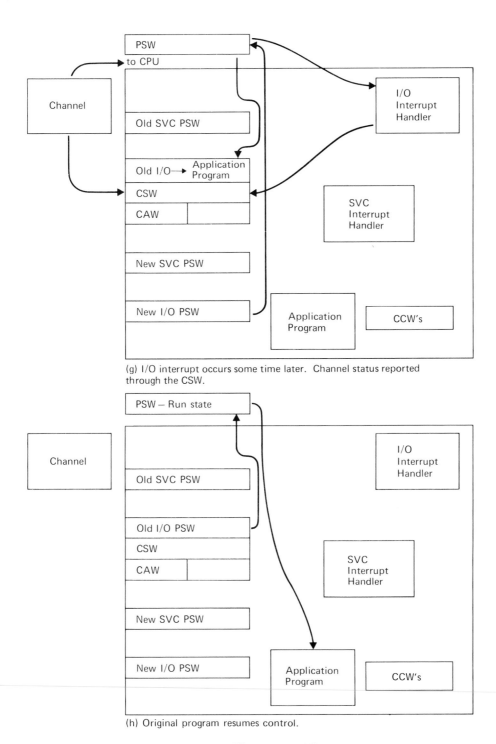

(g) I/O interrupt occurs some time later. Channel status reported through the CSW.

(h) Original program resumes control.

Fig. 15.18 (Cont.)

The Program
Status Word—
EC Mode

When the dynamic address translation (DAT) feature is used on an IBM System/370 computer, the format of the program status word is a bit different. The *extended control* or *EC mode* of the PSW is shown in Fig. 15.19. Let's consider the EC mode of the PSW bit by bit, highlighting how it differs from the BC mode.

The first eight bits of a BC mode PSW are used to hold I/O and external masks. Each channel on the system has its own 1-bit mask to limit I/O interrupts from that specific channel. Most of the time, if I/O interrupts are masked, *all* I/O interrupts are masked; only rarely does it make sense to accept

Fig. 15.19
The program status word (EC mode).

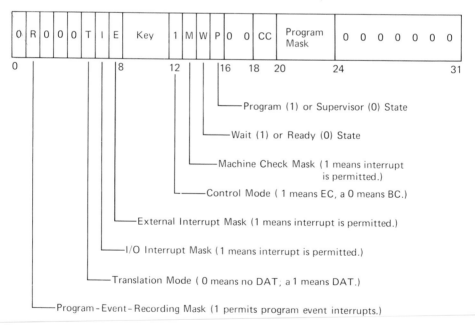

certain I/O interrupts from certain channels while processing another I/O interrupt. Under EC mode, only one bit, bit 6, is used to mask I/O interrupts; if bit 6 is set to 0, *no* I/O interrupts can be accepted. When bit 6 is set to 1, interrupts from specific channels are subject to the control of a series of mask bits in a special system register. External interrupts are still masked by bit 7 in an EC mode PSW (Fig. 15.19).

This frees six of the first eight bits. Two are used. Bit 1 is associated with a new facility of the System/370 series—program event recording (a special debugging feature that we will not cover in detail). Bit 5 controls dynamic address translation. If this bit is set to 0, addresses are not dynamically translated; if it's 1, they are. The other four bits in the first PSW byte are unused and must be set to 0 under EC mode.

With a BC mode PSW, the program's protection key is stored in bits 8 through 11; the protection key occupies the same four bits under EC mode (Fig. 15.19). Bit 12 identifies the mode; it contains 0 for the BC mode and 1 for the EC mode. Under both modes, bit 13 contains the machine check mask, bit 14 the wait state bit, and bit 15 the problem state bit. Thus the contents of the second PSW byte are virtually identical under both modes.

The next two bytes, bits 16 through 31, contained the interrupt cause code under BC mode. When the extended control mode is specified, the interrupt cause code is placed in a special system register, thus freeing these 16 bits. Bits 16 and 17 are unused, and must contain 0. The condition code is placed in bits 18 and 19, while the program mask occupies bits 20 through 23 (Fig. 15.19). Basically, this byte (bits 16 through 23) contains what used to be in bits 32 through 39 under the basic mode. The exception is the instruction length code: there is no such field in the EC mode PSW.

Bits 24 through 39 are unused under EC mode, and must contain 0's. The last three bytes of the PSW (bits 40 through 63) contain the instruction address under both modes.

Why the change? Why is the EC mode PSW so different from the BC mode PSW? The basic control mode was developed when the IBM System/360 computers were first designed in the early 1960s. Technology has changed since then. While a detailed explanation of why each bit position was changed would probably require access to IBM confidential information and would be only marginally instructive anyway, we can assume that the changes were made in the name of greater efficiency on a virtual memory system. Perhaps the EC mode is the real System/370 mode, while the BC mode is retained for those users who operate their computers without virtual memory.

In the EC mode, fully 22 of the 64 PSW bits are unused and must be set to 0—this can hardly be called efficiency! Additional changes to the IBM System/370 computer series might be anticipated, and these changes might involve some of the unused bits. Perhaps at this very moment, in an IBM development laboratory somewhere, new computer systems are using the unused bits. (In fact, as this was being written, IBM announced several new System/370 models that use a 31-bit address occupying bits 33 through 63. A 31-bit address means a two *gigabyte* memory limit!)

Summary _____

This chapter was concerned with defining the hardware environment of an IBM System/370 computer; subsequent chapters will deal with specific operating systems designed to run under this environment. The first major topic was the program status word, the system register that performs the function of identifying the next instruction to be executed on an IBM machine (in an earlier chapter, this function was performed by an instruction counter). Two forms of the PSW are used: the basic control (BC) mode and the extended control (EC) mode. We considered the BC mode of the PSW first.

Memory addressing and instruction formats on an IBM computer were discussed as necessary background. The instruction length code, condition code, and protection key are all found in the PSW.

The next major topic of the chapter concerned the problem of controlling I/O. In general, an application program gives control to an access method, which completes a channel program (one or more channel command words), and transfers control to the operating system. The operating system, in turn, places the address of the first CCW in the channel address word (CAW), and issues a privileged start I/O instruction; as a result, the channel gets control of the I/O operation. As the I/O is completed, the channel notifies the CPU through an interrupt, reporting its status through the channel status word (CSW). As a memory jog, you might remember that instructions or *commands* to the channel are defined in channel *command* words, the channel finds the *address* of its channel program through the channel *address* word, and the channel reports its *status* through the channel *status* word.

Next, we turned to the interrupt concept. On an IBM computer, interrupts are recognized by switching PSWs. For each type of interrupt there is both an old PSW and a new PSW at fixed locations in main memory. In response to an interrupt, the current PSW is dropped into the old PSW field, and the new PSW is made current. Five types of interrupts were discussed in the text: external, I/O, program, SVC, and machine check. A sixth interrupt type, restart, was not covered. Topics related to the interrupt concept included interrupt masking, program states, and interrupt priority.

The chapter ended with a discussion of the format of the EC mode of the program status word. The extended control mode is used when the dynamic address translation feature is implemented.

Key Words

channel address word (CAW)	new PSW
	old PSW
channel command word (CCW)	permanent storage assignments
channel program	privileged instruction
channel status word (CSW)	program interrupt
	program status word (PSW)
external interrupt	
interrupt	protection key
I/O interrupt	SVC interrupt
machine check interrupt	

Exercises

1. The IBM System/370 is a byte-addressed machine. What does this mean?

2. Relate the IBM program status word to the instruction counter described in an earlier chapter.

3. How does the PSW help to determine the order in which instructions are executed?

4. How can an IBM System/370 distinguish the length of its instructions?

5. Explain how I/O is controlled on an IBM System/370. What functions are performed by the following components.

   a) the access method

   b) the channel program

   c) the channel command word

   d) the channel address word

   e) the operating system

   f) the channel status word

6. What is a privileged instruction? Why are such instructions important in controlling I/O?

7. What is an interrupt? How is the interrupt concept implemented on an IBM System/370?

8. Name the five primary types of interrupts recognized on an IBM System/370. Describe the source of each.

9. What are permanent storage assignments? Why are they necessary on a computer like the IBM System/370?

10. Why is it necessary to mask certain types of interrupts at certain times?

11. Explain the priority of interrupts on an IBM System/370.

12. Distinguish between the BC mode and the EC mode. When is each used? How do the PSWs differ?

13. Assume that an IBM System/370 is running under basic control mode. The contents of certain fixed locations in main memory are

Address	Contents in Hexadecimal
0	FF04000BD0013000
8	0000000000000720
16	0000000000000000
24	00510082C0026400
32	FF510008C0031424
40	FF55000BC003F340
48	00510000C004A000
56	00510003C00422FA
64	0000000000000000
72	0000000000000000
80	0000000000000000
88	000500000001A000
96	FF05000000017000
104	FF05000000013000
112	0005000000011000
120	0005000000015000

Sketch a map of main memory showing the location of each of the interrupt handling routines. What kind of interrupt has just happened? What is the address of the "bad" instruction? Can an I/O interrupt happen now? How do you know? Can a privileged instruction be executed? How can you tell that the computer is in a basic control (BC) mode?

16

IBM System/370 Disk Operating System/Virtual Storage

Overview

IBM's Disk Operating System/Virtual Storage (DOS/VS) is an operating system designed to control an IBM System/370 computer. It includes modules to handle interrupts, coordinate job-to-job transition, communicate with channels, handle I/O operations, maintain a series of libraries, compile and link edit programs, and in general supervise a multiprogramming operation. All of these functions must be performed within an IBM System/370 environment. The operating system must provide a mechanism for smooth coordination between the programmer's application module and the PSW, interrupt handling, and channel communication concepts that are built into this computer series. In this chapter, we'll study the key operating system modules that handle these functions.

DOS is used on smaller system/370 computers. The operating system is somewhat limited in scope—the small user is rarely interested in software intended to be "all things to all people," preferring an operating system designed to be efficient in a small to mid-size business environment. This limited scope makes DOS an ideal operating system for our purposes here—it's great for introducing basic concepts.

DOS/VS System Geography

DOS/VS is designed to function in a virtual storage environment. As we begin our analysis of this operating system, it might be wise to start with the contents of virtual memory, considering how the system is mapped to physical storage later. Remember that virtual memory does not actually exist anywhere—virtual memory is a logical model of the system.

Virtual memory is usually larger (by a factor of three or four) than the real memory that will support it; for example, 1000K of real memory might support 3000K of virtual memory. It is possible to divide the virtual memory space into two components (Fig. 16.1). The first part, beginning with address 0, is exactly equal in size to real memory, and is called the *real address area*. Virtual space over and above the amount of real memory is called the *virtual address area*.

The resident operating system, known as the *supervisor,* occupies the low-address region of the real address area (Fig. 16.1). Following the supervisor comes a series of *real partitions,* one (potentially) for each application program partition. Certain types of applications, data communication routines, for ex-

Fig. 16.1
DOS/VS virtual memory geography.

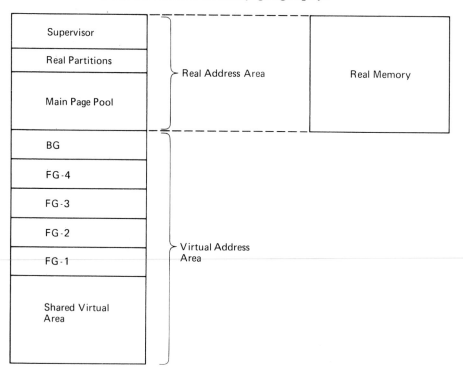

ample, often require that key modules be in real memory, i.e., that they *not* be paged. We'll consider such applications in Chapter 19; for the present, we will simply ignore the real partitions. The rest of the real address area contains the *page pool* in which individual application program pages will reside while executing.

The virtual address area is divided into from one to five application program partitions. First comes the low-priority *background partition* followed by up to four *foreground partitions* (Fig. 16.1, again). The partitions are physically defined in reverse priority order. Following the application program partitions is a *shared virtual area* that holds program load modules designed to be shared by all partitions; a data base manager (another topic from Chapter 20) might be one example.

How are the contents of virtual memory physically stored? The real address area occupies real memory (Fig. 16.2) while the virtual address area resides on external page storage, usually disk or drum. Pages from this external *page data set* are paged into and out from the page frame area of real memory (Fig. 16.2).

In our discussion of DOS/VS, we will be, in effect, "pretending" that programs and the operating system really reside in virtual memory. Remember that they do not actually reside there—virtual memory does not exist, it is merely a model. Concentrating on the model does, however, help to simplify our ability to visualize the functions of the operating system.

SYSGEN and IPL

An operating system does not simply spring into being; it must come from somewhere. The source is a procedure known as SYStem GENeration (SYSGEN).

The manufacturer (in this case, IBM) maintains a complete master copy of the operating system. When a customer decides to purchase or lease a computer, representatives of both IBM and the customer get together and plan the detailed content of the operating system for the customer's own operating environment. By analyzing typical applications and by identifying the specific devices to be attached to the system, it is possible to pinpoint those operating system modules that are of greatest importance to this specific installation; these key modules can be concentrated in the supervisor, the portion of the operating system that is core resident, while less-used modules are given transient status. Tables are created to support the specific I/O devices and the partition configuration chosen by the customer. This "made to order" version of the operating system is then copied to a SYStem RESidence device, usually a disk pack; this SYSRES pack, when transferred to the customer's computer, is the source of the operating system.

As long as the operating system, even a *disk* operating system, remains on a disk pack, it does little or no good; if the operating system is to perform

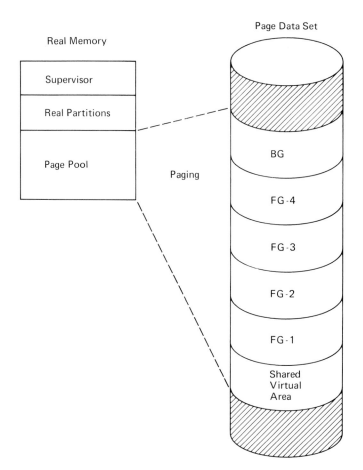

Page Data Set

Real Memory

Supervisor

Real Partitions

Page Pool

Paging

BG

FG-4

FG-3

FG-2

FG-1

Shared
Virtual
Area

Fig. 16.2
Physically storing the contents of virtual memory
under DOS/VS.

useful work, it must be copied from the SYSRES device into core. This objective is achieved through Initial Program Load (IPL).

Loading
Application
Programs

Following IPL, the system is ready to accept application programs. On several earlier versions of DOS, the computer operator could directly control the loading of an application program into a partition by using an operating system module called the single program initiation (SPI) routine. This routine is no longer supported under DOS/VS. With few exceptions, job-to-job or job-step-to-job-step transition is pretty trivial—an execute statement and, perhaps, a few device assignments. To insist that a human operator type these instructions each time a job is run is a very inefficient way of managing a computer system.

By using job control language, individual control statements can be key-punched or typed and subsequently read by an input device, a procedure that consumes far less time than typing every one on-line. A programmer can pre-pare a job deck, using a JOB card to mark the beginning, a "/&" card to mark the end, EXEC cards to identify individual job steps, and ASSGN cards to make I/O device assignments; this job deck thus becomes a self-contained series of program statements and system commands requiring iittle or no operator intervention (beyond, perhaps, mounting tapes or disks and responding to pro-gram messages) from program start to job completion. Job-step-to-job-step transition is handled by job control statements instead of by operator messages, a significantly more efficient procedure.

Why stop with one job? There is no reason why any number of jobs can't be loaded, back to back, into the system's input device and processed in se-quence, one job after another. JOB and "/&" statements serve to separate jobs, and, within a job, the EXEC statements serve to identify individual job steps. Using such a *job stream* approach, job-to-job transition can be handled smoothly and efficiently by a program written to interpret job control state-ments, with a minimum of operator intervention required.

The Job
Control Program

If you read the previous paragraph carefully, you probably noticed the follow-ing statement: "job-to-job transition can be handled smoothly and efficiently *by a program* written to interpret job control statements"; we've simply added italics this time. Program loading and program initiation are not automatic. The *job control program* takes care of these functions in a job stream approach.

The job control program is not a part of the resident operating system; instead, when a job transition point is reached (end of job step), the resident supervisor loads the job control program into the newly freed partition and passes control to this module. Job control then reads control statements, makes any necessary device assignments, prepares the partition for the execution of an application program, and handles other housekeeping functions. When the job control program encounters an EXEC statement, it asks the resident supervi-sor's program-loading routine to read in the requested program and give it control.

Let's review this process through an example, following Fig. 16.3. In Fig. 16.3(a), a program in background partition has just reached successful comple-tion, and this fact has been communicated to the resident operating system through a RETURN macro. The operating system loads a copy of the job con-

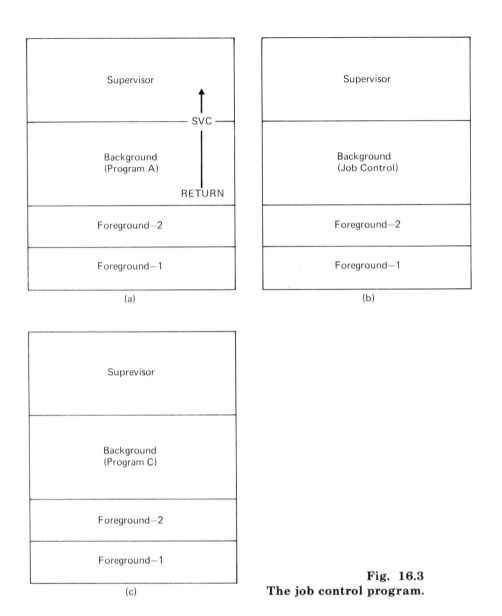

Fig. 16.3
The job control program.

trol program from the SYSRES pack into the background partition. This program overlays the problem program (which has just completed anyway). The job control program, once in memory, (Fig. 16.3b) reads job control statements for the next job step, performing any requested services. Normally, the last control statement in the job step is an EXEC statement; when this is encountered, the job control program turns control back to the resident operating system which loads the requested program from either the system or a private core-image library into the background partition, overlaying the job control program (Fig. 16.3c).

This discussion assumes that the program is loaded into virtual memory. What really happens is that an attempt is made to load all the pages from the new program into real memory. Except for the first few programs following IPL, there simply will not be room in real memory, as a significant number of pages will be in use by active programs. Thus the incoming application program will be paged-out to the external page device. The effective result is to load the program through real memory and onto the page data set.

Spooling and Queueing

What program is loaded next? Under DOS/VS, a separate job stream is maintained for each partition. When a partition becomes free, the job control program is loaded into this partition and reads the job stream associated with this partition. The first job in the job stream identifies the next program to be loaded.

What is the source of the job stream? On a smaller computer system, the source is frequently punched cards or small, relatively slow diskettes. Often, to gain efficiency, the job stream is spooled or queued to disk before being read by the job control program. A single job stream containing jobs for *all* partitions might be read by the spooler program and, based on a job class, queued to the job stream for the appropriate partition. Now, control statements and input data can be read from high-speed disk rather than from a slower device. A popular spooling routine designed to run under DOS/VS is *POWER/VS*. POWER/VS normally occupies the high-priority foreground-1 partition.

Multiprogramming and the Physical I/O Control System _____

Now that we've seen how the supervisor program is loaded via IPL and application programs are loaded by the job control program (job streams), we're ready to consider how DOS handles the multiprogramming problem. I/O—more specifically, the disparity between the speed of an I/O device and the computer's own internal processing speed—is, as you may recall, the key to multiprogramming. Rather than forcing a high-speed CPU to wait for a (relatively) slow I/O device, the CPU switches its attention to another program. By executing several programs concurrently, both throughput and turnaround time can be improved.

Because I/O is the key to multiprogramming, it follows that a study of the input and output functions as handled by a given operating system should provide excellent insight into multiprogramming controls. The *Physical Input/Output Control System* (*PIOCS* for short) of IBM's Disk Operating System does provide such an insight.

PIOCS is implemented through three macros: the *CCB* macro that creates something called a command control block, the *EXCP* or execute channel program macro and the *WAIT* macro. To use PIOCS, the programmer must first write a channel program using channel command words or CCW's as described in the prior chapter. This channel program is stored somewhere in the program partition (Fig. 16.4a). Also in the program, usually in among storage area definitions, the programmer must code a CCB macro. This macro creates a command control block, containing such information as the symbolic name of the actual I/O device, the address of the first CCW in the channel program, and various flags set by the user program or the operating system to indicate the status of an I/O operation.

When the programmer is ready to request an I/O operation, he or she issues an EXCP macro (Fig. 16.4b); this macro results in a supervisor call (SVC), transferring control to the operating system. The reason for this transfer of control is simple—only the supervisor is allowed to issue the SIO instruction needed to actually start an input or output operation. The only operand needed on an EXCP macro is the address of the CCB that, you may remember, contains the symbolic unit address and the address of the associated channel program.

Following execution of the services requested by the EXCP macro, the supervisor returns control to the application program (Fig. 16.4c). Usually, this program quickly reaches a point at which it is unable to continue until the requested I/O operation is completed, and issues a WAIT macro (again, referencing the CCB). This is another supervisor call. Its purpose is to tell the operating system that the issuing program is unable to continue until the operation described in the referenced CCB is completed. The supervisor is thus in a position to place the program into a wait state, remove its most current PSW (the old SVC PSW) from the interrupt queue, save the program's registers, and attempt to turn control over to another application program (Fig. 16.4d).

Where might the old PSW and the registers be stored? Remember (from Chapter 13) the idea of control blocks? Each application program partition has its own control block; under DOS/VS, these control blocks are found in the operating system's parameters area. This is where the old PSW and the registers are stored for future reference.

What if two or more programs are ready to go when our program enters a wait state? This is where partition priority comes in. Foreground-1 has high priority, followed by F-2, F-3, F-4, and the background partition; the program in the highest-priority partition will go first. The supervisor simply searches the partition control blocks in priority order, checking the wait state bit in the most current PSW. If it's still 1, a wait state, the next control block is checked. If it's 0, a ready state, the supervisor loads this "most current" PSW into the computer's current PSW register, giving this program control.

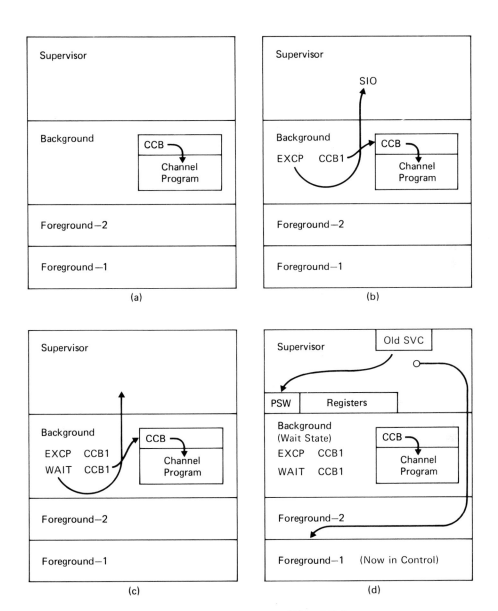

Fig. 16.4

The physical input/output control system.

The Logical
Input/Output
Control System

Very few application programmers are interested in writing their own channel programs and, in fact, most DOS programmers do not, directly, use PIOCS. Instead, they rely on a series macros known, collectively, as the *Logical Input/ Output Control System (LIOCS)*.

The programmer using the logical input/output control system must code a *DTF* macro for each file accessed by a program. The DTF (Define The File) macro generates a DTF table for the file containing detailed information about the data to be accessed—logical record size, block size, record format (fixed-length, variable-length)—and other descriptive information that defines the access method needed to process the data. The final stage in the generation of the macro involves setting up a series of address constants that, eventually, will link the DTF table and the access method logic module.

The linkage editor resolves these "external references" during the link edit step. In building the load module, a copy of the proper access method logic routine is "grafted" onto the program object module; the actual address of this access method routine replaces the address constants generated by the DTF macro. Once the program load module (or phase in DOS) is loaded and begins running, the programmer's GET and PUT or READ and WRITE macros reference the DTF table, resulting in a branch to the access method module included by the linkage editor (Fig. 16.5).

There are three key components to an access method logic module. First, it contains the actual channel program. The second key element of the access method module is the PIOCS instructions (CCB, EXCP, and WAIT macros) needed to support the requested operation—LIOCS *uses* PIOCS. Finally, the LIOCS module contains instructions to support blocking, deblocking, and buffering.

Multiprogramming
Summary

DOS/VS supports multiprogramming. In this mode, as you may recall, a number of programs (a maximum of five under DOS/VS) are loaded into core at the same time; the CPU processes these programs concurrently, switching its attention from one to another much as a chess master handles concurrent opponents. On a computer, multiprogramming takes advantage of the wide disparity between I/O and internal-processing speeds. When a program in the foreground-1 partition issues a request for input or output, the time required to fill this request is relatively long. Most of the time, the program will be unable to continue until the request is filled. Rather than force the entire computer system to wait, this single program is dropped into a wait state and control of the CPU is given to the foreground-2 partition (or some other partition if the F-2 program is also in a wait state).

The key to controlling this kind of multiprogramming is, obviously, I/O. On IBM's System/370, the instruction that actually begins an I/O operation, the SIO or Start I/O instruction, is privileged, meaning that it can be executed only by an operating system module in the first (protection key 0000) partition; thus the programmer *must* surrender control to the operating system. Once the supervisor has control, multiprogramming can be implemented.

Under DOS/VS, the physical input/output control system is the programmer's direct link to the multiprogramming functions of the operating system. The CCB or command control block macro creates a block of information and status flags allowing for communications between the processing program and

Fig. 16.5
A load module using LIOCS.

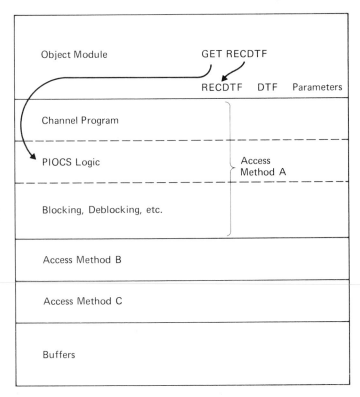

the supervisor's PIOCS logic modules. By coding an execute channel program (EXCP) macro, the programmer causes an SVC instruction to transfer control to the supervisor which issues an SIO instruction and returns control to the processing program. A third PIOCS macro, WAIT, allows the programmer to surrender control to the operating system which can, subsequently, transfer control of the CPU to another partition.

Most programmers do not actually code PIOCS macros. Instead, they code logical LIOCS macros—DTF's, GET's, PUT's, READ's, WRITE's—that link to an access method module grafted onto the load module by the linkage editor. This access method module contains the channel program, PIOCS logic, and blocking/deblocking routines needed by the program.

Incidentally, in many DOS/VS installations, application programmers do not code their own DTF's. Instead, the DTF's are written as system macros or simply prewritten and included in the programmer's source module through a COPY statement, thus allowing the programmer to concentrate on program logic rather than the details of an I/O operation.

Remember that DOS/VS is designed to run in a virtual storage environment. The operating system is stored in real memory, while the application programs reside on the external paging device or the page data set and are paged into real memory as needed. Paging can be viewed as a system function, performed automatically by the hardware under control of the operating system; paging does not change the *logical* flow of control through the system.

Memory Management

Now that we've considered how multiprogramming can be implemented under DOS, it's time to look at some of the problems created by multiprogramming. One of these is memory allocation. When main memory contains a number of unrelated programs, how is this key resource broken up and allocated? DOS/VS is a fixed-length partition operating system; at system generation time virtual memory is divided into a number of fixed-length partitions. The operator, at IPL time, can change the standard configuration but once the system starts running, memory allocation is fixed and constant.

Memory protection is a related problem. How can the system prevent a program in the background partition from destroying data or instructions in the foreground-1 partition? The answer is equally simple—each partition gets its own unique protection key, and any attempt to execute an instruction that would destroy the contents of any storage location outside a program's own protection key region results in a protection interrupt and, most likely, program termination.

Processor Management _____

When main memory contains two or more programs, and two or more are in a ready state, which one gets the CPU first? This internal priority decision is made by the supervisor under DOS/VS. Each partition has its own control block. The supervisor simply checks the control blocks in priority order, starting with the foreground-1 partition and ending with the background; the first partition containing a ready program gets control.

I/O Device Control _____

What if two programs both request input from the same tape drive at roughly the same time? When memory can contain a number of unrelated programs, this problem can exist, and the operating system must be able to handle it. DOS/VS uses three key tables to control I/O device allocation.

The first of these three tables is the *Physical Unit Block* or *PUB table*. Each physical device attached to the system has a single, 8-byte entry in the PUB table; the first byte identifies the channel number, the second identifies the device number, the other six hold various pointers and flags. This table, stored in the table region of the supervisor partition, is created at system generation time and is maintained in channel sequence, with devices attached to channel 0 (the multiplexer) coming first, followed by channel 1, and so on.

As you may recall from the chapter on DOS job control (Chapter 8) the programmer rarely refers to a physical I/O device, using instead, a symbolic name. These symbolic names are kept in a *Logical Unit Block* or *LUB table*— there is one such table *for each partition* active on the system. Individual LUB table entries are stored in a fixed sequence as shown in Fig. 16.6. These entries are each two bytes long, with the first byte pointing to a PUB table entry.

Probably the best way to visualize the functioning of these two tables is through an example (Fig. 16.7). Let's assume that a program in the background partition has just issued an I/O request referencing a device known as SYSIPT. To find the actual device being referenced, the supervisor first looks at the Logical Unit Block (LUB) table for the background partition; since SYSIPT is *always* the second entry in any LUB table, attention is focused on this second block (Fig. 16.7a). The first byte of this entry identifies Physical Unit Block (PUB) table entry number 03 as the one containing the information giving the physical device assigned to SYSIPT for the background partition—it's channel 0, device 14 (OE in hex, Fig. 16.7b). As you may recall from Chapter 15, the Start I/O instruction contains in the operands field the channel and device address of the unit, the PUB table entry is where this information comes from

SYSRDR	Input unit for job control statements
SYSIPT	Input unit for application programs
SYSIN	(Optional) System input device for spooling
SYSPCH	Punched card output unit
SYSLST	Printer output unit
SYSOUT	(Optional) System output device for spooling
SYSLOG	Operator messages output unit
SYSLNK	Disk extent for linkage editor input
SYSRES	System residence device (or extent)
SYSVIS	Disk extent for virtual storage support
SYSCAT	Disk extent for VSAM master catalog
SYSCLB	Private core image library
SYSRLB	Private relocatable (object module) library
SYSSLB	Private source statement library
SYSREC	Disk extent for error logging
SYS000– SYSmax	Other units. Exact meaning is installation dependent

Fig. 16.6
LUB table sequence.

(Fig. 16.7c). Assuming that the channel is free, the channel/device address is moved into a SIO instruction, the instruction is executed, and the channel takes over.

But what if the channel is *not* free? Rather than keep the system waiting, an I/O operation that cannot be started because of a channel-busy condition is placed on a channel queue, a third key I/O control table, for later processing. Later, when an I/O interrupt signals the end of an I/O operation, the supervisor checks the channel queue table to see if any additional operations are pending for the channel; if there are, the supervisor starts the pending request before resuming normal processing.

Individual channel queue entries are four bytes in length; they contain the address of the command control block (CCB) in the requesting program and a pointer to the next channel queue entry. One of the fields in the individual physical unit block (PUB) entries points to the channel queue. Channel queues allow the system to avoid the problem of simultaneous (almost) access to the same device. Other fields in the PUB entry allow a specific device, a tape drive, for example—to be assigned to a given partition for the life of a job, a request that is communicated through an ASSGN statement. Since every I/O operation must go through the PUB table, this gives pretty good control.

This *could* cause a problem. Card input is common to many programs; let's assume that the foreground–1, foreground–2, and background partitions all require card input. Why not attach three card readers to the system? There is,

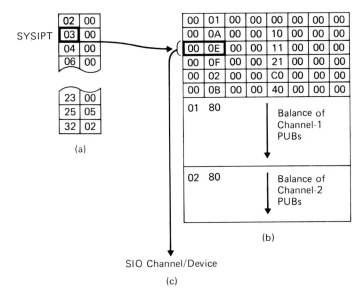

00	01	00	00	00	00	00	00
00	0A	00	00	10	00	00	00
00	0E	00	00	11	00	00	00
00	0F	00	00	21	00	00	00
00	02	00	00	C0	00	00	00
00	0B	00	00	40	00	00	00

SYSIPT

02	00
03	00
04	00
06	00

23	00
25	05
32	02

(a)

01 80   Balance of
              Channel-1
              PUBs

02 80   Balance of
              Channel-2
              PUBs

(b)

SIO Channel/Device

(c)

Fig. 16.7
The relationship between the logical unit control
block table and the physical unit control block
table. (a) The LUB table; (b) the PUB table; and
(c) the SIO instruction.

don't forget, one LUB table for *each* partition; in F–1, SYSIPT might be assigned to PUB entry 1 and thus, indirectly, to channel 00 device 01 (Fig. 16.8),
while in F–2, SYSIPT is tied to PUB entry 2 and channel 00 device 02. In the
background LUB, SYSIPT points to PUB #3 and, indirectly again, channel 00
device 03 (Fig. 16.8).

Spooling is implemented in much the same way. Assuming that the spooling routine resides in the F–1 partition, SYSRDR and SYSIPT for this partition refer to an actual card reader; in all other partition LUB tables, SYSRDR
and SYSIPT refer to the spooled file created by the spooling program. Thus
the programmer is not aware of the actual source of data on a spooled system.
When spooling is used, programmers often mix job control statements and data
in the same job stream. Under DOS/VS, another logical input device, SYSIN,
can be designated as the system input device containing both control statements and data. On output, SYSOUT can be designated as the spooled system
output device.

Throughout this discussion we've been referring to the supervisor in general terms as we discussed the logic of controlling I/O; actually, there are a number of easily identified supervisor *modules* involved. The programmer requests

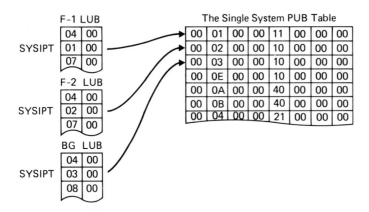

Fig. 16.8
Three-card readers for three partitions.

the help of the supervisor through a supervisor call interrupt which is handled by an SVC interrupt handling routine. The LUB and PUB table relationship, channel queueing functions, and the issuing of SIO instructions are handled by a channel scheduler module. I/O interrupts are handled by an I/O interrupt handler routine that links to the channel scheduler which checks for possible pending I/O operations for the "just freed" channel before returning control to a processing program. These few examples serve to illustrate the point that an operating system is a collection of program modules.

Job Queueing and External Priorities

The fourth major problem discussed in Chapter 13 was job queueing: when space (a partition) becomes available, which program is loaded onto the computer next? Under DOS/VS, a separate job stream is maintained for each partition. This job stream might be read via a partition's private physical device (SYSRDR). As an alternative, a spooling routine such as POWER/VS might read a common job stream and build the individual partition queues on disk; thus the source becomes SYSIN.

When a partition becomes free, the scheduler module of the supervisor will eventually gain control, recognize the free partition, and load the job control program. The job control program reads the job stream associated with the partition it occupies; for example, if the job control program is in partition foreground–2, it will read the job stream for foreground–2. How does the job control program find this job stream? It reads logical device SYSRDR or SYSIN; the LUB table entry for the referenced logical device in foreground–2 will reference a PUB table entry which points to a *specific* physical device, the source of the job stream. The first job defined by this job stream's control statements will be loaded next. (More accurately, the first or next program defined within this job—remember that a single job can define multiple programs through multiple EXEC statements—will be loaded.)

Librarian Functions

DOS/VS supports three levels of program libraries. A *source statement library,* as its name implies, holds source code (assembler or compiler language source statements) in modules called "books." Macro expansions are usually stored on a source statement library; when the macro is referenced in the programmer's source code, the associated book is simply added to the module and compiled or assembled along with the programmer's code. Data structures might be precoded and added to the source module through the use of a COPY statement. The system source statement library resides on the system residence pack; private source statement libraries are also supported, and can reside on almost any secondary storage device.

A *relocatable library* holds object modules. Access method logic, which is added to an object module by the linkage editor as it builds a load module, usually resides on the relocatable library. Subroutines can be added to a module by using the INCLUDE statement we discussed back in Chapter 8. Relocatable library object modules are read by the linkage editor and used in building a load module. As with source statement libraries, the system relocatable library resides on SYSRES. Private relocatable libraries are also supported by DOS/VS.

A load module, the output of the linkage editor, represents a module of machine-level code ready to be loaded and executed—it's a complete, ready-to-run program. Load modules are maintained on a *core image library.* An EXEC statement references a core image library member (called a phase under DOS/VS), instructing the supervisor to load the phase into a core partition and execute it. The system core image library is found on the system residence device and, and once again, private core image libraries are supported.

DOS/VS provides a number of special programs that maintain, service, and copy library members. These programs support such functions as adding, deleting, or renaming members, maintaining library directories, listing or punching library members, creating new private libraries; and reorganizing a library.

Summary

The chapter began with a discussion of DOS/VS operating system geography. Virtual memory was considered first. The real address area contains the supervisor, optional real partitions, and the page pool; the total size of the real area is equal to the size of real memory on a system. The virtual address area, the virtual space over and above the amount of real memory, is divided into a background partition, from one to four foreground partitions, and a shared virtual area. The real address area is physically stored in real memory. The virtual address area is physically stored on an external page data set, usually disk or drum. SYSGEN and IPL procedures were briefly described.

Programs are normally loaded into memory under control of the job control program. When a partition becomes free, the supervisor loads the transient job control program into this partition, and the job control program reads the job stream commands to identify the next program to be loaded. Often, spooling or queueing routines are used to make the process of reading the job stream more efficient.

The key to DOS/VS multiprogramming is the physical input/output control system (PIOCS) which is implemented through three macros—CCB which creates a command control block, EXCP which instructs the supervisor to execute a channel program, and WAIT which returns control to the supervisor so that another program partition can be given control. Few programmers actually use PIOCS, preferring the DTF, GET, and PUT macros of the logical input/output control system (LIOCS). The access method modules of LIOCS are grafted onto a load module at link edit time; these modules contain the necessary channel programs, PIOCS code, and blocking/deblocking and buffering logic.

I/O device allocation is controlled through a number of system tables. The physical unit block or PUB table holds one entry for each I/O device attached to the system. The logical unit block (LUB) table relates symbolic device assignments as used by the programmer to the actual device assignments in the PUB table. If a channel is busy at the time an input or output operation is requested, the request can be kept pending in core by placing it in a channel queue; later, when an I/O interrupt occurs, the interrupt handler routine turns control over to the channel scheduler routine that checks for pending I/O requests on the channel, starting the next one before returning control to a processing program.

Memory management under DOS/VS is similar to fixed partition memory management. Virtual memory space is broken into fixed-length foreground and background partitions at SYSGEN or IPL time; the task of paging the program between real memory and the page data set is a system function that is transparent to the programmer. The supervisor determines internal priority by searching the partition control blocks in a fixed order, from foreground–1 to background. External priorities are set by a job's position in the job stream. Each partition has its own job stream. When the partition becomes free, the job control program will load the next program defined by that partition's job stream.

The final subject covered in this chapter was that of libraries. DOS/VS supports source statement, relocatable, and core image libraries, both system and private.

Key Words

background partition	page pool
CCB (command control block)	physical input/output control system
core image library	Physical Unit Block (PUB)
DOS/VS	
DTF (Define The File)	PIOCS
EXCP (Execute Channel Program	POWER/VS
	real address area
foreground partition	real partition
job control program	relocatable library
job stream	shared virtual area
LIOCS	source statement library
Logical Input/Output Control System	
	supervisor
Logical Unit Block (LUB)	virtual address area
	WAIT
page data set	

Exercises

1. Distinguish between the real address area of virtual memory and the virtual address area of virtual memory under DOS/VS.

2. Sketch a map of virtual memory under DOS/VS, assuming four active application program partitions.

3. How are the contents of virtual memory physically stored under DOS/VS?

4. Explain how application programs are loaded from a core image library under DOS/VS. What does it mean when we say that the job control program is transient?

5. Explain how PIOCS is used to support multiprogramming under DOS/VS.

6. Explain the difference between PIOCS and LIOCS. Which one does the typical application programmer use? Why? When LIOCS is used, where is the PIOCS logic normally found?

7. Briefly describe memory management under DOS/VS.

8. Briefly describe processor management under DOS/VS.

9. Explain how I/O device access is controlled under DOS/VS. Why is there one LUB table for each partition? Why is there a single PUB table for the entire system?

10. Briefly explain how the external priority decision is made under DOS/VS.

11. Distinguish among a source statement library, a relocatable library, and a core image library.

17

IBM System/370 OS/VS1

Overview

In this chapter, we'll be discussing another operating system designed to support multiprogramming in a virtual memory environment on an IBM System/370 computer; it's known as OS/VS1.

We'll see how, through software, such problems as scheduling, memory allocation, CPU access, I/O device control and allocation, data management, and others are handled when memory is occupied by more than one program. Because this is an IBM operating system written to support an IBM computer, software is restricted and limited by IBM's hardware design; thus the operating system must be able to deal with interrupts, program status words, and the channel linkage fields.

The intent of this chapter is to illustrate, in general terms, how a typical operating system works. To do this, we'll have to analyze the operating system in some detail, but we are not really interested in a complete, "bit-level" understanding of what is really nothing more than one solution to a fairly common data processing problem; thus no attempt will be made to cover the detailed function of each and every operating system control block. A certain level of detail is essential if the student is to understand how an operating system works, but too much detail can be confusing. We hope that we have attained a reasonable balance. Read this material carefully, and refer to the illustrations as you read. Finally, try to concentrate on OS/VS1 as a *solution* to the multi-programming problem, and not as a separate problem in itself.

The Basic Structure of OS/VS1

IBM's OS/VS1 is a virtual storage operating system. As was the case with DOS/VS, perhaps the easiest way to begin to grasp the structure of the system is to define the contents of virtual memory first. Remember, once again, that the virtual memory does not actually exist anywhere—it is a logical model of the system.

Virtual memory space can be divided into two major components (Fig. 17.1): the *real address area* and the *virtual address area*. The *resident supervisor* is found at the beginning (address 0) of the real address area, followed by an area to store key system *control blocks*—we'll discuss several of these later. The rest of the real address area is called the *virtual equals real* (or *V = R*) *area,* and the line separating the real address area from the virtual address area is called the *V = R line*. If necessary, an application program can be assigned,

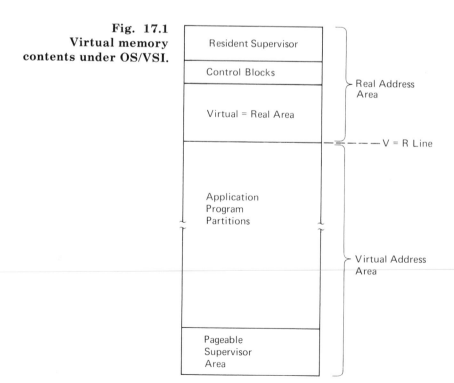

Fig. 17.1 Virtual memory contents under OS/VSI.

in whole or in part, to a real partition within the V = R area, remaining V = R space holds the page pool.

The virtual address area is divided into as many as fifteen fixed length application program partitions stored in reverse priority order; i.e., the lowest priority partition is closest to the real address area, and the highest priority partition is nearest the end of virtual memory. At the very end of virtual memory is space for the *pageable supervisor*—transient supervisor modules are executed from this space.

The contents of virtual memory are physically stored much as they were under DOS/VS. The real address area occupies the available real storage (Fig. 17.2), while the virtual address area occupies external storage: the page data

Fig. 17.2
Physically storing the contents of virtual memory under OS/VSI.

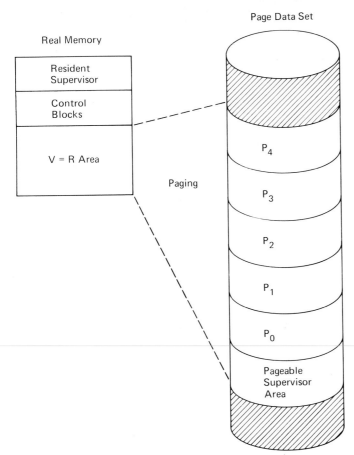

Page Data Set

Real Memory

Resident Supervisor

Control Blocks

V = R Area

Paging

P_4

P_3

P_2

P_1

P_0

Pageable Supervisor Area

set. Paging takes place between the external paging device and that portion of the V = R area not allocated to real partitions; in other words, the page pool.

As was the case with DOS/VS, our discussion of the OS/VS1 operating system will tend to emphasize the contents of *virtual* memory. Remember that virtual memory is merely a convenient logical model of the system; it does not physically exist anywhere.

As an example, let's set up the system we'll be using throughout this chapter. The system contains 500K of real memory supporting 2000K (or two megabytes) of virtual. The operating system and its control blocks require the first 100K, leaving 400K for the page pool; we'll assume that there are no real partitions.

The virtual address area holds, in this example, two application program partitions, each 500K long; the remaining 500K is the pageable supervisor area. We will run three different kinds of jobs on this system. Class A jobs, the most common type, are short-running jobs that will occupy the high-priority partition. Longer running jobs are run in the low-priority partition under Class B. A special class, C, is for jobs requiring tape and disk mounts; these jobs share the low-priority partition. This system is *not* intended to illustrate a *typical* OS/VS1 system; it merely provides a convenient base for a number of examples.

To help improve the efficiency of the system, application programs are spooled to a disk queue (Fig. 17.3); an operating system module performs this spooling function, while another operating system module moves program load modules from the queue and the various libraries into memory. Once in memory, other operating system modules handle interrupts, control communications with the input/output equipment, and perform other services for the application program. In the balance of this chapter, we'll be studying how the application programs and these operating system modules "fit together." We've already discussed, in general terms, most of these operating system modules in prior chapters; the functions will not be new, although the program and table names chosen by IBM may be. In the next few pages, we'll concentrate on IBM's program names and terminology, relating the individual OS/VS1 operating system components to the general functions of an operating system as described in Chapters 5, 6, 13, and 14. Once the key modules have been identified and defined, we'll consider the interrelationship of the operating system and two application programs by analyzing a few seconds of actual system time.

Jobs and Tasks

To a programmer interested in checking and testing a program, the functions of compiling and link editing a job are pretty much beside the point—all he or she wants is a job listing and a set of program results. To the computer, this rather simple job involves three distinct steps, with the compile step accepting source

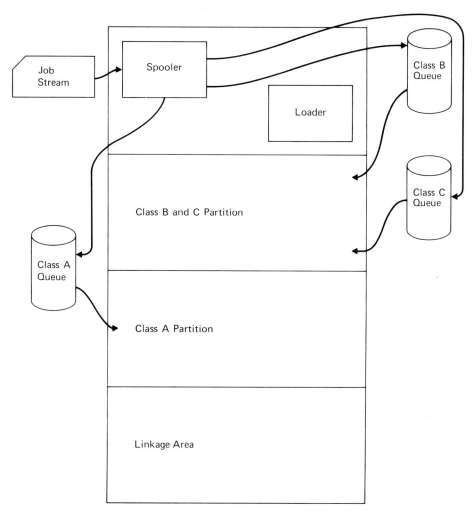

Fig. 17.3
Spooling and job classes.

input and producing object module output, the linkage editor reading the object module and producing a load module, and the load module being loaded and executed in the third step. The programmer looks at a *job*; the computer sees three job steps or *tasks*. A task is what the computer loads and executes. A job consists of one or more related tasks.

Within the operating system, the individual modules concerned with getting a job into the computer, including the functions of loading and starting the routines requested by individual job steps (EXEC statements), are grouped

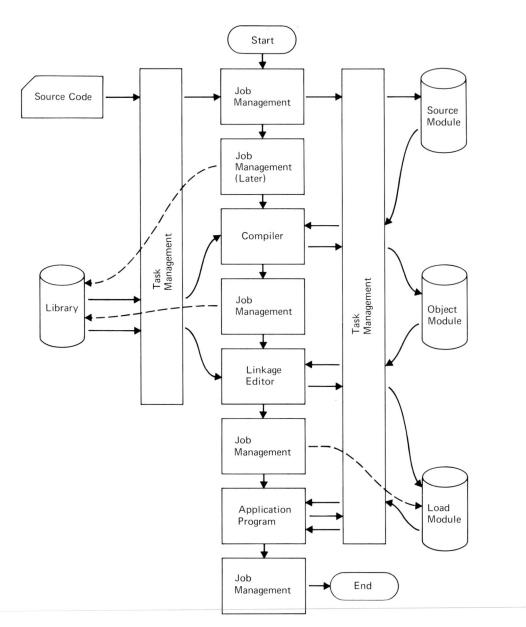

Fig. 17.4
Job management and task management.

under the general term of *job management*. Once a program or routine has been loaded, *task management* takes over the responsibility for operating system support of the program, basically handling interrupts. After the program completes, job management once again takes over, cleaning up the remnants and preparing the partition for another program.

Let's go over that again, step by step, following the flow chart in Fig. 17.4; we'll use a compile, link edit, and go job in our example. First, job management reads the source module, spooling it to a disk file. Some time later, another job management routine, recognizing the fact that a partition is free, reads the first EXEC statement for the job and loads and starts the compiler program. Should the compiler require the help of the operating system (a supervisor call to request the start of an I/O operation for example), help is provided through task management. As its last act, the compiler writes an object module to disk (with the help of task management, of course), after which job management takes over again and cleans up the partition. Job management can now load and start the linkage editor which reads (through task management) the object module and creates and writes, again with the help of task management, a load module. Job management then cleans up, loads the load module, and starts it. As the application program runs, the various interrupts are handled by task management. Upon completion, job management finishes up. Let's take a closer look at the operating system modules that constitute job and task management.

Job Management—The
Master Scheduler

Which job, or specifically job step, should be given control next? This question is answered by the *master scheduler* routine (Fig. 17.5). Most of the time, jobs are scheduled according to a preset rule (like first-in-queue, first-out) or by priority; at times, operator intervention is desirable. The operator can communicate with the master scheduler routine; using this facility, the operator can override standard system action, perhaps giving a "hot" job top priority or cancelling a job giving unacceptable intermediate results or locked in an obvious internal loop. The operator's console, as you may remember, is linked to an IBM computer through the mechanism of an external interrupt; once the interrupt handler routine recognizes the specific cause of the interrupt, it simply turns control over to the master scheduler through a branch instruction.

Job Management—The
Job Entry Subsystem

The *job entry subsystem* (*JES*) is responsible for reading the job stream and placing the jobs on appropriate class queues (Fig. 17.6). As the job is read, JCL statements are scanned for accuracy and, if they are undecipherable, the job is

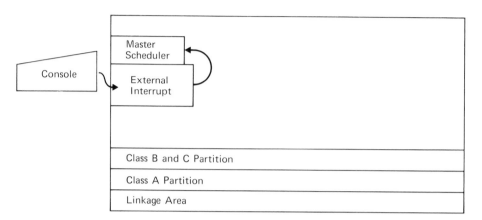

Fig. 17.5
The master scheduler.

cancelled at this point. Cataloged procedures are added to the job stream. A series of tables listing programs by class and within class by priority is created and maintained. Since input card data is part of the job stream, the system input device (SYSIN) comes from this job management function.

Fig. 17.6
JES and job queueing.

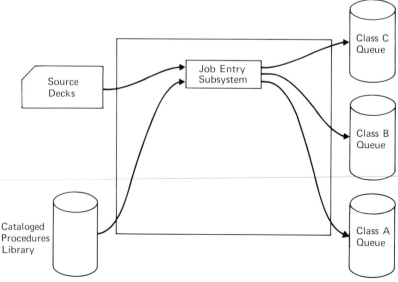

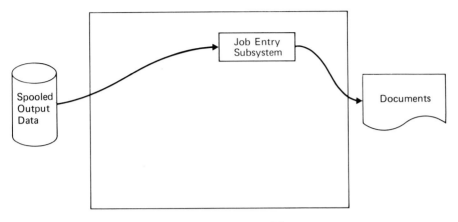

Fig. 17.7
JES and spooled output.

On output, programmers rarely communicate directly with such slow devices as printers or card punches. Instead, the output data are spooled to secondary storage and later printed or punched. Another function of the job entry subsystem is to control the transfer of data from the system devices to an ultimate output device (Fig. 17.7). JES is a new facility of the IBM System/370; in the earlier System/360 series, two operating system modules, the reader/interpreter and the output writer were used to perform these spooling and queueing functions. The job entry subsystem essentially combines the features of System/360 spoolers such as HASP, the reader/interpreter, and the output writer into a single operating system module.

Job Management—The Initiator/Terminator

As a partition becomes available, the *initiator/terminator*, takes a new job step from a class queue and loads it onto the system. An attempt is made to load this job step into real memory; most of the time, sufficient space will not be available, so the new program will be paged out to the page data set.

Under OS/VS1, there is one initiator/terminator for each partition on the system. Like the job control program of DOS/VS the initiator/terminator is a transient module, occupying the application program's partition between job steps. The terminator portion of this module, as you've probably already figured out, performs the clean-up functions at the end of a job step.

When the operator sets up the partitions, he or she indicates the job class or classes that are to run in the partition; the initiator/terminator for that partition works with the designated job class queue or queues only. Once the initi-

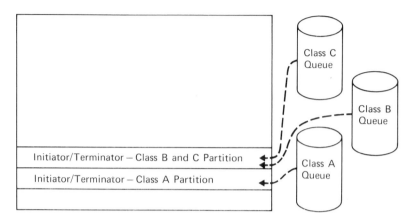

Fig. 17.8
The initiator/terminator.

ator has loaded a job step, task management takes over as the operating system's representative. The terminator routine comes into play at the conclusion of the job step.

To summarize, the job entry subsystem works with the complete *job,* reading all the job stream statements and enqueueing them, while the initiator/terminator concentrates on individual *job steps* (the EXEC statements), fetching them one at a time from the job class queue, performing the essential function of loading the individual job steps, and, following job-step conclusion, cleaning up the partition. The functions of the initiator/terminator are illustrated in Fig. 17.8.

Job Management— Summary

Job management is concerned with starting and finishing things. Under the control of job management, a given job is spooled, scheduled, loaded (by job step), and started. Once an individual job step begins executing on its own, job management is no longer involved; any needed operating system support is provided by task management. Once the application program completes, job management once again takes over, preparing the partition for the next job step.

Task Management

The function of task management is to support a program while it is running. A task management routine starts as a result of an interrupt. The SVC interrupt allows the programmer, through an SVC instruction, to initiate a link to an operating system module that can get an input or output operation started. The I/O interrupt allows the channel to control an I/O operation without the help of the computer, thus freeing the computer to work on another task; the channel simply signals the CPU when an operation is completed. Program errors and timer interrupts are handled by the program interrupt and external interrupt handlers, respectively. Programs are protected from machine errors by the machine-check interrupt handler routine.

We read about these interrupts back in Chapter 15. All the interrupt handler routines grouped together make up task management. Task management routines gain control of the computer as the result of an interrupt; following the completion of a task management routine, control is returned, normally, to the master scheduler, which determines the operating system module or application program to receive control next. Note that the *transition* from one task to another is a job management (master scheduler) function. Task management supports a task while it is running; job management is responsible for transitions.

Interrupts, as you may remember, are implemented through the switching of program status words, with the old PSW field providing a link back to the original program. There is only one old PSW field for each of the five types of interrupts. When a program enters the wait state—following the start of an I/O operation for example—this link must be removed from the PSW queues and stored somewhere in memory; if it isn't and another program is allowed to gain control, this link back to the initial program might be destroyed by a subsequent interrupt of the same type. Task management does this—we'll look at the mechanism shortly. Controlling program status is a task management function.

Tying Things Together— Basic VS1 Control Blocks

To execute a single job step, it is necessary to coordinate a number of job management, task management, and application program routines; how can all these separate subprograms and modules be made to work in concert? These separate routines are tied together and coordinated through a series of control blocks and pointers.

The key to finding most of the important system control blocks and pointers is the *Communication Vector Table* or *CVT* (Fig. 17.9). The CVT is essentially a table of addresses; it contains the address of most of the key control blocks. The communication vector table is itself pointed to by the address stored in the third doubleword in real storage—absolute address 16; this, as you

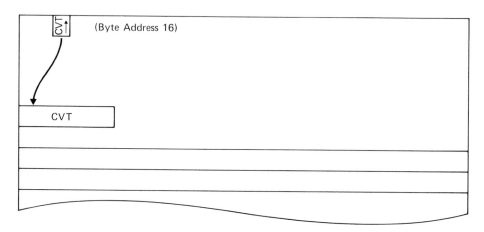

Fig. 17.9
The communication vector table.

may remember from Chapter 15, is one of the system's permanent storage assignments.

Activities within a partition are coordinated by a *task control block* or *TCB*. There is one TCB for each partition (Fig. 17.10). The communication vector table points to the first TCB which contains a pointer to the second TCB (Fig. 17.10)—this is called the TCB queue. On a system with more than two partitions, the CVT points to the first TCB which points to the second TCB which points to the third, and so on. If two or more programs are ready to

Fig. 17.10
The task control block queue.

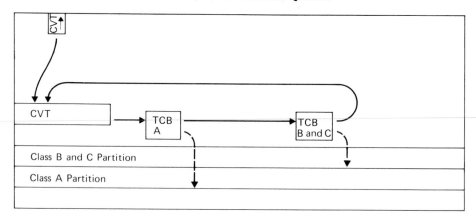

start at the same instant of time, which one goes first? Answer: the one whose TCB shows up earliest on the TCB queue. In our example, since the task control block for the Class A partition is the first one on the queue, Class A jobs have a higher internal priority than do Class B or Class C jobs.

The contents of a given partition are described by a series of *request blocks* spun off the task control block (Fig. 17.11). The existence of an active program within the partition is indicated by a *Program Request Block* or *PRB*. If a supervisor call interrupt is being processed in support of the partition, this fact is indicated by the presence of a *Supervisor Request Block* or *SVRB*. In a simple read-a-card, process-the-data, and print-a-line program, using the system input and output devices, it is not at all unusual for three request blocks to be active at one time—a PRB to indicate the presence of an active program and two SVRBs to show that system access methods are in the process of blocking or deblocking physical records.

Request blocks identify active modules executing in (or in support of) a partition; if the request block queue is empty, so is the partition. One of the

Fig. 17.11
The request block queue.

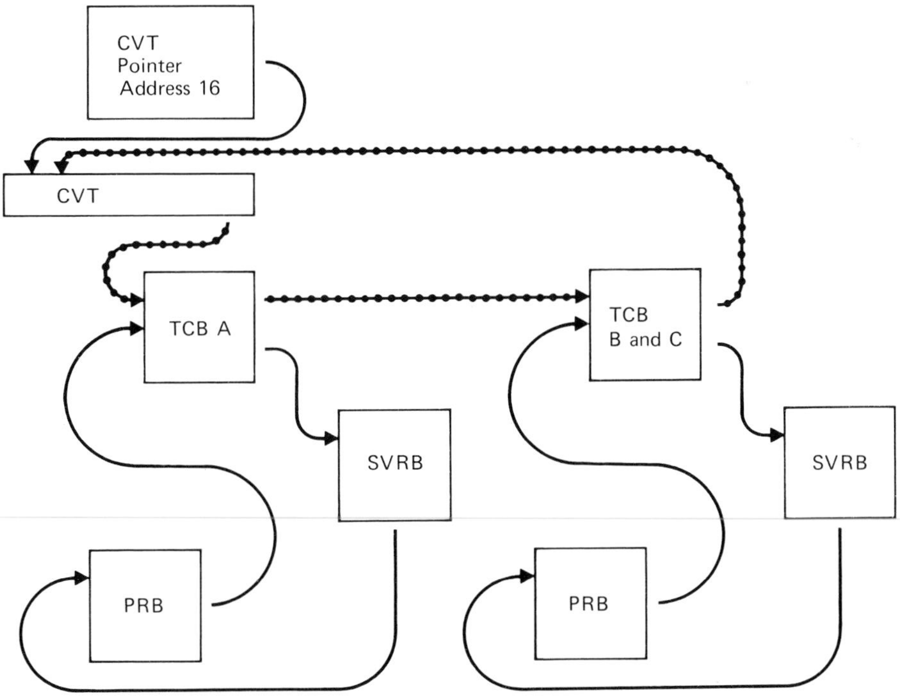

specific functions of the terminator module is to wipe out these request blocks following task completion. Job management finds an empty partition by finding a task control block with no request blocks attached.

An Example

One of the best ways to gain an understanding of these control blocks and pointers is to follow them through a few seconds of computer time. Our computer system is the one we've described earlier in this chapter—two partitions: for Class A and for Class B and Class C. The CVT points to the Class A task control block (Fig. 17.12), giving these jobs top internal priority. As we start our example, both partitions are empty (no request blocks) and a number of programs have already been spooled to the job class queues (on disk). As we start, the master scheduler routine has control (Fig. 17.12).

As we begin this example, remember that the operating system and the key task management control blocks are in real memory, but the application programs actually reside on the external page data set, with a set of active pages in real memory. To simplify the logical flow through the system, we'll diagram what happens in virtual memory. Don't forget that virtual memory is just a model of the physical system.

The master scheduler is going to try to get something started. In the absence of any operator commands, the master scheduler begins looking for an

Fig. 17.12
Our system as we begin our example.

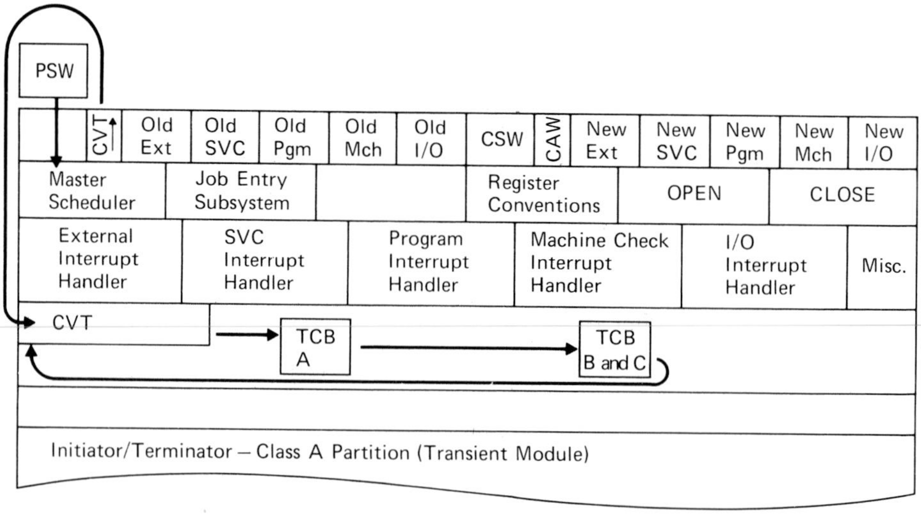

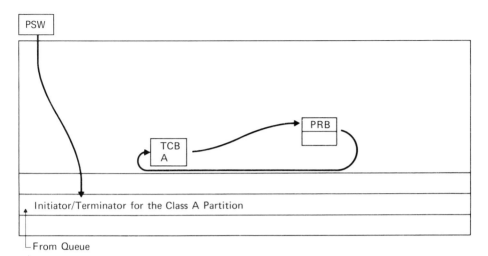

PSW

PRB

TCB
A

Initiator/Terminator for the Class A Partition

From Queue

Fig. 17.13
The initiator/terminator in control.

empty partition. The communication vector table is found through the address stored at real address 16; the CVT points to the first task control block (Class A). The partition controlled by this TCB is free; there are no active request blocks present. Thus the master scheduler causes the initiator/terminator module for this partition to be loaded and transfers control to this job management routine.

The Initiator/Terminator (Fig. 17.13) creates a program request block and attaches it the TCB for this Class A partition. A job is read from the Class A queue and loaded into the partition. For simplicity, we'll forget about the time delay inherent in reading the initiator/terminator and the job step from disk queue and assume that both happen in an instant. You should, however, be aware of the fact that program loading is an I/O operation. What happens is that, on completion of the transfer of the program from a library into memory, the channel issues an I/O interrupt. The interrupt handler routine, in turn, gives control to the master scheduler which, finding a ready program in partition A, gives it control.

After executing several instructions, the application program finds itself in need of data, so it issues a supervisor call instruction (Fig. 17.14), causing an SVC interrupt and passing control to the SVC interrupt handler routine, a part of task management.

This task management routine starts by attaching a supervisor request block (SVRB) to the request block queue (Fig. 17.15), thus indicating that an operating system module is active in support of this partition. The old SVC PSW is then stored in the program request block. The input operation is start-

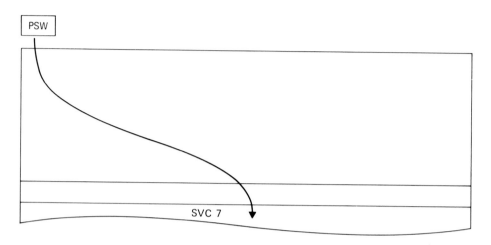

Fig. 17.14
The application program in control.

Fig. 17.15
The SVC interrupt handler takes over.

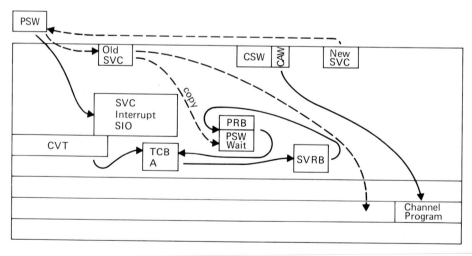

ed in the usual way, with the channel address word being initialized and a start I/O instruction executed. The routine then waits until the channel reports its status through the channel status word. Assuming that the status is positive, the channel takes over the resonsibility for the input operation, and the original program is placed into a wait state; this change in state is accomplished by the SVC interrupt handler which changes the wait state bit (bit 14) in the PSW field in the program request block, and control is returned, via a branch, to the master scheduler.

The master scheduler once again tries to get something started. In the absence of specific operator instructions, it begins looking for either an open partition or a program in the ready state. The CVT is once again the starting point, pointing to the TCB for the Class A partition. The presence of request blocks indicates that the partition is in use; a quick check of the PSW field in the program request block indicates that the program is in a wait state (Fig. 17.16). The TCB also contains a pointer (the address) of the next task control block on the TCB queue; since nothing can be done with this first partition, the master scheduler moves along.

Because there are no request blocks chained off this second TCB, the master scheduler "knows" that the partition is empty. The initiator/terminator routine responsible for this partition (Fig. 17.17) is loaded, and in turn loads a task or job step from the Class B queue—the program request block (PRB) shown in Fig. 17.18 was created by the initiator/terminator to show that a task is now active in this partition. The PSW of Fig. 17.18 shows that the application program in the second partition is in control.

Suddenly, an I/O interrupt occurs, indicating the end of the input operation previously started for the program in the Class A partition; as a result of PSW switching, the I/O interrupt handler, a task management routine, takes control (Fig. 17.19). The old I/O PSW field, don't forget, still points to the

Fig. 17.16
Back to the master scheduler.

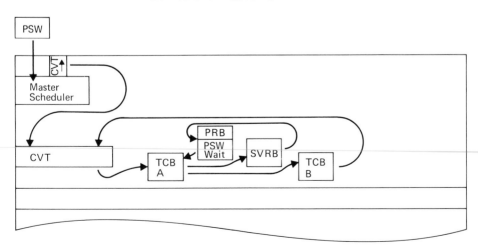

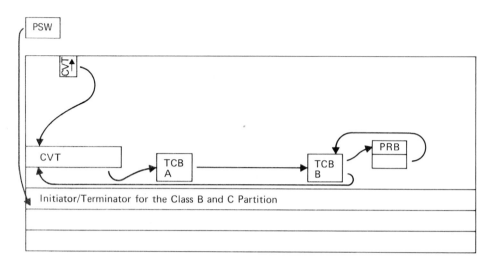

Fig. 17.17
The class B initiator/terminator.

Fig. 17.18
A second application program begins.

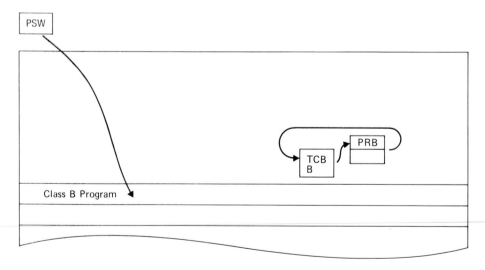

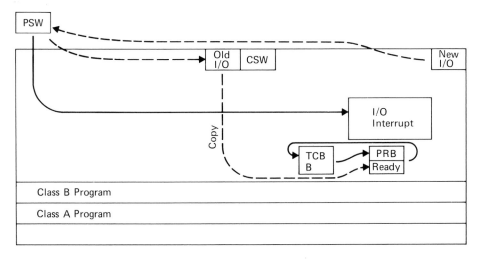

Fig. 17.19
An I/O interrupt occurs.

Class B program, and this program is in a ready state; even so, it's copied to the PRB. The interrupt handler identifies the program connected with the interrupt, program A, and, by following the CVT/TCB/PRB chain, locates its most current program status word and resets its fourteenth bit to indicate a ready state (Fig. 17.20). Once again, control is returned to the master scheduler which begins its usual search of the TCB queue. Discovering that the most current PSW of the Class A program indicates a "ready" state, this PSW is copied from the program request block to the current PSW location (Fig. 17.20 again), thus transferring control to the Class A program. Note that a supervisor call routine

Fig. 17.20
Class B is ready, but class A gets control.

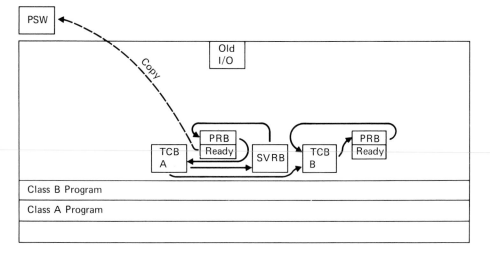

is still actively supporting this partition—you can tell by the presence of an SVRB on the request block queue. This particular I/O operation involved the system input device, and there are a number of unprocessed logical records left in the buffer.

After some time and several instructions, the Class A program reaches the point at which output data must be sent to the printer and thus issues an SVC interrupt. As a result, control is passed to the SVC interrupt handler (Fig. 17.21) which creates another SVRB, starts the output operation, sets the old SVC PSW's fourteenth bit to indicate a wait state, moves this PSW field into the program request block for the Class A partition, and turns control back to the master scheduler (Fig. 17.22).

The master scheduler, once again, begins searching the TCB queue looking for something to start. The program in the first partition is in a wait state, so the master scheduler moves along to the Class B partition. Discovering that the program in this partition is in a ready state, the PSW found in the program request block is simply moved into the current PSW location, thus returning control to the Class B program (Fig. 17.23).

After a bit of time, the Class B program issues an SVC for input data. Task management, specifically the SVC interrupt handler, takes over (Fig. 17.24), creates an SVRB, starts the input operation, sets the old SVC PSW to a wait state, and moves this old PSW to the Class B PRB. And again, it's back to the master scheduler (Fig. 17.25).

Fig. 17.21
An SVC interrupt gets us back to task
management.

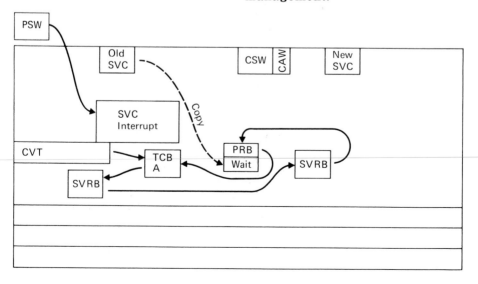

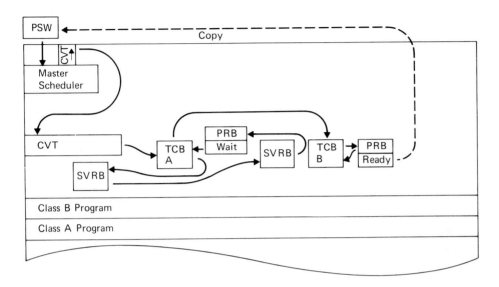

Fig. 17.22
The master scheduler.

Fig. 17.23
The class B program regains control.

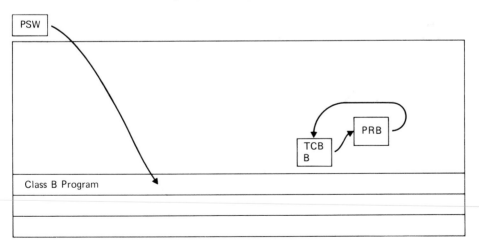

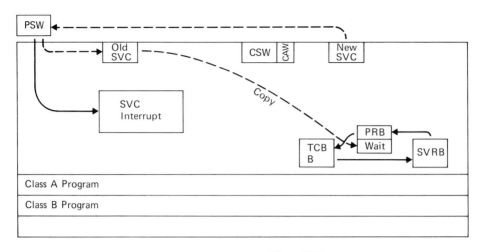

Fig. 17.24
An SVC is issued.

Fig. 17.25
Back to the master scheduler.

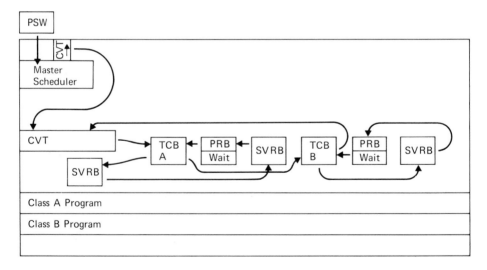

By tracing a path through the CVT, the TCB queue, and the RB queues, the master scheduler discovers that both partitions are active and both contain programs in the wait state. Because no application program is ready to go, control is passed to the JES function of job management (Fig. 17.26), which starts the operation of spooling one more card from the card reader to disk, returning control to the master scheduler (Fig. 17.27). Once again, all partitions are full and waiting. As a last resort, control is passed to the output portion of the job entry subsystem (Fig. 17.28) which starts an output operation, dumping

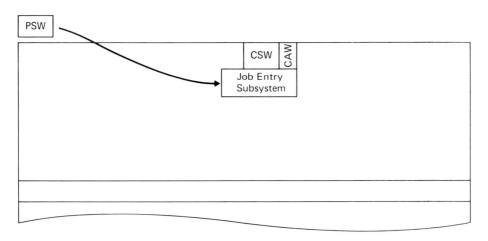

Fig. 17.26
The job entry subsystem gets control and spools
in a record.

Fig. 17.27
The master scheduler again.

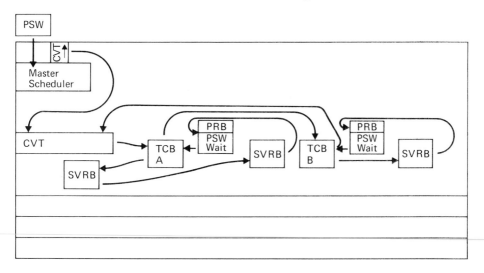

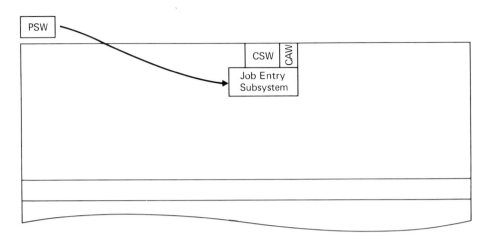

Fig. 17.28
JES outputs a spooled record.

one record from the system output device to the printer before again returning control to the master scheduler (Fig. 17.29). Everything is now waiting, so the system settles into a hard wait (Fig. 17.30) with four I/O interrupts pending.

Finally, an I/O interrupt occurs, starting the task management routine (Fig. 17.31); it's for the Class A program, so the fourteenth bit in the program request block's PSW field is set to a ready state. In this case, let's assume the output data was sent with a blocking factor of one, meaning that the supervisory functions associated with this SVC are completely finished; the SVRB is

Fig. 17.29
Again, the master scheduler.

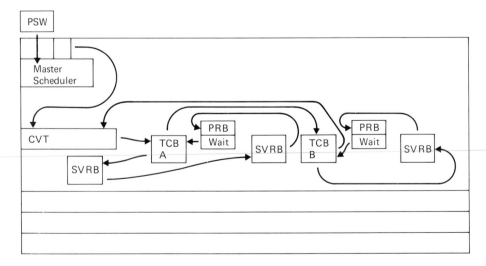

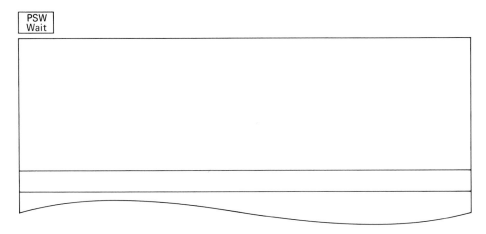

Fig. 17.30
The whole system waits.

Fig. 17.31
An I/O interrupt occurs.

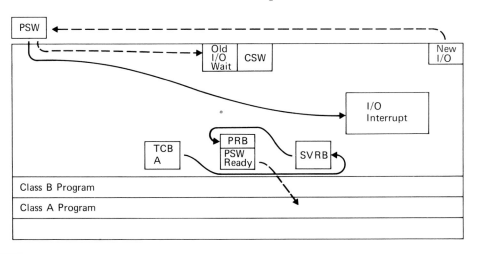

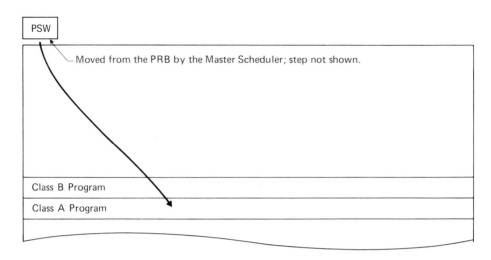

Fig. 17.32
The class A program resumes.

wiped off the request block queue, the PSW found in the program request block is made current, and Program A once again takes control (Fig. 17.32). But only for a while—two instructions into the program is a zero divide; the resulting program interrupt turns control back to task management (Fig. 17.33). The program interrupt handler prepares a dump and turns control over to the terminator routine for the partition. The terminator (Fig. 17.34) wipes out all request blocks and once again links back to the master scheduler. The job management routine resumes its eternal quest to "get something started," following the CVT/TCB chain to the first partition, discovering, through the lack of request blocks, that this partition is available (Fig. 17.35), and linking to the Class A initiator/terminator.

Fig. 17.33
But quickly program checks.

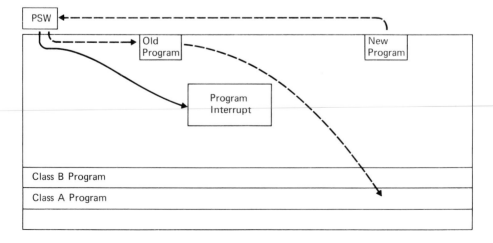

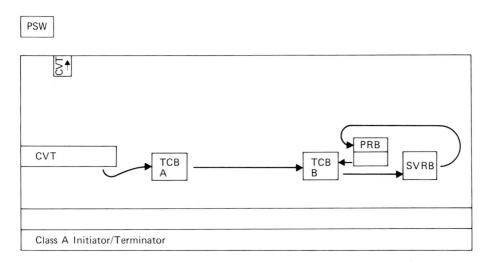

Fig. 17.34
The terminator routine prepares the partition for
the next program.

Fig. 17.35
We leave the systems as the master gets ready
to start another class A program.

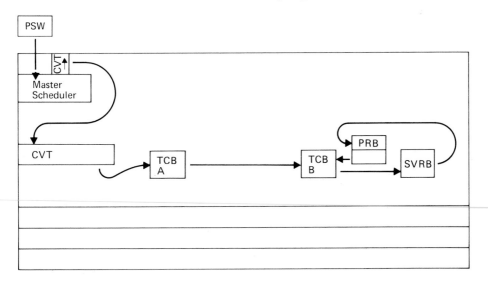

Our Example—
A Summary

In this example, we have followed the changing state of the program status word and other pointers through perhaps one second of computer time on a multiprogramming machine. Let's try to relate some of the things that happened to the general functions of an operating system as discussed in prior chapters.

Scheduling helps to improve the utilization of all the system resources by minimizing time delays due to necessary setup. One key element in implementing any scheduling system involves grouping similar jobs; under OS/VS1, this function is performed by the job entry subsystem, a part of job management. The class parameter assigned by the programmer through a job statement identifies many of the key characteristics of the job; once JES has spooled the job to a queue, the master scheduler routine, another part of job management, can, as its name implies, implement scheduling.

Internal priorities were seen to be a potential problem on a multiprogramming system. When two or more programs are ready to go at the same time, which one goes first? This program is also handled by the master scheduler routine through the simple expedient of causing this program to search the CVT/TCB chain in a fixed sequence as it looks for a ready program.

Register protection—a program that enters a wait state *must* find expected values in the registers when it resumes—is implemented through standard register conventions; although we didn't mention them in our example, register conventions are a part of each operating system module. There is room in both the task control block and in the supervisor request block for saving registers.

Spooling was shown to be at least a partial solution to the problem of dealing with slow-speed input and output devices; under OS/VS1, the job entry subsystem handles spooling. Third generation equipment is so fast that on-line spooling is possible.

The use of channels was shown to be a big help in minimizing the impact of slow I/O operations; essentially, the channel assumes all responsibility for actually controlling the operation, freeing the CPU to do other work in parallel. Task management links the channel and the computer by handling the request for the start of a channel operation through an SVC interrupt and taking care of I/O interrupts, the channel's signal that an operation has been completed.

Task management also handles program interrupts. Memory protection, a topic not covered in our example, is implemented by having the CPU check to make sure that the sending and receiving addresses of a potentially destructive instruction (such as a move) both lie in the same partition, i.e., both have the same protect key (remember the PSW's protect key field?). If they don't, it's grounds for a program interrupt—task management. Timer interrupts, a hedge against endless loops, are one variety of external interrupts and are handled by this task management function. Operator intervention through the console also causes an external interrupt, resulting in a branch to the master scheduler, a job management routine.

The potential problem of two or more programs wanting the same input or output device at the same time is handled by job management; for example, two jobs requesting the same tape drive are simply not loaded at the same time. The exact procedure for implementing this control will be discussed within the next several pages. Data management is another topic we'll cover soon.

In short, OS/VS1 is nothing more than a collection of programs, program modules, and routines designed to implement the functions that must be performed by a multiprogramming operating system on an IBM System/370. The module names and the structure of the various control blocks and pointers are unique to OS/VS1, but the functions being performed are common to all multiprogramming operating systems.

I/O Controls under OS/VS1

In a serial-batch system, all input and output devices are available to the program in control of the system. As soon as we progress to multiprogramming, conflicts are inevitable. These conflicts must be resolved, and they are—by the same job and task management routines we've already discussed. To implement these I/O device controls, the operating system builds and maintains a series of special control blocks and pointers; we'll look at some of the key ones in the next few paragraphs.

I/O Control—The Unit Control Block

If an operating system is to control the allocation and scheduling of input and output devices, it's only reasonable that the operating system have a list of available devices; this list is provided through the *Unit Control Block* (*UCB*), specifically through a chain of UCB's (Fig. 17.36). Under OS/VS1, each device attached to the computer has its own unit control block. Each UCB contains such information as channel and device address, the device type (3410, 3330, 3211, etc.), and various sense and status fields. This table is created at system generation time. There is one UCB for each and every I/O device attached to the system; a device without a unit control block, as far as the operating system is concerned, does not exist.

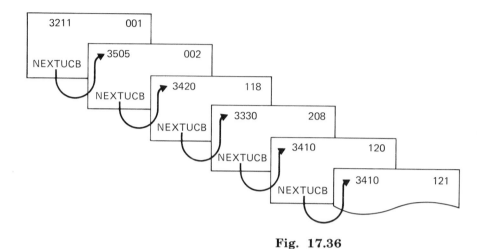

Fig. 17.36
Unit control blocks.

As a job is read by the reader/interpreter, requests for I/O support (made via DD statements) can be checked against the UCB queue; if a request is made for a device that is not on the system (probably an error in coding the JCL statement), there is no sense in even spooling the job. As a job or job step becomes ready for loading, the initiator/terminator can check the UCBs to make sure that a given device is available before loading the step. Should a job step require exclusive use of a device—a tape drive, for example—the fact that the device is not available for other jobs can be noted in the UCB, thus informing other initiator/terminators (one per partition, remember) that a job step requesting "this" device should not be loaded but, instead, be kept waiting a bit longer. Job management works with the unit control block to make sure that two or more jobs do not try to use the same I/O device at the same time. It can also be used by task management to avoid the problem of multiple access to the same shared device (disk, for example).

I/O Control—The Task
Input/Output Table

The *Task Input/Output Table (TIOT)* is created by job management just prior to the loading and starting of a job step or task; essentially, it's a list of all the DDNAMEs on all the DD statements included in the job step. Along with the DDNAME is a series of pointers that allow the system to find all the parameters coded on the DD statement. A schematic of a Task Input/Output Table is shown in Fig. 17.37.

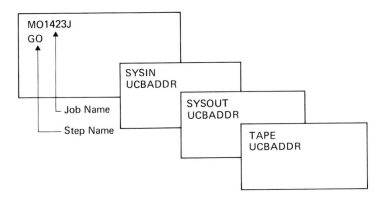

Fig. 17.37
The Task Input/Output Table (TIOT)

I/O Control—The
DCB and DEB

We've already looked at the data control block in some detail—it's a series of constants, coded within the programmer's own module, describing such things as the access method to be used in a given I/O operation, the logical record and blocksizes, record formats, the DDNAME assigned to the JCL statement describing the physical device, and other characteristics of the data. There is one data control block for each device accessed by the job step.

The *Data Extent Block (DEB)* is an extension of the data control block. While the DCB is entirely within the programmer's own region and thus subject to programmer modification and control, the DEB is not generally programmer-accessible.

I/O Control—The
OPEN Macro

Most programmers are aware of the *OPEN* macro in a negative sense—if I don't code it, my program blows up on the first read. The OPEN actually performs a much more positive function. When the programmer codes an OPEN, he or she is indicating that the program is about ready to begin requesting input or output operations on a particular device. Within the application program, the OPEN takes the form of an SVC instruction coupled with some constants and addresses identifying the data set (through the DCB) to be opened—the programmer usually sees just the word OPEN, especially in a high-level compiler language, but the pointers and the SVC are there. The SVC instruction causes an SVC interrupt, thus signaling the operating system of the programmer's intentions.

You may remember, from our discussion of the DD statement, that not all data control block parameters need be coded within the program DCB; many can be coded in the DCB parameter of the DD. It is necessary to get these DD statement DCB subparameters into the program data control block at some time; this is one of the functions of OPEN. You may also remember that it is not normally necessary to code any DCB parameter on a DD statement when retrieving an already existing data set; this is because information such as logical record length, blocksize, and record form can be found in the data set label. Moving this information from the label into the program DCB is another OPEN function.

The OPEN works something like this. First, any parameters coded as zero in the program data control block (uncoded fields are zero fields) are filled from the DCB parameter of the associated DD statement. The DDNAME is one parameter that must be coded in the program DCB; thus the OPEN routine has the "associated" DDNAME and the proper DD can be located through the task input/output table which contains a list of all the DDNAMEs (and thus DD statements) included in the job step's JCL.

After merging in the DCB parameter fields from the DD, the OPEN routine performs its label checking functions; at this time, any DCB fields that are still zero can be filled from label information on an existing data set. (Incidentally, the OPEN creates a label for a new data set.) Following execution of the OPEN routine, the basic I/O control blocks are complete and ready to support an input or output operation (Fig. 17.38).

Fig. 17.38
The OPEN routine builds basic control blocks for supporting I/O.

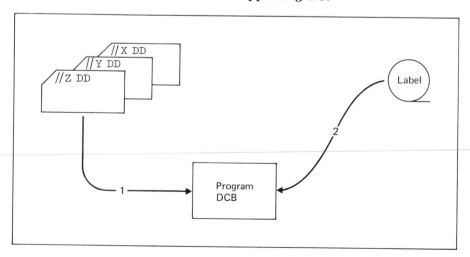

The OPEN routine is a part of task management; it gains control as the result of a supervisor call interrupt. The OPEN routine is usually one of the resident operating system modules.

I/O Control—The Application Program/ Channel Program Link

Actual physical I/O operations are, as we know, controlled by a channel; the channel gets its instructions from a channel program—one or more CCWs. Individual channel programs, for (hopefully) obvious reasons, are not the type of software routines that the typical programmer should be allowed to modify or change. For this reason, channel programs are placed either in the region of memory assigned to the operating system or in the access method routines grafted onto the load module by the linkage editor. The programmer must have some control over the I/O operation, of course; the data control block is within the partition and can be modified.

We've already looked at the data extent block or DEB; it's basically an extension of the data control block. One key function performed by the DEB is to provide a link between the DCB (the application program) and the unit control block identifying the specific input or output device involved in this operation (Fig. 17.39). The DCB and the channel program are tied together by

Fig. 17.39
I/O control blocks.

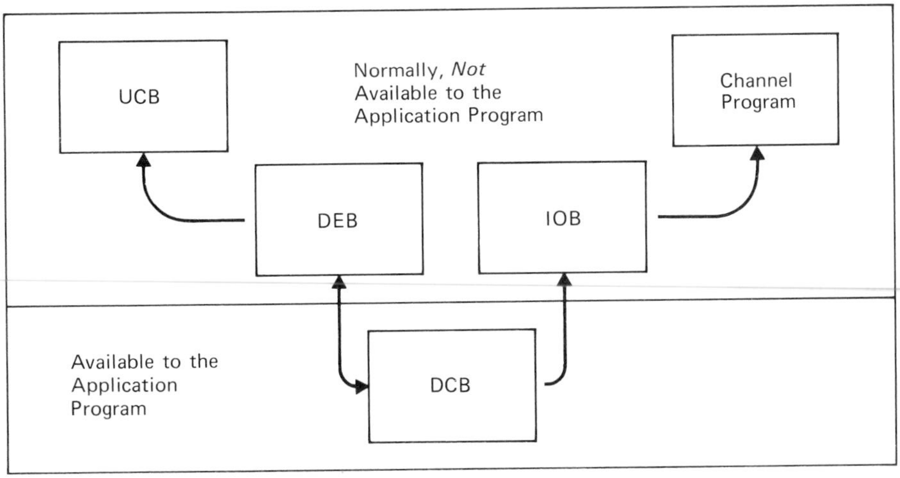

another control block, the *Input/Output Block* or *IOB* (Fig. 17.39 again); we haven't discussed this control block in detail, and we won't. The important point to remember is that we now have a complete link between the application program and the channel program; the routine requesting an I/O operation and the routine that will actually implement this request have been tied together.

Data Management

Data management is concerned with such things as access methods, libraries, catalogs, and so on. OS/VS1 supports all of these concepts.

Much of data management—access methods and buffering techniques in particular—is added to an actual load module by the linkage editor; the code for these routines is often found on a direct access library. To simplify access to several key libraries, an activity normally calling for a JOBLIB or STEPLIB DD statement, information needed to achieve a linkage is stored in the communication vector table. The SYS1.LINKLIB (a DSNAME, nothing more) is one such library, containing routines used by the linkage editor. Another library accessed through the CVT is the SYS1.SVCLIB, which holds SVC and other transient operating system routines not part of the resident operating system.

SYSIN and SYSOUT, the system input and system output devices, are a part of data management. These two data sets provide an excellent example of the difficulty involved in separating functions into neat, clean categories. Data are placed on the system input device by a job management routine, and moved from the device into memory under the control of task management. Yet, the system input device is part of data management. Direct communication between the various pieces of the operating system is the rule rather than the exception.

System Generation and Flexibility

What operating system modules should be included in the resident supervisor? One possible answer, recognizing the inherent time delays involved in moving a module from a direct access device into real memory, is "All of them." Unfortunately, operating system modules, like any software routine, take up space and the more real memory we assign to operating system modules, the less we have available for paging the application programs. Computers do not exist for the purpose of running an efficient operating system; computers exist to execute application programs, and the operating system performs a support function.

The other extreme is to keep most or all of the operating system on disk or drum and bring modules in as needed; this frees real memory, but the time delay arising from direct-access I/O each time a transient operating system module is needed leads to inefficiency. This is done on some smaller computers using a disk operating system, but on a larger, faster computer, it's impractical.

Somewhere between these two extremes is the "best" solution. On a large computer running numerous, small, brief programs, the "best" solution might be close to the "all in real" alternative. A scientific machine running long, compute-bound programs might lean toward a minimum-nucleus operating system. OS/VS1 was designed by IBM to be a general-purpose operating system, capable of supporting both types of applications.

The modular nature of OS/VS1 is the key to this flexibility. Certain routines and control blocks *must* be resident; beyond this, individual modules may be made resident or part of the system library at the option of the user. IBM provides the basic system and options; the user builds a customized system during system generation.

OS/VS1 Limits

Multiprogramming exists because of the speed disparity between the computer and its I/O devices; by placing a number of programs in storage at the same time and allowing the CPU to switch its attention from program to program, much of what would be wasted "wait" time can be utilized. The operating system exists to handle the inevitable conflicts.

We've been looking at a system with two programs in memory. In a two-program system, there will be times when both are waiting; additional system efficiency could be gained by introducing a third program. The same argument might be used to justify a fourth program, a fifth, and so on. As the number of programs in memory increases, the amount of time when the computer is left with nothing to do (because all programs are waiting for something) must drop. There is a limit—eventually, interference between programs will become so great as to offset the advantages of adding more programs—but up to this point the more programs we have in memory, the greater the utilization of the computer.

Under OS/VS1, there are a few more practical limits. The address of the last byte in the largest possible IBM System/370 machine is, in hex, $(FFFFFF)_{16}$, a limit arising from the use of three-byte or 24-bit addresses in the PSW and throughout the machine; that's about 16 million bytes. What it means is that the biggest address that can possibly be referenced, even in *virtual* memory, is about 16 million. When the IBM System/360 system was developed in the mid-1960s, 16 million bytes was simply unimaginable—a 512K machine was considered big. Today, 16 megabytes is considered a limiting factor.

Look for changes in the next generation of IBM machines; in fact, IBM recently announced a system on which the instruction address portion of the PSW is expanded to 31 bits. Imagine a computer with over two *billion* bytes of main memory!

The number of programs that can be loaded into virtual memory at one time is a function of the available real memory space. There is a limit on the amount of virtual memory that can be supported by a given computer system. The normal ratio is in the neighborhood of three to four times the real memory space; in other words, for example, a computer with one megabyte of real memory can probably support between three and four megabytes of virtual memory. If we assume a three-megabyte virtual system, the first million bytes are assigned to the real address area, leaving two million for application program partitions. Assuming an average partition size of 200K (not a large partition), we would have room for only ten application program partitions.

Why not increase the virtual-to-real ration? Why not support a five-megabyte virtual system on a one-megabyte real computer? (After all, it's only virtual memory.) More virtual space would mean more virtual partitions; more partitions would mean more application programs concurrently sharing the CPU, and hence more throughput. The problem, however, is that with a high virtual-to-real ratio, most of the pages in each program must remain on the external page data set. Every time a program in real memory references a page that is on virtual memory, a page-out/page-in operation is necessary. More programs on virtual, with the same amount of real space, means that less of each program will be in real; thus the probability that a reference will be made to a nonresident page increases as the virtual-to-real ratio increases. As a result, the need for paging increases, very quickly leading to *thrashing,* with the system spending so much time paging in and paging out that it literally has no time to do any useful work. The amount of real memory limits the amount of virtual memory that can be supported, and thus limits the number of partitions that can be defined.

There is one other limitation. Each partition must have its own protection key. The protection key field in the PSW is four bits long. There are only 16 different combinations of four bits, (0000) through (1111). The operating system uses protect key (0000), leaving keys for 15 application-program partitions. IBM is, of course, aware of this limitation. As IBM announces new products, you might anticipate that more concurrent application programs will be supported.

Summary _____

In this chapter, we considered another operating system designed to run in a virtual environment on an IBM System/370 computer—OS/VS1. The structure of this operating system is similar to that of DOS/VS, with its virtual memory being divided into a real address area containing the resident supervisor, real partitions, and the page pool, and the virtual address area containing the application program partitions and a supervisor transient area. The line dividing the real address area from the virtual address area under OS/VS1 is called the virtual equals real (V = R) line; the real partitions plus the page pool make up what is called the virtual-equals-real area.

The difference between a job and a task was then described. Job management is concerned with loading jobs and job steps (or tasks) onto the computer. Task management supports the job steps after they have been loaded. The key modules that support job management were discussed one at a time; they include the master scheduler, the job entry subsystem (JES), and a transient module called the initiator/terminator. The master scheduler implements the internal priority decision, identifies empty or available partitions, loads the initiator/terminator in an empty partition, and communicates with the operator. The initiator/terminator controls the loading of the "next" job step from a library, reading and interpreting the job control language statements from the job stream as a guide. The job entry subsystem enqueues jobs and spools both input and output data. The main modules that make up task management are the interrupt handler routines.

The primary control blocks that are used to link the various components of the operating system were described next. Many of the key system constants or control areas are recorded in or addressed by the communication vector table. The contents of a given partition are defined (in general terms) by a task control block. The specific functions active in a given partition are described by a chain of request blocks spun off the task control block. TCBs are linked in a fixed order, with the CVT pointing to the first TCB, the first TCB pointing to the second, and so on. Internal priority is determined by the master scheduler as it follows this chain; the high-priority partition is first, and the low-priority partition is at the end of the chain. The chapter then turned to an in-depth example of the flow of control through a second or so of computer time; if you can follow this example, you have a good feel for what an operating system does.

I/O controls were considered next. We briefly covered the unit control block, with one entry for each physical device on the system. The task input/output table holds information, taken from a job step's DD statements, describing the I/O device requirements of the step. We showed how two new control blocks, the data extent block and the input/output block, are used to link the channel program, the data control block, and the unit control block. The OPEN macro was seen as a key element in this linkage process.

Data management was discussed briefly. A key element of OS/VS1 is its flexibility—it is intended to be a general-purpose operating system. We discussed how a customized version might be created at system generation time.

The chapter ended with several comments on the limitations of the OS/VS1 operating system and (more specifically) IBM's System/370 hardware. The amount of available real memory limits the size of virtual that can be supported. The size of the virtual memory, in turn, limits the number of application program partitions. The biggest address that can be referenced on an IBM System/370, roughly 16 million, is another limiting factor. The size of the memory protection key is still another.

Key Words

communication vector table (CVT)

control block

data extent block (DEB)

initiator/terminator

input/output block (IOB)

job

job entry subsystem (JES)

job management

master scheduler

OPEN

pageable supervisor

program request block (PRB)

real address area

request block

resident supervisor

supervisor request block (SVRB)

task

task control block (TCB)

task input/output table (TIOT)

task management

unit control block (UCB)

virtual address area

virtual equals real (V = R) area

virtual equals real (V = R) line

Exercises

1. Under OS/VS1, what are the contents of the real address area of virtual memory? of the virtual address area?
2. What might be found in the area assigned to the pageable supervisor?
3. Distinguish between a job and a task.
4. Distinguish between job management and task management.
5. What are the functions of job management?

6. What are the functions of task management?

7. What does the job entry subsystem (JES) do? Describe the relationship, if any, between JES and the master scheduler.

8. The initiator/terminator is a transient module. Why? What does this mean?

9. How does the master scheduler discover if a partition is free or busy? Mention all the tables, control blocks, and pointers involved in this process.

10. Add a third partition (for class D jobs) to the example system developed in the text. Explain how this third partition might change the flow of control through the system.

11. Describe the series of control blocks involved in linking an application program's DCB to a unit control block and a channel program. What is the function of each of these control blocks?

12. How are DD statement DCB subparameters and label information merged with the program DCB?

13. OS/VS1 is designed to be a general-purpose operating system. What does this mean?

14. A key objective of a multiprogramming operating system is to maximize the number of different programs occupying memory. With more programs sharing the CPU, greater throughput can be gained. Briefly describe some of the factors that limit the number of programs that can run under OS/ VS1.

Trends and Alternatives
in Operating System Design

Overview

Change may well be the only constant in the computer field. In this chapter, we will investigate a number of trends and then project the impact of these changes on operating system design.

The design of an operating system is, of course, influenced by the hardware architecture of a particular computer system. We begin the chapter with a discussion of some alternatives to the IBM hardware covered in the last three chapters, quickly leading to an analysis of two likely hardware trends—toward big machines and toward small machines.

The trend toward large machines often involves the use of multiple virtual memories and the virtual machine concept. The small machine trend is concerned with microcomputers and personal computers; declining cost is the key variable here. Networks are sometimes used to link small computers to larger machines; this is one trend that should tend to bridge the gap between large and small machine development. Multiprocessing is another, with multiple processors sharing a single memory and sharing the responsibility for supporting application programs. The chapter ends with a brief discussion of the migration of overhead functions from software to hardware.

Alternative Architectures _____

An operating system rests on a hardware foundation. Clearly, the structure of the operating system will depend on the structure of that hardware. If the equipment differs from IBM equipment, then the operating system will differ from an IBM operating system. Many students find it difficult to distinguish between an example and a general principle. Having just read three chapters devoted to a series of examples based on the IBM System/370 series of computers, the student has a tendency to think that every computer is controlled by a program status word and that all computers recognize interrupts by switching PSWs. This is simply not the case. The IBM System/370 is but one example; other computer manufacturers do things differently.

Interrupts

One of the most important differences between the various suppliers of computer mainframes lies in the way they deal with interrupts. Some computers are designed to handle only one or two different types of interrupts; IBM can handle five on its System/360 and System/370 series; the Xerox Data Systems Sigma 5/7 series is capable of working with up to 224 interrupt levels. As an upper limit, imagine one interrupt for each different I/O device, a separate SVC-like interrupt for starting an I/O operation with each individual device attached to the system, several different program interrupts (one for each type), and so on. The big advantage to multiple interrupts is speed—it is possible to link directly to the specific operating system module designed to handle a particular variety of interrupt rather than first going to a general module (perhaps a branch table) whose only function is to link to the desired routine. The cost of the multiple-interrupt approach is measured in a loss of some flexibility. The interrupt is normally implemented through hardware; hardware is fast but a bit tougher to change than a program.

The sheer number of interrupts is not the only place in which manufacturers differ; the IBM approach of old PSW's and new PSW's for each interrupt type is not universal. One popular variation involves maintaining stacks or queues of pending interrupts in special registers or in core; as each additional interrupt arrives, it is simply added to the list. Many different approaches have been tried. Let's take a quick look at two of them.

Interrupt stacking involves maintaining an array of interrupts either in main memory or in special registers. Let's assume that we have a system with a stack big enough to hold five interrupts (Fig. 18.1a). The top of the stack is, in this example, the current program status word (or its equivalent); we'll assume

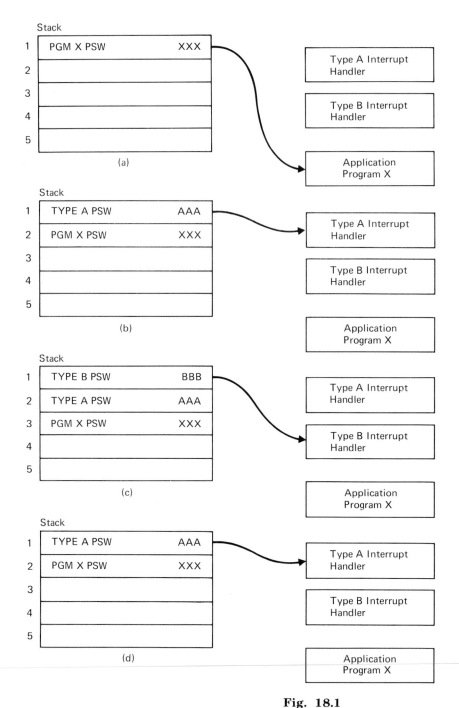

Fig. 18.1
Interrupt stacking. (a) Program X in control. (b)
Type A interrupt occurs. (c) Type B interrupt
occurs. (d) After processing Type B interrupt,
control returns to the Type A interrupt handler.

that instructions in program X are being executed as we begin. Suddenly an interrupt occurs. In response, the system hardware pushes the current PSW down to the second stack position (a push-down stack), and inserts the interrupt PSW at the top of the stack (Fig. 18.1b). The interrupt PSW will contain the address of the first instruction in its interrupt handler routine; thus control of the computer passes to the interrupt handler, location AAA in our example.

After several instructions in this routine have been executed, another interrupt occurs. As a result, the original program is pushed down to stack position three, the first interrupt PSW is pushed down to stack position two, and the new interrupt's PSW is moved into the top position (Fig. 18.1c). Now, the second interrupt is being processed. As this second interrupt processing routine reaches completion, the system pops the stack, moving all the elements on the stack up by one position (Fig. 18.1d); the routine that handles the first interrupt is now in control. Eventually, control will return to the application program.

Note that we did not distinguish between the interrupt types in this example. Unlike the IBM System/370 technique of switching PSW, interrupt stacking does not require a physical differentiation between various interrupt types; every interrupt, no matter what its source, is simply placed at the top of the stack. Interrupts, from whatever source, are handled in reverse order of occurrence—last in, first out.

Another problem we did not discuss was interrupt masking. On an IBM System/370, an I/O interrupt closely following another I/O interrupt could, by destroying the contents of the old I/O PSW field, wipe out the link back to the original program; thus we mask interrupts. With stacking, a subsequent I/O interrupt does not destroy anything—it is simply placed at the top of the stack. As a result, multiple I/O interrupts can be accepted concurrently; other "in-process" interrupts or control fields are simply moved down the stack with their contents preserved.

There is, of course, a limit to interrupt stacking: the size of the stack is finite. If we have allowed room for five stack elements, only five interrupts can be processed concurrently. On a computer that uses interrupt stacking, a great deal of thought goes into defining the ideal stack size; the result is usually quite efficient. Still, the number of elements on the stack is a limiting factor.

It is possible to add a bit of sophistication to the interrupt stacking process. For example, assume that each interrupt is assigned a priority. As the interrupt enters the system, the stack can be searched for the first element with a lower priority. Rather than automatically being placed at the top of the stack, the new interrupt can be placed just before the first stack element with a lower priority (just after the interrupts with a higher priority). In this way, the stack is processed in priority order.

Where do the interrupts come from? Some are generated by a channel or other peripheral device. Others—supervisor calls and program checks—come from within the program. On the IBM System/370, the address of each interrupt handler routine is stored in a fixed main memory location as a constant; actually, there is a table of such constants. An alternative might be to store the interrupt at its source: within the I/O control unit or the channel, for example. In this way, the interrupt signal itself could contain all the information needed to link to the appropriate interrupt handler routine. On some systems, a user is allowed to define customized interrupts. For example, assume that we have written a program to answer the telephone. We could design an electronic device to respond to the signal of the telephone ringing and generate an interrupt with the address of this telephone-answering program. The result, coupled perhaps with a speech generator, would be an automatic telephone-answering computer.

An alternative to interrupt stacking is *interrupt queueing*. With stacking, a new interrupt normally enters at the top of the stack; the last interrupt to occur is the first one processed. With queueing, a new interrupt is placed at the bottom of the queue; the *first* interrupt accepted is the first processed.

Basic interrupt stacking can be implemented by simply keeping track of the top of the stack. With queueing, both the top (the current PSW) and the bottom (the location of the "next" interrupt) must be defined. Thus interrupt queueing normally involves the use of two pointers: one to the current element and one to the next available element (Fig. 18.2). Queueing is just a bit more complicated than stacking.

The use of pointers does, however, have its advantages. How, for example, is an element pushed down on a stack? The process normally involves shifting the contents of the stack registers or storage locations by one element; pushing an element back up involves the same process in the opposite direction. With queueing and pointers, the physical shifting of the queue elements is no longer necessary; instead, the addresses in the pointers can be changed. For example,

Fig. 18.2
Interrupt queueing.

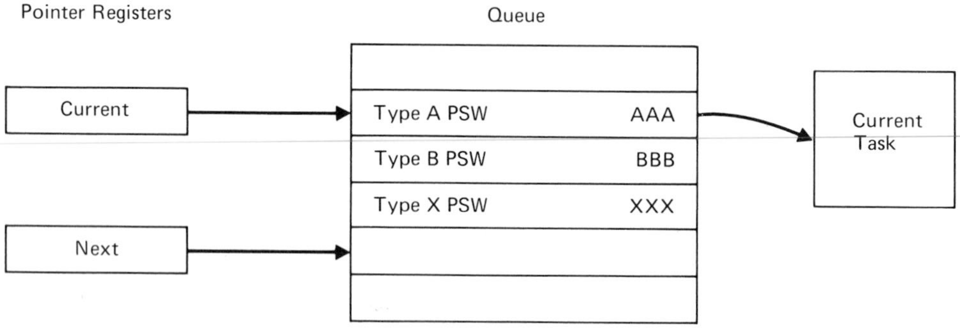

as a new interrupt is added to the queue, the address in the end-of-queue pointer can be incremented by one element. As processing in a given module is completed, the address of the current element can also be incremented, thus pointing to the next queue entry. What happens when either pointer reaches the end of the queue? If, for example, the queue consists of ten elements, there simply is no eleventh. The solution is simple: when a pointer value reaches the end of the queue, it is reset to point to the top of the queue, a technique sometimes called wrap-around.

An operating system written for a computer that uses interrupt stacking or interrupt queueing will be different from an operating system written for a machine like an IBM System/370. Consider, for example, the problem of internal scheduling. Scheduling is a function of a module's position on the stack or the queue; the search sequence of a set of partition control blocks would no longer be the critical factor. Interrupt handler routines would no longer look to a fixed location in memory (different for each type of interrupt) for old PSW information; instead, with stacking, the equivalent of IBM's old PSW field would always be in the second stack element. With queueing, it is possible that a program might avoid interruption until it issued a WAIT macro (remember, first-in first-out). Try to imagine other ways in which the flow of logic through the operating system might be affected by a change in interrupt technique.

I/O Linkages

Interrupts are not the only factors that vary from computer to computer; the mechanism for communicating with a channel can vary significantly among manufacturers as well. In Control Data Corporation's CYBER series, for example, the central processing unit shares the spotlight with a number of peripheral processors one of which handles all the problems of input and output. The peripheral processors are all independent and can work in parallel with the central processing unit; the logical equivalent of CCW's, the CAW, CSW, and the SIO instruction can be set up and executed while the central processor is handling other business, as can the handling of the eventual I/O interrupt.

On some computers, certain I/O devices are actually addressed much as main memory. For example, consider a microcomputer system with a sectored diskette attached through an I/O interface unit. Assuming a uni-bus architecture, the CPU might send a signal requesting that the contents of sector 52 be placed on the bus; the result would be the transfer of one sector (usually 256 characters) into main memory. Compare the simplicity of this I/O linkage with the "access method/CCW/SVC/CAW/SIO/interrupt/CSW" linkage on an IBM System/370; much of the logic needed to implement this linkage is moved to the I/O interface unit on the smaller system. The cost of simplicity is reduced flexibility; the I/O operation described above is limited to a particular type of 256-character sectored diskette, while IBM's I/O linkage could be used to access *any* record from *any* device. Still, there is a great deal to be said for simplicity. Fixed-block architecture, a topic to be covered later in the chapter, represents a move in this direction on the bigger machines.

Trends in Computer Development

IBM equipment and IBM architecture represents but one approach to implementing computer technology. We could go on and on with examples of competitive architectures, but such a discussion would add little to the development of the material in this text. The point is simple: do not confuse an example with the underlying principle.

Change may well be the only constant in the computer field. The machines of tomorrow will be quite different from the machines of today. The specific example will change; it will become obsolete. The underlying concept will, however, remain basically the same. The computer of the future will still recognize interrupts. *How* interrupts are recognized and what action is taken in response on a given machine will change, but the concept won't. Future computers will still commmunicate with I/O devices. Programmers will still request logical I/O, and the logical request will still be converted, in some way, to a physical I/O request. The details of implementation will change; the concepts will not. If you know only the details of implementation, your knowledge will soon become obsolete. However, if you understand the concept, learning the new technology will be relatively easy because it will be based on the same elementary principles.

What will the future hold? It is always dangerous to predict the future, particularly in a field as dynamic as the computer field. A key technological breakthrough could be just around the corner, and could completely upset all current plans and projections. (For example, a decade ago, who could have predicted the impact of microcomputers?) Still, it is possible to project future technology based on what is happening today. Recent product announcements, rumors and news items, and the published results of current research can be combined to support an educated guess as to the future direction of the field. What might we anticipate?

Two major trends seem to dominate. One is toward larger and larger computers with almost unimaginable speed and memory capacity. The other is toward personal microcomputers—small machines with limited power but very low cost. These trends seem diametrically opposed: large and small. As we shall see, however, the two trends do converge. Using modern network technology, the small computers of tomorrow will be able to link with a large machine, acting (whenever necessary) as a type of intelligent terminal. Another interesting area of convergence involves the use of small computers as component parts of the big machines—multiprocessing. In the balance of this chapter, we'll consider these two trends and their convergence.

The Large Machine Trend: The Supercomputers

One of the more exciting areas of computer development today is the very large, very powerful computer. Let's briefly consider one specific example of this trend. When the IBM System/360 was released in the mid-1960s, the architecture was designed around a 32-bit word, with a 24-bit address. Because of this 24-bit address, the system was limited to roughly 16 megabytes of main memory. In 1964, a machine with 500K of main memory was considered large; 16 megabytes was simply unthinkable.

Look back to the chapter on the IBM principles of operation, and consider the difference between the BC mode and the EC mode of the PSW. Under the BC mode, 24 bits are allocated to the instruction address. Under the EC mode, the same 24 bits are set aside for the instruction address but, by shifting the location of other PSW fields, the eight bits immediately preceding the instruction address (bits 32 through 39) are set to zero. Recently (October 1981), IBM announced a new processor with "extended architecture." Under extended architecture, the address used within the system expands to 31 bits. Old programs can still run under the new architecture; the first, or high-order, eight bits of an old program's address are simply assumed to be zero when the 24-bit address is expanded to 31 bits. With a 31-bit address, it is possible to address in excess of two *billion* bytes (two *gigabytes*) of main memory!

The direction is toward larger computers. Memory capacity increases. The hardware becomes faster and faster. We have moved from the integrated circuit, to large-scale integration (LSI), to very large-scale integration (VLSI); as speed and capacity have increased, the machines have gotten smaller, more reliable, and (relatively) less expensive. Current research is focused on such exotic techniques as superconductivity; components and connectors are measured in microns rather than millimeters; machine cycle time could well push into the picosecond range. All these trends clearly point in the direction of larger and larger (in terms of capacity) machines.

There are implications to this trend. As speed and capacity increase, the speed disparity between the computer and even the improved peripheral devices of the future will become greater and greater. Multiprogramming provides at least a partial solution to this problem by allowing the CPU's resources to be shared by a number of concurrently executing programs. Increased processor speed calls for more levels of multiprogramming—more concurrent programs on line. How might this objective be achieved?

The Virtual
Machine Concept

Under a standard virtual operating system such as OS/VS1, the virtual memory is a model of the system. Physical storage, of course, involves real memory and an external page device, but the programmer can ignore the physical reality and view a program as moving from a library into virtual storage, where it is executed. Addresses on virtual memory are imaginary. The task of mapping these imaginary addresses to real memory and external page memory is a relatively straightforward exercise in applied mathematics. In other words, given a virtual address, the associated real address can be *computed* by using a well-defined algorithm.

Under OS/VS1, a single virtual memory is mapped onto a single real computer. The mapping process is nothing but applied mathematics. The central processing unit simply executes instructions in a sequence controlled by the content of the PSW; the dynamic address translation feature computes addresses based on the contents of a set of segment and/or page tables. The source of the instructions, the partition or program they belong to, is irrelevant to the hardware. There is no reason why a single real computer cannot support *several* virtual memories (Fig. 18.3). Given a super operating system to provide control, the CPU can be made to switch its attention from virtual storage 1 to virtual storage 2 just as easily as it switches its attention from partition 1 to partition 2 under more standard multiprogramming. Such systems do exist; two common examples are IBM's *OS/VM* (virtual machine) and *OS/MVS* (multiple virtual storage). Imagine 15 virtual memories *each* holding 15 application program partitions, and you have many more concurrent programs on line.

What would we expect to find in one of the virtual memories of an OS/VM system? Basically, it would be much like the virtual memories we have already discussed. In the real address area, we would expect to find an operating system and a page pool, along with optional real partitions. The virtual address area would hold the application program partitions or regions.

How would the contents of a virtual memory be stored? With *multiple* virtual memories, it would *not* be possible to store in real memory the real address area of each virtual memory; this is the essential difference between a single-level virtual system and one with several virtual memories. Instead, both the *virtual operating system* and the virtual application program partitions would be stored on an external paging device and paged into real memory un-

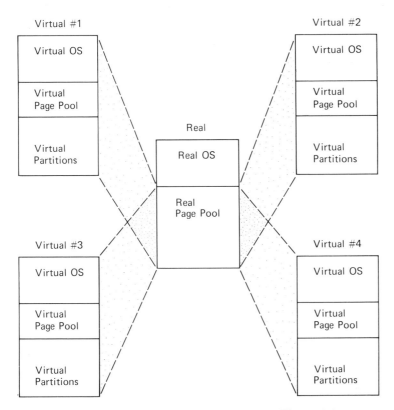

Fig. 18.3
Multiple virtual memories on a single real machine.

der the control of a main control program, the *real* operating system. That's right: the virtual operating system would be subject to paging!

How might the main control program transfer control from virtual operating system to virtual operating system? Time slicing is one possible solution. The main control program might begin by giving control to virtual machine number one. VM-1's operating system, perhaps DOS/VS, would then assume responsibility for controlling the execution of programs in the VM-1 background and foreground partitions. Eventually, after a preset interval or slice of time has passed, the main control program would take control away from the first virtual machine and transfer control to the operating system of virtual machine number two (an OS/VS1 system, perhaps) for a slice of time. Using a round robin polling technique, the main control program could give each virtual machine a shot at the CPU in much the same way that each terminal user gets to access the CPU under a time-shared system.

We could encounter several problems with such a system. Consider, for example, dynamic address translation. With a single-level virtual system, a page existed on the external page device, and the addresses on this page were expressed in virtual terms—the segment/page/displacement address relative to the beginning of virtual memory. When this page was transferred into real memory, dynamic address translation (table look-up) was needed to convert the virtual address to a real address. Basically, as a page was loaded into real memory, the real entry point address was placed in a page table; later, as the instructions on the page were executed, the dynamic address translation feature broke the virtual address into page and displacement components (or segment/page/displacement components) and used the page number to search the page table for the base address.

When looking at multiple virtual memories or multiple virtual machines, we might *visualize* a process whereby a page would be transferred from a virtual partition into a virtual page pool in virtual memory, and then transferred from the virtual page pool into real memory for execution. It doesn't physically work that way, of course; current program pages are transferred directly from the external page device into real memory. The point is that when using the virtual memory model of a system we can *visualize* a two-step process.

What exactly is involved in each step? Dynamic address translation. What is dynamic address translation? It is the algorithmic process of mapping virtual addresses into real addresses. The key is the segment and page tables in real memory. A single virtual system executes this mapping function once. A multiple virtual system would execute the mapping function more than once. Generally what happens is that the main control program maintains, for each virtual machine, a set of *shadow* segment and page *tables* that reflect all the computations that would be implied if a page really were moved to a virtual page pool, dynamically translated, and then transferred to the real page pool and dynamically translated again. Since the mapping—the dynamic address translation—is simply the solution of an algorithm, we can do the computations to reflect a page's position in a virtual page pool *without actually transferring* the page to the virtual page pool. The key point is that mapping the contents of virtual memory (a model) into real memory is a straightforward mathematical function. In other words, once the math has been worked out, dynamic address translation is not a problem on a virtual machine system.

Controlling access to the I/O devices is, however, a very real problem. The number of physical devices attached to a computer system is finite. It might be possible to assign certain devices to a specific *virtual* machine simply by not listing these devices on the unit control block (or equivalent) queues of the other virtual machines; such dedicated devices could operate under control of a virtual operating system. This solution, however, is unworkable for any device that must be physically shared among the various virtual machines—the disks, for example. Allowing two different operating systems to attempt to concurrently access the same physical device is every bit as dangerous as allowing two different applications programs to do so.

Generally what happens is that the main control program—the master operating system that is resident in real memory—traps or intercepts any I/O operations generated by or generated in support of one of the virtual operating systems. A virtual operating system is given a set of *virtual devices;* i.e., imaginary I/O peripherals. The virtual operating system, working just like a real operating system, issues a start I/O instruction referencing one of these virtual devices. The *virtual* SIO, however, does not communicate directly with the channel. Instead, it is intercepted by the real operating system, which actually handles the real or physical I/O operation, communicating directly with the channel and, if necessary, enqueueing the virtual I/O request until the external physical device becomes available.

With multiple virtual memories or virtual machines, a great deal of paging is going to occur. This can become quite inefficient. Partly in response to this problem, the suppliers of large computer systems have begun to move in the direction of *fixed block architecture* on secondary storage. With a standard disk pack, physical records can be almost any size. As a result of this flexibility, the hardware and software elements that control the I/O operation must be flexible or general purpose in nature. With fixed block architecture, physical records are all the same size—for example, 4K. Given fixed block architecture, and assuming a 4K block, *every* physical record will be stored as *exactly* 4K bytes on disk. *Every* output operation will transfer exactly 4K bytes to disk. *Every* input operation will transfer exactly 4K bytes from secondary storage. Given the consistent nature of such I/O operations, less logic is needed. In fact, it is possible to skip several steps in the logical-to-physical I/O translation with fixed block architecture, because the length (at least) is a constant rather than a variable. This simplifies I/O.

A page is a fixed length piece of a program. There is no reason why the page size and the fixed block size cannot be made the same. The result is simplification of the paging process, leading to somewhat improved efficiency.

Using relatively simple fixed block architectures, it is possible to shift much of the logic normally housed in the access method and the various interrupt handler routines to a hardware chip, and to place this chip in the channel or the I/O control unit. Moving the logical details outside the computer decreases the amount of work the computer must do to support I/O. The result is greater CPU efficiency. We'll return to the idea of this migration from software to hardware later in the chapter.

Microcomputers and the Trend toward Small Machines

There is another trend that is apparent in the computer field today—the trend toward microcomputers. The big reason for this trend is declining cost. The modern consumer can purchase a surprisingly powerful microcomputer system for under $1000, and the cost seems to be dropping. Many foresee the home or personal computer as *the* appliance of the 1980s. Small, video game computers are already very common. Outside the home, microcomputers are found in automatic bank teller terminals, supermarket checkout stations, and a variety of other everyday business applications. There is little question that microcomputers are proliferating, and few experts predict an end to this trend.

At first glance, the growth of the microcomputer industry would seem in direct conflict with the development of the big machines. Is the computer of the future going to be a large, centralized multiprogrammed or time-shared super computer, or a small personal machine? Actually, the answer is probably both.

There is a great deal to be said for the personal computer. The pocket calculator provides an excellent parallel. A decade ago, inexpensive pocket calculators were not available. The typical college student had access to several excellent desk calculators in a library or a laboratory, but few students used these calculators. They were simply not convenient. Today, with good calculators available for less than $20, almost everyone has one, and they are commonly used. No matter how good centralized facilities might be, they can never match the availability and convenience of a personal machine. The same can be said for computers. Centralized data processing will always be less convenient than personal data processing. This argument would seem to favor the micros.

There is one problem with a microcomputer, however: limited capacity. A small machine cannot be used to store a large data base. An occasional need for large-scale computations may well tax the limits of a micro. There are tasks that a microcomputer cannot handle; a large machine can do everything a micro can, but not vice versa. This argument would seem to favor the supercomputers.

Networks

Many experts see a marriage of microcomputer and super computer technology in the near future. For example, consider the equipment that might be available to the soon-to-graduate programmer. On his or her desk is a microcomputer. Source programs are entered into the micro under control of a text editor, are edited for certain obvious syntax errors, and are stored on diskette. Once the complete program has been entered, the programmer, by typing a few commands into the micro, can transmit the source code to a large, centralized machine where it is compiled and tested; the results are sent back to the micro for analysis by the programmer. This programmer would enjoy the availability and convenience of a personal microcomputer *and* the power of a large mainframe. Such systems are available (and not uncommon) today.

When two or more independent computers are linked by communication lines, they form a *network*. One form of network might involve several microcomputers basically used as "stand-alone" machines, but with the ability to establish access with a large, centralized computer when such support is needed. An example might be a large insurance company with satellite micros or minis in each sales office linked to the central corporate data base via telephone lines. Such tasks as billing, proposal development, and sales office accounting can be handled throughout the business day on the small, local machine. At the end of the business day, all activity can be reported to the central machine, thus allowing the insurance firm to update its data base. Essentially, we are looking at the marriage of small and large computer technology.

Not all networks involve the linkage of large and small computers; many involve communication between computers of roughly equal size. For example, a firm with three major corporate data processing centers might link its three large computers to form a ring network. The problem of handling peak demands at center A could be minimized by sending some of the extra work to the computers in centers B and C; in effect, the three computers could share the work load. Another significant advantage to such a network configuration is *backup*; if one computer "goes down," the other two machines can assume much of its work until the problem is corrected.

Multiprocessing

Another area in which we can begin to see small and large computer development converging is *multiprocessing*. The term multiprocessing refers to two or more processors sharing a common memory. With multi*programming*, we had two or more programs and a single processor. Because there is only one processor, it is impossible to execute two or more instructions simultaneously. With multi*processing*, we have two or more *processors*. Each processor can function independently; thus we can have two or more instructions executed simultaneously on a multiprocessor machine.

Consider, for example, the problem of controlling I/O. The process as we have considered it to date involves several hardware and software components. Basically, the application program issues a request for logical I/O that results in a branch to the access method. The access method converts the logical request to a physical request (often by completing a channel program), and transfers control to the operating system. The operating system starts the I/O operation and communicates with the channel; once the I/O has been successfully started, the application program can be placed in a wait state, and another program given control. Eventually, the channel sends an I/O interrupt to the CPU, and the application program is ready to resume processing.

What happens while the channel is in control of the I/O operation? It is performing computational functions, counting characters and incrementing an address. At the same time (simultaneously), the central processing unit is executing instructions in support of a different program. The channel is a special-purpose minicomputer. Two processors, the CPU and the channel, share main memory. Because they are independent processors, they can function independently. Two processors can execute two different instructions simultaneously.

The relationship between the channel and the CPU is a limited form of multiprocessing. Although the formal definition—two or more processors sharing a common memory—is technically met, the fact that the channel's processor is so limited when compared with the CPU causes most computer experts to place the CPU/channel relationship closer to processor/peripheral link than a processor/processor link. Still, based on what you have learned to date, the relationship between the channel and the CPU provides a good starting point for a discussion of multiprocessing.

What would happen if we were to make the channel more powerful? Assume, for example, that we are going to replace the channel with a microcomputer, a complete micro with its own programmable memory (Fig. 18.4). The

Fig. 18.4
For certain I/O operations, the channel can be
replaced by an I/O processor.

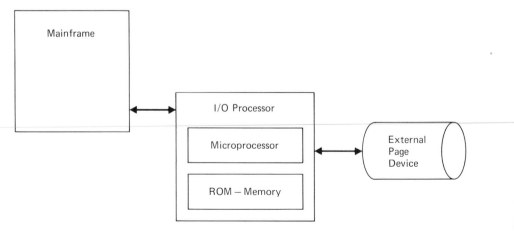

I/O device, we'll assume, is a fixed block architecture disk device used to support paging; 4K blocks will be transferred between main memory and secondary storage. Consider the logic that would be involved in supporting such an I/O operation.

We might start with the OPEN macro. During OPEN time, the physical cylinder/track address of the start of the page data set is defined and stored in the program's data control block (or equivalent): no change here.

Once the start address has been established, we can consider the actual paging operation itself. Although paging is an operating system function and thus largely transparent to the programmer, the steps involved in transferring a page between main memory and secondary storage must be much the same as the steps involved in transferring a physical record between a program's partition and the external device—we are, after all, dealing with the same computer. What steps would (logically) be involved in making this transfer?

Let's assume that the pages are physically stored as 4K blocks. The first page on the page data set would be relative page 0; the second page would be relative page 1; the third page would be relative page 2; and so on. Given the start-of-file address and the relative page number, the disk address of the desired page can be computed. Given this absolute address on disk, along with the physical record length (a constant, 4K) and the address where the page is to be placed in main memory (the page frame), the channel program can be completed. Normally, this is done in the access method. With our new micro-controller, we can code all the logic in the microcomputer's memory (Fig. 18.5), in effect

Fig. 18.5
The I/O processor (see Fig. 18.4).

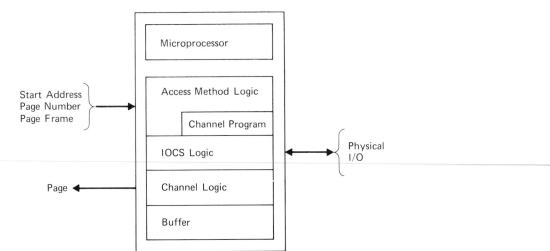

shifting the "access method" logic outside the traditional computer. The equivalent of an access method on this new machine would simply pass the physical file start address and the page frame address to the I/O processor, much as a main program passes parameters to a subroutine, and the secondary processor would do the rest.

What about the operating system and the IOCS? On a traditional computer, the operating system logic is needed to establish the necessary communication link to the external device, a process that involves the exchange of a number of well-defined protocol signals. There is no reason why the responsibility for handling these protocol details cannot be assigned to the I/O microcomputer (Fig. 18.5).

What about the channel? It counts characters and updates a main memory address. In addition, the channel passes specific commands along to the I/O control unit. These logical functions can also be incorporated into the control program of the I/O microcomputer (Fig. 18.5, again).

Consider the I/O microcomputer carefully. We have taken major components of the access method logic, the operating system IOCS logic, and the channel logic and shifted them to the I/O micro. This independent processor is now capable of performing a great deal of relatively complex logic. Within the main computer, the equivalent of the access method is reduced to little more than a subroutine call. The function of the operating system becomes little more than passing the necessary parameters to the micro. The bulk of the I/O control logic is then executed by the micro, *in parallel* with the main processor, which can turn its attention to another program. Clearly, the microcomputer-based I/O controller does a great deal more than the old channel did; it is a legitimate processor in its own right. Both it and the CPU have access to the same main memory. When two or more processors share a common memory, we have multiprocessing.

Control Data Corporation has implemented this type of multiprocessing on its 6000 or Cyber series computers. In addition to the traditional *main processing unit,* the CDC machines contain a number of *peripheral processors* to control, in parallel, such functions as I/O, communication with the operator, and several others. Other manufacturers are beginning to take a similar approach on their mainframes. Each peripheral processor is an independent microprocessor or miniprocessor in its own right. They share a common main memory. Although the main processor may well provide overall control, we still have a multiprocessing configuration.

In effect, what is happening is that microcomputers and microprocessors are becoming *components* of the larger machines. As an operating system or system software function becomes well defined and stable, why not transfer this logic to an independent processor? Rather than tying up the CPU with detailed system control logic, why not allow the CPU (or MPU for main processing unit) to "farm out" these functions to smaller, less expensive subprocessors? In this way, more of the CPU's time can be allocated to supporting the application programs, and less of this precious and limited resource will be tied up in overhead. In fact, this is what is happening. System software and operating system logic is migrating from software to hardware (or firmware), moving from main memory to the read-only memory (ROM) of a secondary processor.

The large computer of the near future may well resemble the architecture sketched as Fig. 18.6. Sharing the mainframe with the CPU or MPU will be several secondary processors. Some, the I/O processors, will handle the details of converting a logical I/O operation to a physical operation; we described their function above. A data base processor will handle all communications with the central data base. Spooling will be handled by a spooling processor, thus completely relieving the main processor of any responsibility for communicating with the slower I/O devices. When an application program calls for computations involving arrays, the main processing unit will set up the arrays but will not perform the actual array computations. Instead, once defined, the arrays will be passed to an array processor, where the rules of linear algebra will be applied. Communication with local and remote terminals will be the responsibility of a communication processor. We can even expect FORTRAN and other language processors that will be able to directly *execute* (much as a modern

Fig. 18.6
The architecture of a possible future
multiprocessing system.

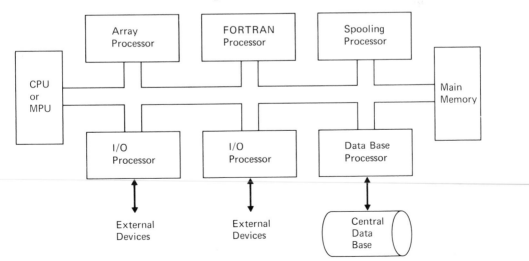

interpreter does) source statements, a tremendous benefit during program debug.

The important point is that because each of these processors is a separate *processor*—a separate source of electronic "intelligence"—all of these functions will be performed *simultaneously*. In any given instant of time, one or more I/O operations may be in process, the data base may be in the process of being accessed, an input job stream may be being read, an array may be being inverted, a programmer may be debugging a FORTRAN program, a clerk may be entering a transaction through a terminal, *and* a payroll computation may be in the process of being executed by the main processor, each in support of a different application program. With multiple processors, simultaneous events can occur.

Obviously, only on a very large, multiprogrammed or time-shared computer could so many simultaneous events be possible. Multiprocessing, at least in this example, is being superimposed on top of multiprogramming. We might, for example, start an I/O operation for partition 1, set up an array and give control to the array processor for partition 2, and begin executing instructions through the main processor in support of partition 3; three simultaneous events would involve three independent processors, but the control—the responsibility for assigning work to these processors—would rest with something very much like a traditional multiprogramming operating system. Multiprocessing implies large-scale computation.

But consider the individual processors. An array processor is a very special-purpose machine designed to perform a single set of functions, a series of standard array manipulations. A data base processor is another special-purpose machine designed to accept requests in a particular format and access a particular data base. It is microcomputer technology that makes such single-function hardware economically feasible. In other words, the big computer of the future may well be a collection of small computers. The trend toward large machines and the trend toward small machines are not incompatible. They do come together.

Event Synchronization

The fact that events can occur simultaneously does create several new problems. Consider, for example, I/O control. There is little problem with starting the I/O operation; the I/O processor will not be given control until the application program requests the supervisor's help. The problem occurs at the end of the I/O operation. The application program cannot resume processing until the I/O operation is finished. But the responsibility for controlling I/O belongs to an independent device. How can the application program know when the I/O is finished? Although it is true that the channel will send an interrupt when that event occurs, how would the program know whether or not the interrupt had been sent yet?

Consider another example. As part of an application program, we set up an array and pass it to the array processor via the operating system. Having started the array processor, the operating system returns control to our application program, and we resume processing. Eventually, we reach a point at which we cannot continue until we have the output from the array processor. If the array processor has finished its work, we can continue processing; if it has not, we must drop into a wait state. How can we tell?

The problem is one of *event synchronization*; we must coordinate the timing of independent events. Because many of the examples of the past several chapters have been based on the IBM System/370 series, we might continue with that series to illustrate event synchronization. To use an admittedly unrealistic but understandable example, let's imagine that a programmer wishes to have the operating system start an I/O operation and, while the channel is controlling the operation, wants to regain control and execute a number of instructions in a computational subprogram. If both the I/O operation and the subprogram complete at the same instant of time, there is no problem. If the I/O operation completes first, again there is no problem—in both cases, the application program can continue normally. What happens, however, when the subroutine finishes before the I/O operation? If you think about it, you'll see that the application program must wait until the I/O is finished before continuing (Fig. 18.7).

How can the computer know which of two parallel modules has completed first? On the IBM System/370, this problem of event synchronization is handled by a special control block called an Event Control Block or ECB. In our example, the fact of I/O completion would be noted in an ECB through the execution of a POST macro (probably by an operating system module). The application program, upon completion of the "parallel" subprogram, checks the ECB. If it has been "posted," the parallel operation is finished and processing can continue; if not, the application program issues an SVC and drops into a wait state. The WAIT macro we discussed in an earlier chapter generates the logic needed to check the event control block and, based on the contents, either issue or bypass the supervisor call that drops the program into a wait state.

A similar approach might be needed to synchronize the activities of a number of independent processors. The main processor, probably acting under control of its operating system, would be responsible for this coordination. The secondary processors would report their status to the main processor, probably through a set of system control registers. The main processor could pass information on the status of one of the other processors to an application program either through a control register or through something like an event control block.

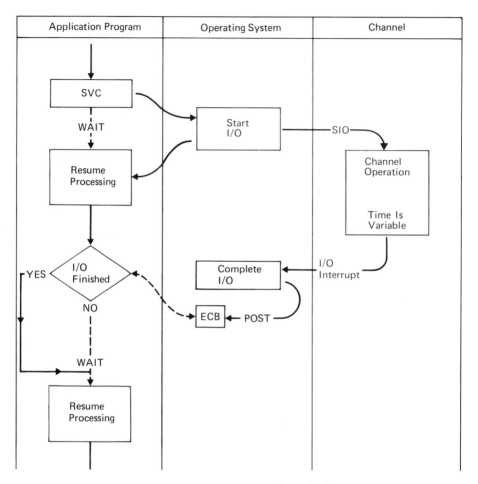

Fig. 18.7
Event synchronization.

The Migration
from Software
to Hardware

How do all these trends impact operating system design? At one level, the new functions of controlling and coordinating the operation of complex network or multiprocessing configuration are clearly operating system functions calling for new operating system components. There is, however, a much more significant trend taking place. Many of the functions performed by operating system software are migrating to hardware.

Consider, for example, the input/output processor example developed earlier in the text. The memory of the independent I/O processor contained much of the logic that had previously been found in the access method, the IOCS, and the channel. The memory of the independent processor is likely to be read-only memory, ROM. In effect, a copy of the logic is burned permanently into an integrated circuit chip: it's hardware. Major elements of system software have been transferred from their traditional, volatile software state to permanent hardware.

This same trend can be seen in a number of operating system modules. Basically, when a software module becomes stable, it makes sense to shift the logic to read-only memory. The hardware is faster and nonvolatile (you don't have to IPL hardware). Gradually, most of the key system software modules we have studied in this text will migrate to hardware, thus substantially changing the nature of an operating system. Earlier, we said that an operating system serves as a hardware/software interface. Given this migration, the dividing line between hardware and software becomes increasingly fuzzy. In fact, some computer people use the term *firmware* to describe these ROM-based "permanent software" modules.

On the larger computers, the operating system logic often moves to a peripheral processor, thus allowing overhead functions to be performed in parallel. Not even microcomputers are immune to this trend, however. CP/M, a microcomputer operating system widely regarded as a standard, is available in ROM form. On such a system, the operating system can, for all practical purposes, be viewed as part of the hardware, available as soon as the machine is turned on.

Look for a continuation of this trend, with more and more of what we call system *software* moving to hardware. The computer of the near future could be a very interesting machine.

Summary ———————————————————————————

The chapter began with a discussion of a few alternatives to the IBM architecture described in Chapters 15 through 17. Interrupt stacking, interrupt queueing, and the use of an independent processor to control I/O were considered. The IBM architecture and the operating systems built on that architecture is merely an example, and the example should not be confused with the general concept.

We then turned our attention to a number of trends that are apparent in the computer field. Technology seems to be advancing in two opposite directions—toward big machines and small machines. In reality, these trends converge.

A great deal of current research (and several recent announcements) seem to point in the direction of supercomputers, extremely large (in terms of memory capacity) and fast machines. We considered the use of multiple virtual memories as a technique for making more programs concurrently available to such a computer. Dynamic address translation for multiple virtual memories merely involves the application of a mathematical mapping function more than once. To avoid the problem of multiple simultaneous accesses to the same physical I/O device, the virtual machines are assigned a set of virtual I/O devices, with the real operating system trapping and controlling all requests to begin an I/O operation. Fixed block architecture was briefly described as a technique that could make paging more efficient.

The trend toward small machines is driven, to a large extent, by the declining cost of microcomputers. It is likely that the microcomputer of the future will include a communications option that will allow it to access a large machine when necessary. A network will provide the communication link between processors. This communication link between the large machine and the small machine is one way in which the two trends described earlier converge.

The technologies also converge on modern multiprocessing systems, where small processors often become components of a larger mainframe. Multiprocessing involves two or more processors that share a common memory. In a multiprocessing configuration, key overhead functions such as I/O control, data base access, telecommunication control, and others are shifted from software operating system modules controlled by the main processor to peripheral or secondary processors in the mainframe. Since the processors are separate *processors,* these overhead functions can be performed in parallel with the main processor and other peripheral processors' functions. On a multiprocessing system, it is possible to perform two or more functions simultaneously.

The chapter ended with a brief discussion of the tendency of operating system and other system software to migrate to hardware or firmware.

Key Words

event synchronization	network
fixed block architecture	OS/MVS
gigabyte	OS/VM
interrupt queueing	peripheral processors
interrupt stacking	shadow tables
main processing unit (MPU)	virtual device
multiprocessing	virtual operating system

Exercises ————————————————————————

1. Explain interrupt stacking. What advantages does interrupt stacking enjoy over the IBM approach?

2. Contrast interrupt stacking and interrupt queueing.

3. How might fixed block architecture (or the use of sectored disk) simplify the process of converting logical I/O to physical I/O?

4. Why is it so important that you learn the underlying principles of operating systems rather than simply the details of operating system implementation on a particular vendor's machine?

5. Describe some of the characteristics of the large computer of the near future.

6. Briefly explain the concept of implementing multiple virtual memories on a single real machine.

7. What exactly is virtual memory? What is dynamic address translation?

8. Explain how access to I/O devices is controlled on a multiple virtual system.

9. Why is microcomputer use expanding as rapidly as it is?

10. What is a network? Explain how networks tend to pull together the trends toward large and small computers.

11. What is multi*processing*?

12. With multiprocessing, why is it possible for two or more events to be processed simultaneously?

13. Explain how multiprocessing tends to pull together the large and small computer trends.

14. Explain event synchronization. Why is something like event synchronization necessary on a multiprocessing machine?

15. Briefly describe and explain the migration of overhead functions from software to hardware. Why is this migration taking place?

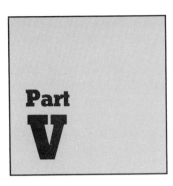

System Software

Overview of Part V

In the past few chapters, we've been discussing a number of general-purpose operating systems supplied by the computer manufacturer and designed to handle a wide range of applications. The reason for the general-purpose nature of these operating systems is not hard to fathom—such software packages are expensive to develop, the only way to recover these development costs is to sell many copies, and the only way to sell many copies is to be general. Within certain limits, these operating systems can be customized—core resident and transient modules can be selected, priorities reset, memory reallocated, and so on—but the fact that the package is designed to cover a wide range of applications and job mixes is what makes it a general-purpose operating system.

Not all applications fit this general-purpose mold. In Chapter 19, we'll consider software packages designed to deal with the problem of data communication. In Chapter 20, we'll turn our attention to data base management software. Both types of software were originally developed as "add-on" packages to the general-purpose operating systems, intended to expand the capabilities of a standard computer system. In Chapter 21, we'll consider a variety of commercial software packages.

19

Data Communication Monitors

Overview

In this chapter, we will consider the hardware and software needed to support data communications. Many current applications require terminals that are linked to a central computer by some form of communication line. Another data communication application is the CPU-to-CPU link that is characteristic of a network.

We begin with an overview of several basic data communication concepts, highlighting those aspects of the technology that make data communication different from normal data transfers. Three key elements are found in most data communication software—polling, line protocols, and partition management. We'll discuss each of these concerns one at a time, and then combine them to form a data communication monitor. Finally, we'll discuss a number of trends in the data communication field.

The Need for Data Communications

The idea of a network—two or more computers linked by communication lines—was introduced in Chapter 18. Earlier, in Chapter 13, several basic time-sharing functions were discussed; an implied element of the time-shared system was a group of terminals linked, in some way, to the computer. In both cases, we essentially skipped over the details of data communication. Actually, data communication creates a number of unique problems of its own, and many of these problems must be handled by special system software.

There are some subtle differences between linking a terminal to a computer and linking two computers. Rather than complicate our discussion needlessly with a series of "howevers" and "on-the-other-hands," we'll concentrate on the terminal/computer link first, and briefly summarize the CPU to CPU link at the end of the chapter.

We already know how a *local* terminal is linked to a computer: it uses the standard control unit and channel as its I/O path, with the normal access method and operating system modules providing on-the-computer intelligence. The only real difference between the local terminal and a *remote* terminal is that a communication link (a telephone line, for example) is placed between the terminal and the control unit. What is it about transmitting data over the communication line that makes the remote terminal so different?

Basic Data Communication Concepts: Modulation/ Demodulation

Within a computer, data can be represented as individual pulses of electricity; a pulse of current is a 1-bit and "no" pulse is a 0-bit. Since the individual components of a computer system are generally pretty close to one another, this does not present a problem. When we attempt to send information over a long distance, however, several things happen. First, the signal tends to drop in intensity, to "die down," because of the resistance of the wire, much as a bicycle coasts to a stop on a level surface. The second problem is that the signal tends to pick up interference. If you've ever tried to listen to a distant radio station, or if you've ever heard other voices in the background on a long-distance telephone call, then you have experienced this interference, called *noise.*

An electronic signal traveling along a wire or a radio signal traveling through the air will lose strength and pick up noise. As it gets further and further away from the source, the signal gets weaker and weaker, and the noise becomes more intense until eventually the noise overwhelms the signal and the signal is lost. When this happens, no information can be transmitted.

But our telephone system allows us to talk from coast to coast and even halfway around the world, and we see television programs from virtually every spot on earth (not to mention the moon and Mars). If signal loss and noise create problems for long-distance data communications, how can we explain these obvious discrepancies? Data *can* be transmitted over long distances. In order to transmit information over long distances, however, it is necessary to boost the signal occasionally.

Boosting an electronic signal is, however, not quite that simple. Some signals are easier to boost than others. As it turns out, the easiest signal to boost is in the form of a sine wave. The "electronic pulse" within the computer is one of the most difficult patterns to boost. Thus, in transmitting computer data over any communication facility, the data are first converted from the computer's internal "pulse of current" form to a wave pattern. The process of converting from a binary pattern to a wave pattern is called *modulation*. The process of converting back is called *demodulation*.

The device that performs the conversion from pulse to wave and back to pulse form is called a *data set* or *modem* (Fig. 19.1); the word modem is an acronym that stands for *m*odulator/*dem*odulator, a name that accurately describes the functions performed by this device. Normally, there is a data set or modem on each end of the communication line (Fig. 19.2). These devices must be present because of the electronic incompatibility between a computer and common communication facilities.

Fig. 19.1
A typical data set or modem. (Photograph
courtesy of Anderson Jacobson, Inc.)

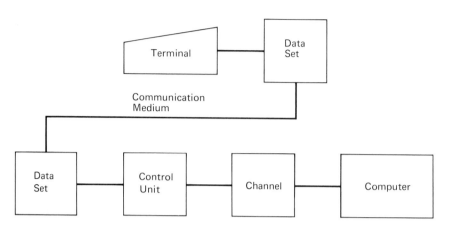

Fig. 19.2
The hardware involved in connecting a remote
terminal to a computer.

Common Data
Communication Media

Now that we have identified the various parts of a remote terminal network let's turn our attention to the communication facilities. We'll start with the telephone system. Our national telephone network connects just about every point in the world, and it's extremely reliable and dependable.

The type of telephone line that we all use for voice communication is called a voice-grade line. It can also be used for data communication. A voice-grade line normally transmits between 2000 and 2400 bits of data per second. A man named Emile Baudot was an early pioneer in the data communication field; in his honor, the basic unit of *data transmission* speed, one bit (more accurately, one signal event) per second, is called a baud, making a voice-grade line a 2400-baud line.

If a line speed of 2400 baud isn't enough, it's possible to transmit the data at a higher frequency. To preserve compatibility with the switching equipment of the telephone company, even multiples of 2400 (4800, 7200, and 9600 baud) are commonly used. Special modems are needed to transmit at these higher rates. If 9600 baud is not enough, wide-band channels with data transfer rates ranging from 19,200 to one million baud can be leased. If 2400 baud is more than is needed, telegraph channels from 75 to 300 baud are available. There really is a broad range of alternatives.

In many cases, the need for data communications is not continuous; short occasional bursts of connect time are all that is needed. In such cases, the user will typically take advantage of the regular public telephone system, dialing the computer, making a connection, and hanging up the phone when the work is finished. This approach is called dial-up.

Dial-up can get expensive if the call is long distance. Even if the call is local, many data communication users are not willing to accept the noise, interference, occasional busy signal, and other problems that are inherent in the dial-up approach. As an alternative, it's possible to lease a *private line*. This is very common when line speeds in excess of 2400 baud are involved.

When you say "hello" into a telephone receiver, it is not your actual sound waves that are transmitted over the line. Instead, the sound waves are converted into an electronic wave form that "represents" the actual data being transmitted. In other words, the telephone line transmits an analog signal rather than a true signal.

We use analogs every day. The height of a column of mercury in a thermometer really isn't the temperature, it just represents the temperature. The needle on your automobile's control panel really isn't the speed, it just represents the speed. The signal passing over a telephone wire isn't the sound wave—it is merely analogous to the sound wave.

Most of our telephone equipment transmits analog signals. Most computers are digital in nature, representing data as patterns of binary numbers. This is the basic incompatibility that makes equipment like modems necessary.

Actually, it is possible to transmit digital data. A 1-bit can be sent as a normal sine wave; a 0-bit can be sent as the absence of a normal sine wave. The signal can be boosted by simply retransmitting it, sending out strong wave pules for each 1-bit and filtering all noise from the 0-bit signal. Given today's technology, digital data transmission is actually superior to traditional analog transmission, which tends to amplify the entire signal, including any noise that may have been picked up.

Why, then, hasn't the telephone company switched to digital? Simply because they have such a tremendous investment in existing analog equipment—equipment that, incidentally, works quite well. As new facilities are added, however, most do use digital technology.

There are alternatives to the telephone system. Data can be transmitted between two points via radio waves, and many organizations doing a significant amount of data communication have installed private microwave relays. When microwave is used, transmission is restricted to a "line of sight"; in other words, if any large solid object gets in the way, microwave transmission will not work. The earth, as we all know, is round; it curves. The curvature of the earth limits the maximum distance of data transmission, making expensive relay stations necessary (Fig. 19.3). In an attempt to circumvent this problem, data communication satellites have been placed in orbit allowing installations located anywhere in the United States to send data, via microwave, to any other spot (Fig. 19.4). Eventually, this satellite network will be worldwide.

Fig. 19.3
Since microwave data
transmission is limited
to a "line of sight,"
relay stations must be
used to compensate for
the curvature
of the earth.

Fig. 19.4
Satellites can also be
used for microwave
data communication.

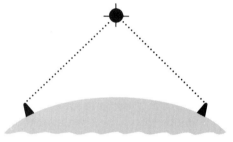

The Speed
Disparity Problem

Let's return to a typical keyboard terminal/data set/voice-grade line/data set/ computer system network. At the computer's end, data can be manipulated at speeds of four million characters per second and more. A voice-grade line is rated at 2400 baud; if we assume an eight-bit code, we get 300 characters per second, which is significantly less than four million. What about the terminal? Typical terminals are rated in the range of from 20 to 30 characters per second and, given the typing speed of most people, the rated speed is probably an exaggeration.

We have a 20-character-per-second device attached to a 300-characters-per-second line which, in turn, is attached to a four million-characters-per-second computer. That's certainly an enormous range! How can we possibly deal with this speed incompatibility? We can use buffers and we can handle a number of terminals at the same time. Let's deal with the first part of the solution first.

Most terminals contain a buffer (Fig. 19.5). Typically, a terminal's buffer is just big enough to hold one line of data. As the user types at a certain rate of speed, the individual characters go into the buffer. The RETURN key usually signals the end of a line, be it a partial or a full line. When the RETURN key is depressed, all of the data are in the buffer in an electronic form. This means that they can be transmitted at electronic speeds—300 characters per second is

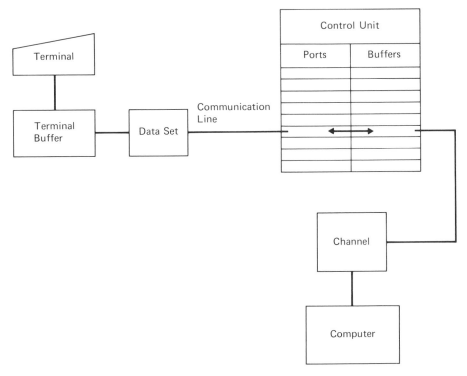

Fig. 19.5
On a typical data communication network,
buffering takes place at both the terminal and
the control unit ends of the line.

easy. Output data can be written into the buffer at a rate of 300 characters per second and transferred to the printed page or CRT screen at a rate of 20 or 30 characters per second. With a buffer in the middle, both the terminal and the telephone line can work at peak speed.

What happens at the other end of the line? Once the data have passed through a modem, they enter a control unit to begin their trip into the computer. A modern transmission control unit, often called a front-end device, is made up of a series of ports and associated buffers (Fig. 19.5). A port is nothing more than a connection point for a communication line and usually contains the modem. We already know what a buffer is. Data enter the control unit at a rate of 300 characters per second and are moved into the buffer associated with the "port of entry." Once all the data are in the buffer, the transmission control unit can signal the channel which in turn can signal the computer (an interrupt, remember?) that data are available for transfer into the computer. As soon as the computer is ready, the data transfer can be achieved at close to the computer's internal speed. Going back out, data can be dropped in one of the transmission control unit's buffers at four million characters per second, parceled out to the communication line at 300 characters per second, dumped into the terminal's buffer at 300 characters a second, and printed at a rate of 20 characters per second.

But this is only half the story. If the computer supplies data to the transmission control unit at a rate of four million characters per second and the communication lines at the other end of the control unit can accept only 300 characters per second each, how many lines can the front-end transmission control unit handle? At four million per second in and 300 per second per line out, the transmission control unit could, in theory, take care of a full 13,333 lines at the same time (or at least concurrently)! Most front-end machines do not operate nearly this high—25 to 100 lines is a more reasonable range. But the idea that a single control unit can easily keep pace with a number of lines should be obvious to you. Buffering makes it possible.

Getting back to the terminal end of the line, we might note that attaching a single 20- or 30-character-per-second terminal to a 300-character-per-second line represents a bit of a speed mismatch, too. It's possible to put a multiplexor or concentrator at the terminal end (Fig. 19.6) and assign to this piece of hardware the responsibility for controlling several terminals, concentrating their data transmission requirements, and getting closer to full utilization of the communication line.

The Intelligent Component—Data Communication Software

Consider a typical data communication system such as the one pictured in Fig. 19.6. Several pieces of hardware are involved, including numerous terminals, multiplexers, data sets, a transmission control unit, a channel, and the computer. Just coordinating all of this hardware is difficult. In addition, each terminal may well represent a different application that must be assigned a different work space in main memory. Keeping track of these work spaces is another complicating factor. Controlling and coordinating such complexity requires intelligence and, at least on a computer, intelligence is normally found in the software.

Some computer systems are designed specifically to support this multiterminal mode of operation; the time-sharing systems of Chapter 13 are an example. On such systems, many of the details of data communication are handled by the hardware, with operating system modules doing the rest.

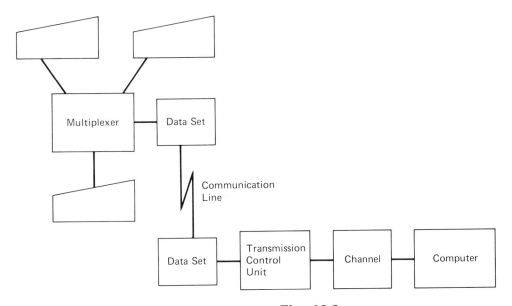

Fig. 19.6
It is possible to improve the utilization of a
communication line by placing a multiplexer at
the remote end. The multiplexer serves to
concentrate the transmission activities of several
terminals or other devices over a single line.

It is possible to run a multiple terminal application on a large multiprogramming system as well. Normally, a special software package called a *data communication monitor* is loaded into one of the partitions, usually a high-priority or foreground partition. This data communication monitor, in turn, assumes responsibility for taking care of the problems implied by multiple terminals and data communications.

What types of problems are handled by the data communication monitor? First, with all the terminals attached to such a system the software must, in some way, establish a clear and unambiguous link between the computer and *a particular* terminal. Most data communication monitors select the terminal to be accessed through a *polling* process. Communicating with a specific terminal involves several different pieces of equipment, and a very precise series of electronic signals must be exchanged with each before data communication can proceed. Monitoring and transmitting these *line protocols* is another responsibility of the data communication software package.

Once data communication has been established, the user at a remote terminal must have software to communicate with, often in a private work space.

The terminal user is typically active for a very small percentage of the time; thus the data communication monitor must be able to roll-in and roll-out user work spaces as required. Keeping track of the status and location of work spaces for dozens of users—some active and some waiting—is not unlike keeping track of the application program partitions on a virtual memory system. In performing this *partition management* function, the data communication monitor is not unlike an operating system within its own partition.

On many systems, much of the responsibility for polling and line protocols is shifted from the data communication monitor to the transmission control unit or front end processor. On a multiprocessing system, partition management may well be handled by a secondary processor. These functions, however, do require logic and (electronic) intelligence, and must be performed by some form of processor executing a program (be it software or firmware). Let's consider each of these logical functions one at a time.

Polling

Given dozens, perhaps even hundreds of terminals, which one gets to communicate with the computer next? On most data communication systems, this decision is made by polling the terminals. Imagine, to use a simple round robin polling example, a stack containing one entry for each active terminal. The polling logic of the data communication monitor starts at the top of the stack, issuing the equivalent of a start I/O instruction to the first terminal. If this terminal is ready to transmit data, it does. If not, a "start I/O" is sent to the second device on the list, then the third, and so on. Rather than returning to the top of the stack following each interrupt, the polling logic simply picks up where it left off, searching the complete table or stack from top to bottom, and then returning back to the top. In this way, each terminal receives roughly equal priority.

How does the system "know" when a given terminal is ready to transmit data? Assume that you are the user seated at a remote terminal. How do you indicate that you are ready to transmit data? You probably type a complete line of data into the terminal's buffer and then hit the RETURN button. The RETURN button, in effect, turns on a switch. If the poll signal arrives and this switch is off, you have *not* yet hit the RETURN button, and thus are not ready to transmit data. If, when the signal arrives, the switch is on, you *have* hit RETURN, and the data are transmitted to the computer.

One of the problems associated with this kind of polling is the time delay inherent in establishing contact with a terminal. Under control of the data communication monitor, the computer sends a poll signal to the terminal. If a signal is returned, fine, but what if no signal comes back? Is the terminal broken or down? Is the terminal active but not yet ready to transmit data? Or is the data communication link just slow? Usually, the terminal will be given a reasonable period of time in which to respond; if it doesn't, the monitor assumes that the terminal is not ready, and moves to the next terminal on the polling list. This does take time, and although the computer can certainly work on other things during this wait period (multiprogramming), it does represent overhead. Significant efficiencies can be gained by moving the responsibility for at least part of the polling process out to the front-end processor.

One commonly used approach has the front-end processor performing the polling function at the terminal level. This peripheral device sends polling signals to the terminals and, under its control, the terminals transmit their data into the front-end processor's buffers (Fig. 19.7a). Thus the data communication monitor does not have to worry about polling the actual terminals. Instead,

Fig. 19.7
**Key components of the polling function can be
shifted to the front-end device. (a) The front-end
device polls the terminal. (b) The computer, later,
gets its data directly from the front-end device.**

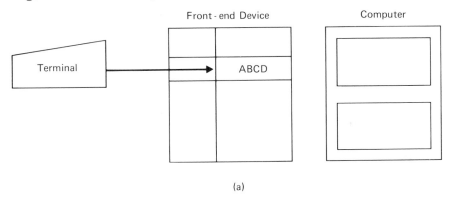

(a)

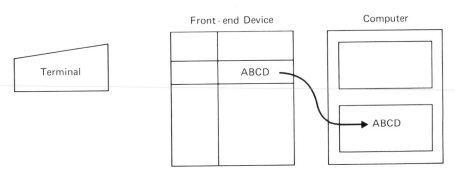

(b)

it can poll the front-end processor's buffers, which either do or do not contain current data (Fig. 19.7b). Because the monitor does not have to wait for the terminal's response, it can move on to the next potential source of data input much more quickly. The result is less time lost to overhead and, usually, better response for all the terminals.

A variation of this technique involves dropping the terminal's buffer and allowing the terminal data to be entered directly into the front-end buffer. The RETURN key sends a form of attention interrupt to the front end device, which sets the interrupt switch. Later, the data communication monitor will accept the input when it polls the front-end buffers. Although apparently much more efficient at the polling level, this approach (as we shall see) can have negative implications for line speed and protocol complexity.

Line Protocols

A second major function of the data communication software is to transmit and monitor line protocol signals. A line protocol is a standard set of precisely defined signals that must be exchanged by two pieces of hardware before they can begin to communicate. Data are transmitted in the form of electronic signals at very high rates of speed. In most cases, the individual bits are distinguished by timing circuits; i.e., if no signal arrives in the next 15 nanoseconds, assume a 0-bit. Given the importance of timing, the two communication devices must be carefully synchronized before the data can be transmitted. This is a key function of the line protocol.

Perhaps the best way to visualize a line protocol is to follow a typical example. Let's assume, as is often the case, that the front-end processor is responsible for establishing a link with a terminal. Several steps such as the following might be involved.

1. The front end sends a poll signal to the terminal: do you have any data?
2. The terminal, assuming it has data in its buffer, sends a response: yes.
3. A synchronization signal is sent to the terminal.
4. The synchronization signal is echoed back to the front end.
5. The front end sends a transmit command.
6. The terminal transmits the data surrounded by message characters. (More about them later.)
7. The front-end device runs a parity check on the data.
8. The front-end device sends either a message received or a retransmit message to the terminal.

If retransmission is necessary, the process goes back to step 6, and tries again; this cycle could be repeated several times.

The *message characters* described in the example above perform a very important function. They surround the data, both preceding and following the message as it goes over the line (Fig. 19.8). These message characters serve much the same function as "hello" and "good-bye" in human communication; they mark the beginning and the end of the actual data transmission.

A particular line protocol consists of a set of data transmission commands (poll, send, retransmit, etc.), a well-defined format for message characters, and a precise sequence in which commands and the message must be transmitted. Many different protocols are in common use today; there is no universally accepted standard. As a result, it is not always possible to communicate between a given terminal and just any computer; individual vendors tend to offer their own systems that are largely incompatible with the products of any other vendor. Slowly but surely, a few protocols are becoming de facto standards simply because of the number of installations using them. Perhaps we will have a small number of standard protocols before the end of the decade.

Some protocols support *serial* data *transmission,* with one bit following another over a single line. Some support *parallel transmission* with several bits being transmitted, in buslike fashion, in parallel over several lines. With *asynchronous* data transmission, the data are transmitted one character at a time, with a complete set of protocol signals and message characters for each single character. This is the problem we referenced earlier (p. 446) when we were discussing the possibility of a terminal sending data directly into the front-end buffer rather than into its own buffer. *Synchronous* data communication requires a single set of protocol signals and message characters for the *complete* message; thus the ratio of overhead signals to data signals is much lower. Because the line speed is finite (so many bits per second) the less overhead (protocol signals and message characters) we must transmit, the more data we can transmit. Synchronous data communication makes more effective use of the line. Unfortunately, the equipment to support synchronous communication must be better (i.e., more expensive) than the equipment needed to support asynchronous communication simply because it must stay "in sync" with a longer message.

Fig. 19.8

When transmitting data, message characters are normally placed in front of and behind the data.

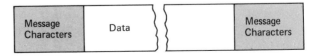

The protocol used in a given application will be a function of the computer, the peripheral devices, and the communication medium used. If we could standardize the hardware, we could standardize the protocols. We haven't done that yet.

Transmitting and monitoring protocol messages is a rather trivial data processing operation but, given the need for taking variable action based on those signals, electronic intelligence is required. The data communication monitor can (and sometimes does) assume this responsibility, using the central processing unit. On larger systems, the protocol responsibility is shifted from the main computer to a front-end processor. In fact, it is not uncommon to see a minicomputer being used as the front end for a large mainframe.

Partition Management

The characteristics of a multiple terminal, time-sharing application were discussed in some detail in Chapter 13. Basically, the typical time-shared system supports a large number of concurrent users who make brief and widely spaced demands on the computer's resources. To ensure that no one user dominates the system, time slicing is employed. A user is given control of the central processing unit for a limited period of time. If control of the processor is voluntarily surrendered before the time period expires, fine; the system simply moves on to the next user. If processing continues beyond the time limit, however, the user program is interrupted and placed at the end of the queue, and the next program given control.

Another problem with a time-shared system is memory allocation. With large numbers of users, there is simply not enough space in main memory to give each user a sufficient work area. Taking advantage of the typically long intervals between transactions, a user's work space is rolled out to secondary storage as soon as processing is completed. Later (on the average, at least 30 seconds later), when the next transaction from this user arrives, there is plenty of time to roll the work space back in to main memory. In this way, several different users can share the same physical main memory work space.

On a time-shared system, time slicing and roll-in/roll-out are functions of the operating system. On a large multiprogrammed system, these functions are assigned to the data communication monitor. A single partition, usually a high-priority or foreground partition, is assigned to the data communication monitor. Within this partition, the monitor acts as a *partition manager,* performing, at a lower level, many of the functions of an operating system. Specifically, it imposes time slicing on the application programs, perhaps by setting a timer as the user's module begins processing, and accepting a real or simulated timer interrupt if the time slice is exceeded. The data communication monitor also assigns work space to the user programs and controls the roll-in/roll-out function.

The Data
Communication
Monitor

Let's briefly assemble the pieces of the data communication monitor software package. It contains the logic needed to perform three primary functions (Fig. 19.9)

1. polling,

2. transmitting and monitoring line protocols,

3. partition management.

In addition, this software package sometimes contains such secondary, application-dependent modules as a query facility, a report generator, a text editor, statistical routines, and many others, but the three primary functions are the keys.

These are operating system functions on some machines, in particular on those computers that were designed with time-sharing in mind. On the large multiprogramming computer, the data communication monitor effectively acts like an operating system running under another operating system. This mode of operation entails a great deal of overhead; it is relatively inefficient. Why is the data communication monitor a separate program? Why have these functions not been incorporated into the large, general-purpose operating system?

The basic reason is cost. Developing and writing an operating system is expensive. The cost is recovered from the customers. The more customers that might be expected to use an operating system, the lower the cost per customer. The biggest market for computers is the general business market. The large multiprogramming operating systems were designed for this market. Until recently, a very small percentage of the business organizations who compose this market needed data communications. Thus it made little sense to build data

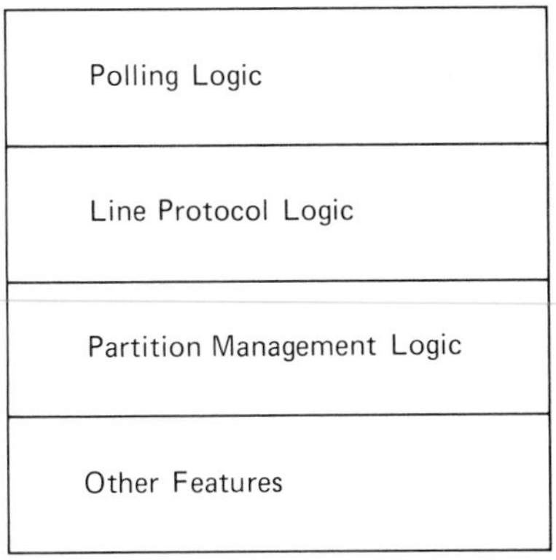

Fig. 19.9
The components of a
typical data
communication
monitor.

Polling Logic
Line Protocol Logic
Partition Management Logic
Other Features

communications into the operating system. Instead, by writing a data communication monitor to run *under* the large, general-purpose operating system, the vendors found it possible to service the occasional customer who needed data communications without burdening the majority of their customers who did not.

One major result of this marketing approach was the appearance of independent software houses who sold nonvendor supplied data communication monitors. Several of these independent software products are excellent, and have been outstanding commercial successes. Very simply, the major vendors failed to fill a need, and a number of (usually) young entrepreneurs moved in to fill the vacuum. The software industry remains a "land of opportunity" to the intelligent and highly motivated individual even today.

Trends in Data Communication

The traditional batch orientation of the so-called general-purpose market is beginning to change. More and more organizations are using on-line data entry, on-line information retrieval, and other terminal-oriented techniques. Gradually, data communication is becoming part of the mainstream, rather than a peripheral or special-interest application. As it does, the structure of both the data communication monitor and the operating system that supports the monitor will change.

The first change, already well under way, will be to shift more and more of the responsibility for polling and line protocols outside the mainframe and onto the front-end processor. Certain partition management functions will begin to work their way up into the operating system, perhaps at first as SYSGEN options. Eventually, look for large computer systems with a multiprocessing architecture including (perhaps optionally) a data communications *processor* to take care of the polling, protocol, and partition management functions.

Other changes are occurring outside the computer. Personal microcomputers are dropping in price; we are rapidly approaching the point where the cost of a microcomputer is comparable to the cost of a simple terminal. In the future, a significant amount of data processing will be done on micros, with these machines acting as terminals when access to a large machine is necessary. A student might, for example, enter a program into his or her microcomputer under the control of a text editor and then dial up a large mainframe to have the source code compiled. Economically, "off-loading" trivial tasks such as data entry makes a great deal of sense; direct interaction with a human being at a keyboard has never been a particularly effective way to use a large mainframe computer. In the past, data communication was not a key part of a general-purpose operating system because it was not seen as cost effective. Given the dawning microcomputer revolution, data communication may become an essential part of such an operating system simply because data communication will become extremely cost effective. The microcomputers described above sometimes acted as computers and sometimes as terminals. As far as the central computer is concerned, such devices are terminals, and are controlled as terminals; what happens before the data communication link is established is irrelevant.

A network consists of two or more computers linked by communication lines—computer/computer communication. Line protocols are still needed on such systems, but polling and partition management may well be unnecessary. Often, two central processing units communicate with each other through a special type of interrupt that activates an operating system module. For example, on the IBM System/370, CPU to CPU communication involves an external interrupt.

One intriguing possibility for network development involves a rather extreme level of off-loading. At the top of the network is a super computer that has no (repeat, no) I/O devices. Below the "star" computer are a number of lesser computers that do have peripherals. Essentially, the idea is to allow the smaller, less expensive machines to communicate with the relatively slow input and output devices, editing and concentrating the data before transmitting them, in buslike fashion, to the large mainframe. Imagine an extremely powerful, high-speed, high-capacity central computer concurrently executing thousands of different programs stored on hundreds of different lower-level computers!

Data communication would be a critical element on such a system. Almost certainly, the polling and protocol functions described in this chapter will be implemented in hardware on this system, with partition management controlled by a secondary processor within the mainframe. System software tends to migrate to hardware, but the function does not change.

Summary

This chapter was concerned with the software used to support data communication. We began with a brief overview of several key data communication concepts, including modulation, various communication media, and the speed disparity problem. We then turned our attention to the data communcation software.

Multiple-terminal applications can be supported on a large multiprogramming computer system by loading a data communication monitor in a foreground or high-priority partition. The data communication monitor performs three key functions: polling, dealing with a line protocol, and managing the partition.

The polling function is concerned with establishing communication between the computer and a given terminal. Often, round robin polling techniques are used, with each terminal having roughly the same priority. A few alternatives to round robin polling were briefly discussed. On many systems, much of the responsibility for polling the terminals is shifted from the data communication monitor to the front-end device.

A line protocol is a set of transmission commands and message characters that must be exchanged between devices before data communication can take place. The data communication monitor accepts, transmits, and acts upon these protocol signals in establishing the terminal/computer link. On many systems, responsibility for the line protocol is assigned to the front-end device.

Partition management is concerned with such problems as time slicing and roll-in/roll-out. In effect, the data communication monitor functions much as an operating system within its own partition. An anticipated trend is the shifting of partition management functions to a secondary processor on a multiprocessing machine.

With the rapid development of network technology, the data communication function will, more and more, become an integral part of a general-purpose computer system. As these trends continue, look for the functions currently performed by the data communication software to migrate to hardware or firmware.

Key Words

data communication monitor	message characters
	modem
data set	modulation
line	noise
	partition management
line protocol	polling
local	remote

Exercises

1. Distinguish between the terms local and remote.
2. Why are modulation and demodulation necessary when communicating over existing data communication media?
3. Distinguish between an analog signal and a digital signal.
4. Why is buffering an important factor in data communication?

5. What functions are performed by a front-end device or transmission control unit?

6. List the primary functions performed by a data communication monitor software package.

7. What is the purpose of polling? Why is something like polling necessary on a multiple terminal application? Why does it make sense to shift much of the responsibility for polling to the front-end device?

8. What is a line protocol? Why does it make sense to shift line protocol responsibility to the front-end device?

9. What is partition management? Why is it necessary? In performing the partition management function, a data communication monitor has been compared to an operating system within its own partition. Why? What parallels can you see?

10. Why isn't data communication software a standard part of most general-purpose operating systems?

20

Data Base Management

Overview

Data communication software was initially developed as an addition to the standard operating systems, providing support that, until recently, was needed by only a small percentage of computer users. Today, data communication is becoming more and more common, and may soon be a critical element of what is called a general-purpose system. In this chapter, we turn our attention to a similar software product—a data base management system.

We begin with a discussion of the problem that a data base management system is intended to solve. Many existing computer systems were developed application by application, with little thought given to the potential for integrating these applications. As a result, files are normally customized to the application. This leads to a number of inefficiencies. Data are simply not available to support certain new applications. The same element of data is often found in several different places, and this data redundancy leads to inaccuracy. Programs are data dependent, with programmers often more concerned with the details of I/O than with the real application. The central data base concept, typically implemented through a data base management software package, represents an increasingly popular solution.

After describing the problems associated with pre–data base application development, the central data base concept will be introduced. The way in

454

which the data base approach solves each of the problems will be discussed. We then turn our attention to the implementation of the data base concept, describing the functions performed by a typical data base management system.

Early Computer Applications—Cost Justification

Payroll was, for many firms, one of the very first computer applications. The reason for using a computer to do payroll is easy to pinpoint. The computations for a ten-employee payroll might take an hour if done manually; a 100-employee payroll might be expected to consume ten hours; a 1000-employee payroll gets us up to 100 hours or two and one-half full-time people. As the firm grows, the personnel time (and thus cost) of processing payroll grows, and it doesn't take too much imagination to see that by automating this highly repetitious task and doing it on a computer, these costs can be brought under control. Payroll is easy to cost justify—if we don't get a computer, we'll need 25 full-time payroll clerks within two years. Add the advantages of speed and accuracy, and there's no way any large firm can avoid using a computer for payroll processing.

Other early computer applications—accounting, ledgers, accounts payable, accounts receivable, inventory, bill-of-material processing, report generation—are equally easy to cost justify on their own merits. A basic argument in each case is cost reduction: It's less expensive to do the job on a computer than to do it manually.

Most firms believe in cost justifying any new project; if the expected benefits do not outweigh the cost of achieving those benefits, no sense investing the money or personnel. These early computer applications fit beautifully into the cost justification mold, with each single computer application standing on its own. Programmers quickly learned that core minimization and CPU-time minimization were very important, measurable attributes of a good program and, given the relatively slow speeds and limited storage of early computers, these were important. This approach did, however, lead to a method of organizing data which, as we shall see, has come back to haunt many companies.

Let's consider an example. Manufacturing has need for a new expediter, and management in all sincerity feels that this is a perfect opportunity for moving a woman into a position of some responsibility. Data processing has been asked to aid in the search, and to provide, within the next two weeks, a compilation of information that is certainly available on the computer—namely, a list of all female employees who have at least five years of experience with the company, a college degree, some experience in a manufacturing department, and some managerial training. A reasonable request? Not so says the data-processing department—six months and $30,000.

Why? How could a simple list of existing data possibly require six months of programming effort? Easy. A good part of the basic data is on the personnel file, but work history (some experience in a manufacturing department) is on a history file considered to be highly confidential by the personnel department. It will take at least three weeks to negotiate the release of this data. Further complications are expected to arise from the fact that the history file hasn't been very well maintained. If an employee was a college graduate when first hired, it's recorded on the personnel file, but if a degree were earned after initial employment this information would be found only on the education department's external education file. This wouldn't be so bad except that information in the personnel file is organized by social security number while the education department uses its own key—there is no way to merge these two files except by matching names (which might work well if both files reflected name changes due to marriage, but they don't). Management training is even tougher. The firm has an internal program, with a simple list of attendees maintained in chronological order. Voluntary education is a second possible source of such training, but the voluntary education department uses its own (strange) course codes and maintains lists of attendees haphazardly, at best. Again, external training at a local college or university would show up on the education department's external education file.

The programming department sees a need for combining information from several different files into a single new file and writing a program to select records from this new file. Each source file must be read by a separate, new program which creates a new, partial record; these partial records must be merged into the new file format requiring another new program before the desired program can be executed. Thus six months and $30,000 for a list of maybe 50 names. And accuracy cannot be guaranteed because of name changes and poor file maintenance.

How could such a thing happen? When data are stored on a computer, they are supposed to be available; we all learned that in our "introduction to the computer" course. The reality is often quite different. The data are not available or, if available, are not accurate. Why?

The Customized File Approach _____

The basic problem begins with the application-by-application approach to developing computer-based systems. Each single application stands on its own, with little or no central planning to provide a context for these applications. As a result, efficiency is defined at the application level. The "ideal" program is one that uses a minimum amount of main memory, a minimum amount of CPU time, and a minimum amount of I/O.

One of the best ways to achieve program-level optimization is to customize the data files to fit the application. Thus a typical organization has a set of payroll files, a set of billing files, a set of accounts payable files, and so on. It is the very independence of these files, the lack of integration of all this information, that creates problems.

Data Redundancy and the Lack of Data Integrity

Perhaps the most obvious problem arising out of the customized file approach is that of *data redundancy*. With so many independent files, it is almost certain that the same element of data will appear in several different places. For example, consider the files that are found at your college or university. The chances are that information concerning *you* appears on several different files. For billing purposes, your name and address appear on the bursar's records. Your name and address are also on the registrar's files, your department-of-major's file, the files belonging to any social groups you have joined, housing files, library files, alumni files, automobile registration files, and probably several others. What happens if your address (or your name) changes? The correction will be made on some of the files, perhaps even most of the files, but the chances are that the correction will not be made on *all* the files. Thus there will be two (or more) different versions of the same data element: in this example, your name and address. When two or more values exist for the same element of data, the *integrity* of that data is subject to question.

How can we get two different values for the same data element on the same computer? Obviously, to continue with the same example, at least one version of your name and address must be wrong. Remember that the files are independent, and the applications that access these files are independent. When does the bursar *need* your name and address? Probably, just before the beginning of the term, when bills are mailed. When does the registrar need your name and address? At the *end* of the term, when grade reports are mailed. The two applications have different timing requirements. As a result, they will update their files at different times. Thus, at times, they will have different values for your name and address.

How important is your name and address to the bursar? If you don't get your bill, the school does not get paid; the bursar considers your name and address very important, and will make a serious effort to make certain that it is correct. How important is your name and address to the registrar? If you don't get your grade report, you will be mildly inconvenienced, but a simple telephone call or visit to the administration building will usually solve the problem.

Since the penalty for bad data is not as great for the registrar, it is not reasonable to assume that the registrar's office will make as much of an effort to ensure the accuracy of name and address data as the bursar does. Your department probably has your name and address on file too; how important is this information to them? How often does a department try to contact students at their homes? Only occasionally. If you have moved, your department probably has the wrong address for you. Because of their need for the data, these three groups used quite different editing and verification standards; they are simply not equally careful in maintaining a particular data element.

A student's name and address is perhaps a trivial example of data redundancy and the resulting lack of data integrity (although it is probably not trivial to the student). Consider another very important statistic: the number of majors in a given department. To the department, this number is extremely important, as it determines or influences the number of instructors who will be hired to teach in that department. The department tends to count as majors all those students who are taking its major course sequence. When a student changes majors, the new major department adds that student to its records as soon as the necessary paperwork is signed. The registrar is concerned with a student's department of major only when that student applies for graduation. Thus the registrar is in no hurry to update its count of students by major. The result is two different versions of the "truth." As a direct consequence, "we don't trust their data and they don't trust ours." The *data integrity* is subject to question.

Such problems are, of course, not limited to the university. Any time the data files are custom-designed to fit each application, data redundancy will be found. Given redundant data, and given the different timing and editing standards of the independent applications, different values of the "same" data element will be stored on the same computer. With different versions of the "truth," how can we trust the data?

Data Ownership: The "Mother, May I?" Problem

Individual users tend to define data integrity strictly in terms of their own application. The bursar's office will take steps to ensure that the financial data are accurate. The registrar will carefully verify academic data. Each user is concerned with the integrity of the data that are relevant to that user's application. One way to guarantee the integrity of a given file is to limit access to that file. Thus the bursar's files are available only to the bursar's office; by denying others access, the risk of incorrect data being introduced by an untrained individual is minimized. Another factor is security; the bursar's records contain certain highly confidential information, and limiting access helps to preserve this confidentiality. The reasons for denying access to data are many, and they are easy to justify. Such a localized, "this application" definition of data integrity does, however, lead to another problem.

Who *owns* the data? The answer is not always clear. Operations controls the hardware on which the data are stored; thus operations has a legitimate claim. Without software to create, maintain, and manipulate the data on the files, there would be no files; thus systems and programming might claim ownership. The user, on the other hand, is responsible for the integrity of the data, and thus has the right to define the conditions for data access. All three groups—operations, systems and programming, and the user—can reasonably claim ownership. Split responsibility never works very well.

To access a given file, it is often necessary to get the approval of the user, computer operations, and the programmers. The result is red tape and bureaucracy: the "Mother, may I?" problem. The bursar may have the most accurate file of student names and addresses but because the bursar's records contain other, confidential information, no one else is allowed to access these records. The result is the creation of other files containing the same information, redundant data. This takes time, and costs money. The fact that data exist on the computer does not necessarily mean that they are easily accessible.

Thus we see why the programming department says "six months and $30,000" when asked to compile an apparently simple one-time report. Imagine trying to assemble a jigsaw puzzle after someone has spread the pieces all over the neighborhood. To complicate matters, not only must you find the right pieces, but once you find one, you must negotiate with a neighbor for the right to use it! Customized files tend to limit *data accessibility*.

Data-Dependent
Programs

Programs designed to access custom files are *data-dependent*. Consider, for example, the standard master file update application. Two files, a master file and a transactions file are input to this program, which matches the transactions to the appropriate master file record and creates a new master file. Much of the logic of the program is concerned with input and output. To the user, such problems as matching records, first record processing, and last record processing are irrelevant. All the user really wants are the results in the form of valid pay checks or bills. The programmer is really solving two problems: the user's data manipulation problem and the problem of moving data between primary and secondary storage. If the structure or organization of the data changes, the standard master file update program will not work. The program is clearly data-dependent.

Often, data dependency is more subtle. Consider, for example, the problem of how dates are stored on many customized files. To save space (remember, space minimization is one of the objectives of this approach), the year is often stored as a two-digit number—84 rather than 1984. Imagine a program that ages inventory, compiling statistics on stock that is over 90 days old, from 60 to 90 days old, and so on. The logic of this program would involve a comparison with the current data. What happens on January 1, 2000? The two-digit year is 00. Does 85 mean 15 years in the past or 85 years in the future? Beginning on January 1, 2000, any logic based on a comparison with the current date will not work!

Why not simply change the date field to hold a four-digit year? Because hundreds of programs have already been written to expect a two-digit date, and they would all have to be changed. As if that is not enough, hundreds of other programs that do not even reference the date in their logic do read a record that contains the date. Changing from two to four digits means a change in the logical record length. The result: *every* program that even reads a record containing the date would have to be changed, whether that program used the date or not. Clearly, all these programs are data-dependent.

The zip code provides another example of the potential impact of data dependence. Recently, the United States Postal Service announced its intent to begin using a new nine-digit zip code. Significant improvements in postal service, coupled with a drop in certain postal costs, were anticipated, but the users of the postal service, in particular the larger business firms, fought the change. Why? Basically because of the high cost associated with modifying existing computer programs and files to accommodate the new, longer zip code. Cost estimates in the *billions* of dollars were not uncommon.

Whenever a data file is customized to meet the needs of a particular program, that program, in turn, becomes locked to its data. Any change in data content, data structure, or file organization can imply a need to modify the program. As a result, management is often faced with three almost equally unacceptable choices: (1) patch the present system, (2) write a new system from scratch, or (3) risk falling behind the competition. Simple maintenance becomes impossible because such a significant portion of the program is locked to the physical structure of its custom files.

Actually, all the programmer really wants is a set of values for certain data elements that are relevant to the logic of a program. The details associated with physically retrieving that data—the file organization, the job control language, the special parameters on the I/O macros—are really secondary. in fact, a surprising number of programmers really do not understand these details; they just use them, by rote. Although it is difficult to identify the precise cost of this data dependency, it may well be greater than data redundancy, the lack of data integrity, and the problem with data accessibility combined.

How might we solve these problems? Increasingly, it appears that data base management might be the answer.

The Central Data Base Concept _____

Most of the problems cited above were a direct result of the traditional approach to developing computer applications, one at a time, with no coordination or central planning. The big problem was seen to be the customized file, with its data integrity, data ownership, and data dependency implications.

Why not group all of an organization's data resources to form a large, integrated *central data base*? To control access to this data base, we might provide a *data base management system* and require all input and output operations to flow through this software module. The result could well be a solution to many of the data access problems cited above. Clearly, with a single, centralized data base, the problems of data redundancy and data integrity would be minimized. Centralized data implies centralized control, thus solving the data ownership problem. With all programs accessing a common data base, any changes in the physical structure of the data would impact only the data base manager; the application programs could be relatively data independent. Let's investigate how the central data base concept might help to solve each of these problems.

Data Integrity

On a centralized data base, we would store a single version of each *element* of data. A school, for example, might store a student's name and address on the data base. Any application requiring the student name and address would get it from this central source. With a data base, if your name or address were to change, it would be corrected once, on the data base, and everyone would have the correct information.

Clearly, the idea of a central data base almost eliminates the problem of data redundancy. Redundant data are data that are stored in several different places. The data base concept implies that an element of data will be stored once, in the central data base. Reduced data redundancy means improved data accuracy.

Another factor that would tend to improve the accuracy of data on a data base is ease of verification. With multiple, customized files, the user department might be held responsible for editing or verifying input data, at a *record* level. Certain critical fields would, we might expect, be carefully scrutinized, but other fields less critical to the application would receive less careful consideration. This is one reason why different values often exist for redundant data fields. With a data base, the department or user group most concerned with the accuracy of a given data element can be assigned verification responsibility for that *field,* and no group would have to be concerned with the accuracy of data elements of secondary importance. Key department verification of *each* individual data element would lead to much greater data integrity.

For example, consider sales data. Who is most concerned with seeing that a given sales transaction is entered on the system? Assuming that the salesperson is paid on a commission basis, the answer is clear—the salesperson. We might assign to the salesperson the responsibility for entering sales data.

Reducing data redundancy and clearly defining responsibility for the accuracy of each data element will tend to improve data integrity. Earlier, we saw that one way to help ensure the integrity of a particular customized file was to limit access to that file. Often, the justification was the confidential nature of one or more fields in a record. A key feature of the central data base approach is a data base management system lying between the application program and the data base. With this module in place, *all* access to the data base can be routed through a common control mechanism. Security, at the field or data element level, can be implemented in the data base management system. With this kind of control, a given application program can be restricted to authorized data elements only. Security is no longer an excuse for denying data access.

Data Ownership

Another direct result of the central data base approach is a very clear definition of data ownership. With all of the organization's data collected into a single central data base, it becomes relatively easy to define the data as an *organizational resource,* owned by the *entire* organization. In fact, in today's increasingly complex world, information may well be the organization's most valuable resource.

How might we achieve the objective of clearly defining data ownership? Let's begin with pre–data base, customized files. The Information Management function of most large organizations using this approach will probably resemble Fig. 20.1. The manager of MIS (Management Information Systems) probably

Fig. 20.1
The pre-data base structure of the MIS function.

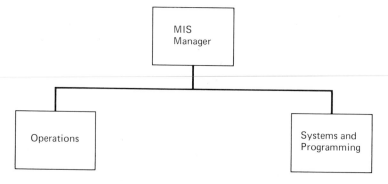

reports to the controller; sometimes, the MIS manager is a vice-president, porting directly to the president. Reporting to the MIS manager are two functional groups. *Operations* is responsible for the hardware, performing such functions as operating the computers, maintaining the hardware, and entering the data. *Systems and programming* is responsible for planning, implementing, and maintaining the software. Who is responsible for the data? *Physical* data responsibility goes to operations—it owns the hardware on which the data are stored. *Logical* data responsibility belongs to systems and programming—it writes the programs that create and maintain the data. Who is responsible for data integrity? Often, the user. Thus we have a split responsibility and split control. The result is the "Mother, may I?" problem described earlier in the chapter.

With the data resources centralized, centralized control suddenly becomes possible. Many organizations have restructured their MIS function (Fig. 20.2), adding a new department, the *data base administrator* or *DBA*. Operations is still responsible for the hardware, and systems and programming still controls software. The data base administrator controls the data. What are the three primary elements of *any* computer system? Hardware, software, and data. With this new organizational structure, the primary responsibility for each of these major system elements is clearly and unambiguously defined.

Centralized control, unfortunately, carries a certain risk. An unconstrained data base administrator could arbitrarily limit access to the organization's data, becoming a data czar. This is where the data base management system comes into play (Fig. 20.3). The data base management system is a software module that lies between the application program and the data base. The rules for accessing the data base are implemented in the data base management system. The task of the data base administrator is thus one of seeing that the rules for

Fig. 20.2
The structure of the MIS function when the centralized data base approach is used.

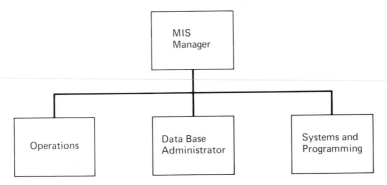

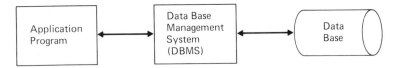

Fig. 20.3
The data base management software comes
between the application program
and the data base.

data base access, as defined by company policy, are accurately reflected in the data base management system.

Security precautions provide a good example. Because every attempt to access the data base must pass through the data base management system, security rules can be implemented in this software module. Before a given program is allowed to access a particular element of data, the security level of the application can be compared with the security level of the data element, and the request either honored or denied. For example, a first-level manager might be allowed to access personnel data on his or her employees, but details on higher-level managers might be off-limits.

It seems almost a paradox, but the tighter, more centralized control made possible by the data base approach leads to greater *data accessibility*. With security in place, confidentiality is no longer an excuse for denying access to the data. With improved data integrity, the "we can't trust their data" problem disappears. Suddenly it becomes possible to honor unanticipated requests for information. In fact, many data base systems have implemented *query languages* that allow nontechnical users to extract information from a data base using Englishlike questions. Another popular option is *report generator* software which allows the nontechnical user to structure and actually execute simple one-time programs to generate special-purpose reports from the data base.

Data-Independent
Programs

The problems of data integrity and data ownership are quite apparent to the computer professional. (Ask any programmer if he or she has ever had to program around a political roadblock, or if different values of what should be the same data element ever appear.) The problem of data dependency is a bit more subtle. As we saw earlier, the programmer using customized files is really solving two problems: data access *and* the user's application. Unfortunately, the programmer rarely sees these two problems as independent—data access and the user's application are so tightly linked that they become a single problem in the programmer's mind and in the code. This is why, when the file organization changes, it is so often necessary to rewrite rather than maintain the program. Programmers do *not* view such rewrites as maintenance. Instead, such projects are seen as new system development.

Management takes a somewhat different view. If an organization has an existing system to generate valid pay checks, and a change in the law makes a new payroll system necessary, programming sees a need for a development project. Management, on the other hand, sees a considerable sum of money being spent to allow the organization to continue doing what it already was doing— generating valid paychecks. Management sees a need for the maintenance of an existing system, and (quite correctly) sees the need to redesign and recode the entire payroll system as highly inefficient. The argument that a change in data structure makes the logic of the existing program totally obsolete is not particularly impressive to nontechnical management. Computer professionals, all too often, are so close to the data dependency problem that they cannot see it.

How might a centralized data base help to make application programs data independent? Consider, once again, a pre–data base application. The programmer requests logical I/O (Fig. 20.4) by transferring control to an access method. The access method converts this logical I/O request to a physical I/O request and passes this request to the operating system, which issues the instructions needed to control the physical I/O. The key problem with this approach is that the programmer's "logical" *record* must physically exist somewhere; in other words, if the employee's name and address are required, the programmer must read a record *containing* the name and address. Fields such as name and address simply do not exist independent of that record; the record defines a structure; the record defines the context in which the desired data elements can be found.

Fig. 20.4
**Without a data base management system, the
programmer codes logical *record*-level I/O.**

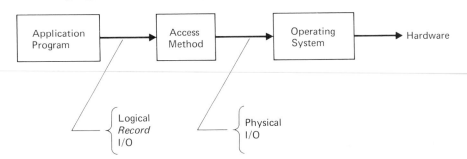

With the centralized data base approach, a data base management system is placed between the application program and the access method (Fig. 20.5). The data base management system still uses the standard access methods, and still accesses the data base through the operating system, but the application program is insulated from this linkage. The application program can now request true logical I/O. For example, if the program needs an employee's name and address, only the name and address would be requested from the data base management system. This software package would translate the application program's request for values for these two data elements into the necessary record requests, issue the necessary traditional I/O operation or operations, accept the input data records, extract the relevant field or data element values, and pass them back to the application program. Thus the programmer could ignore the details of physical I/O.

Consider very carefully the distinction between traditional logical I/O and true logical I/O. When a programmer reads a traditional record from a traditional file using a traditional access method, that record must physically exist. The data might be stored as a large physical record composed of several logical records. A large logical record might be spread over two or more physical records. The point is that the logical record holds the data in a fixed structure, and when the programmer requests a logical record, the entire record will be transferred into (or out from) the program. The fact that the programmer may not need every field in that logical record is not relevant; the record's structure within the computer will be identical to the record's structure on the external, physical storage device. Using the traditional approach, the programmer must accept the entire record as it is physically stored, or accept none of it.

A data base management system supports true logical I/O. If the programmer needs only certain data elements, the programmer can create a logical record or data structure that contains only those data elements. The data base

Fig. 20.5
With a data base management system,
the programmer can code logical
***data element*-level I/O.**

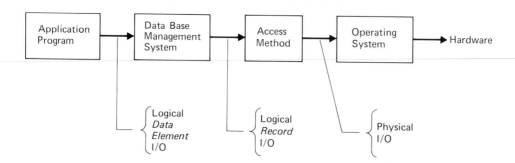

management system accepts the programmer's request for data, issues the necessary physical I/O commands, and assembles the data elements requested by the programmer. It is possible that the programmer's request may match the physical structure of the data on the external device. More often, however, the logical record requested by the programmer does not physically exist until the data base management system assembles the pieces. Thus the programmer can ignore the physical stucture of the data.

What if the physical organization of the data were to change? Since the application programs are not concerned with the physical organization of the data, they will not be affected. Rather than modifying hundreds of different programs, the new data structure could be implemented by modifying only one: the data base management system. This is what we mean by the term data-independence.

Consider, once again, the nine-digit zip code problem. For those organizations with a centralized data base in place, the change to a longer zip code, while still a problem, is certainly not insurmountable. A minor change would have to be made in the data base software, and modifications would have to be made in those programs that actually use the zip code, but the programs that do not use the zip code would not be impacted. Without the centralized data base approach, all programs that access a record *containing* the zip code would have to be modified whether they used the zip code or not.

The idea of data independency is an *extremely* important concept, especially to the future computer professional. It directly influences programmer productivity, a key concern of management in these days when the demand for programmers is much greater than the supply. Increasingly, the attitude of both management and technical people is changing. The emphasis is shifting away from *computer* efficiency (with its implied concentration on the machine) and toward problem solving (with a concentration on meeting user requirements). This trend will have a profound impact on the job of the future systems analyst or programmer.

The Central Data Base: Advantages

Let's briefly summarize the advantages derived from the central data base approach. First, perhaps most importantly, applications can be relatively data-independent; the programmer can ignore the physical structure of the data. Second, data responsibility and authority are clearly defined, often in the person of a data base administrator. Finally, data integrity is improved through reduced data redundancy, better data verification and control, and better security. The result of all these factors is that the data resources of the organization are accessible to the entire organization.

The Central Data
Base: Disadvantages

No improvement is without its cost, and data base management is no exception. Concerns range from the overhead associated with the data base, through the impact of the data base approach on the programmer, and on to the cost of the data base itself.

The data base management system is positioned between the application program and the traditional access methods. Speaking positively, the data base approach insulates the application program from the data, thus promoting data independence. From a more negative perspective, the use of a data base represents one more level of overhead. Rather than communicating directly with the access method, the program must now go through the data base management system. Overhead implies execution time and memory space. There is little question that a well-written program accessing customized files will run faster than a well-written program performing the same data processing functions but accessing its data through a data base management system.

The basic problem with this argument is that it tends to define efficiency in primarily hardware terms. The objective of the organization is not to minimize the cost of running payroll on the computer. The objective of the organization (with respect to payroll) might be better stated as minimize the total, long-run costs of producing valid paychecks. The total cost would certainly include the on-the-computer costs of concern to the single application people, but other costs would be considered as well—for example, coding costs and long-term program maintenance costs. Of even greater concern is the relationship between the payroll application and the organization's other information processing needs. From a total organization point of view, the "efficiency" argument loses a great deal of its appeal.

By insulating the programmer from the need to worry about I/O, the use of data base management techniques does tend to simplify the coding process. From a management perspective, this is clearly a positive result, with implications for improved programmer productivity. To the programmer, the impact of data base management often seems negative. By simplifying the task of writing code, the use of data base management makes the job of the programmer seem more mundane. Programmers complain about the loss of an opportunity to exercise their creativity. Some choose to leave the organization, moving to firms that provide more of a technical challenge. In these days of high demand for programmers, the organization must consider this risk.

Actually, there is more to programming than writing code. In fact, excessive concentration on the "neat" technical details may be one reason why programmers have historically had such a difficult time communicating with their users. Data base management does not impact the portion of a program concerned with actually solving the user's needs; it impacts that part of the program that is concerned with I/O. In other words, from a management perspective, the alleged impact of data base management on programmer creativity affects a secondary function, I/O, and does not affect the primary function of the program. We still need creative people to translate user needs into technical terms, but must that creativity be extended to the details of file manipulation? Perhaps what we really need at this level is *precision,* and not creativity. Frankly, except for the implied "I'll take my marbles and go home" threat of programmers who know they are in short supply, the creativity argument is irrelevant.

There is, however, one very strong argument against the data base approach—cost. The data base management system, that critical software package, is a very complex program that is beyond the capabilities of most installations. Commercial data base management systems can be purchased or leased, but they are quite expensive. The cost of developing or leasing and installing a data base management system can easily hit $50,000 or more.

The cost of the control software is insignificant when it is compared to the cost of developing the data base, however. In a relatively brief period of time, all the data stored in hundreds of previously customized files must be merged to form the data base. The application programs, perhaps hundreds of them, that accessed the customized files, must be rewritten or modified to access the data base. These phase-over costs can be enormous, perhaps ranging into the hundreds of thousands of dollars.

These costs are concrete. They are short-run costs, representing dollars that must be spent now, rather than at some vague time in the future. Unfortunately, the benefits derived from the central data base approach—data integrity, data availability, and data independent programs—are less concrete and more in the future. Management is asked to spend a great deal of short-run money for a somewhat questionable long-run payoff. Not surprisingly, many organizations have decided not to change.

Unfortunately, the problem will only get worse. Each year, new applications are added, meaning that the switch to data base will cost more next year than this year. A few decades after the end of World War II, the United States, with its largely obsolete steel-making facilities, found it very difficult to compete with Germany and Japan and their rebuilt steel plants. To the American steel industry, the cost of upgrading facilities was prohibitive, but so was the cost of *not* upgrading. In the future, the decision to switch from customized files to a data base approach may be viewed in much the same light.

Implementing the
Data Base Concept

How might we go about implementing the data base concept? Let's begin with the data base management system, the software package that sits between the application program and the data base. How does this software product work?

The key idea is to allow the programmer to request elements of data at a purely logical level, without regard for the physical organization of that data. For example, when writing a program to generate the special report described earlier in the chapter, the programmer might begin with a request something like the following:

```
FOR EACH EMPLOYEE IN THE COMPANY,
GET NAME, SEX, HIGHEST-DEGREE, PRESENT-DEPARTMENT
PAST-DEPARTMENTS, MANAGEMENT-COURSES, DATE-OF-HIRE.
```

The request might be in the form of a simple CALL macro. It might look like the list-directed I/O of BASIC or FORTRAN. Perhaps special data base macros will be used. The point is that the programmer can simply ask for the *specific* data needed to support the application, and only for that data. The assumption is that the data base management system will, in some way, figure out where those data elements are physically stored, assemble the requested values, and return them to the application program. *How* this task is performed is the data base management system's problem. What was previously a very difficult program thus becomes very easy to write: get the data, test the fields, and selectively write the output before returning to the top of the loop.

Obviously, the data must still be stored in the form of physical records; data base management does not imply a new set of secondary storage hardware. Physical storage implies physical records moving back and forth between main and secondary memory under control of the standard hardware and software components of the computer system. In other words, in spite of the fact that the programmer can now request logical fields or structures, physical records must still, at some point, be read or written. In general, the data base management system uses the standard access methods (Fig. 20.6). Given a logical request for values for selected data elements, the data base management system determines the identity of the logical record or records containing these fields,

Fig. 20.6
**The data base management system uses the
standard access methods.**

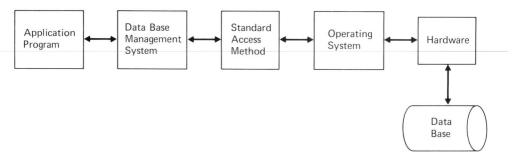

and issues the necessary record-level I/O operations to a standard access method. The access method, as before, converts the logical record request to a physical record request, transfers control to the operating system, and so on. Once values for all the requested data elements have been assembled (note that several physical I/O operations may be required), the data base management system returns the data elements to the application program.

Clearly, the data base management system must have a mechanism for finding the physical record that contains a particular data element. One common technique is to use pointers to link the physical records. Consider, for example, the record structure described in Fig. 20.7. Physically, each employee in the organization has a master record containing such key information as name, address, department, and so on. Buried in this master record are a series of pointers to other, secondary records such as a work history record, an external education record, and an internal education record. Faced with a need for generating a report listing all employees who meet certain criteria the programmer might write a simple loop beginning with a request for input listing the relevant data elements. The data base management system would accept this request, determine (either from the specific command or from the context of the request) what the programmer needed, read the employee master record, read any necessary secondary records, compile the data needed by the programmer, and return these data to the application routine.

Fig. 20.7
The physical structure of a typical data base.

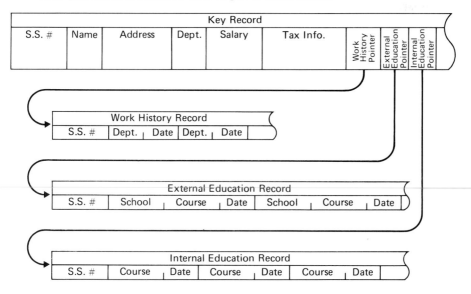

As an alternative to pointers buried in the records, the data base management system might maintain a detailed set of indexes telling it where each data element is physically stored. On some applications, the use of pointers leads to an excessive amount of physical I/O, as the system chases through a long chain of pointers. It is often less time-consuming to search a set of indexes in main memory to locate the desired physical element of data. On the other hand, the indexes take up a great deal of main memory, and maintaining the indexes can be a significant problem. The "best" technique will be a function of the application.

Data Base Organization

Following a chain of pointers through a data base implies a series of physical I/O operations. How might we follow such a chain? How is the data base physically structured?

Once again, different data base systems structure the data in different ways. Many use a *hierarchical organization.* For example, a university might include student information as part of its data base (Fig. 20.8). A student master record would link to secondary academic, financial, housing, activity, and other records, each one providing more details about the student. The secondary records might themselves point to lower-level records; for example, a student's academic record might point to course description records. Look at the data structure illustrated in Fig. 20.8, and it should be obvious why this is called a hierarchical organization.

In more general terms, the record at the top of the hierarchy is called the *parent.* Data elements in the second level are the *children* of the associated parent. A second-level record can itself be a parent with lower-level children.

One limitation to the hierarchical structure is the fact that, while it is possible for a parent record to have many children, a child record can have only one parent. In many typical business applications, this limitation is not a problem, as the data requirements are themselves hierarchical. Not all data base applications follow this pattern, however. As a result, an alternative *network organization* is quite popular.

Under a network organization (Fig. 20.9), a parent record can still have many children, but a given child record can have many parents. This one-to-many and many-to-one relationship is what makes the network structure different. With a hierarchical organization, it is necessary to start at the top and work down, through the hierarchy. With a network organization, it is possible to start almost anywhere, and move either up or down.

Consider, for example, a university data base. If we want to key on the student, using the student master as our parent record, we might be able to define a hierarchy of data, with each student record linked to a number of

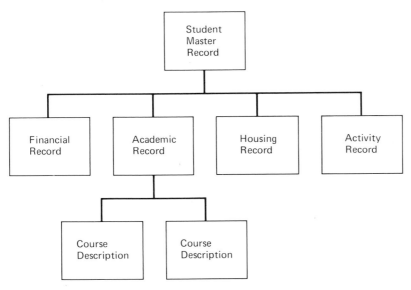

Fig. 20.8
A hierarchical data base organization.

children that provide academic, financial, residential, and other details about that student. What if we were to decide to start with the functional group rather than with the students? Assume, at some level in the data base, we have parent records for the bursar, the registrar, student housing, and so on. Where would we place the student? With a hierarchical organization, we would need a

Fig. 20.9
A network data base organization.

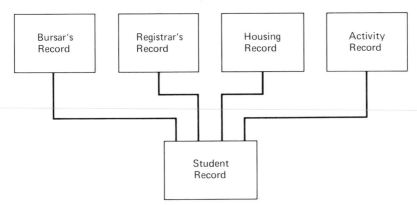

separate student record for *each* parent—redundant data. With a network organization, all the parent records would simply reference *the same* student record—one child with many parents.

A considerable amount of development work is currently being done on the *relational data base* concept. Rather than relying on physical pointers or detailed indexes to define the relationships between and among data elements, the relational data base approach is based on the mathematical theory of relations. We won't attempt to develop that mathematical theory in this text; you should be aware, however, that there is a very good chance that you will be using relational data bases in the future.

The Data Base
Management System

We have discussed the logical functions of the data base management system. Physically, where is it found?

System software or support software often follows a relatively predictable path. It begins as application software, supporting a particular application in a particular installation (Fig. 20.10). Assuming that the product is good, detailed documentation and user specifications are written, and the software is offered for sale or lease as a *program product*. When sales reach a critical level, it becomes possible to move the program product into the operating system, where it becomes *system software*. Finally, after the logic of the application has stabilized for a reasonable period of time, it migrates to hardware. Data communication monitors are following this path; so are data base management systems.

Initially, the data base management system was little more than a sophisticated access method (Fig. 20.11), added to a load module by the linkage editor and supporting a single application program in a single partition. This approach is still used on many small computer systems. Today, many data base management systems are placed in a common area of memory where they can be shared by all the application program partitions (Fig. 20.12). The use of a common data base management system has the advantage of forcing *all* data base I/O from *all* partitions to pass through *the same* control module. This is the physical implementation of the concept of centralized control.

Fig. 20.10

The development stages of system software.

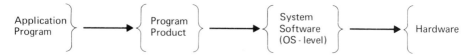

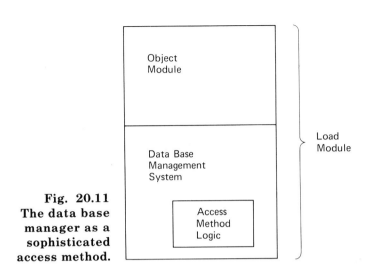

**Fig. 20.11
The data base
manager as a
sophisticated
access method.**

**Fig. 20.12
The data base management system as shared
logic occupying a common area.**

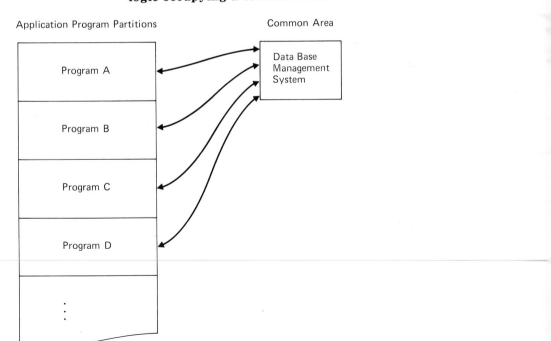

To the computer manufacturer, the use of data base program products occupying a common partition creates a problem simply because any independent software house can develop and market such a program product. Thus, for competitive reasons, the manufacturer is going to try to move its own data base management software into the operating system. With standard system software to provide data base capability, the customer will be less likely to purchase that same capability from an independent supplier. Why pay for the same thing twice? The limit to this trend is the migration of system software to hardware. The data base processor, either in the form of an independent back-end machine or an independent secondary processor in a multiprocessing configuration, is probably the wave of the future.

Summary

This chapter began with a discussion of the application-by-application approach to developing computer systems. The need for individual application cost justification almost invariably leads to customized data files. These customized files, in turn, lead to a variety of problems, destroying the integrity of the data, causing the question of data ownership to be unclear, almost guaranteeing that application programs will be data dependent and, in general, assuring that the organization's data resources will *not* be readily available.

The central data base approach helps to solve all these problems. By eliminating or minimizing data redundancy and by allowing functional groups to worry about the accuracy of only the data elements that affect them, the central data base approach can significantly improve data integrity. The very fact that the data base is centralized implies a possibility of centralized control and ownership, often under a new computer professional, the data base administrator. The use of a data base management system allows the programmer to concentrate on purely logical, data element-level I/O, thus ignoring the physical details of how the data are stored; the result is data-independent programs.

There are, of course, disadvantages to the data base approach. Technical people often attack the efficiency of data base I/O, and complain about the impact of the data base concept on their creativity. Management tends to reject both arguments. The cost of the data base management package and the cost of creating the data base and modifying existing programs to access the data base are much more relevant to management.

To the programmer, a data base management system allows I/O operations to be specified at a purely logical, data element level. The data base management system accepts the programmer's logical data requests, figures out where the appropriate data elements are physically stored, and issues the necessary logical *record* I/O operations to a standard access method. Some data base management systems use pointers to link physical files; others use indexes. Some use a hierarchical organization to define the relationships between and among data records; others use a network organization. A considerable amount of current research is directed at establishing a relational data base.

Initially, data base management software was implemented as a sophisticated access method, occupying an application program partition as part of the load module. Most current data base management systems are stored in a common partition in memory, with all application programs sharing the same data base software. Eventually, look for the data base logic to migrate into the operating system, and from there into hardware.

Key Words

child	data integrity
central data base	data redundancy
data accessibility	hierarchical organization
data availability	
data base	network organization
data base administrator (DBA)	parent
	program product
data base management system	query language
	relational data base
data dependent program	report generator
data element	system software

Exercises

1. Why does the need to cost justify *individual* applications generally lead to customized data files?
2. What is data redundancy? How does data redundancy tend to destroy data integrity?
3. With files customized to the application, who owns the data? Why? Why does this hurt data accessibility?
4. Programs that access custom designed data files are data dependent. Why? Why is this a problem?
5. How does the central data base approach help to improve data integrity?
6. How does the central data base approach help to more clearly define data ownership? Who is the data base administrator?

7. How does the central data base approach improve data accessibility?

8. How does the central data base approach promote data independent programs? Why is data independence valuable?

9. Why does management tend to reject the efficiency argument against data base management? Why does management reject the programmer creativity argument?

10. Why is cost a critical management concern when it comes to data base management?

11. Explain how a data base management system converts true logical I/O to physical I/O.

12. Explain how pointers can be used to link related records. Explain how indexes can be used.

13. Distinguish between a hierarchical data base organization and a network data base organization.

14. Where is the data base management software located? In other words, where in main memory is it stored?

A Brief Survey of Commercial Software

Overview

Commercial software is one of the most rapidly growing components of the computer marketplace. In this chapter, we will briefly survey a variety of software products.

What Is Commercial Software?

When we think of software, we tend to think of custom programs written to solve specific problems within an organization. As the use of computers becomes more common, more and more programs are written. As a result, when a modern organization begins to contemplate the development of a new software package, it is likely that someone else has already written a similar set of programs. Why reinvent the wheel? If some other organization has already written the necessary software, why not simply buy the programs? With the ever-increasing cost of software development, this argument makes sense. As a result, *commercial software* sales have increased dramatically over the past several years.

What exactly is commercial software? We might begin by contrasting commercial software with *custom software*. Custom software is developed to solve a specific problem within a given organization. Usually, an organization's custom software is designed and written by the organization's system and programming staff. At times, a system will be designed internally, with the coding and testing subcontracted to a service bureau or to a consulting firm. Occasionally, the entire system is designed and implemented by external consultants, but the key idea does not change: the system is designed to deal with a specific application within a specific organization. The software is *not* generalized; it is highly special-purpose.

Commercial software is purchased from outside the organization. It is leased or purchased as a *finished* package; in effect, rather than structuring the software to fit the application, the application is restructured to fit the software. Data base management systems and data communication monitors are good examples. The software comes first. An organization that wishes to use a data base manager or a data communication monitor will typically study the available software packages, select the one that best fits their environment, and then modify existing internal software and operating procedures to fit the new package. Often, minor changes will be needed to *customize* the commercial software package to the application, but such changes represent a very small percentage of the total code.

There is an impressive array of commercial software available today, and the list is growing almost daily. The future computer professional should be aware of this source of software; it is a viable alternative to custom software development. A key problem in many organizations is the shortage of qualified professional programmers; the result is a backlog of work in most systems and programming departments. Commercial software is an excellent way to help clear that backlog.

The rest of this chapter will consist of a brief survey of a variety of commercial software products. Product groupings are arbitrary; many commercial software products cut across any classification scheme. The program products are described in generic terms, with few references to specific suppliers or software development firms. For those who are interested in more specific information, *DATAMATION* magazine publishes an annual systems software rating (usually in the December issue) that ranks a large number of software products by name. Additional details can be found in the *Auerbach Reports* and in the *Datapro Reports,* which can be found in the reference section of most technical libraries.

System-level Support Software

Some commercial software packages work at the operating system level. Perhaps the most obvious examples are the complete operating systems designed to run (usually) on small to mid-sized computers for which only very limited operating system support is provided by the vendor. One example that we studied earlier in the text was CP/M.® It was developed by an independent software house to fill a void in the microcomputer market, and has become almost a standard.* Another is UNIX,® an operating system designed to support certain minicomputers.†

Other products are designed to enhance the performance of a standard operating system. Although most vendors make a sincere effort to develop highly efficient operating systems, a project of this magnitude is bound to contain a few areas of inefficiency. The performance-enhancing software basically consists of additions or revisions to the standard operating system designed to correct one or more of these rough spots.

Closely related to the performance-enhancing software are a number of very good job stream managers, spoolers, and schedulers. Disk space managers are also available. In general, it is possible to find a software product aimed at optimizing the utilization of almost any one of the system resources. We might place data base and data communication software in this category.

One major problem facing a number of computer installations is that of converting from one operating system to another. To aid in this process, several conversion aids are available; for example, some convert DOS job control and macros to OS form. Another alternative is to use an emulator, a software module that allows programs written for one system to run on another (for example, some firms are still running second generation programs on a third generation machine by emulating the old machine on the new one).

Backup and security are major problems in most computer centers; thus packages to provide backup and security support are quite common. Perhaps the most popular backup software is designed to dump and restore on-line files. Most computer centers copy all on-line files to magnetic tape at least once a day; in the event of computer failure, the tapes allow the system to be restored to (at worst) yesterday's state. The dump/restore software supports very efficient disk-to-tape and tape-to-disk I/O. Security packages may include such features as user number or password checking, various levels of authorization codes, and even data encryption.

Finally, we might consider a number of accounting packages as a form of operating system support. These packages aid in job costing for accounting purposes: those who use a computer's resources should pay for that use. Other packages measure computer use, keeping track of such features as CPU utilization, channel utilization, and the like. In addition to providing a basis for accounting charges, such information can prove useful in estimating the capacity of a computer system.

---

*CP/M is a Registered Trademark of Digital Research.
†UNIX is a Registered Trademark of Bell Laboratories.

Software
Development
Support

Many packages are concerned with supporting the professional programmer as he or she develops custom programs. Given the current shortage of qualified programmers, the productivity of those who are working is of prime concern to management. These software development aids tend to improve programmer productivity, and that is the primary motivation for their use.

We might begin with the usual compilers, assemblers, and interpreters. Clearly, they are aids to programmer productivity, as anyone who has ever tried to program in binary can attest. The compilers have, however, been around for quite some time. At a standard level, they are not viewed as commercial software.

There are, however, a number of improvements to the standard compilers that are commercially available. Optimizing compilers, for example, take standard source code and generate not just object code but highly efficient object code. A programmer might need several days to smooth out the rough spots in an otherwise working application program. A good optimizing compiler can do almost as good a job in a matter of minutes. Optimizing compilers are not normally used during program debug. Instead, the program is debugged under a standard compiler and, once the code is acceptable, submitted to the optimizing compiler. Typically, the optimizing compiler takes much longer than the standard compiler. The result, however, is reasonably efficient code at little marginal cost.

Another type of compiler-support product is the precompiler or preprocessor. Such products allow the programmer to enter code in a shorthand form and/or interactively. Imagine, for example, a COBOL precompiler. Rather than typing the rather long statements required by COBOL, the programmer might enter shortened versions of the source code, with the precompiler expanding the code to standard COBOL form. Another feature of many precompilers is a statement-level syntax check—an incorrect statement will be flagged as it is entered, allowing the programmer to correct it before the code is submitted to the compiler. Closely related to the precompilers are a number of structured code generators. These allow the programmer to enter code in a reasonable form, and then modify the code to fit a standard structured format. This is as much a documentation aid as a coding aid.

A major problem is encountered when new applications are developed for small microcomputers: very simply, the micro is often not big enough to hold both the compiler and the source code. A cross compiler allows the programmer to create code for one computer on another computer; for example, a cross compiler designed to run on a large mainframe computer might produce object-level code for a different manufacturer's microcomputer.

Other software products are designed to provide special requirements support. For example, coding the character by character contents of a CRT screen is a tedious process in most compiler languages. A screen format generator might allow the programmer to simply type the contents of a complete screen and then issue a command; the results would be a complete set of constants and variables generated from the screen contents. On a good screen generator, the programmer simply does the layout, and the software does the rest.

The commands for generating graphic output can be quite complex in many programming languages. Graphics packages can greatly simplify this task.

Documentation and maintenance are, in general, not the typical programmer's favorite tasks. As a result, documentation and maintenance are often poorly done, if they are done at all. Several software packages can provide at least some support. Flowchart generators can scan source code and develop reasonable flowcharts to describe the logic. A data dictionary can be used to keep track of references to a given data element by literally every program used on a given computer. Other packages convert code from one language to another; for example, one converts IBM COBOL to UNIVAC COBOL, or RPG to COBOL. These converters can save a great deal of maintenance effort when an installation changes computers or operating systems.

Library managers typically control source statement, object module, and load module libraries, and make it easy for the programmer to access, modify, add modules to, and delete modules from the library. Such librarian support is particularly valuable with on-line debugging.

Debugging aids are also available. A trace feature can be added to many of the common languages, allowing the programmer to generate a trace of the logic path followed by a given program. Dump analysis routines are designed to accept a standard system dump and provide the programmer with an easily read analysis of the probable cause. The wave of the future, however, may well be the on-line debugging routines that literally allow the programmer to step through his or her logic, line by line. Another common debugging problem is the generation of test data to adequately exercise the logic; commercial test data generators can prove most useful in solving this problem.

Finally, we should mention utility programs and sort/merge routines; no computer installation would be complete without them.

Support for Nonprogrammers

One of the most rapidly growing areas in the commercial software market is software designed to support the nonprogrammer. Report generators are a good example of end-user software. With a good report generator, a nontechnical

user can specify the content of a desired report, submit it to the report generator, and allow the system to do the rest. Only the most limited sense of computer logic is required. Query languages support similar nontechnical information
retrieval applications in an on-line environment.

A rapidly developing computer application is *word processing* or text processing. Word processing systems allow the nontechnical person to enter and
edit text, usually through a CRT and keyboard, by using little more than basic
typing skills. Often, a variety of printers can be used to provide draft, letter, or
even camera-ready text. Once the text is entered onto the computer, it can be
transmitted to other computers or terminals in a form of electronic mail; additional system software can be purchased to provide this support.

The nontechnical user can also obtain limited graphic support. On many
systems, sets of statistics can be automatically converted to bar chart or pie
chart form. On others, the user can literally draw graphics on a CRT screen
with a light pen. These charts and graphs, often in full color, can be used effectively in formal presentations or as illustrations in a term paper.

A very common nontechnical use of the computer involves developing tables of data; for example, a table of mortgage payments, or car payments, or
savings account balances. Often, one element of the table is generated directly
from the value of the prior element. There are packages that greatly simplify
the generation of such tables; perhaps the best known is called VisiCalc®.*

Some nontechnical packages are aimed at the scientific user; for example,
the scientific subroutines that are supported in many languages, particularly
FORTRAN. Various mathematical and simulation aids are also available. To
call such software nontechnical is a bit misleading, as the applications themselves are often highly technical. In this context, however, the term "technical"
refers to the computer. The engineer or applied mathematician may well be
highly skilled in his or her own technical discipline, but may not be interested
in learning the details of another technical discipline, the computer field.

Other scientific packages serve as design aids. For example, there are programs that allow the electronics expert to draw and test electronic circuits on a
CRT screen. Other packages provide drafting support and more general graphic
support.

Application Software

The commercial software covered to this point has been support software, used
by the technical or nontechnical person to achieve a finished product. With the
growth in the use of inexpensive microcomputers, more and more users with

---

*VisiCalc is a Registered Trademark of Personal Software, Inc.

almost no computer expertise are becoming interested in software. As a result, the demand for complete application-level programs has skyrocketed. Many of the standard business applications—payroll, accounts receivable, accounts payable, ledger—are available on almost all of the better-known microcomputer systems (not to mention the larger systems). In addition, such consumer products as games and educational packages are quite popular today.

These packages are aimed at the unsophisticated user. Such individuals are simply not interested in learning the details of computer programming. They want a package that works—period! Perhaps they do not possess the skills necessary to be a computer programmer. Perhaps they are simply not interested, preferring to channel their energies elsewhere. In any event, they tend to view the computer in much the same way as most people view a television set or a home appliance—plug it in, turn it on, and it should work. This submarket needs *turnkey systems*; literally, all these users want to have to do is turn the key. There is a tremendous potential for growth in turnkey systems development.

The Commercial Software Market

We have not even come close to describing all the software currently available in the commercial market, and the market is growing day by day. Commercial software is here to stay; it is a highly viable segment of our economy. Why? Home-grown software is expensive, and besides, why reinvent the wheel? With the continuing growth in the use of microcomputers, the demand for commercial software can only expand. There are tremendous opportunities for the bright, self-motivated man or woman in this field.

One key factor that virtually assures continued growth is the relatively low level of capital required to enter this marketplace. For the price of a personal microcomputer, a few thousand dollars, the skilled individual can begin to generate commercial software. Literally thousands of independent programmers are earning their livings writing such software today, and thousands of others earn extra income.

Many experts believe that commercial software will become the "cottage industry" of the late twentieth century. Significant numbers of programmers will not work for the large business organizations but will instead stay at home and write their own programs. Some will sell their services to the large organizations, writing custom software for a fee. Others will write and market commercial software. We already have several large organizations that market commercial software products, paying the authors a royalty similar to the royalty paid to writers or recording artists. Perhaps someday there will be almost as many software stores as there are record or book stores.

The point is simple: The opportunities for a bright, self-motivated individual who is capable of writing software that other people might want to buy are virtually unlimited. Some people like the security and social implications of a large corporation. Others do not, preferring independence and risk. There is room for both types in the computer field.

Summary

This chapter consisted of a brief survey of commercial software. Commercial software is written outside the organization and purchased or leased as a finished product. Some packages provide operating system support. Others are aimed at making the application programmer more productive. Increasingly, software support is available to the nonprogrammer; perhaps the limit to this trend is the development of turnkey software. This market will continue to grow, and represents a tremendous opportunity for the bright, self-motivated programmer.

Key Words

commercial software	turnkey system
custom software	word processing

Exercises

1. Contrast custom software and commercial software.
2. Why is the commercial software market growing?
3. Why is commercial software designed to support system or program development so popular?
4. Why, do you suppose, is software support for the nonprogrammer so popular?
5. What is a turnkey system?
6. Discuss the concept of a commercial software "cottage" industry.

Number Systems, Data Types, and Codes

The Binary Number System

Modern digital computers are designed to work with binary data; thus a basic appreciation of the binary number system is essential if one is to gain an understanding of how a computer really works. Because the decimal numbering system is far more familiar to most of us, let's start our discussion of binary numbers by taking a close look at a few decimal numbers.

Consider the two numbers 3 and 30; both contain the same character, a three, but we all know that we are looking at two different numbers. What's the difference between the three in the number 3 and the three in the number 30? The answer, as any schoolchild knows, is position; the first three is in the "units" column and the second three is in the "tens" column. Closer analysis reveals the fact that the number thirty (30) is really another way of saying three tens and no ones.

Let's put it another way. *Any* decimal number consists of a series of digits—0, 1, 2, 3, 4, 5, 6, 7, 8, 9 in some order—written in very precise positions; the number twenty-three is written as 23 while another combination of the same two digits, 32, represents a different number. The value of a given sequence of digits is found by multiplying each digit by its place or positional value and summing these products.

Consider, for example, the number 3582; what is really represented by this combination of digits is

```
 2 times     1 =     2
+8 times    10 =    80
+5 times   100 =   500
+3 times  1000 =  3000
                  ────
                  3582
```

In general terms, *any* number is simply the sum of the products of its digit and place values; in the language of mathematics,

Number = $\sum$ (digit value times place value).

Take a closer look at the sequence of place values: 1, 10, 100, 1000, 10000, 100000, 1000000, 10000000, and so on. The pattern is pretty obvious. Using scientific notation and taking advantage of the fact that any number raised to the zero power is one, the place values in the decimal number system can be represented as a series of powers of ten (the base) raised to sequential integer powers. (See Fig. A.1) Decimal fractions, 0.25 for example, have as their place values negative powers of ten.

$$2 \text{ times } 10^{-1} = 2 \text{ times } 1/10 = 0.2$$
$$+5 \text{ times } 10^{-2} = 5 \text{ times } 1/100 = \frac{0.05}{0.25}$$

A few concepts stand out in our discussion of the decimal number system. First is the idea of place or positional value represented by the base (10) raised to sequential integer powers. The use of the digit zero to represent *nothing* in a given position is a second key concept. Third, a total of *ten* digits, 0 through 9 is needed to write decimal numbers. Finally, only values less than the base, in this case ten, can be represented in a single position.

There is nothing to restrict the application of these rules to a base-ten number system. If the positional values are represented by powers of two instead of ten, we have the framework of a base-two or binary number system. Such a framework is pictured in Fig. A.2.

As in the decimal system, the digit zero is needed to represent *no value* in a given column. In addition to the zero digit, the binary number system uses only one other digit, a 1, to form numbers. Why only two digits? As in the decimal system, only values less than the base, in this case 2, can be represented in a single column; thus only the digits zero and one are needed. The binary

Fig. A.1
Decimal place values. | 10^6 | 10^5 | 10^4 | 10^3 | 10^2 | 10^1 | 10^0 | 10^{-1} | 10^{-2} | 10^{-3}

2^8	2^7	2^6	2^5	2^4	2^3	2^2	2^1	2^0	2^{-1}	2^{-2}	2^{-3}	2^{-4}
Decimal		64	32	16	8	4	2	1				

Fig. A.2
Binary place values.

number 1100101 is, using the digit-times-place-value rule, equal to the following decimal number.

$$
\begin{array}{rl}
1 \text{ times } 2^6 = 1 \text{ times } 64 = & 64 \\
+1 \text{ times } 2^5 = 1 \text{ times } 32 = & 32 \\
+0 \text{ times } 2^4 = 0 \text{ times } 16 = & 0 \\
+0 \text{ times } 2^3 = 0 \text{ times } 8 = & 0 \\
+1 \text{ times } 2^2 = 1 \text{ times } 4 = & 4 \\
+0 \text{ times } 2^1 = 0 \text{ times } 2 = & 0 \\
+1 \text{ times } 2^0 = 1 \text{ times } 1 = & \underline{1} \\
& 101
\end{array}
$$

The number 2 is written as a 10 in binary; the number 4 is 100; ½ is written as 0.1 which is

$$1 \text{ times } 2^{-1} = 1 \text{ times } \tfrac{1}{2} = \tfrac{1}{2}.$$

Any whole number can be written in binary. Not all fractions can be written exactly in binary, but that's no surprise when you remember that not all fractions can be written exactly in decimal—one third, for example.

We humans, at least in this part of the world, use the base-ten system because that's the number system we are used to. There is nothing inherently "better" about base ten.

For a computer, an electronic device, there is a tremendous advantage to using the binary number system; since data can be represented by only the two digits, 0 and 1, the computer can work with the simple on/off logic of electrical circuits. Binary is truly an electronic number system.

Other number systems, notably octal (base eight) and hexadecimal (base sixteen), have gained popularity in the computer field. The octal system uses powers of eight to represent positional values (Fig. A.3) and denotes values of

Fig. A.3
Octal of base-eight place values.

8^8	8^7	8^6	8^5	8^4	8^3	8^2	8^1	8^0	8^{-1}	8^{-2}	8^{-3}	8^{-4}

Fig. A.4
Hexadecimal of base-
sixteen place values.

| 16^5 | 16^4 | 16^3 | 16^2 | 16^1 | 16^0 | 16^{-1} | 16^{-2} | 16^{-3} |

numbers by using the digits 0, 1, 2, 3, 4, 5, 6, and 7 within this framework. The hexadecimal system (Fig. A.4) uses powers of sixteen and the digits 0, 1, 2, 3, 4, 5, 6, 7, 8, 9, A, B, C, D, E, and F. The hexadecimal number $(FF)_{16}$ is:

$$\begin{array}{rl} 15 \text{ times } 16^1 = & 240 \\ +15 \text{ times } 16^0 = & 15 \\ \hline & (255)_{10} \end{array}$$

The reason why these two number systems are so important in the world of computers is the ease of conversion between octal and binary or hex and binary. Each octal digit is equivalent to exactly three binary digits (Fig. A.5); each hexadecimal digit converts directly to four binary digits (Fig. A.6) Thus octal or hexadecimal can be used as a sort of shorthand for viewing binary data, and this fact has a tremendous impact on the printed volume and readability of such data (Fig. A.7).

Numerical Data

Because binary numbers are so well suited to electronic devices, it is not surprising that many computers are most efficient when working on binary numbers. Many machines have been designed around a basic unit of binary data called a word—usually 16, 24, or 32 bits (binary digits), although almost any

Fig. A.5
Octal-to-binary
conversion table.

Octal	Binary	Octal	Binary
0	000	4	100
1	001	5	101
2	010	6	110
3	011	7	111

Fig. A.6
Hexadecimal-to-binary
conversion table.

Hex	Binary	Hex	Binary
0	0000	8	1000
1	0001	9	1001
2	0010	A	1010
3	0011	B	1011
4	0100	C	1100
5	0101	D	1101
6	0110	E	1110
7	0111	F	1111

Binary

110010101011	000101001000	101100001111
011001100001	100000100011	011101010100
000100000000	011111110000	000010000101
100100100100	100001011111	100000011001

Fig. A.7
Octal and hexedecimal
as binary shorthand.
Note that octal and
hexadecimal are much
more compact and
readable than
binary is.

Octal	**Hexadecimal**
6253 0510 5417	CAB 148 B0F
3141 4043 3524	661 823 754
0402 3760 0205	102 7F0 085
4444 4137 4031	924 85F 819

word length can be (and probably has been) used. One bit, usually the high-order bit, is set aside to hold the sign (0 for +, 1 for negative numbers) with the binary number occupying the remaining bit positions. There is no provision for a decimal point in such numbers, decimal alignment being the responsibility of the programmer. Word size sets an absolute limit on a given computer's range. A machine with a 32-bit word, for example, can handle a number consisting of a sign followed by thirty-one binary 1's (a number equal to the decimal number 2,147,483,647), while a 16-bit machine's limits are $(0111111111111111)_2$ or 32,767 in decimal.

Simple binary integers are fine for many computer applications but, at times, numbers larger than the fixed word limit and fractional quantities are needed. In the world of science, extremely large numbers (astronomical distances) and very small numbers (subatomic measurements) are written using scientific notation, a decimal fraction followed by a power of ten; the speed of light, 186,000 miles per second, might, for example, be written as 0.186×10^6.

Large numbers, small numbers, and fractions can be stored on a computer by using an approximation of scientific notation. Since computers do not normally work in decimal, powers of ten cannot be used, but a system based on the number "2" gives reasonable results. On the IBM System/360 and System/370, for example, a fullword of 32 bits is set aside for each "floating point" number. The high-order bits (Fig A.8) holds the sign of the fractional portion. The next seven bits hold a binary power of *16* having the same meaning as the power of ten in normal scientific notation. The remaining 24 bits hold the fractional portion of the number.

To simplify the handling of the decimal point, numbers are normally represented as binary values multiplied by a power of 16, with the first significant bit following the binary point (as opposed to decimal point); thus the function of decimal point manipulation is completely handled by the characteristic.

To improve accuracy, IBM has created an extended precision form for its floating-point numbers; an extra 32-bit word is added to the normal floating-

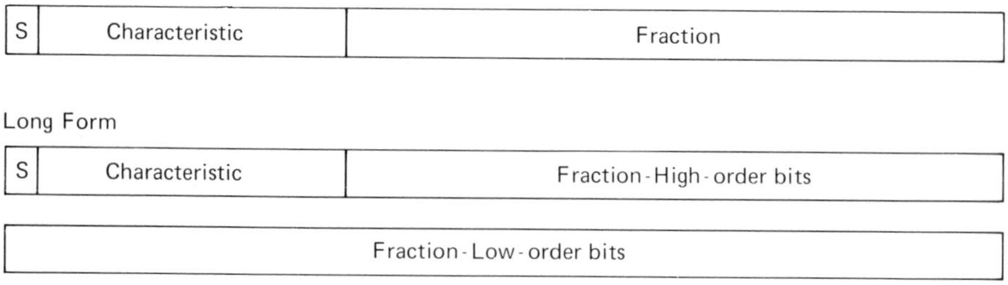

S	Characteristic	Fraction

Long Form

S	Characteristic	Fraction - High - order bits

Fraction - Low - order bits

Fig. A.8
IBM floating-point-data formats.

point field, increasing the fractional portion of the number from 24 to 56 bits.
Other manufacturers provide similar features.

Computer Coding

For economic reasons, card readers, printers, and other input/output devices
are designed to send data to and from the computer as a string of independent
characters. The number 12 is treated, for example, as a 1 and a 2, *not* as a
twelve. Since each character is treated as a separate entity, each character can
be represented by a unique code. Looking first at numeric data, each decimal
digit can be represented by its binary equivalent (see Fig. A.9); four bits are
used for each digit even when some are nonsignificant largely because it's simpler to design an electronic device to handle the same number of bits at all
times. The number twelve, using this coding scheme on the individual digits,
would be 00010010. If this number were treated as a pure binary number and
converted to decimal, its value would be $2^1 + 2^4$, which is 18 and *not* 12. Fortunately, most computers contain special circuitry for converting binary coded
decimals into pure binary. Some machines can perform arithmetic on binary
coded data; IBM, for example, refers to such data as packed decimal.

Many computer applications require alphabetic as well as numeric data;

	Decimal	Code	Decimal	Code
	0	0000	5	0101
	1	0001	6	0110
Fig. A.9	2	0010	7	0111
Binary-coded decimal	3	0011	8	1000
numbers.	4	0100	9	1001

thus something more than the simple numeric code described above is needed. An early solution to this problem was the six-bit BCD code shown in Fig. A.10. In this code, individual characters are represented by a series of six bits—two "zone" bits and four "numeric" bits. The letters A through I are assigned zone bits 11; since A is the first letter in this group, its BCD numeric part is 0001. The second letter, B, is 11 0010. J through R are assigned zone bits 10 and S through Z zone bits 01; again, the numeric bits show the character's relative position within the group. All things considered, the BCD code makes a great deal more sense than the code developed by Mr. Morse for his telegraph.

The code, to restate a point made previously, allows input and output devices to treat each character as an independent entity; the computer, under program control, puts these individual characters together to produce meaningful data. Any code will do, as long as it is consistently applied. Two codes enjoying great popularity on modern computers are IBM's Expanded Binary Coded Decimal Interchange Code or EBCDIC (pronounced ebb-see-dic) and the ASCII-8 code of the American National Standards Institute (Fig. A.11). Both are eight-bit codes.

Fig. A.10

**The six-bit BCD code. Certain unused
combinations of bits are used to represent
punctuation marks and other special symbols.**

Character	Code	Character	Code
A	11 0001	S	01 0010
B	11 0010	T	01 0011
C	11 0011	U	01 0100
D	11 0100	V	01 0101
E	11 0101	W	01 0110
F	11 0110	X	01 0111
G	11 0111	Y	01 1000
H	11 1000	Z	01 1001
I	11 1001		
		0	00 1010
J	10 0001	1	00 0001
K	10 0010	2	00 0010
L	10 0011	3	00 0011
M	10 0100	4	00 0100
N	10 0101	5	00 0101
O	10 0110	6	00 0110
P	10 0111	7	00 0111
Q	10 1000	8	00 1000
R	10 1001	9	00 1001

Character	EBCDIC Binary	EBCDIC Hex	ASCII–8 Binary	ASCII–8 Hex
A	1100 0001	C1	0100 0001	41
B	1100 0010	C2	0100 0010	42
C	1100 0011	C3	0100 0011	43
D	1100 0100	C4	0100 0100	44
E	1100 0101	C5	0100 0101	45
F	1100 0110	C6	0100 0110	46
G	1100 0111	C7	0100 0111	47
H	1100 1000	C8	0100 1000	48
I	1100 1001	C9	0100 1001	49
J	1101 0001	D1	0100 1010	4A
K	1101 0010	D2	0100 1011	4B
L	1101 0011	D3	0100 1100	4C
M	1101 0100	D4	0100 1101	4D
N	1101 0101	D5	0100 1110	4E
O	1101 0110	D6	0100 1111	4F
P	1101 0111	D7	0101 0000	50
Q	1101 1000	D8	0101 0001	51
R	1101 1001	D9	0101 0010	52
S	1110 0010	E2	0101 0011	53
T	1110 0011	E3	0101 0100	54
U	1110 0100	E4	0101 0101	55
V	1110 0101	E5	0101 0110	56
W	1110 0110	E6	0101 0111	57
X	1110 0111	E7	0101 1000	58
Y	1110 1000	E8	0101 1001	59
Z	1110 1001	E9	0101 1010	5A
0	1111 0000	F0	0011 0000	30
1	1111 0001	F1	0011 0001	31
2	1111 0010	F2	0011 0010	32
3	1111 0011	F3	0011 0011	33
4	1111 0100	F4	0011 0100	34
5	1111 0101	F5	0011 0101	35
6	1111 0110	F6	0011 0110	36
7	1111 0111	F7	0011 0111	37
8	1111 1000	F8	0011 1000	38
9	1111 1001	F9	0011 1001	39

Fig. A.11

The eight-bit EBCDIC and ASCII codes. Once
again, unused bit combinations are used to
represent punctuation marks and other special
symbols; these symbols are not shown here
because the pattern of the code is not as obvious.
A full listing of these codes can be found in
almost any reference manual.

A Summary of DOS Job Control Statements

The primary reference for this chapter is IBM Publication #GC33-5376, DOS/ VSE System Control Statements. Portions of several of the generalized job control statements are taken directly from this publication. The excerpts are reprinted by permission from International Business Machines Corporation.

Statements

ASSGN assigns a logical I/O unit to a physical device.

```
//   ASSGN SYSxxx,address  ⎡⎛,X'ss'        ⎞⎤
                           ⎢⎜,UA           ⎟⎥
                           ⎢⎜,IGN          ⎟⎥
                           ⎢⎨,SYSyyy       ⎬⎥
                           ⎢⎜,device-class ⎟⎥
                           ⎣⎝,device-type  ⎠⎦
```

where

SYSxxx is the symbolic unit name;
address is the physical device address expressed as

495

X'cuu' where c = channel and uu = device, or

UA which indicates that unit is unassigned, or

IGN which indicates that the device is to be ignored (i.e., disabled), or

SYSyyy, which assigns SYSxxx to the same device as SYSyyy, or
device-class, for example DISK or READER, or
device-type, for example 3330 or 2501.

A number of optional operands can be coded as well.

CLOSE closes a logical unit.

```
//  CLOSE   SYSxxx  ⎡⎡.X'cuu'[.X'ss']⎤⎤
                    ⎢⎢.UA            ⎥⎥
                    ⎢⎨.IGN           ⎬⎥
                    ⎢⎢.ALT           ⎥⎥
                    ⎣⎣.sysyyy        ⎦⎦
```

where parameters have the same meaning as in ASSGN.
DATE places a date in the communication region.

```
//  DATE    mm/dd/yy
```

or

```
//  DATE    dd/mm/yy
```

EXEC indicates end of control information for a job step and identifies the core-image library program (phase) which is to be loaded and executed.

```
//  EXEC    [programname].GO
```

or

```
//  EXEC    PROC = procname
```

where

programname is the name of the program to be loaded and executed. If blank, the load module just produced by the linkage editor is assumed,

GO indicates that the output of a compiler is to be link edited and executed, and

procname is the name of a cataloged procedure.

EXTENT defines an area or extent of a direct access file.

```
//   EXTENT   [symbolic-unit],
              [serial-number], [type],
              [sequence-number],
              [relative-track],
              [number-of-tracks],
              [split-cylinder-track],
```

where

     symbolic unit is the SYSxxx form symbolic = unit name of the desired volume. (If omitted, the unit from the last EXTENT is used. If this is the first or only EXTENT, the unit from the DTF is used.)

     serial number is the volume's serial number. (If omitted, the serial number from the last EXTENT is used. If this is the first or only EXTENT and no serial number is coded, the serial number is not checked.)

     type is 1 for a data area, 2 for an overflow area, 4 for an index area, and 8 for a split-cylinder data area;

     sequence number is the relative location of this extent within a multi-extent file;

     relative track is relative track address of the track where the data extent (indexed sequential file) is to begin;

     number of tracks indicates the number of tracks to be assigned to this file;

     split-cylinder track indicates the upper track number for split-cylinder sequential files.

JOB indicates start of a job.

```
//   JOB   jobname [accounting information]
```

where

     jobname is the 1–8 alphanumeric character name of the job;

     accounting information is optional with the installation. (If specified, separate from the jobname by a blank.)

LBLTYP defines the amount of main storage to be reserved at link edit time or at execution time for label processing.

```
//   LBLTYP   ⎧TAPE[ (nn) ]⎫
              ⎨            ⎬
              ⎩NSD(nn)     ⎭
```

where

TAPE(nn) is used to indicate that only tape labels and no nonsequential DASD file labels are to be processed;

NSD(nn) indicates that nonsequential disk file labels are to be processed. (This also allows for other types as well. The nn indicates the largest number of extents to be processed for a single file.)

OPTION specifies job control options.

```
//   OPTION   option1[,option2,...]
```

where

typical *options* include: LOG or NOLOG, DUMP or NODUMP, LINK or NOLINK, DECK or NODECK, LIST or NOLIST, LISTX or NOLISTX, SYM or NOSYM, XREF or NOXREF, ERRS or NOERRS, CATAL, STDLABEL, USRLABEL, PARSTD, 48C, 60C (60-character set), and SYSPARM.

RESET resets certain I/O assignments to the standard assignment, within the partition.

```
              ⎧ SYS    ⎫
              ⎪        ⎪
//   RESET    ⎨ PROG   ⎬
              ⎪ ALL    ⎪
              ⎪        ⎪
              ⎩ SYSxxx ⎭
```

where

SYS resets all system logical units;

PROG resets programmer logical units;

ALL resets all logical units;

SYSxxx resets the specified unit.

RSTRT allows programmer to restart a checkpointed program.

```
//   RSTRT   SYSxxx,nnnn[,filename]
```

where

SYSxxx is the symbolic name of the device on which checkpoint records are stored;

nnnn identifies the checkpoint record to be used for restarting;

filename is the symbolic name of a disk file used for checkpoint (disk volumes hold multiple files).

UPSI allows the programmer to set program switches in the communications region:

```
// UPSI  nnnnnnnn
```

where

nnnnnnnn represents the desired settings of the eight program switch bits—a 0 sets the associated switch to 0, a 1 sets the switch to a 1, and an X leaves the switch setting unchanged.

The symbol, /*, is an end-of-data file marker.

The symbol, /&, is an end-of-job marker.

Linkage Editor Control Statements

PHASE assigns a phase name and gives main storage load address for the phase.

INCLUDE indicates that an object module is to be included. If the operands field is blank, the module is on SYSIPT; i.e., it's in object deck form.

ENTRY provides for an optional phase entry point.

ACTION specifies linkage-editor options.

Summary of Job Control Language for the IBM System/360 and System/370 Operating System

The primary references for this chapter follow.

G. D. Brown, *System/370 Job Control Language,* Wiley, 1978.

R. Hannula, *System 360/370 Job Control Language and the Access Methods,* Addison-Wesley, 1977.

IBM Publication # GC28-0618, *OS/VS JCL Reference.*

The format for describing the individual JCL statements was based on the IBM *OS/VS JCL Reference* material, and is used with the permission of the International Business Machines Corporation.

General JCL Rules

JCL Statement Format

//name operation operands comments
Fields are separated by one or more blanks.

Valid names: A jobname, stepname, or DDname may consist of from one to eight alphanumeric characters, the first of which must be alphabetic or one of the national characters (#, @, or $).

500

Continuation of a JCL Statement

1. Break after any comma, including the comma on the original line.
2. Code "//" in the first two columns of the continuation line.
3. Resume the coding of parameters anywhere between positions four and sixteen of the continuation line.

Rules for using parentheses: When the first subparameter is the only one coded, parentheses are not needed. When more than one subparameter or a positional subparameter other than the first one is coded, parentheses are needed.

The JOB Statement

Function: Job separation. Secondary functions allow the programmer to pass accounting information and other parameters to the system. (See Fig. C.1.)

Fig. C.1
The job statement—general form.

//Name	Operation	Operand	P/K
//jobname	JOB	[([acct'] [,acctg information])]	P
		[programmer's name]	P
		$\text{MSGLEVEL} = (\begin{bmatrix} 0 \\ 1 \\ 2 \end{bmatrix} \begin{bmatrix} ,0 \\ ,1 \end{bmatrix})$	K
		[COND = ((condition), . . .)]	K
		[RD = request]	K
		$\text{RESTART} = (\begin{Bmatrix} * \\ \text{stepname} \\ \text{stepname.procstep} \end{Bmatrix}[,\text{checkid}])$	K
		[PRTY = nn]	K
		[MSGCLASS = x]	K
		[TYPRUN = HOLD]	K
		[TIME = (minutes,seconds,)]	K
		[CLASS = jobclass)	K
		$[\text{REGION} = (\begin{Bmatrix} \text{nnnnnK} \\ \text{value}_0\text{K} \end{Bmatrix}[,\text{value}_1\text{K}])]$	K
		[ROLL = (x,y)]	K

Legend:
P Positional parameter.
K Keyword parameter
{ } Choose one.
[ ] Optional; if more than one line is enclosed, choose one or none.

Parameters:
accounting information.
This is an installation-dependent positional parameter, normally containing an account number followed by other accounting information. It's optional but can, at the installation's request, be made a required parameter.

programmer's name
This second positional parameter consists of a one- to twenty-character name composed of letters, numbers, and a period. If the field contains any other characters (a blank, for example) it must be enclosed in a set of apostrophes.

MSGLEVEL=(jcl, allocations)

Specifies the printing of job control statements and device allocation messages. The two positional subparameters are interpreted as follows.

JCL	Meaning
0	Print JOB statement only.
1	Print all JCL including that generated by cataloged procedures.
2	Print only JCL in job stream.

Allocations	Meaning
0	Print messages only if job abnormally terminates.
1	Print all messages.

COND=(condition,...)
This parameter is normally coded on an EXEC statement. If coded on the JOB statement condition parameters on subsequent EXEC statement are cancelled.

RD=request
Allows for automatic restart and suppression of checkpoints.

RESTART=stepname
Requests step restart.

PRTY=nn
Priority within job class—low is zero; high is 13.

MSGCLASS=x
Allows the programmer to specify the device to which job scheduler messages are to be spooled.

TYPRUN=HOLD
Holds the job in the input queue until the operator issues a RELEASE command.

TIME=(minutes, seconds)
The TIME parameter is normally coded on an EXEC statement. If coded on the JOB statement, it sets a time limit for the entire job.

CLASS=jobclass
Specifies the job's class.

REGION=nnnnnK
This is another parameter that is more commonly coded on an EXEC statement. If coded on the JOB statement, the parameter sets an upper limit for the entire job; therefore you must allow enough space for the biggest job step.

ROLL=(x,y)
Allows the roll-in/roll-out feature to be implemented. The first subparameter indicates if this program can be rolled-out; respond with "YES" or "NO." The second subparameter indicates if this program can cause another program to be rolled-out; once again, respond "YES" or "NO."

The EXEC Statement

Function: Identifies the specific program (directly or through a cataloged procedure) to be executed. (See Fig. C.2.)

Parameters:
PGM=program name or PROC=procedure *name or just plain procedure name.*

This is the first positional parameter, and it fulfills the primary function of the EXEC statement. If no keyword is coded, PROC is assumed.

COND=(condition1,condition2,...)
Allows the programmer to specify conditions for bypassing the job step.

PARM=value
Allows the programmer to pass parameters to a program.

ACCT=(accounting information)
This is a rarely used parameter that allows the programmer to provide jobstep accounting information. Accounting information is usually passed through the JOB statement.

//Name	Operation	Operand	P/K
//[stepname]	EXEC	$\begin{cases} \text{PGM = program name} \\ \text{PGM = *.stepname.ddname} \\ \text{PGM = *.stepname.procstepname.ddname} \\ [\text{PROC = }]\text{ procedure name} \end{cases}$	P
		$\text{COND = }(\begin{cases}\text{(condition)}\\\text{EVEN}\\\text{ONLY}\end{cases}[,\text{(condition)},\ldots])$	
		$\text{COND.procstep = }(\begin{cases}\text{(condition)}\\\text{EVEN}\\\text{ONLY}\end{cases}[,\text{(condition)},\ldots])$	
		$\left[\begin{array}{l}\text{PARM = value} \\ \text{PARM.procstepname = value}\end{array}\right]$	K
		$\left[\begin{array}{l}\text{ACCT = (acctg information)} \\ \text{ACCT.procstepname = (acctg info)}\end{array}\right]$	K
		$\left[\begin{array}{l}\text{RD = request} \\ \text{RD.procstepname = request}\end{array}\right]$	K
		$\left[\begin{array}{l}\text{DPRTY = (value 1, value 2)} \\ \text{DPRTY.procstepname = (value 1, value 2)]}\end{array}\right]$	K
		$\left[\begin{array}{l}\text{TIME = (minutes,seconds)} \\ \text{TIME.procstepname = (min,sec)}\end{array}\right]$	K
		$\left[\text{REGION = }(\begin{cases}\text{nnnnnK}\\\text{value}_0\text{ K}\end{cases}[,\text{value}_1\text{ K}])\right.$	
		$\left.\text{REGION.procstepname = }(\begin{cases}\text{nnnnnK}\\\text{value}_0\text{ K}\end{cases}[,\text{value}_1\text{ K}])\right]$	
		$\left[\begin{array}{l}\text{ROLL = (x,y)} \\ \text{ROLL.procstepname = (x,y)}\end{array}\right]$	K

Legend:
P   Positional parameter
K   Keyword parameter.
{ } Choose one.
[ ] Optional; if more than one line is enclosed, choose one or none.

Fig. C.2
The EXEC statement—general form.

RD=request
As on the JOB statement, this parameter allows for automatic restart and suppression of checkpoints.

DPRTY=(valuel,value2)
The dispatching priority determines which of the several programs concurrently resident in core on a multiprogramming system gets first access to the CPU in the event of conflicts.

TIME=(minutes,seconds)
Sets a time limit for the job step.

REGION=nnnnnK
Sets a limit on the amount of main storage available to the jobstep.

ROLL=(x,y)
As with the JOB statement ROLL parameter, this parameter allows the programmer to specify if this job step can be rolled-in and rolled-out (x) and if this job step can cause another to be rolled-in and rolled-out (y).

The DD statement

Function: Specifies details—physical location, logical configuration—of data sets. (See Fig. C.3.)

Fig. C.3
The DD statement—general form.

//Name	Operation	Operand

// [ddname
procstepname.
ddname]
	DD	[DSNAME = identification
		DSN = identification]
		[UNIT = (unit information)]
		[UCS = (UCS information)]
		[VOLUME = (volume information)
		VOL= (volume information)]
		[DCB = (attributes)
		DCB = ({ dsname
		   *.stepname.ddname
		   *.stepname.procstep.ddname } [,attributes])]
		[LABEL = (label information)]
		[DISP = ([status] [,disposition])
		SYSOUT = x
		SYSOUT = (x [,progname] [, form$^{\#}$])]
		[SPACE = (direct access space)
		SPLIT = (direct access space)
		SUBALLOC = (direct access space)]
		[SEP = (ddnames)
		AFF = ddname]

		{ * DATA } [,DCB = ([BLKSIZE = block] [,BUFNO = number])]
		DUMMY, . . .
		DDNAME = ddname [,DCB =([BLKSIZE = block] [, BUFNO = number])]

Legend:
{ }   Choose one.
[ ]   Optional; if more than one line is enclosed, choose one or none.

Parameters: *DSNAME* or *DSN* Identifies a data set by name.

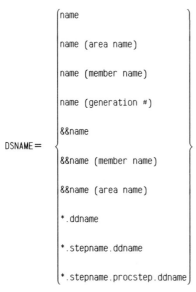

DSNAME =
- name
- name (area name)
- name (member name)
- name (generation #)
- &&name
- &&name (member name)
- &&name (area name)
- *.ddname
- *.stepname.ddname
- *.stepname.procstep.ddname

UNIT

Requests a particular type of physical I/O device:

```
       (  [address]  [.P]  [.DEFER] [.SEP=(list of ddnames)])
UNIT=     type       .n
       [group]     [.  ]
```

Units can be requested by actual channel/device address (address), by IBM model number (2400 is a particular model of tape drive—this is the "type" option), or by a general group name as defined by the installation. The second form

```
UNIT=AFF=ddname
```

allows the data set to be mounted on the same physical device used by a previous data set (referenced by DDNAME) in the job.

Getting back to the first form of this parameter, the second positional subparameter allows the programmer to specify parallel mounting of all the volumes in a multivolume file by indicating the actual number of volumes; if the number of volumes is specified in the VOL subparameter, the programmer simply codes "P." The DEFER subparameter, the third positional subparameter, postpones issuance of a volume mount message until the actual OPEN macro is executed. The SEP subparameter is a keyword subparameter that indicates to the system that data sets listed as part of the subparameter are to be placed on physically separate devices—if, for example, a program were to access both input and output disk data sets, the SEP subparameter could cause these data sets to be maintained on separate disk volumes, thus minimizing head movement.

UCS

This parameter allows for the mounting of a special print chain or print train for a nonstandard character set on a 1403 printer.

```
UCS=(character set code⌈.FOLD⌉[.VERIFY])
               ⌊.    ⌋
```

VOLUME or VOL

Allows for the specification of volumes; i.e., specific tape volumes or disk volumes.

```
VOLUME=([PRIVATE]⌈,RETAIN⌉⌈,volseq#⌉⌈,volcount⌉[,]⌈SER=(list of serial #s)         ⌉)
                 ⌊,     ⌋⌊,      ⌋⌊,       ⌋    |REF=dsname                         |
                                                   |                                   |
                                                   |REF=*.ddname                       |
                                                   |                                   |
                                                   |REF=*.stepname.ddname              |
                                                   |                                   |
                                                   ⌊REF=*.stepname.procstep.ddname⌋
```

The primary option is the SER or REF subparameter that allows the programmer to specify either a specific volume or a group of volumes directly, by serial number, or indirectly by referring back to a prior job step. The PRIVATE subparameter gives exclusive use of the data set to the requesting program. The RETAIN subparameter keeps the volume mounted between job steps. The third positional subparameter allows the programmer to indicate that processing is to begin with a volume other than the first one on a multivolume file. The fourth positional subparameter allows the programmer to specify the number of volumes in a multivolume file.

DCB

Specifies details about actual data format.

LABEL

Specifies the label type as well as the relative file number on a multifile tape volume and indicates whether the file is to be accessed for input or output.

LABEL=([data set seq#] [,SL] [,PASSWORD] [,IN] [.] [EXPDT=yyddd])
        [,SUL] [L,] [L,OUT] [RETPD=nnnn]
        [,NSL]
        [,NL]
        [,BLP]
        [L,]

The first subparameter, which is positional, indicates the relative file number on a multifile volume; if blank, relative file # 1 is assumed. The second positional subparameter identifies the label type. Specifying "IN" or "OUT" as the third positional subparameter allows the programmer to override a program specification of INOUT access in the OPEN macro for BSAM files; it's of primary importance to FORTRAN programmers. The final subparameter allows for the specification of an expiration date or retention period.

DISP

Specifies the status and disposition of a data set. The first positional subparameter indicates the status of the data set at the beginning of the job step. The second subparameter indicates what is to be done with the data set at the conclusion of the job step, while the third subparameter indicates the disposition in the event of abnormal jobstep termination.

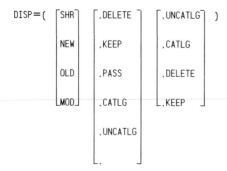

DISP=([SHR] [,DELETE] [,UNCATLG])
       [NEW] [,KEEP] [,CATLG]
       [OLD] [,PASS] [,DELETE]
       [MOD] [,CATLG] [L,KEEP]
             [,UNCATLG]
             [L,]

SYSOUT

Specifies the use of a system output device. Since the disposition of the system output devices is specified by the system, the DISP parameter is not coded.

SPACE

Specifies the amount of direct access space to be allocated to a data set. The first form

```
SPACE=(ABSTR,(quantity,address[,directory]))
```

allows the programmer to specify actual, absolute track addresses for his or her data set; the second and third positional subparameters indicate the number of tracks and the absolute address of the first track to be assigned. The final subparameter allows for the assignment of directory space for an indexed sequential or partitioned data set.

The specification of absolute tracks is a rare option under OS; more commonly, the second form of the SPACE parameter is used.

```
SPACE=( ⎡TRK      ⎤ .(quantity⎡,increment⎤⎡,directory⎤)⎡,RLSE⎤⎡,CONTIG⎤[,ROUND])
        ⎨CYL      ⎬         L,           L,index   J  L    ⎢ ,MXIG ⎥
        ⎣blocksize⎦                                        ⎢ ,ALX  ⎥
                                                           L,      J
```

Using this form, the programmer can request tracks (TRK), cylinders (CYL), or blocks of a given size. Following specification of the type of space allocation required, the programmer requests an amount of space, asking first, through a series of positional subparameters, for a primary allocation, next, for a secondary allocation in the event that the primary allocation proves to be insufficient, and finally for directory or index space. Note that, in terms of punctuation, the entire "quantity" request is treated as a single positional subparameter, with the quantity, increment, and index sub-subparameters being enclosed in a set of parentheses.

The RLSE subparameter allows the programmer to return all unused space to the system at the conclusion of the job step. CONTIG allows the programmer to request contiguous space, MXIG allows for the allocation of the largest contiguous free area on the volume (as long as it's larger than the request), and ALX provides the five largest contiguous free areas on the volume (again, with a "larger than the request" restriction). ROUND causes space allocated by blocks to be aligned on cylinder boundaries.

SPLIT

Allows a space allocation to be split among several different physical volumes, thus minimizing head movement in the processing of a data set.

```
SPLIT=  ⌠n
        │
        │(n,CYL,(quantity[increment]))
        ⟨
        │%
        │
        ⌡(%,blocksize,(quantity[.increment])))
```

Space can be split in terms of the number of tracks per cylinder or the percentage of tracks per cylinder to be assigned to a given data set. Normally, a number of SPLIT parameters are coded on a series of separate DD statements indicating, in essence, how an initial space request is to be subdivided.

SUBALLOC

Allows space on the same physical volume to be suballocated among a number of data sets.

```
SUBALLOC=[ ⌠TRK      ⌡.(quantity⌠.increment⌡[.directory]) ⌠.ddname                        )
           ⟨CYL      ⟩           ⌊.          ⌋             ⟨.stepname.ddname
           ⌡blocksize⌠                                     ⌡.stepname.procstepname.ddname
```

SEP and AFF

The SEP parameter allows the programmer to specify channel separation between two data sets. The AFF parameter allows the programmer to copy a SEP parameter from another DD statement.

DUMMY

Causes the I/O operations specified on the DD statement to be bypassed.

* or DATA:

The asterisk or (*) character in the operands portion of the DD statement indicates that data follows in the job stream; this parameter is often used to indicate that punched card data is to be read through the system input device.

DATA implies the same thing, but allows for the inclusion of cards with //
punched in the first two columns.

DDNAME:

Postpones definition of data set parameters until a subsequent DD statement
with the specified DDNAME is encountered.

Special DD statements

The JOBLIB
statement

```
//JOBLIB   DD   DSN=library-name,DISP=SHR
```

allows programs in a private library to be loaded and executed. The JOBLIB
statement follows the JOB statement and makes the library available to all
subsquent job steps; the JOBLIB and the SYSCHK statements are the only
DD statements that can legally precede the first EXEC statement.

The STEPLIB
statement

```
//STEPLIB   DD   DSN=library-name,DISP=SHR
```

like the JOBLIB statement, allows programs in a private library to be loaded
and executed. The STEPLIB statement follows the EXEC statement and is
effective for a single job step only.

The SYSABEND
statement

```
//SYSABEND DD SYSOUT=class
```

provides an abnormal termination dump of the system nucleus.

The SYSCHK
statement

```
//SYSCHK   DD   DISP=OLD,DSN=checkpoint-library
```

describes a checkpoint library data set. Follows the JOB statement and the
JOBLIB statement if present.

Index

513